Street by Street

BLACKPOOL PRESTON

CHORLEY, CLEVELEYS, FLEETWOOD, LEYLAND, LYTHAM ST ANNE'S, POULTON-LE-FYLDE

Bamber Bridge, Clayton-le-Woods, Coppull, Freckleton, Kirkham, Knott End-on-Sea, Longton, Preesall, Thornton, Warton

Ist edition May 2001

Published by AA Publishing (a trading name of Automobile Association Developments Limited, whose registered office is Norfolk House, Priestley Road, Basingstoke, Hampshire, RG24 9NY. Registered number 1878835).

Mapping produced by the Cartographic Department of The Automobile Association.

ISBN 0 7495 2617 3

A CIP Catalogue record for this book is available from the British Library.

Printed by GRAFIASA S.A., Porto, Portugal

Ref: ML075

Key to map pages ii-iii

Key to map symbols iv-1

Enlarged scale pages 2-7

Street by Street 8-95

Index – towns & villages 96

Index – streets 97-117

Index – featured places 117-120

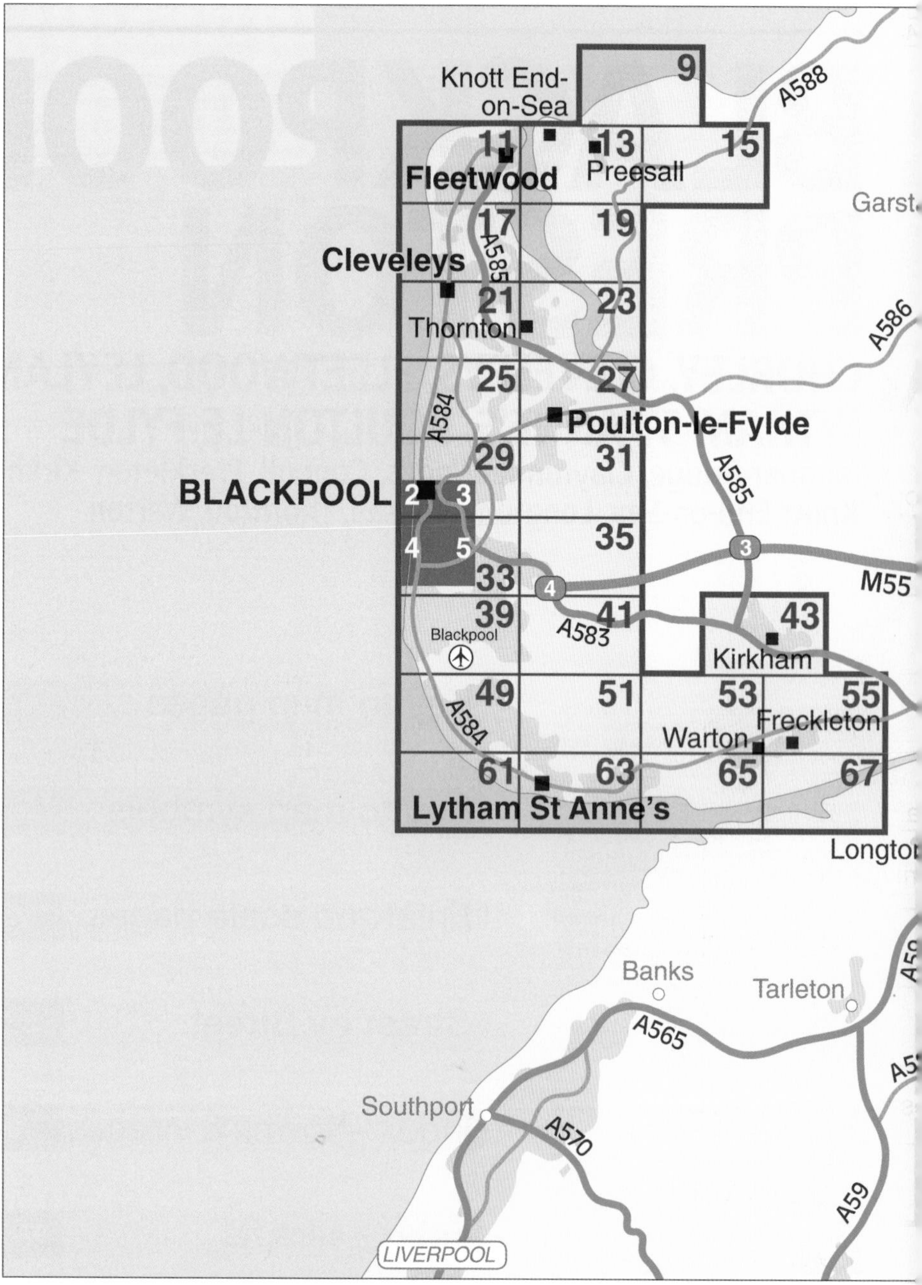

Knott End-on-Sea
9
11 13 15
Fleetwood
Preesall
A588
17 19
Cleveleys
A585
21 23
Thornton
A586
25 27
Poulton-le-Fylde
A584
29 31
BLACKPOOL
2 3
A585
4 5
35
33
3
4
M55
39 41
A583
43
Blackpool
Kirkham
49 51 53 55
A584
Freckleton
Warton
61 63 65 67
Lytham St Anne's
Banks
Tarleton
A565
Southport
A570
A59
LIVERPOOL

Enlarged scale pages 1:10,000

6.3 inches to 1 mile

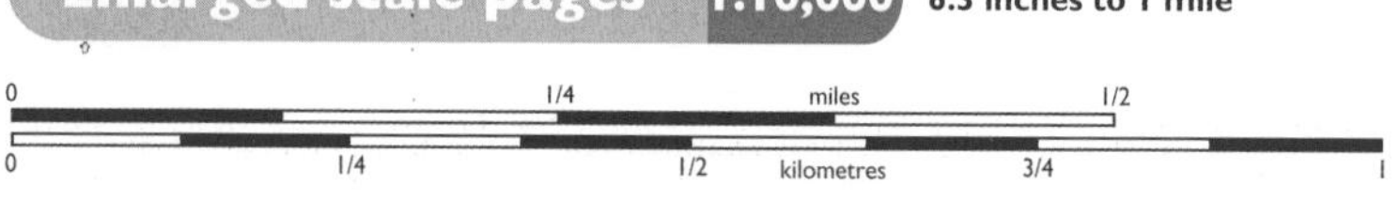

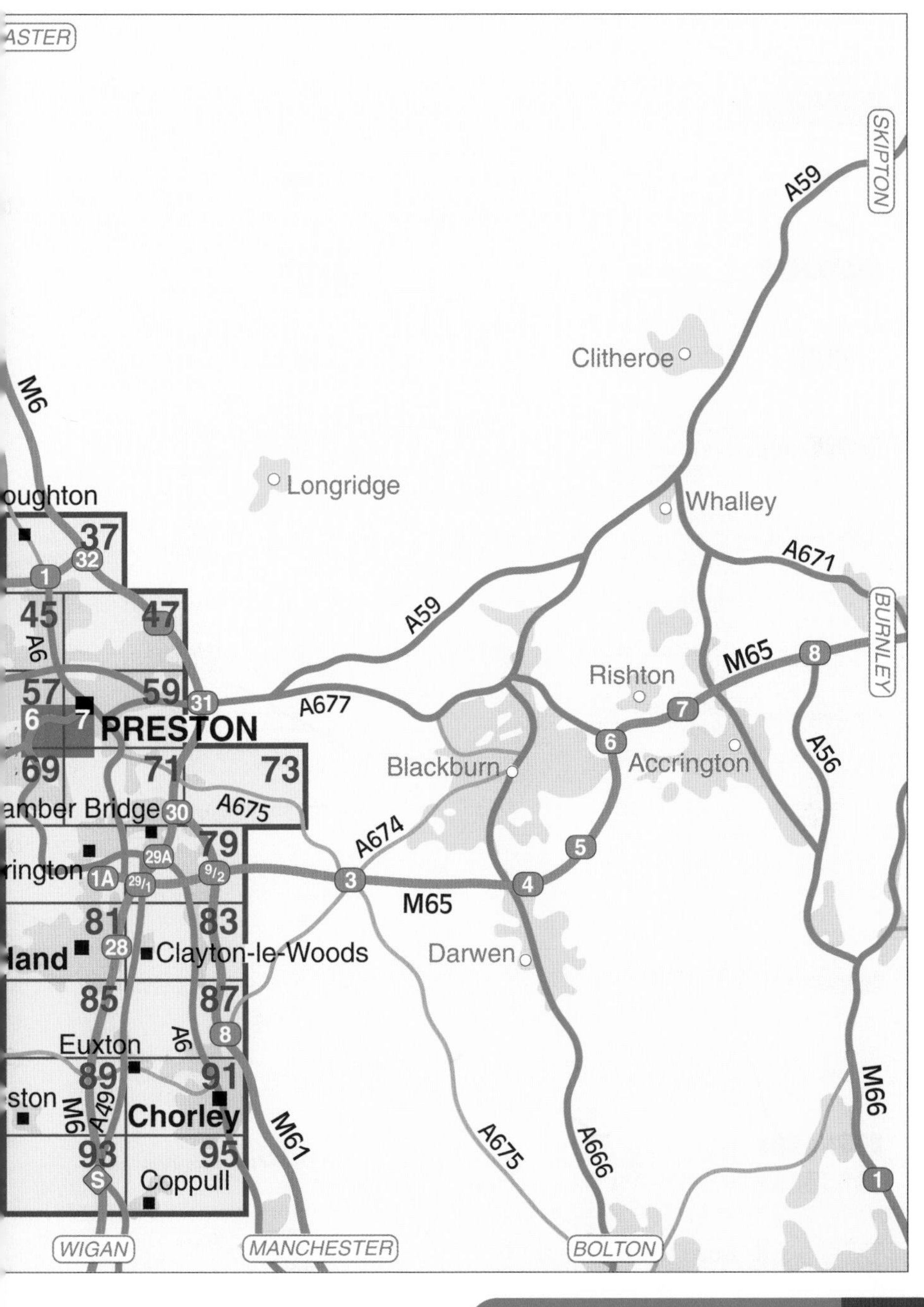

4.2 inches to 1 mile

Scale of main map pages 1:15,000

0 1/4 miles 1/2 3/4 1

0 1/4 1/2 kilometres 3/4 1 1 1/4 1 1/2

Junction 9

Motorway & junction

Services

Motorway service area

Primary road single/dual carriageway

Services

Primary road service area

A road single/dual carriageway

B road single/dual carriageway

Other road single/dual carriageway

Restricted road

Private road

One way street

Pedestrian street

Track/ footpath

Road under construction

Road tunnel

P

Parking

P+

Park & Ride

Bus/Coach station

Railway & main railway station

Railway & minor railway station

Underground station

Light Railway & station

Preserved private railway

LC

Level crossing

Tramway

Ferry route

Airport runway

Boundaries- borough/ district

Mounds

93

Page continuation 1:15,000

7

Page continuation to enlarged scale 1:10,000

River/canal, lake, pier

Aqueduct, lock, weir

465 Winter Hill — Peak (with height in metres)

Beach

Coniferous woodland

Broadleaved woodland

Mixed woodland

Park

Cemetery

Built-up area

Featured building

City wall

A&E — Accident & Emergency hospital

Toilet

Toilet with disabled facilities

Petrol station

PH — Public house

PO — Post Office

Public library

Tourist Information Centre

Castle

Historic house/ building

Wakehurst Place NT — National Trust property

Museum/ art gallery

Church/chapel

Country park

Theatre/ performing arts

Cinema

2
D4
1 Queen Vera Rd
D1
1 Back Pleasant St
2 Lynn Gv
C2
1 Cocker Sq
2 Lansdowne Pl
D5
1 Adelphi St
2 Carter St
3 Coronation St
4 Leopold Gv
E4
1 Back Cookson St
2 Charles St
3 Milbourne St
4 Winstanley Gv
A
B
28
C
D
E
1
2
3
4
5
6
7
4
1 grid square represents 250 metres
PROMENADE
A584
Wilton Pde
Imperial St
Back Eaves St
Dickson Road
Egerton Road
Cheltenham Road
Eaves St
Bute Av
Richmond Rd
Clifford Rd
Ashburton Rd
Cocker Trading Est
Pleasant St
Cross St
Mount St
Lewtas St
Yates St
Back High St
High St
Exchange St
Wall St
Howard Street
Cocker St
Lord St
Back Lord St
Banks St
General St
Francis St
Blackpool North Station
Hotel
Walker St
Springfield Rd
Abingdon Street
Queen St
A586
HIGH ST
TALBOT RD
COOKSON ST
War Memorial
North Pier
Blackpool Borough Council
Deansgate
Topping St
King St
CLIFTON ST
ABINGDON ST
Town Hall & Municipal Blds
Cheapside
Birley Street
Corporation St
Mkt
ABC Cinema
CHURCH ST
Superbowl Leisure Parcs
Church St
Grand Theatre
Blackpool Football Club
Winter Gardens
Victoria Street
Adelaide St
Surg
Medical Centre
Tower World
Houndsmill Shopping Cen
Blackpool Tower
Blackpool Council Register Office
PROM
Adelaide Street
Albert Rd
ALBERT RD
CORONATION ST
Charnley Rd
Hull Road
Vance Rd
Coral Island
A5099
NEW BONNY ST
Lifeboat Station
Havelock St
Livingstone Rd
Sealife Centre
Bonny Street
Police Station
Richardson St
Rishton St
Brunswick St
Louis Tussauds Waxworks
Blackpool County Court
Chapel St
CENTRAL DRIVE
Bethesda Rd
Kay St
Pier St
Coop St
York St
Cent Pier
Dale Street
Shannon St
Foxhall Rd
Dale Mews
Yorkshire Street
Louise St
Erdington Rd
Kent Rd
Middle St

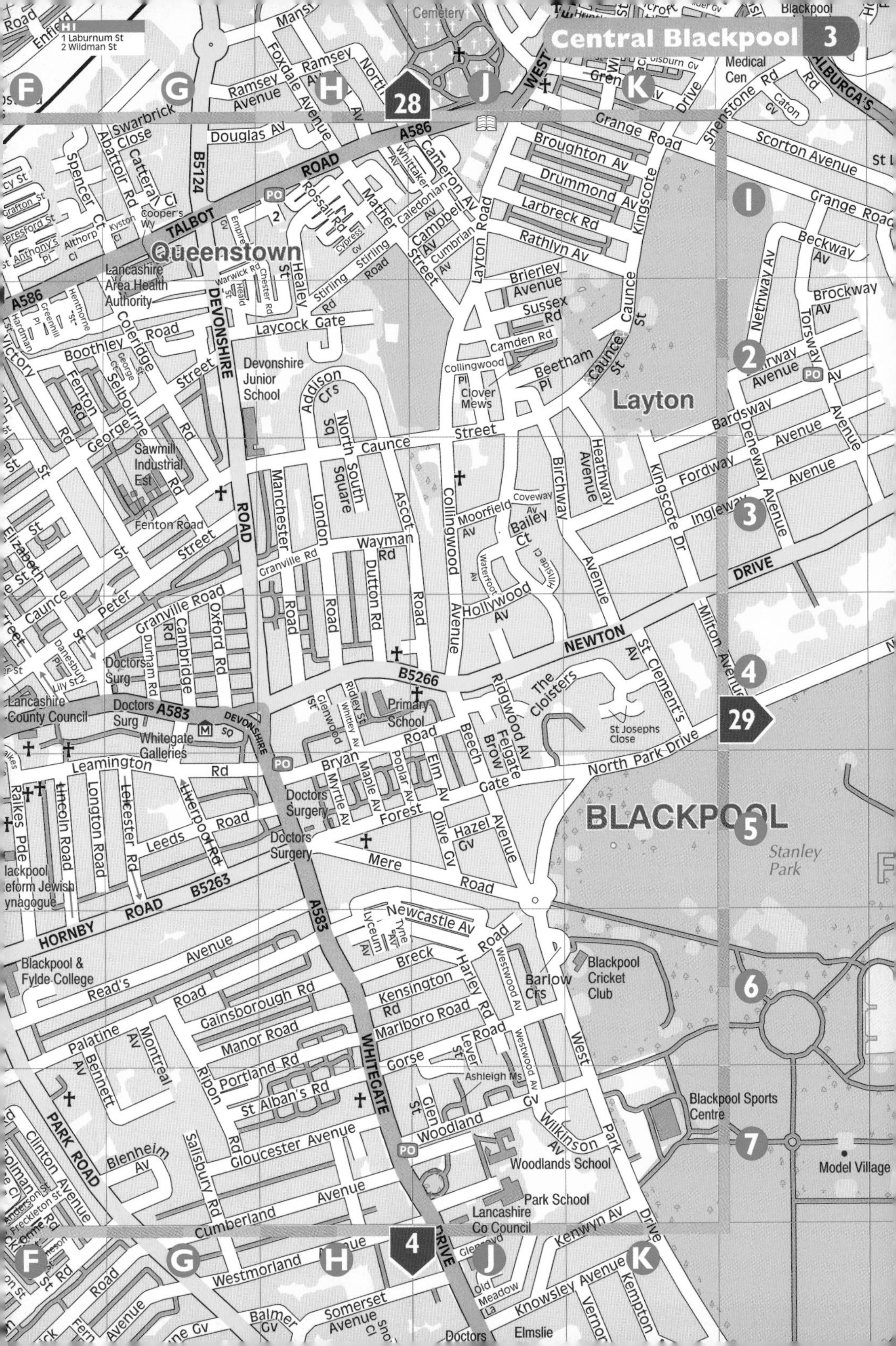
Queenstown
Layton
BLACKPOOL
Stanley Park
Devonshire Junior School
Lancashire Area Health Authority
Lancashire County Council
Whitegate Galleries
Blackpool & Fylde College
Blackpool Cricket Club
Blackpool Sports Centre
Model Village
Woodlands School
Park School
Lancashire Co Council
Sawmill Industrial Est
Primary School
HI
1 Laburnum St
2 Wildman St
28
29
4

4
D1
1 Back Shannon St
C6
1 Commercial St
2 Frazer Gv
3 Gordon St
4 Lawrence St
C1
1 Bickerstaffe St
2 Singleton St
D3
1 Bk Clarendon Rd
2 Back Moon Av
D4
1 Bk Woodfield Rd
2 John St
3 West View Av
D6
1 Back Waterloo Rd
E1
1 Grasmere Rd
2 Salthouse Av
Central Pier
South Pier
Louis Tussauds Waxworks
County Court
Police
Brunswick St
Chapel St
Pier St
York St
Shannon St
Yorkshire Street
Bairstow St
Foxhall Sq
Princess
Dale Mews
PROMENADE
A584
LYTHAM ROAD
B5262
A5073
CENTRAL DRIVE
Bethesda Rd
Odeon Cinema
Islamic Community Centre
Blackpool Borough Council
Tram & Bus Depot
Sealife Centre
Rigby Road
Sands Way
Seaside Way
Lune Gv
Kirby Rd
Trafalgar Rd
Lonsdale Road
Clarendon Rd
Blackpool Football Club
Barton Av
Gadsby St
Nelson Rd
Wellington Rd
Moon Av
Hyde Rd
Bloomfield Rd
Woodfield Av
Woodfield Rd
Amberbanks Gv
Lowrey Ter
St Chad's Road
Crystal Rd
Austin Gv
Ruskin Av
Clare St
Elland Pl
Doctors Surgery
Alexandra Road
Adrian Street
Duke Street
Haig Road
Ball St
Castlegate
Shaw Rd
Britannia Pl
Miller St
Royle St
Bagot St
Wolsley Rd
St Bede's Av
Hilton Av
Price St
Westbourne Av
Seymour Rd
Blackpool South Station
Bath St
Victoria Market Hall
Moore Street
Byron Street
Hill St
Rawcliffe St
Bond Street
Bright St
Montague St
Dean Street
Station Road
Station Ter
Yeadon Way
Parking
Osbourne Rd
Hampton Rd
Windsor Av
Brighton Av
Mersey
1 grid square represents 250 metres

Central Blackpool
5
G6
1 Devon St
2 Rugby St
3 Taunton St
4 Truro St
K2
1 Godwin Av
F
G
H
J
K
I
3
32
33
2
4
5
6
7
Woodlands School
Park School
Lancashire Co Council
Model Village
Cumberland
Gloucester Avenue
Woodland
Salisbury Rd
Westmorland Avenue
Kenwyn Av
Knowsley Avenue
Kempton Av
Vernon Av
Somerset Avenue
Balmer Gv
Lune Gv
Jeffrey Sq
Knox Grove
Snowdon Cl
Brecon Cl
Bankfield Gv
Doctors Surgery
Elmslie Girls School
Beechfield Avenue
Haslemere Av
East Md
West Pk Dr
East Pk Dr
A587
Aldwych Av
Carsluith Av
Hereford Av
Royal Bank Rd
Latham Av
Lightbown Av
Lindsay Av
Royal Av
Halifax St
Lomond
Great Marton
SOUTH PARK DRIVE
Preston Old Rd
Airedale
Martin Gallery
Wren Gv
WHITECATE DRIVE
Stratford Place
Ferguson Rd
Kirkham Avenue
Thorn Gv
Avenue
Marton Medical Centre
Honister Av
Newlands Av
Higham Gv
Briercliffe Avenue
St John Vianney RC Primary School
A583
Barclay
Oscar St
John Hl
Johnson Rd
Phillip St
Ord Av
Newhouse
Rosary Av
Anger's Hl Rd
Ryson Av
George Avenue
Penrose Avenue
Meadway
Baines Endowed C of E School
Welbeck Av
Colwyn
Vicarage Lane
Burton
Shortridge Rd
Surgery
Bostonway
Lowesway
Burns Pl
Scott Cl
Skiddaw Rd
Avenue
Eastside
Westside
Halton
Longway
Stretton Av
Thursfield Av
Daggers Hall La
Fairway Road
Terance Rd
Morley Rd
Troughton Crs
Hawes Side
Crossland Road
Brook St
Acton Rd
Ilford Road
Arnott Rd
Wanstead Crescent
Picture Gallery
HAWES SIDE LANE
B5261
Ellesmere
Dalewood Av
Rectory Rd
Rybum Av
Belgrave Rd
Branston Rd
Vicarage
St Edmund's Rd
Whittam Av
WATERLOO ROAD
A5073
Oxford Medical Centre
Kirkstall Av
Pine Av
Laurel Av
Mayfair Road
Glastonbury
Greenwood
Fir
Dover Ct
Dover Road
Grove
Brun Gv
Wood Pk
Wood Rd
Baldwin Grove
Stoke Av
Beardshaw Av
Boardman Av
Cunliffe Road
Hartford Av
PARK ROAD
B5390
Road
St Ives Av
St Vincent Av
Grove
Kingsland Gv
Dinckley Gv
Sharow Grove
Thirsk Grove
Auburn Grove
Condor Grove
Thornber Grove
Levens Gv
Bela Gv
Wyre Gv
Lune Gv
GRASMERE ROAD
Westmorland Avenue
Keswick Road
Fern Gv
Queen Victoria Road
Condor Gv
Grasmere Road
Rose Av
Lilac Av
Chadfield Rd
Bloomfield Road
Palmer Av
Bloomfield Medical Centre
Mayor
Marina Av
Arkholme Av
Finsbury Avenue
ANSDELL ROAD
B5261
Nuttall Rd
Hodder Av
Dunsop Cl
Harris Av
Waterloo Primary School
Eccleston Rd
Threlfall Road
Westfield Road
Malvern
Arnside Av
Harlech Av
Hebden Av
Weston Pl
Waterloo Medical Centre
Waterloo Crown Bowling
Durley Rd
Hudson Road
Dunelt Road
Shetland Road
Falmouth Road
Orkney Rd
Eaton Avenue
Lunedale Av
ROAD
Hall Av
Romney Av
Winchester Av
Scudamore Crs
Aylesbury Av
Lyndhurst Av
Avenue
Chislehurst
St Annes Road
Exeter St
Aintree Rd
Frederick St
Newbury Av
Dorset St
Truro St
Silverwood Av
Starbeck Av
Fernhurst Avenue
Marton Drive
Mirfield Gv
Tranmere Rd
Hemingway
FY4
Marsden Road
Swindon Av
Malham Av
Pickmere Av
Rd
Edwell Av
Houghton Av
Walverden Av
Harcourt Road
Avenue
Howe Av
Bean Av
Powell
Loftos Av
Wick Av
Watson Road
HAWES SIDE LA
Townley Av
Macauley
Burnside Av
Hathaway
Cuthberts Primary School
PO

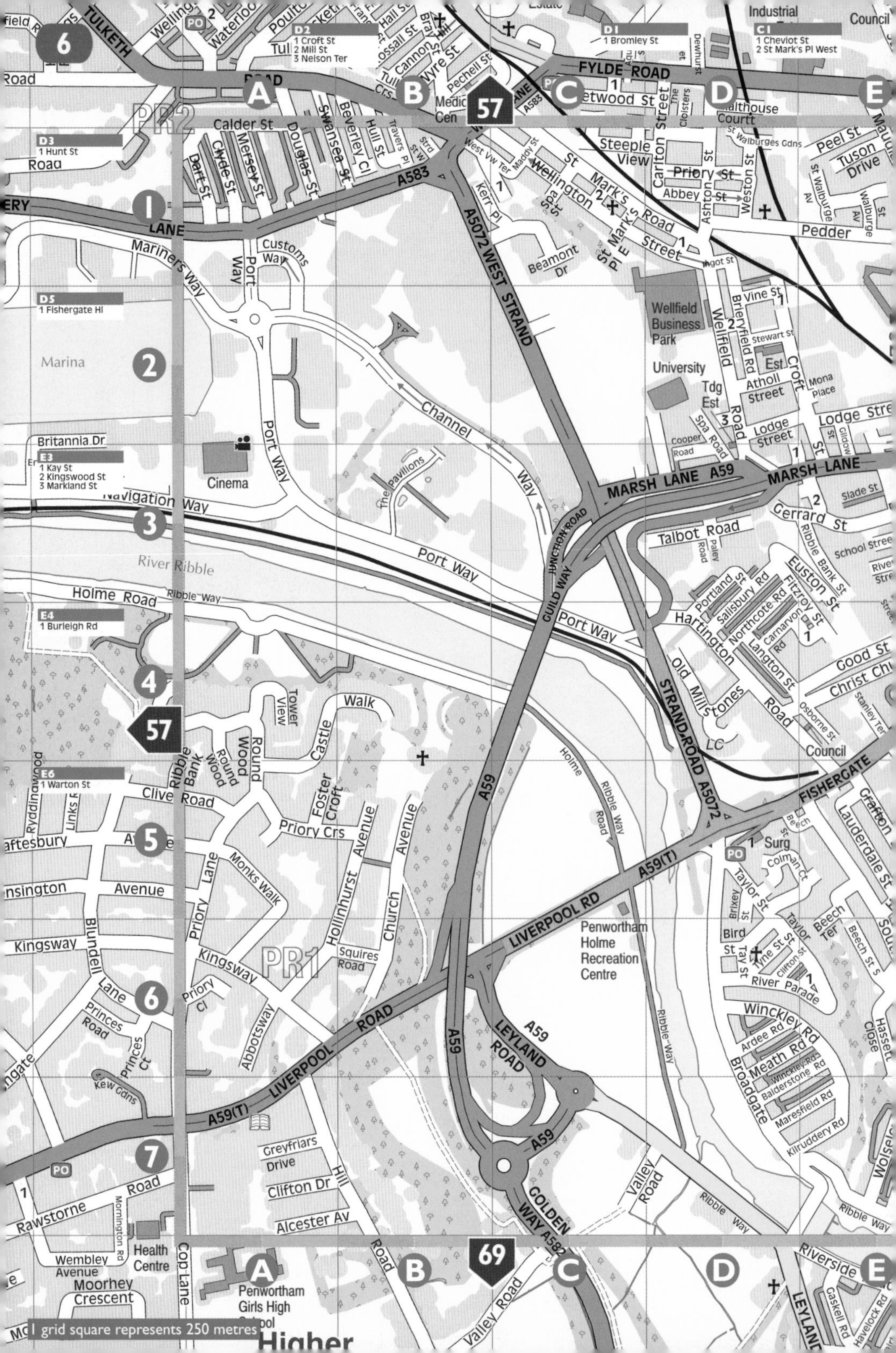
6
57
69
D2
1 Croft St
2 Mill St
3 Nelson Ter
D1
1 Bromley St
C1
1 Cheviot St
2 St Mark's Pl West
D3
1 Hunt St
D5
1 Fishergate Hl
E3
1 Kay St
2 Kingswood St
3 Markland St
E4
1 Burleigh Rd
E6
1 Warton St
TULKETH ROAD
FYLDE ROAD
MARSH LANE A59
A5072 WEST STRAND
STRAND ROAD A5072
LIVERPOOL RD
A59(T)
LIVERPOOL ROAD
LEYLAND ROAD
GOLDEN WAY A582
FISHERGATE
GUILD WAY
JUNCTION ROAD
Port Way
Channel Way
Navigation Way
Mariners Way
Customs Way
Marina
Cinema
River Ribble
Holme Road
Ribble Way
Penwortham Holme Recreation Centre
Wellfield Business Park
University
Penwortham Girls High School
Health Centre
Kingsway
Priory Lane
Clive Road
Blundell Lane
Hollinhurst Avenue
Church Avenue
Greyfriars Drive
Clifton Dr
Alcester Av
Rawstorne Road
Wembley Avenue
Moorhey Crescent
Cop Lane
Valley Road
Riverside
Broadgate
Winckley Rd
Meath Rd
Talbot Road
Hartington Road
Old Millstones
Gerrard St
Lodge Street
Atholl Street
Pedder Street
St Mark's Road
Wellington St
PR1
PR2
1 grid square represents 250 metres

F1
1 Kendal St
2 Moss St
3 Pollard St
4 Stocks St
G2
1 Back Seed St
2 Chandler St
3 Clayton's Ga
4 Simpson St
G3
1 Charnley St
H1
1 Bispham St
2 Lancaster Rd
3 Melbourne St
4 Sizehouse St
H2
1 Trinity Pl
H3
1 Chapel Wks
H4
1 Chaddock St
2 Temple Ct
H5
1 Back Starkie St
J1
1 Hardwicke St
J2
1 Cottage St
2 Crooked La
J3
1 Bostock St
2 Tithebarn St
J4
1 Wolseley Pl
J5
1 Bushell Pl
K1
1 Danewerke St
2 Egan St
3 South Meadow St
K5
1 Avenham Pl
2 Frenchwood St
K4
1 Knowsley St
2 Norwich Pl
K3
1 Back Grimshaw St
2 Greaves St
3 Pembroke Pl
4 Rose St
58
70
F
G
H
J
K
1
2
3
4
5
6
7
University
Harrington St
Singleton Row
Crown St
Warwick St
North St
Lawson St
Elizabeth Street
Lancaster Rd
Melling St
Lund Street
Law Courts
North Rd
Park Mill Place
Alma Street
St Paul's Rd
Mosque
School
St Ignatius' Sq
Meadow St
Constable St
Holstein St
East View
St Paul's Sq
Radio Stn
Deepdale Surgery
Queens Retail Park
PRESTON
Ring Way
A6
A583
A5071
Corporation St
Friargate
Fylde St
Kendal Street
Gt Shaw Street
Walker St
Police
Saul St
Coll
Clnc
Ct
Tenterfield St
Playhouse
UniThtr
Market St W
Council
Mkt Halls
Old Vicarage
Central Bus Stn
Carlisle St
Tithebarn St
St Johns Cen
Town Hall
Guildhall
Lord St
Ward's End
Church St
Corn Exchange
George's Rd
War Mem
Harris Mus
St Georges Shopping Centre
Fox St
Lune Street
Surgeon's Ct
Fishergate
The Theatre Coffee Shop
Fishergate Shopping Cen
Preston Station
Butler Street
Christian Rd
Chapel St
Mount St
Winckley Sq
Cannon St
Glover's Ct
Avenham St
Bolton's Court
Syke St
Avenham Lane
Cross St
Starkie St
Bairstow St
Chaddock St
Berwick Road
Oxford St
Charlotte St
Sch
Grimshaw Street
Manchester Rd
Shepherd St
Oakham Ct
Frenchwood CP School
Frenchwood Knoll
Cardinal Newman
Christ the King High School
Selborne St
Herschell Street
Bank Parade
Latham St
Ribblesdale Place
Medical Centre
Surg
East Cliff Road
East Cliff
Lancashire County Council
Preston Sports Club
Ribble Way
River Ribble
Old Tram Road
Boulevard
Preston Cricket Club
Lower Penwortham

A
B
C
D
1
2
3
4
5
Beach Road
Pilling Lane
Muffy's Platt Farm
Tongues Lane
Woodland Crs
Rosslyn Avenue
Kingston Cl
Hawkshead Road
Eskdale Gv
Kent Cl
Grasmere Road
Thirlmere Cl
Ambleside Av
Lancaster Av
Buttermere Dr
Wilkinson Wy
Pilling Lane
Meadow Av
Pinewood Av
Larch Av
Maplewood Av
Rosemount Av
Cedar Av
Thornhill Av
Beechfield Av
Rosslyn Crs
Rosslyn Crescent East
LANCASTER ROAD
Over Wyre Medical C
Tongues Farm
PREESALL
13
1 grid square represents 500 metres

E
F
G
H
I
2
3
4
5
Fluke Hall La
Fluke Hall
Fluke Hall Lane
Sandfield Cottage
Fluke
Libby Lane
Pilling St John C of E School
Beech House
Duck Street
Carr House Farm
Wheel Lane
Townson Hill
14
Hooles Farm
Pasture House Farm
Smallwood Hey
St Johns Avenue
Lane
Smallwood Hey Road

C5
1 Brant Ct
2 Wraywood Ct

C4
1 Arndale Cl
2 Greendale Cl

D3
1 Curtis Dr
2 Garland Gv
3 Leven Av
4 Monroe Dr
5 Stanley Ga

D4
1 Birkbeck Pl
2 Brathay Pl
3 Honister Cl
4 Troutbeck Av

D5
1 Pool Ct

E2
1 Arden Gn
2 Birnam Gn
3 Duncan Pl
4 Malcolm Pl
5 Manor Wd
E3
1 Lonsdale Crs
2 Oxford Wy
3 Westwood Av
E4
1 Brentwood
2 Hatfield Gdns
3 Hatfield Wk
4 Langwood
5 Westhead Wk
FLEETWOOD
E5
1 Southfleet Pl
F1
1 Elsinore Cl
F2
1 Albany Rd
2 Seymour St
3 Wolsley Rd
F3
1 Eastwood Av
2 Keating Ct
F4
Street names for this grid square are listed at the back of the index
F5
1 Kilbane St
G2
1 Delta La
2 Dock St
3 North Albion St
4 Tennyson Rd
5 Willow St
G3
1 Deepdale Rd
H1
1 Aughton St
2 Cross St
3 Garfield St
4 Lower Lune St
5 North Albert St
6 North Church St
7 Windsor Ter
H2
1 Kemp St
2 St Peter's Pl
Outer Promenade
The Esplanade
Bold Street
Fleetwood Hospital
Wyre Borough Council
Queen's Terrace
Pharos St
Kent St
Lancashire Co Council
Fleetwood Museum
Victoria Street
Adelaide St
Fleetwood Health Centre
Dock Street
Poulton Road
A587
Station Rd
Bridge Road
Amounderness Way
A585(T)
Siding Road
Dock Avenue
Broadway
Shakespeare Road
Shakespeare CP School
St Wulstans RC School
Fleetwood Hesketh High School
Fleetwood Football Club
Victoria Business Park
Copse View Business Park
Copse Road
Park Avenue
Radcliffe Road
Nelson Road
Highbury Avenue
Southwood Av
Cambridge Road
Oxford Road
Hatfield Avenue
Greenfield Road
Broomfield Road
Whinfield Avenue
Heathfield Road
Westfield Av
Fleetwood Road
Lindel Road
Hazeldene Rd
Lingfield Rd
Fairfield Ct
Wingrove Rd
Harbour Close
Maritime St
Denham Wy
Flakefleet Avenue
Southfleet Av
Larkholme Avenue
Meadow Av
Orchard Dr
Homestead Dr
Penrhos Av
Witton Av
Leyburn Av
Northfleet Av
Infant School
Primary School
Harris St School
College
Mount Road
Promenade Road
Carr Road
Abbotts Wk
Milton St
Dronsfield Road
Agnew Road
Abercrombie Road
Galloway Rd
Darbishire Road
Warren Av N
Warren Av S
Lowther Rd
Manor Rd
Macbeth Road
Hamlet Road
Ribble Rd
Lune Road
Mersey Rd
Bramley Av
Borrowdale Av
Coniston Avenue
Poulton Rd
Cop Lane
Preston Street
King Street
Queen St
Walmsley St
Poulton St
Lord St
Warren St
FY7
Fleetwood Cricket Club
St Edmunds RC Junior
Wood Street
12
17

C1
1 Elterwater
A1
1 Custom House La
D1
1 Keswick Gv
Knott End-on-Sea
A
B
C
D
1
2
3
4
5
11
18
Fleetwood Hospital
Wyre Borough Council
Lancashire Co Council
Fleetwood Museum
Queen's Terrace
Victoria Street
Dock Street
Church St
Albert St
Crown La
High St
Warren St
North St
Mill Lane
BOURNE MAY ROAD
ESPLANADE
BARTON SQ
B5270
LANCASTER
Qualle
Wayside
Ashton Av
Worsley Cl
Westbourne Road
Salisbury Av
Barton Av
Holme Road
Fairway Gdns
Parksway
Wyresdale Rd
Holmefield Rd
Links
Bleasdale Rd
Road
Hackensall Road
The Glen
Plantation Avenue
Over Wyre Medical Cen
Coniston Avenue
Kingston Cl
Eskdale
Hawkshead
Ennerdale Cl
Rydal
Lancaster Cl
Ambleside Av
PO
Hackensall Hall
Whinny Lane
Meadow Lane
New Heys Farm
Brine Wells
Coat Walls Farm
Clods Ca
Brine Wells

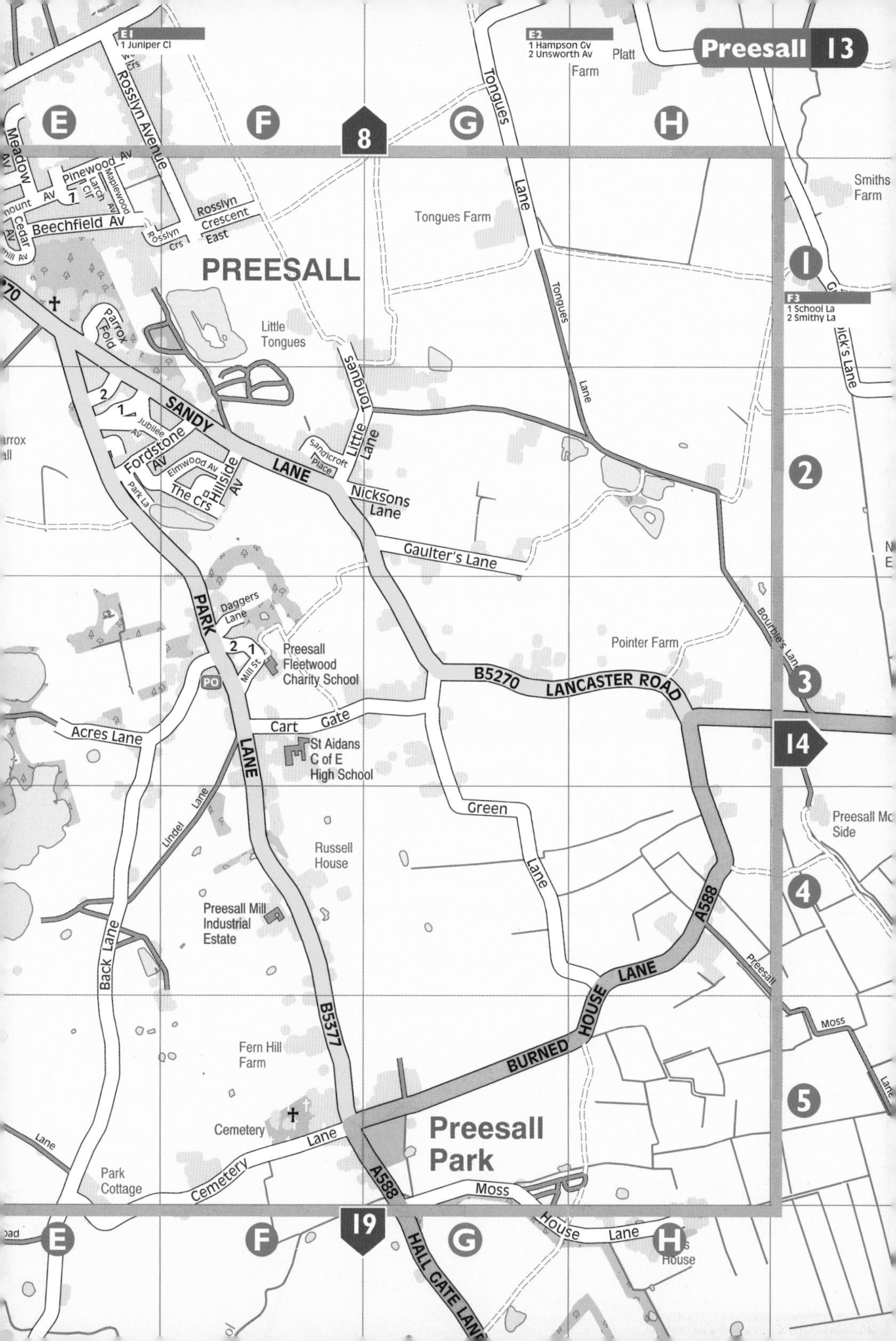
E1
1 Juniper Cl
E2
1 Hampson Gv
2 Unsworth Av
F3
1 School La
2 Smithy La
PREESALL
Preesall Park
Rosslyn Avenue
Rosslyn Crescent East
Pinewood Av
Larch Cl
Maplewood
Beechfield Av
Meadow
Cedar Av
Tongues Lane
Tongues Farm
Platt Farm
Smiths Farm
Little Tongues
Parrox Fold
SANDY LANE
Jubilee Av
Fordstone Av
Elmwood Av
The Crs
Hillside Av
Park La
Sandicroft Place
Little Tongues Lane
Nicksons Lane
Gaulter's Lane
Bourbles Lane
Pointer Farm
B5270 LANCASTER ROAD
PARK LANE
Daggers Lane
Mill St
PO
Preesall Fleetwood Charity School
Acres Lane
Cart Gate
St Aidans C of E High School
Green Lane
Lindel Lane
Russell House
Preesall Mill Industrial Estate
Back Lane
A588
BURNED HOUSE LANE
Preesall Moss Lane
B5377
Fern Hill Farm
Cemetery
Cemetery Lane
Park Cottage
Moss House Lane
HALL GATE LANE
House
E
F
G
H
1
2
3
4
5
8
14
19

14
9
13
A
B
C
D
1
2
3
4
5
Townson Hill
Smithson's Farm
Hooles Farm
Smallwood Hey
Wheel Lane
Pasture House Farm
Hools Lane
Smallwood Hey Road
Green Dick's Lane
Ned's Lane
Lamb's Lane
Shaws
Shaw's Lane
New England
Bourble's Lane
HEAD DYKE LANE
A588
Preesall Moss Side
Preesall Moss Lane
Moss House
Carter's Farm
Old Tom's
1 grid square represents 500 metres

Pilling St Johns C of E School
PO
Broadfleet Close
The Surgery
School Lane
Pilling
Taylor's Lane
LANCASTER
Fisher's Row
Stable Yard
A588
Cherry Tree Cl
St Johns Avenue
Carr Close
Horse Park Lane
Lancaster Road
Drive
Stakepool
St Williams RC School
Moss House
PO
Stake Pool
Pilling Water
Garstang
Carr Lane
Fold House
DYKE LANE
HEAD
A588
Scronkey
Bradshaw Lane
Pilling Moss
Bradshaw Lane Head
New Union Farm
Rigby
E
F
G
H
1
2
3
4
5

C5
1 Beechcroft

C1
1 Lynton Ct

D1
1 Hornby Av
2 Medway Av

D4
1 Way Ga

Cleveleys 17
E1
1 Cedar Av
E2
1 Ayr Ct
E4
1 Ripon Cl
F1
1 Hazel Av
2 Maple Av
F4
Street names for this grid square are listed at the back of the index
F5
1 Barnfield Cl
2 Folkestone Cl
3 Portsmouth Cl
G3
1 Venture Rd
G4
1 Borage Cl
2 Dunlin Cl
3 Fieldfare Cl
G5
1 Keeper's Hey
2 Pickmere Cl
H5
1 Hapton St
2 Orchard Cl
3 Walker Wy
E
F
G
H
11
18
21
1
2
3
4
5
Larkholme Avenue
Penrhos Av
Meadow
A585(T)
Fleetwood Cricket Club
Brook St
Hawthorn Av
Broadwater Av
Laurel Av
The Crs
St Edmunds RC Junior School
Wood Street
Fleetwood Rd
Jameson Road
Blackpool and Flyde College
FLEETWOOD ROAD
Rossall Lane
SALL LANE
B5268
Burn Hall Industrial Estate
Enterprise Way
AMOUNDERNESS WAY
Thistle Cl
Woodruff Cl
Bluebell
Chaffinch Cl
Pheasant Wood Dr
Celandine
Trefoil Cl
Elder Cl
Sorrel Cl
Snipe Cl
Milburn Av
Ingleby Close
Redcar Av
Myrtle Av
Heron Cl
Plover Cl
Kestrel Cl
Woodcock Cl
Northumberland Av
Selby Av
Mallard Close
Redwing Av
Swallow Cl
Curlew Cl
Whitecrest Av
Cheviot Av
Newcastle Av
Seaton Av
Ringway
Blaydon Av
Sunderland Av
Rochester Av
Brampton Av
Belford Av
Berwick Av
Bourne Way
Bourne Road
FLEETWOOD ROAD
NORTH
Saltash Rd
Crystal Rd
Gamble Road
Wembley Rd
Butts Rd
Burn Naze
Edward St
Rock St
John St
Northfold CP School
North Drive
Brooke Gv
Beck Gv
Burn Gv
Kirkby Av
Allonby Av
Halton Avenue
Allandale Av
Cornwall Av
Warwick Av
Kent Av
Croasdale Drive
Whimbrel Dr
Breeze Cl
The Maltings
Poachers Wy
The Covert
Mayfield Avenue
Teal Cl
Tower Cl
The Chase
Kildare Av
Springfield Drive
Widgeon Cl
Partridge Av
West Drive
Fairclough Road
Taywood Rd
Ormerod Street
Heys Street
Red Marsh Drive
Redmarsh School
Lincoln Av
Wolsey Cl
Ingleway
Hampton Pl
Gorse Av
May Bell Av
Central Drive
Eversleigh Av
Coleridge Av
Milton Av
Masefield Av
Tennyson Av
Reta Dr
Cookson Rd
Mildred Cl
Trinity Gdns
Fairholmes Way
Holmes Road
Sacred Heart School
Great Arley Swimming Pool
Special School
Brookside
PO

18
A
B
12
C
D
1
2
3
17
4
5
Brine Wells
Height o' th' Hill
Brown's Lane
Burrow's Lane
Burrow's Farm
River Wyre
Saltash Rd
Road
Butts Rd
Butts Close
Rock St
Burn
Ormerod Street
Red Marsh Drive
Heys Street
School
Crabtree Road
Redmarsh School
Great Arley
Brookside
22
1 grid square represents 500 metres

Preesall Park
Cemetery
Cemetery Lane
Park Cottage
Moss House Lane
Moss House
HALL GATE LANE
Grange Pool
Back Lane
Grange Lane
The Grange
Heads
Stalmine
Douglas Avenue
Smithy Lane
Smithy Close
Carr
Lynwood Drive
Hillside Dr
Fair Way
Fell Wy
Harwood Cl
Lynwood Dr
Malvern Av
Hanley Cl
Ash Lea Gv
The Surgery
MILL LANE
Birch Gv
Crook Dale La
Old To
Crook Da
Stalmine Moss S
Moss Side Lane
Dobson's
Moor End
End Lane
Carr End
STRICKLAND'S LANE
Trees Farm
A588
Lane
Ned's
Bowse's Hill Farm
High Gate Lane
Cold Row
Staynall Lane
Carr Cl
LANE
Staynall
Sower Carr
Sower Carr Lane
Brickhouse Lane
New Road
Wardley's Lane
Brick House La
Brick House Farm
Crombleholme Farm
13
23
E F G H I
1 2 3 4 5
H2
1 Pennine Wy
PO

20
D2
1 The Close
2 The Croft
3 Ramper Ga
4 Runnymede Av
5 St George's La
C5
1 Lodge Cl
2 Micklegate
D1
1 Ritherham Av
C4
1 Melton Pl
C1
1 Beachcomber Dr
2 Kensington Rd
C2
1 Kings Rd
2 Slater Rd
D3
1 Lakewood Av
2 Welwyn Pl
D4
1 Derwent Pl
2 Fleetwood Rd
3 Wingate Pl
4 Wray Gv
D5
1 Delphene Av
A
B
C
D
16
24
1
2
3
4
5
CLEVELEYS
Little Bispham
Norbreck
ROSSALL ROAD
A587
KELSO AVENUE
FLEETWOOD ROAD
PROMENADE
Princes Way
Promenade South
Lower Walk
Victoria Road West
Wyre Borough Council
Cleveleys Health Cen
Doctors Surgery
Norbreck Primary School
Chiropody Surgery
School
College Av
Anchorsholme La W
1 grid square represents 500 metres

E1
1 Leicester Ga
E5
1 Evesham Cl
2 Poolhill Cl
F1
1 Rosemary Av
E3
1 Murchison Gv
F2
1 Rowland Cl
F3, F5, G2
Street names for these grid squares are listed at the back of the index
F4
1 Back Epsom Rd
2 Idlewood Pl
3 Lockhurst Av
4 Quarrybank
5 Sanderling Cl
G1
1 Greenmount Av
G4
1 Green Oak Pl
H1
1 Bonney St
2 Crabtree Orch
3 Fairholmes Cl
4 Lowesway
5 Trunnah Gdns
H2
1 Churchill Cl
2 Crowder Av
3 Grasmere Av
4 Linadale Av
H3
1 Devonshire Ms
2 Heather Cl
3 Sandown Rd
H4
1 Bankfield Ct
2 The Paddock
H5
1 Briarwood Ct
17
22
25
Anchorsholme
Norcross
FY5
Burn Naze
Northfold CP School
VICTORIA ROAD WEST
VICTORIA ROAD EAST
AMOUNDERNESS WAY
FLEETWOOD RD NORTH
FLEETWOOD ROAD SOUTH
TRUNNAH RD
West Drive
North Drive
Marsh Farm
Thornton-Cleveleys Rugby Union Football Club
Primary School
Lancashire Country Council
Doctors Surgery
Marsh Mill Mus
Picture Gallery
Sacred Heart School
Great Arley Swimming Pool
Redmarsh School
Special School
Anchorsholme Primary School
Lancashire County Council
Blackpool & Fylde College
Whiteholme Road
Norcross Lane
Devonshire Avenue
Church Road

B4
1 Cheltenham Crs
2 Tuxbury Cl
3 Wensleydale Cl
B5
1 Ashcombe Ga
2 Balfour Cl
B2
1 Elmside Cl
2 Oakwood Cl
B3
1 Ainsdale Av
2 Chatsworth Cl
3 Fairhaven Cl
4 Lambs Hill Cl
5 Rosewood Cl
A4
1 Dalesford Cl
2 Dorchester Cl
3 Maple Av
4 Sandiways Cl
A2
1 Ferndale Cl
2 Prescot Pl
3 Springbank Av
A3
1 Edgeway Pl
2 Elmwood Dr
3 Mayfair Gdns
C4
1 Chiswell Gv
C5
1 Cranbourne Gv
2 Millersdale Cl
River Wyre
18
21
26
Trunnah
Stanah
THORNTON
Little Thornton
Breedy Butts
Stanah Country Pa
Redmarsh School
Special School
Red Marsh Drive
Hillylaid Road
Stanah Road
River Road
Raikes Road
Underbank Road
Stanah Gdns
Stanah CP Infant School
Stanah CP Junior School
Baines Endowed CP School
Millfield High School
Doctors Surgery
Lancashire County Council
LAMBS ROAD
STATION RD
SKIPPOOL ROAD
B5412
B5439
A585(T)
AMOUNDERNESS WAY
FLEETWOOD ROAD SOUTH
New Road
Links Gate
Woodhouse Rd
Thornton Cleveleys Cricket Club
Wyre Road
Lime Grove
Devonshire Avenue
Belvedere Road
Sunningdale Dr
Parkstone Av
Wentworth Dr
Tarnway
Tarn Road
Gladeway
Southdown Dr
Hillside Cl
Broughton Way
Newton Grove
Carleton
1 grid square represents 500 metres

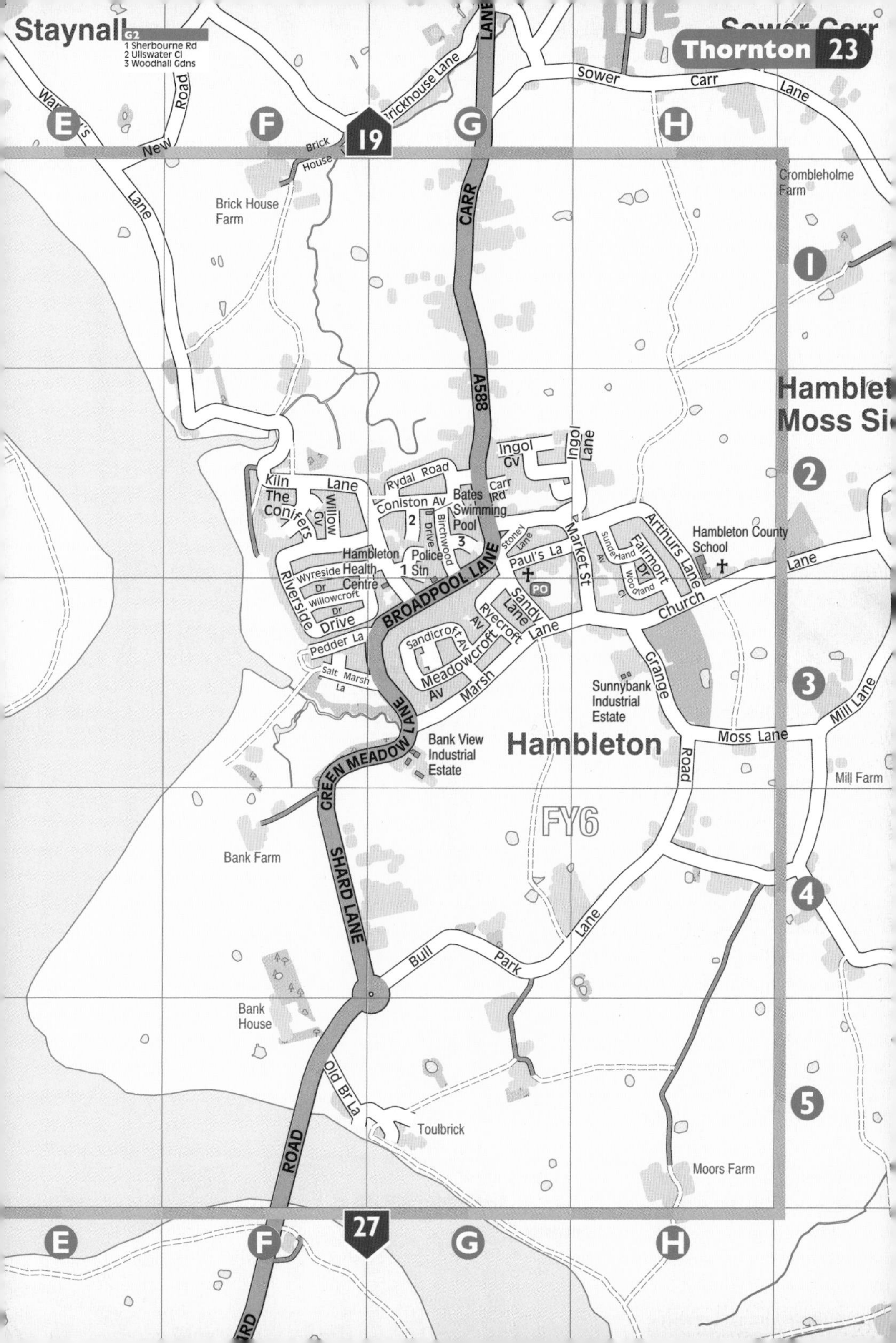
Staynall
G2
1 Sherbourne Rd
2 Ullswater Cl
3 Woodhall Gdns
Sower Carr
New Road
Brickhouse Lane
Brick House
Lane
Brick House Farm
CARR LANE
A588
Sower Carr Lane
Crombleholme Farm
Hamblet Moss Si
Ingol Gv
Ingol Lane
Rydal Road
Kiln Lane
The Conifers
Willow Gv
Coniston Av
Carr Rd
Bates Swimming Pool
Drive
Birchwood
Hambleton Health Centre
Police Stn
Riverside Drive
Wyreside Dr
Willowcroft Dr
Stoney Lane
Paul's La
Market St
Sunderland Av
Fairmont Dr
Woodland Cl
Arthurs Lane
Hambleton County School
Lane
Church
PO
BROADPOOL LANE
Pedder La
Salt Marsh La
Sandicroft Av
Meadowcroft Av
Ryecroft Av
Sandy Lane
Marsh Lane
Grange Road
Sunnybank Industrial Estate
Moss Lane
Mill Lane
Mill Farm
GREEN MEADOW LANE
Bank View Industrial Estate
Hambleton
FY6
Bank Farm
SHARD LANE
Bull Park Lane
Bank House
Old Br La
Toulbrick
Moors Farm
ROAD
RD
E F G H I
1 2 3 4 5
19
27

C1
1 Lanark Av
B3
1 Arundel Av
2 Carlton Gv
3 Daventry Av
4 Pennystone Rd
5 York Rd
C3
1 Bayswater
2 Cedric Pl
3 Melville Rd
D1
1 Oakland Av
D2
1 Cherrydale
2 Denebank
3 Norwich Pl
D3
1 Millom Av
D4
1 Normandie Av
Norbreck
20
28
Bispham
Queen's Promenade
Promenade
Chiropody Surgery
Westcliffe Infant School
Devonshire Road
Primary School
Doctors Surgery
World Wide Travel & Theatre Agency
Bispham Endowed Junior School
Golf Course
Shaftesbury Avenue
Hotel
Doctors Surg
Leys Road
B5265 Warbreck
1 grid square represents 500 metres

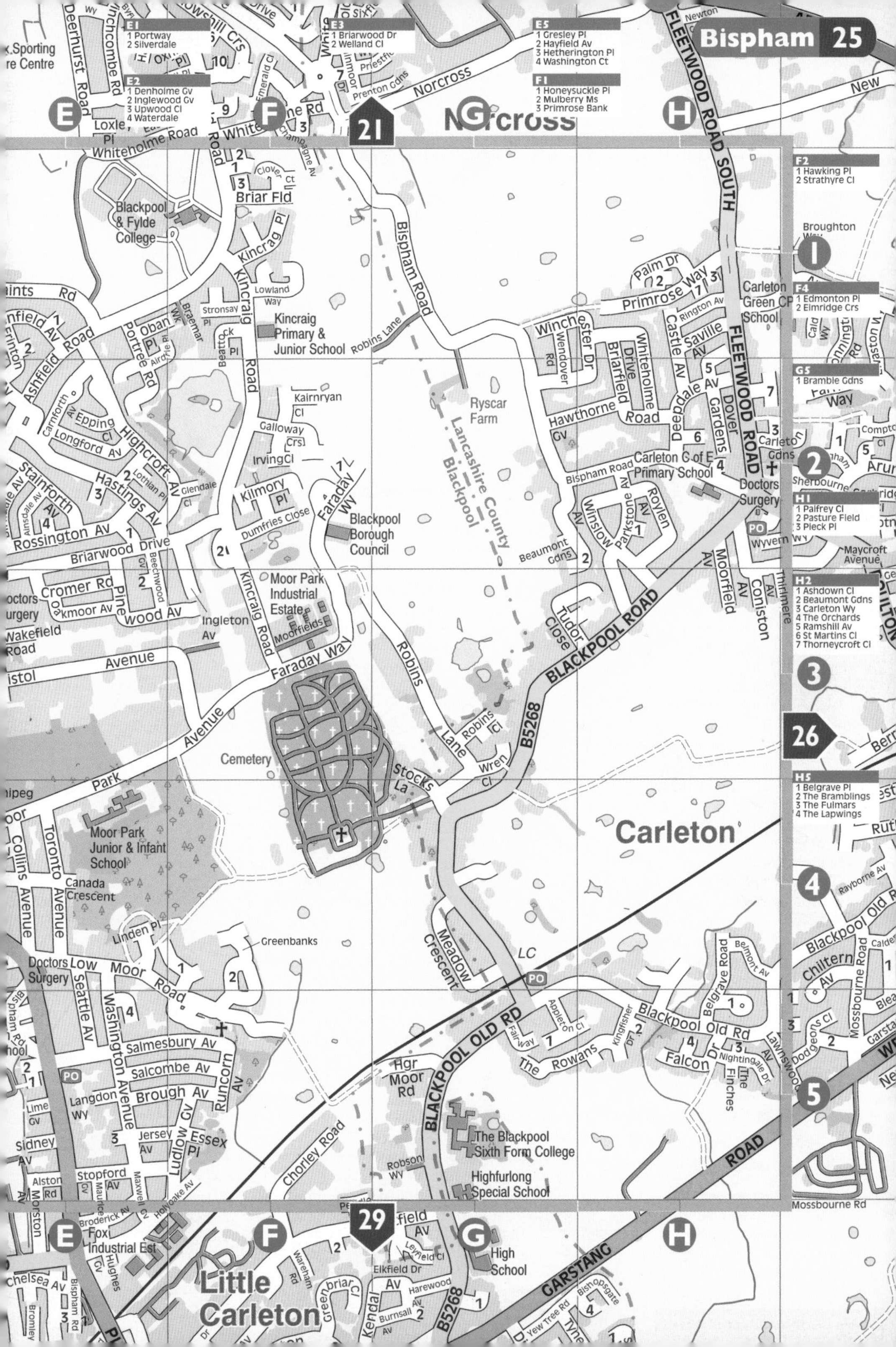
E1
1 Portway
2 Silverdale
E2
1 Denholme Gv
2 Inglewood Gv
3 Upwood Cl
4 Waterdale
E3
1 Briarwood Dr
2 Welland Cl
E5
1 Gresley Pl
2 Hayfield Av
3 Hetherington Pl
4 Washington Ct
F1
1 Honeysuckle Pl
2 Mulberry Ms
3 Primrose Bank
F2
1 Hawking Pl
2 Strathyre Cl
F4
1 Edmonton Pl
2 Elmridge Crs
G5
1 Bramble Gdns
H1
1 Palfrey Cl
2 Pasture Field
3 Pleck Pl
H2
1 Ashdown Cl
2 Beaumont Gdns
3 Carleton Wy
4 The Orchards
5 Ramshill Av
6 St Martins Cl
7 Thorneycroft Cl
H5
1 Belgrave Pl
2 The Bramblings
3 The Fulmars
4 The Lapwings
Norcross
21
26
29
Blackpool & Fylde College
Kincraig Primary & Junior School
Blackpool Borough Council
Moor Park Industrial Estate
Ryscar Farm
Lancashire County
Blackpool
Cemetery
Moor Park Junior & Infant School
Carleton
Carleton Green CP School
Carleton C of E Primary School
Doctors Surgery
The Blackpool Sixth Form College
Highfurlong Special School
High School
Little Carleton
Fox Industrial Est
Fleetwood Road South
Fleetwood Road
Blackpool Road
Blackpool Old Rd
Garstang Road
B5268
Bispham Road
Kincraig Road
Faraday Way
Robins Lane
Stocks La
Park Avenue
Whiteholme Road
Highcroft Av
Rossington Av
Briarwood Drive
Moor Road
Chorley Road
Meadow Crescent
Primrose Way
Deepdale Av
Hawthorne Road
Low Moor Road
Washington Avenue
Mossbourne Rd
Greenbanks
Canada Crescent

26
22
25
30
A2
1 Canterbury Cl
2 Knaresb'ough Cl
3 Maldern Av
4 The Paddock
5 Taylors Cl
A1
1 Carisbrooke Cl
2 Hadleigh Rd
A4
1 Brentwood Av
2 Garstang Cl
3 Roseway
A5
1 Cottam Pl
2 Dodgeons Cl
3 Glenholme Gdns
B3
1 The Lanterns
2 Longfield Pl
3 Prudy Hl
B4
1 Church St
2 Elizabeth Ct
3 Market Pl
4 Queen's Sq
C3
1 Crescent Rd
C4
1 Greenbank
2 Regents Ter
3 Windsor Ct
Breedy Butts
Skippool
POULTON - LE - FYLDE
Thornton Cleveleys Cricket Club
Breck CP School
Wyredale School
St Johns RC Primary School
Wyre Borough Council
Fylde Cricket Club
Cemetery
Hodgson High School
Poulton-le-Fylde Station
Doctors Surgery
Poulton C of E School
Carr Head CP School
Blackpool & Fylde College
Baines School
A585(T)
AMOUNDERNESS WAY
FLEETWOOD ROAD SOUTH
BRECK ROAD
STATION ROAD
POULTON RD
TITHEBARN ST
B5267
A588
A586
GARSTANG ROAD
WEST
B5412
1 grid square represents 500 metres

Old Br La
Toulbrick
Moors Farm
ROAD
E
F
23
G
H
I
Shard Bridge
SHARD
A588
NE A585(T)
2
River Wyre
3
MAINS LANE
Honeypot La
Pool Foot Lane
A585(T)
GARSTANG ROAD
GARSTANG
tle
ulton
Little
Singleto
4
AST
Cemetery
B5260
Drive
Bracewell Avenue
Wyrefields
Beacon Road
Avenue
LODGE
5
LANE
E
F
31
G
H
Singleton C of E Schoo
PO
Main
Carr Lane
B5260
STATI
ches

C5, D3
Street names for these grid squares are listed at the back of the index
B3, B4, B5, C3
Street names for these grid squares are listed at the back of the index
B2
1 East Boothroyden
2 Northfield Av
3 Redvers Ter
4 St Paul's Rd
C2
1 Avon Pl
2 Seacrest Av
C4
1 Back Cookson St
2 Butler St
3 Edelston Rd
4 Eden St
5 Fairhurst St
6 Greenhill Pl
7 Handley Rd
8 Hardman St
9 Henthorne St
10 Howard St
11 Lang St
12 Larkhill St
13 Seed St
14 Swainson St
15 Whiteside St
D1
1 Milford Av
D2
1 Blackfen Pl
2 Danson Gdns
3 Newman Rd
4 Penhill Cl
5 Rice Gv
D4
1 Chester Rd
2 Fenton Rd
3 Heald St
4 Healey St
5 St George Ct
6 Stirling Rd
D5
1 Durham Rd
2 Glenwood St
3 Myrtle Av
4 Poplar Av
5 Ridley St
6 Whitley Av
24
32
North Shore
PROMENADE
A584
Blackpool & Fleetwood Tramway
WARBRECK HILL ROAD
DEVONSHIRE ROAD
B5124
B5265 WARBRECK
North Pier
War Memorial
Town Hall & Municipal Blds
Superbowl Leisure Parcs
Tower World
Winter Gardens
Houndsmill Shopping Cen
Blackpool North Stn
Gynn Gallery
Claremont Junior & Infant School
Knowle Preparatory School
Cocker Trading Estate
Lancashire Area Hlth Authority
Sawmill St Industrial Estate
Whitegate Galleries
Reform Jewish Synagogue
Register Office
Blackpool Borough Council
CHURCH ST
GROSVENOR ST
COOKSON ST
ABINGDON ST
CORONATION ST
B5390
B5263
A583
1 grid square represents 500 metres

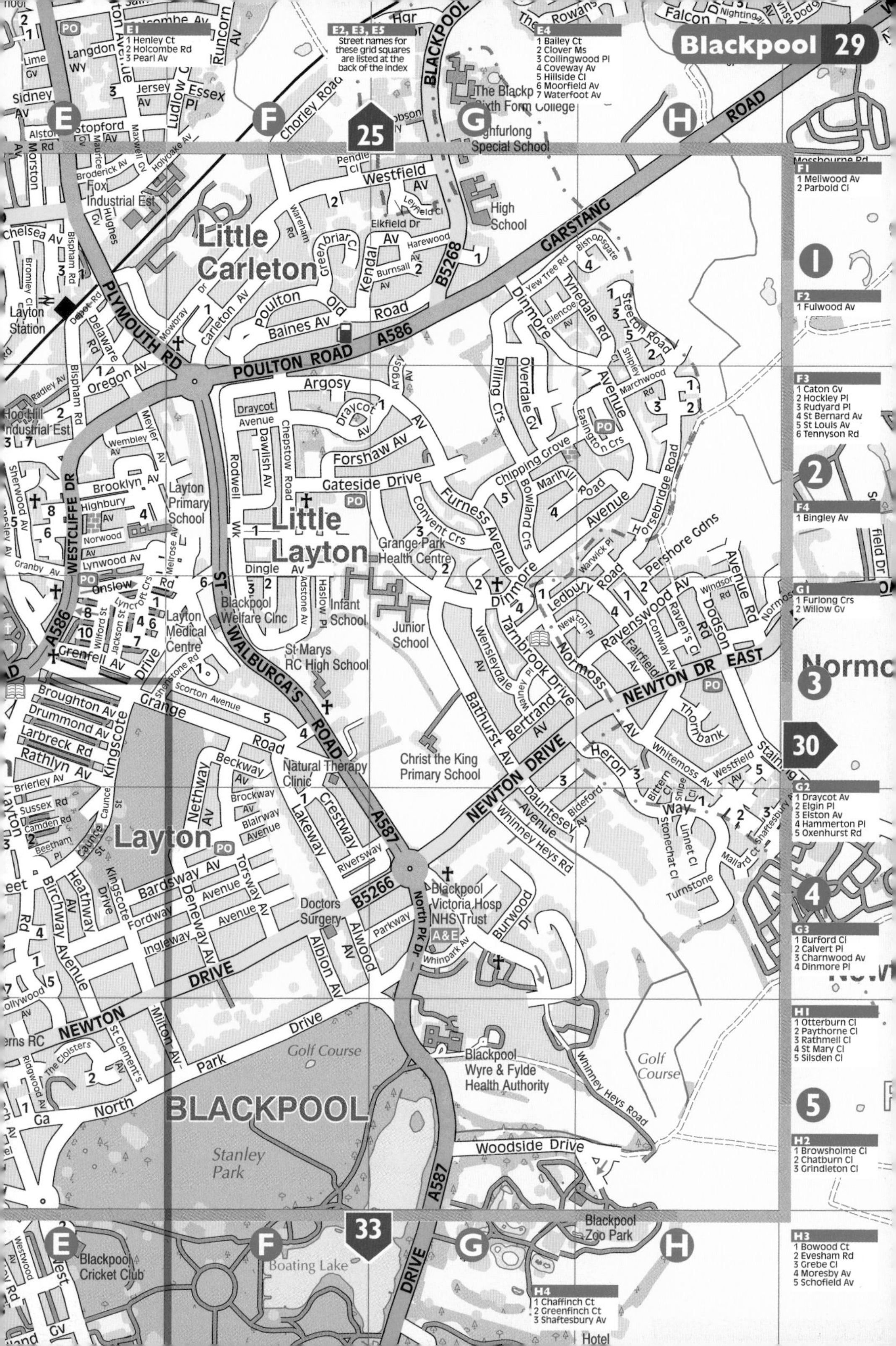

Blackpool 29
E1
1 Henley Ct
2 Holcombe Rd
3 Pearl Av
E2, E3, E5
Street names for these grid squares are listed at the back of the index
E4
1 Bailey Ct
2 Clover Ms
3 Collingwood Pl
4 Coveway Av
5 Hillside Cl
6 Moorfield Av
7 Waterfoot Av
F1
1 Mellwood Av
2 Parbold Cl
F2
1 Fulwood Av
F3
1 Caton Gv
2 Hockley Pl
3 Rudyard Pl
4 St Bernard Av
5 St Louis Av
6 Tennyson Rd
F4
1 Bingley Av
G1
1 Furlong Crs
2 Willow Gv
G2
1 Draycot Av
2 Elgin Pl
3 Elston Av
4 Hammerton Pl
5 Oxenhurst Rd
G3
1 Burford Cl
2 Calvert Pl
3 Charnwood Av
4 Dinmore Pl
H1
1 Otterburn Cl
2 Paythorne Cl
3 Rathmell Cl
4 St Mary Cl
5 Silsden Cl
H2
1 Browsholme Cl
2 Chatburn Cl
3 Grindleton Cl
H3
1 Bowood Ct
2 Evesham Rd
3 Grebe Cl
4 Moresby Av
5 Schofield Av
H4
1 Chaffinch Ct
2 Greenfinch Ct
3 Shaftesbury Av
25
30
33
Little Carleton
Little Layton
Layton
BLACKPOOL
Layton Station
Fox Industrial Est
Hoo Hill Industrial Est
High School
Highfurlong Special School
Layton Primary School
Layton Medical Centre
Blackpool Welfare Clnc
Infant School
Junior School
Grange Park Health Centre
St Marys RC High School
Natural Therapy Clinic
Christ the King Primary School
Doctors Surgery
Blackpool Victoria Hosp NHS Trust
A&E
Blackpool Wyre & Fylde Health Authority
Golf Course
Stanley Park
Boating Lake
Blackpool Cricket Club
Blackpool Zoo Park
Hotel
POULTON ROAD
GARSTANG ROAD
PLYMOUTH RD
WESTCLIFFE DR
ST WALBURGA'S ROAD
NEWTON DRIVE
NEWTON DR EAST
Woodside Drive
Whinney Heys Road
North Park Drive
Gateside Drive
Furness Avenue
Dinmore Avenue
Normoss
Grange Road

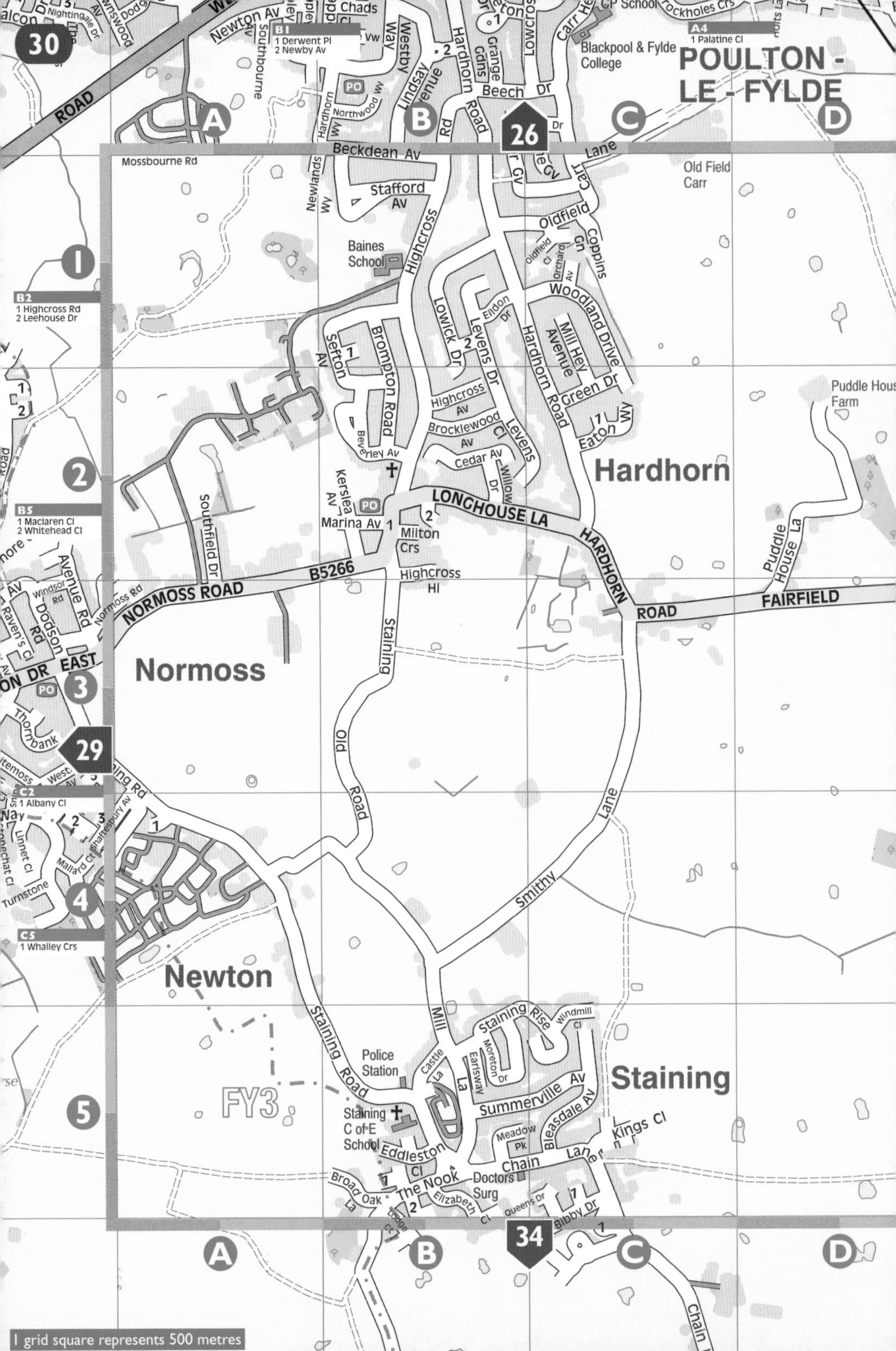

30
POULTON - LE - FYLDE
Hardhorn
Normoss
Newton
Staining
FY3
26
29
34
B1
1 Derwent Pl
2 Newby Av
A4
1 Palatine Cl
B2
1 Highcross Rd
2 Leehouse Dr
B5
1 Maclaren Cl
2 Whitehead Cl
C2
1 Albany Cl
C5
1 Whalley Crs
Blackpool & Fylde College
CP School
Baines School
Police Station
Staining C of E School
Doctors Surg
Old Field Carr
Puddle House Farm
NORMOSS ROAD
B5266
LONGHOUSE LA
HARDHORN ROAD
FAIRFIELD
Beckdean Av
Mossbourne Rd
Stafford Av
Highcross Rd
Hardhorn Road
Beech Dr
Carr Lane
Oldfield
Coppins
Woodland Drive
Mill Hey Avenue
Green Dr
Eaton Wy
Lowick Dr
Levens Dr
Sefton Av
Brompton Road
Highcross Av
Brocklewood Av
Cedar Av
Willow Dr
Beverley Av
Kerslea Av
Marina Av
Milton Crs
Highcross Hl
Southfield Dr
Staining Old Road
Smithy Lane
Mill La
Staining Road
Staining Rise
Windmill Cl
Moreton Dr
Earlsway
Castle La
Summerville Av
Bleasdale Av
Kings Cl
Meadow Pk
Chain Lane
Eddleston Cl
The Nook
Broad Oak La
Elizabeth Cl
Queens Dr
Bibby Dr
Lodge Ct
Puddle House La
Dodson Rd
Avenue Rd
Windsor Rd
Normoss Rd
Thornbank
Linnet Cl
Mallard Ct
Turnstone
Shaftesbury Av
Newton Av
Southbourne
Lindsay Avenue
Westby Way
Northwood Wy
Newlands Wy
Grange Gdns
Chads
A B C D
1 2 3 4 5
1 grid square represents 500 metres

E
F
27
G
H
LANE
Singleton C of E Scho
PO
Carr Lane
Carr Lane
The Beeches
Singleto
Main Dyke
Avenham Hall
ROAD
STATION
OAD
B5266
Fairfield Rd
Todderstaffe Hall
LC
Hawes House
Preese Hall
Grantham Rd
Aston Street
Cosford Street
Weeton County Primary School
Henderson Rd
PO
1
2
3
4
5
E
F
35
G
H

32
B5
1 Brighton Av
B3, B4, C4
Street names for these grid squares are listed at the back of the index
B2
1 Back Shannon St
2 Bickerstaffe St
3 Butler Rd
4 Cragg St
5 Dale Ms
6 Louise St
7 Middle St
8 Singleton St
B1
1 Adelaide St
2 Bank Hey St
3 Brunswick St
4 Havelock St
5 Kay St
6 New Bonny St
7 Richardson St
8 Sheppard St
9 Winifred St
C1
1 Anderson St
2 Freckleton St
3 Livingstone Rd
4 Pennine Cl
5 Stanley Rd
6 Westwell Gv
C2
1 Chadwick St
2 Fern Gv
3 Jameson St
4 Orme St
5 Salthouse Av
C3
1 Bela Gv
2 Levens Gv
3 Palmer Av
4 Sands Wy
D1
1 Lyceum Av
2 Tyne Av
D2
1 Balmer Gv
2 Dinckley Gv
3 Kingsland Gv
4 Snowdon Cl
D3
1 Arkholme Av
2 Chadfield Rd
3 Condor Gv
4 Hartford Av
5 Lilac Av
6 Marina Av
7 Nuttall Rd
D4
1 Aylesbury Av
2 Devon St
3 Dunsop Cl
4 Harlech Av
5 Hebden Av
6 Rugby St
7 Scudamore Crs
8 Taunton St
9 Truro St
10 Weston Pl
11 Winchester Av
D5
1 Edwell Av
2 Frederick St
3 Houghton Av
4 Malham Av
5 Newbury Av
6 Swindon Av
7 Walverden Av
A
B
C
D
1
2
3
4
5
28
38
North Pier
Blackpool Tower
Coral Island
Lifeboat Station
Sealife Centre
Louis Tussauds Waxworks
Central Pier
South Pier
Ripleys Believe It or Not Museum
Winter Gardens
Church St
Church St
Devonshire Sq
Hornby Road
Blackpool & Fylde College
Albert Rd
Coronation St
Read's Av
Palatine
Park Road
Police Stn
Blackpool Co Court
Central Dr
Princess Street
Odeon Cinema
Islamic Community Cen & Mosque
Blackpool Borough Council
AMF Bowling
Grasmere Road
Tram & Bus Depot
Blackpool Football Club
Bloomfield Medical Cen
Bloomfield Road
Lytham Road
Central Drive
Promenade
Waterloo Road
Blackpool South Stn
Victoria Mkt Hall
Doctors Surgery
St Cuthberts Primary School
South Shore
Yeadon Way
Ansdell Road
Station Road
Watson Road
A584
A5099
A5073
B5262
B5390
B5263
A583
1 grid square represents 500 metres

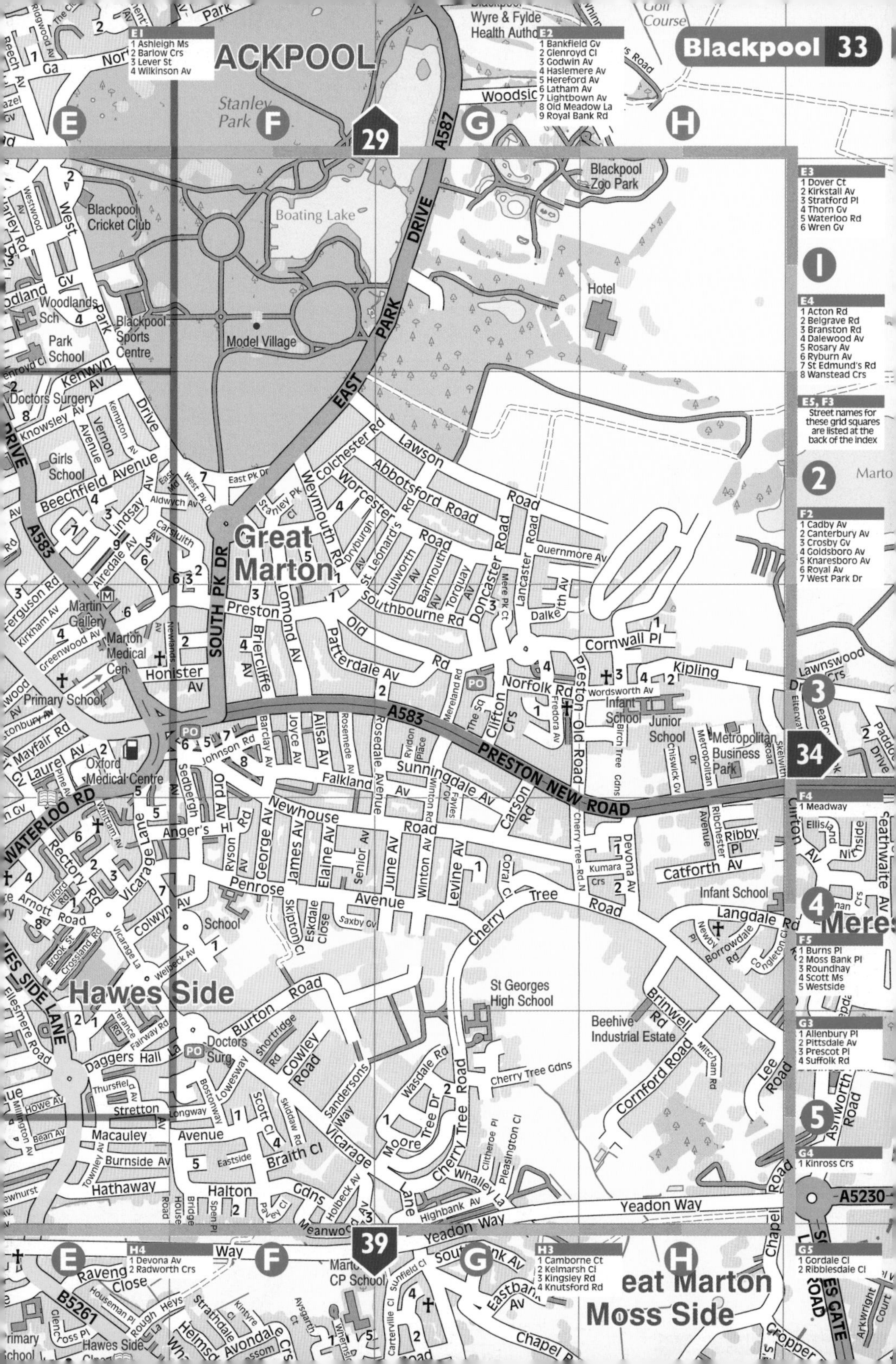
E1
1 Ashleigh Ms
2 Barlow Crs
3 Lever St
4 Wilkinson Av
E2
1 Bankfield Gv
2 Glenroyd Cl
3 Godwin Av
4 Haslemere Av
5 Hereford Av
6 Latham Av
7 Lightbown Av
8 Old Meadow La
9 Royal Bank Rd
E3
1 Dover Ct
2 Kirkstall Av
3 Stratford Pl
4 Thorn Gv
5 Waterloo Rd
6 Wren Gv
E4
1 Acton Rd
2 Belgrave Rd
3 Branston Rd
4 Dalewood Av
5 Rosary Av
6 Ryburn Av
7 St Edmund's Rd
8 Wanstead Crs
E5, F3
Street names for these grid squares are listed at the back of the index
F2
1 Cadby Av
2 Canterbury Av
3 Crosby Gv
4 Goldsboro Av
5 Knaresboro Av
6 Royal Av
7 West Park Dr
F4
1 Meadway
F5
1 Burns Pl
2 Moss Bank Pl
3 Roundhay
4 Scott Ms
5 Westside
G3
1 Allenbury Pl
2 Pittsdale Av
3 Prescot Pl
4 Suffolk Rd
G4
1 Kinross Crs
G5
1 Gordale Cl
2 Ribblesdale Cl
H3
1 Camborne Ct
2 Kelmarsh Cl
3 Kingsley Rd
4 Knutsford Rd
H4
1 Devona Av
2 Radworth Crs
29
34
39
E
F
G
H
I
2
3
4
5
BLACKPOOL
Stanley Park
Wyre & Fylde Health Authority
Golf Course
Blackpool Zoo Park
Boating Lake
Blackpool Cricket Club
Blackpool Sports Centre
Model Village
Hotel
Woodlands Sch
Park School
Doctors Surgery
Girls School
Great Marton
Martin Gallery
Marton Medical Cen
Primary School
Oxford Medical Centre
Hawes Side
School
Doctors Surg
St Georges High School
Beehive Industrial Estate
Wordsworth Infant School
Junior School
Metropolitan Business Park
Infant School
Marton CP School
Great Marton Moss Side
A587
A583
A5230
B5261
EAST PARK DRIVE
SOUTH PK DR
PRESTON NEW ROAD
WATERLOO RD
HAWES SIDE LANE
Yeadon Way
Preston Old Road
Cherry Tree Road
Vicarage Lane
Lawson Road
Abbotsford Road
Worcester Road
Doncaster Road
Lancaster Road
Quernmore Av
Southbourne Rd
Old Patterdale Av Rd
Norfolk Rd
Cornwall Pl
Kipling Dr
Newhouse Road
Penrose Avenue
Burton Road
Cowley Road
Brinwell Rd
Cornford Road
Langdale Rd
Catforth Av
Falkland Av
Sunningdale Av
Beechfield Avenue
Knowsley Av
Kenwyn Av
Honister Av
Macauley Avenue
Hathaway
Burnside Av
Halton Gdns
Stretton Av
Daggers Hall La
Raveng Close
Chapel Rd
Lee Road
Ashworth Road

Staining
FY3
A4
1 Birkside Wy
2 Crummock Pl
3 Dalegarth Cl
4 Langdale Pl
5 Rossett Av
A3
1 Bassen'waite Rd
2 Dovedale Av
B4
1 Oakleaf Wy
2 St Monica's Wy
C1
1 Chain La
Station
Summerville Av
Bleasdale Av
Meadow Pk
Kings Cl
Eddleston
Chain Lane
Doctors Surg
Broad Oak La
Lodge Ct
Elizabeth Cl
Bibby Dr
30
Chain Lane
Main Dyke
Lancashire County
Blackpool
Marton Mere
Kipling Drive
Lawnswood Crs
Elterwater Pl
Meadowbrook
Paddock Drive
Wheatlands Crs
Metropolitan Dr
Metro Bus Park
33
Mythop Road
Little Marton
PRESTON NEW ROAD
Clifton Av
Ribchester Avenue
Ribby Pl
Ellis Rd
Nithside
Seathwaite Av
Castlerigg Pl
Loughrigg Ter
Doctors Surg
Grizedale Road
Bowfell Cl
Kentmere Dr
Ambleside Rd
Acorn Ms
Winster Pl
Infant School
Langdale Rd
Newby Pl
Borrowdale Rd
Congleton Cl
Annan Crs
Mereside
Cartmell Rd
Langdale Road
Lindbeck Road
Deepdale Road
Ennerdale Road
Mickleden Rd
PO
Mardale Av
Rusland Av
Branstree Road
Bowness Avenue
Hawkshead Ter
Troutbeck Crs
A583
Mitcham Rd
Spen Farm Business Park
Clifton Road
Lee Road
Ashworth Road
Blackpool Borough Council
Clifton Road
Junction 4
Clifton Retail Park
A5230
M55
40
Chapel Road
SQUIRES GATE LINK ROAD
Brunel Way
Arkwright Court
Peel Hill
Peel Hill
A B C D
1 2 3 4 5
1 grid square represents 500 metres

Hawes House
E
F
31
G
Preese Hall
H
I
2
Mythop Road
ythop
3
Mythop Road
Knowslev
4
Weet
St Mi
Prim
5
M55
41
Moss House F
E
F
G
H
Moss House Lane
Moss House Lane

B2
1 Greensway
2 Mere Cl
A2
1 Sunningdale
B3
1 Victoria Ct
B5
1 Newbury Cl
2 Newbury Gn
3 Severn Hl
C5
1 Hazelmere Rd
2 Laburnum Dr
3 Old Cft
D5
1 Hill Crest Av
2 Woodlands Dr
Barton Hall
Crow Hall
Stanley Cft
B5269
Normandy Rd
Lowcroft
Moss House Rd
Broadfield
Moorcroft
Sandygate La
Ashford Crs
West Crescent
Northway
Stone Park Road
Wentworth Dr
Av
Fairways
Kingsway Av
Greensway
WOODPLUMPTON
Pringle Wd
Downing Ct
Broughton High School
A6
Willow Tree Av
Pinewood Av
LANE
Broughton
Old Hall
PO
GARSTANG ROAD
Bank Hall
Hotel
Broughton C of E Primary School
Broughton Park Private Hospital
Church Lane
D'Urton Lane
Broughton House
Junction 1
M55
B6241
Lightfoot Green Lane
EASTWAY
Our Lady & St Edwards RC Primary School
Hazelmere
Lime Chase
Lightfoot Cl
Lightfoot Lane
GARSTANG RD A6
Parklands Grove
Highfield Dr
Parklands Dr
Brookfield Dr
South Gv
South Dr
Preston Grasshoppers Rugby Football Club
Sandyforth Lane
Oakwood Drive
Newark Pl
Beech Drive
Beech Drive Surg
LIGHTFOOT LANE
Sharoe Green
45
Cheriton Fld
Shalgrove Field
Belton Hl
Marlborough Dr
Ashwood Road
Carnoustie Close
Greenacres
Harris CP School
Marston Moor
Hillcroft
Marston Close
Brookside Rd
Sharoe Green Dr
Clanfield
Brooklands
1 grid square represents 500 metres

E5
1 Langfield Cl
2 Longfield
F5
1 Broughton
Tower Wy
WHITTINGHAM LANE
B5269
Whittingham
House
Short
Lane
Dean House
Pudding Pie Nook
Lane
Cowell's Farm
Pudding
Pie Nook
Junction 32
Haighton Top
Lane
D'Urton
D'Urton Lane
Highrigg Dr
Broughton
Hall
Midgery Lane
EASTWAY
TWAY
Briar Bank Rw
Haywood Cl
Levensgarth
Langport Cl
Longley Cl
Ashness Cl
Eskdale Cl
Tiverton Cl
Meadowfield
Kennet Dr
Av
Tower Lane
Southey Cl
Barnacre Cl
Ashleigh Ct
Oliver's Pl
Caxton Rd
Pittman
Pittman Ct
Way
M6
Fernyhalgh Lane
46
St Peters
Primary Sch
Drive
Singleton
Cl
Tower Gn
Gatesgarth
Av
Lane
Tower
Deborah Av
Pennines
The Howgills
Faraday
Williams
Way
E
F
G
H
1
2
3
4
5

1 grid square represents 500 metres

Squires Gate 39
E1
1 Annaside Cl
2 Burgess Av
3 Reaney Av
4 Southworth Av
5 Teenadore Av
E2
1 Margate Av
E3
1 Alpine Av
2 Elswick Pl
3 Inskip Pl
F1
1 Aysgarth Ct
2 Bakers Ct
3 Gregson Cl
4 Marshdale Rd
5 Moorview Ct
6 Moss Wy
F2
1 Milldyke Cl
2 Millfield Rd
3 Moorgate
4 Windmill Pl
F3
1 Belverdale Gdns
2 Broadfield Av
3 Dugdale Ct
4 Myerscough Av
5 Sycamore Av
6 Thornhill Cl
G1
1 Bamburgh Cl
2 Carisbrooke Av
3 Corbridge Cl
4 Nairn Cl
5 Westbank Av
G2
1 Dumbarton Cl
2 Dunvegan Cl
3 Florence St
4 Lauriston Cl
5 Limechase Cl
6 Taymouth Rd
G3
1 Laundry Rd North
G4
1 Worthington Rd
33
40
49
Great Marton Moss Side
Common Edge
Great Marton Moss
FY4
Yeadon Way
Squires Gate Link Road
A5230
B5261
Common Edge Road
Progress Way
Lane
Hathaway
Halton Gdns
Braith Cl
Vicarage Lane
Moore Tree Dr
Cherry Tree Rd
Highbank
Meanwood
Southbank Av
Eastbank Av
Chapel Rd
Marton CP School
Ravenglass Close
Hawes Side Clnc
Rough Heys La
Strathdale
Helmsdale Rd
Wharfedale
Avondale Crs
Blossom Av
Highfield Road
Lowfield Road
Holgate
Walkers Hl
Askrigg Cl
Midgeland Road
Stockydale Road
Jubilee La N
Dickie's La
Cropper
Johnsville Av
Crompton Av
Webster Av
Doctors Surg
Sedgfield Cl
Bowgreave Cl
Glenapp Av
Roxburgh Rd
Kincardine Av
Lochinch Close
Brookfield Av
Harold Av
Bennett's Lane
Stanmore Av
Hampshire Pl
Henson Av
Kingsmede
Regal Av
Edgeway
Drakelowe Av
Collyhurst Avenue
Willowbank Av
Moss House Road
New Hall Av
Jubilee Lane
Alpine Av
Avenue
Plumpton Road
Nateby Av
Newlyn Av
School
Longridge Avenue
Westby Avenue
Weeton Avenue
PO
Chestnut Av
Burbank Cl
Fisher's Lane
Ecclesgate Road
St Nicholas Road
St Nicholas C of E School
School Road
Kitty Lane
Sandy Lane
Squires Gate Industrial Estate
Sycamore Trading Estate
Oakwood Close
Jepson Way
Common Edge Rd
Division Lane
Moss Edge Lane
Blackpool
Lancashire County
Queensway
The Hamlet
Appealing La
Hogton Cl
Calder Cl
Cottam Cl
Honister Square
Whitethorn Mews
Linden Ms
Snowdon Road
Fieldway
Edge Lane
E
F
G
H
I
2
3
4
5

40
Ashworth Road
Clifton Road
Blackpool Borough Council
Clifton Retail Park
Clifton Road
Junction 4
A
B
C
D
A5230
34
M55
Chapel Road
SQUIRES GATE LINK ROAD
Brunel Way
Arkwright Court
Peel Hill
Peel Hill
1
Cropper Rd
Dickie's La
Bambers La
Jenny La
Old House Lane
South
Lane
Dickie's
Bambers Lane
2
FY4
Cropper Road
Whitehill Road
Jubilee Lane
3
School Road
39
Wild Lane
Peel Road
Lane
4
Midgeland Road
5
Division Lane
Pe
Peel Road
Anna's Road
50
A
B
C
D
Lane
1 grid square represents 500 metres
Lytham

E2
1 Bentley Dr
2 Lancia Crs
3 Lotus Dr
M55
E
F
35
G
H
Moss House Farm
Moss House Lane
Moss House Lane
Lotus Drive
PRESTON NEW ROAD A583
PRESTON NEW ROAD
A583
Staining Wood Farm
Little
Plum
Westby Road
Ballam Road
51
Lower
Ballam
North Farm
1
2
3
4
5

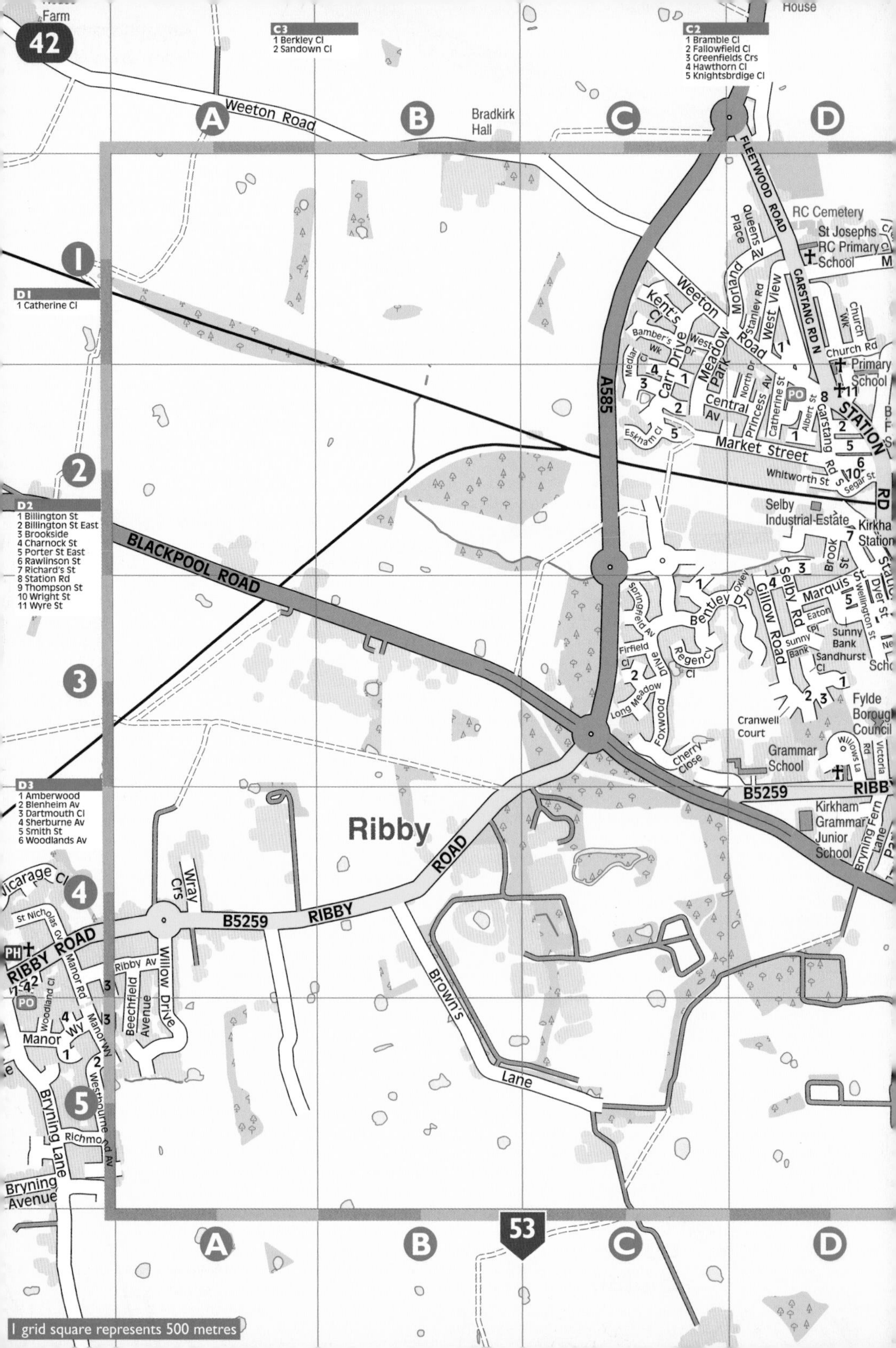

42
53
Farm
House
C3
1 Berkley Cl
2 Sandown Cl
C2
1 Bramble Cl
2 Fallowfield Cl
3 Greenfields Crs
4 Hawthorn Cl
5 Knightsbrdige Cl
D1
1 Catherine Cl
D2
1 Billington St
2 Billington St East
3 Brookside
4 Charnock St
5 Porter St East
6 Rawlinson St
7 Richard's St
8 Station Rd
9 Thompson St
10 Wright St
11 Wyre St
D3
1 Amberwood
2 Blenheim Av
3 Dartmouth Cl
4 Sherburne Av
5 Smith St
6 Woodlands Av
Weeton Road
Bradkirk Hall
FLEETWOOD ROAD
RC Cemetery
St Josephs RC Primary School
Queens Av
Place
Morland Av
Stanley Rd
West View
GARSTANG RD N
Church Wk
Church Rd
Primary School
Weeton Road
Kent's Cl
Bamber's Wk
West Dr
Meadow Park
North Dr
Princess Av
Catherine St
Albert St
Medlar Cl
Carr Drive
Central Av
Garstang Rd S
STATION RD
Eskham Cl
Market Street
Whitworth St
Segar St
A585
Selby Industrial Estate
Kirkham Station
Brook St
Station
Dyer St
BLACKPOOL ROAD
Springfield Av
Bentley Dr
Oxley Cl
Selby Rd
Gillow Road
Marquis St
Wellington St
Eaton Pl
Sunny Bank
Sandhurst Cl
Firfield Cl
Regency Cl
Drive
Long Meadow
Foxwood
Cherry Close
Cranwell Court
Fylde Borough Council
Grammar School
Willows La
Victoria Rd
B5259
RIBBY
Kirkham Grammar Junior School
Bryning Fern Lane
Ribby
ROAD
Vicarage Cl
St Nicholas Gv
Wray Crs
B5259
RIBBY
RIBBY ROAD
PH
PO
Manor Rd
Ribby Av
Willow Drive
Beechfield Avenue
Woodland Cl
Manor Wy
Westbourne Rd
Brown's Lane
Bryning Lane
Richmond Av
Bryning Avenue
A B C D
1 2 3 4 5
1 grid square represents 500 metres

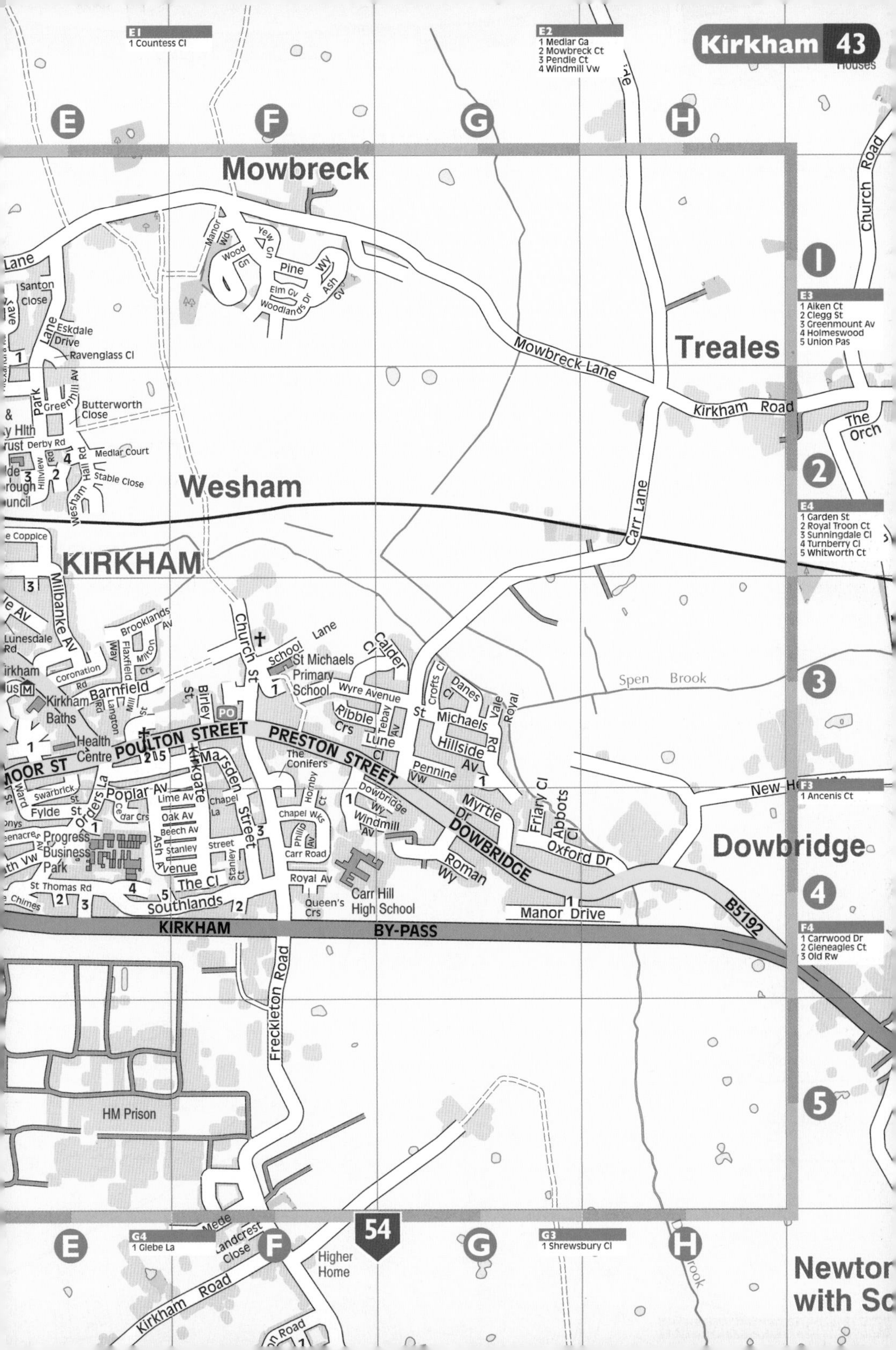
Kirkham 43
E1
1 Countess Cl
E2
1 Medlar Ga
2 Mowbreck Ct
3 Pendle Ct
4 Windmill Vw
E
F
G
H
Mowbreck
Treales
Wesham
KIRKHAM
Dowbridge
E3
1 Aiken Ct
2 Clegg St
3 Greenmount Av
4 Holmeswood
5 Union Pas
E4
1 Garden St
2 Royal Troon Ct
3 Sunningdale Cl
4 Turnberry Cl
5 Whitworth Ct
F3
1 Ancenis Ct
F4
1 Carrwood Dr
2 Gleneagles Ct
3 Old Rw
G4
1 Glebe La
G3
1 Shrewsbury Cl
1
2
3
4
5
Church Road
Mowbreck Lane
Kirkham Road
Carr Lane
The Orch
Spen Brook
New Hey Lane
Manor Wd
Yew Gn
Wood Gn
Pine Wy
Ash Gv
Elm Gv
Woodlands Dr
Santon Close
Eskdale Drive
Ravenglass Cl
Park Lane
Greenhill Av
Butterworth Close
Derby Rd
Medlar Court
Stable Close
Hillview Rd
Wesham Hall Rd
Milbanke Av
Lunesdale Rd
Brooklands Av
Flaxfield Way
Milton Crs
Coronation Rd
Barnfield
Church St
School Lane
St Michaels Primary School
Calder Cl
Crofts Cl
Danes Cl
Royal Vale
Wyre Avenue
Ribble Crs
Tebay Av
Lune Cl
St Michaels Rd
Hillside Av
Pennine Vw
Kirkham Baths
Health Centre
Langton Rd
Mill St
Birley St
PO
POULTON STREET
PRESTON STREET
MOOR ST
Kirkgate
Marsden Street
The Conifers
Hornby Ct
Dowbridge Wy
Windmill Av
Myrtle Dr
DOWBRIDGE
Friary Cl
Abbots Cl
Oxford Dr
Roman Wy
Ward St
Swarbrick St
Fylde St
Orders La
Poplar Av
Cedar Crs
Lime Av
Oak Av
Beech Av
Ash Av
Stanley Avenue
Chapel La
Street
Stanley Ct
Chapel Wks
Phillip Av
Carr Road
Royal Av
Queen's Crs
Carr Hill High School
Progress Business Park
St Thomas Rd
The Cl
Southlands
Manor Drive
B5192
KIRKHAM BY-PASS
Freckleton Road
HM Prison
54
Mede
Landcrest Close
Higher Home
Kirkham Road
Newton with Sc

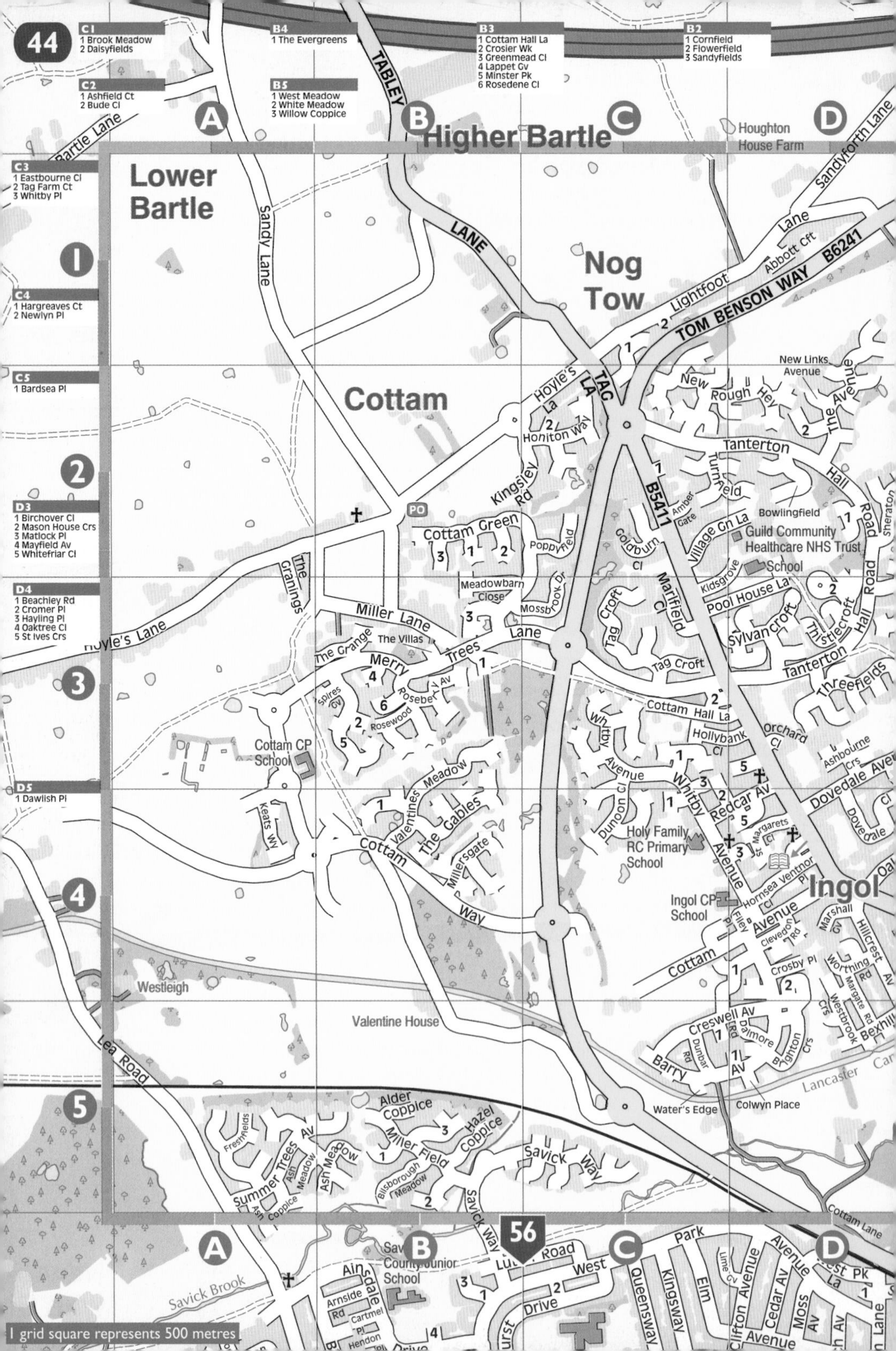
C1
1 Brook Meadow
2 Daisyfields
C2
1 Ashfield Ct
2 Bude Cl
B4
1 The Evergreens
B5
1 West Meadow
2 White Meadow
3 Willow Coppice
B3
1 Cottam Hall La
2 Crosier Wk
3 Greenmead Cl
4 Lappet Gv
5 Minster Pk
6 Rosedene Cl
B2
1 Cornfield
2 Flowerfield
3 Sandyfields
C3
1 Eastbourne Cl
2 Tag Farm Ct
3 Whitby Pl
C4
1 Hargreaves Ct
2 Newlyn Pl
C5
1 Bardsea Pl
D3
1 Birchover Cl
2 Mason House Crs
3 Matlock Pl
4 Mayfield Av
5 Whitefriar Cl
D4
1 Beachley Rd
2 Cromer Pl
3 Hayling Pl
4 Oaktree Cl
5 St Ives Crs
D5
1 Dawlish Pl
A
B
C
D
1
2
3
4
5
Higher Bartle
Lower Bartle
Houghton House Farm
Bartle Lane
Sandy Lane
TABLEY LANE
Sandyforth Lane
Nog Tow
Lightfoot Lane
Abbott Cft
TOM BENSON WAY B6241
Cottam
Hoyle's La
TAG LA
New Links Avenue
New Rough Hey
The Avenue
Honiton Way
Tanterton Hall Road
Kingsley Rd
B5411
Turnfield
Amber Gate
Bowlingfield
PO
Cottam Green
Poppyfield
Goldburn Cl
Village Gn La
Guild Community Healthcare NHS Trust
School
Sheraton
The Granings
Meadowbarn Close
Mossbrook Dr
Tag Croft
Marlfield Cl
Kidsgrove
Pool House La
Sylvancroft
Thistlecroft
Hoyle's Lane
Miller Lane
The Villas
Lane
The Grange
Merry Trees
Rosebery Av
Tag Croft
Tanterton
Threefields
Spires Gv
Rosewood
Cottam Hall La
Whitby Avenue
Hollybank Cl
Orchard Cl
Ashbourne Crs
Dovedale Ave
Cottam CP School
Valentines Meadow
Redcar Av
Dovedale Cl
Keats Wy
The Gables
Dunoon Cl
Holy Family RC Primary School
St Margarets Cl
Millersgate
Cottam Way
Avenue
Hornsea Cl
Ventnor Pl
Ingol
Ingol CP School
Filey Pl
Cottam Avenue
Clevedon Rd
Marshall Gv
Hillcrest Av
Crosby Pl
Worthing Rd
Westleigh
Margate Rd
Westbrook Crs
Valentine House
Creswell Av
Dalmore Rd
Brighton Crs
Bexhill
Dunbar Rd
Barry Av
Lancaster Canal
Lea Road
Water's Edge
Colwyn Place
Alder Coppice
Hazel Coppice
Freshfields
Summer Trees Av
Ash Meadow
Miller Field
Savick Way
Bilsborough Meadow
Ash Coppice
Cottam Lane
56
Park
Savick County Junior School
Ainsdale
Luton Road
West Park
Avenue
Queensway
Kingsway
Elm
Lime Gv
Clifton Avenue
Cedar Av
Moss Av
West Pk La
Savick Brook
Arnside Rd
Cartmel Pl
Hendon Pl
Drive
1 grid square represents 500 metres

E4
1 Fir Tree Av
F1
1 Rowton Heath
F2
1 Johnspool
F3
1 Chalfont Fld
F4
1 Rossall Rd
2 St Anthony's Cl
F5
1 Banks Rd
2 Grange Rd
3 Green Ga
4 Melbert Av
5 Millbank
6 Squire's Gate Rd
7 The Turbary
G1
1 Hurstway Cl
G2
1 Hawkhurst Crs
G3
1 Colebatch
2 Greyfriars Av
G4
1 Alvern Crs
2 Edgehill Dr
G5
Street names for this grid square are listed at the back of the index
H2
1 Cross Green Rd
2 Northlands
H3
1 The Handbridge
H4
1 The Chines
2 Empress Av
3 The Friars
4 Strathmore Rd
5 Warwick Cl
6 Withy Pde
H5
1 Brackenbury Rd
2 Cornthwaite Rd
3 Hardcastle Rd
4 Houldsworth Rd
36
46
57
Sharoe Green
Cadley
Tanterton
LIGHTFOOT LANE
Lightfoot Lane
Hazelmere
Highfield Dr
Parklands
Ashfield
Martinfield
Longley Cl
Meadowfield
Broadwood
Beech Drive
Beech Drive Surg
Marlborough Dr
Compton Gn
Alford Fold
Belton Hl
Birchwood Dr
Chestnut Dr
Ashwood Road
Hillcroft
Marston Moor
Marston Close
Lansdown Hill
Roundway Down
Cheriton Fld
Shalgrove Field
Menai Dr
Brookside Rd
Green Dr
Green Drive
Marina Drive
Brooklands Av
Clanfield
Polefield
Heversham
Sharoe Green Lane
Doctors Surgery
PO
Edenway
Greenway
Hurstway
Northway
Broadway
The Dingle
The Dell
The Court
Scott's Wood
Janice Drive
The Turnpike
Ingle Head
Barnsfold
Ridgemont
Stour Lodge
Black Bull Lane
Hawkhurst Av
Raleigh Rd
Methuen Av
Princes Dr
Royal Av
Yewlands Dr
Yewlands Crs
Yewlands Av
Windsor Dr
Clarence Av
Queens Dr
Greystock Av
Harrison Road
Hall Road
Shire Bank Crs
Regent Pk
Regent Court
Royal Preston Hospital
A&E
Corpus Christi RC High School
Vincents
Fulw
Archb Temp
Crofts
A6
GARSTANG ROAD
Fulwood High School
Fulwood Leisure Centre
Queens Drive Primary School
Esher Pond
Nine Elms
Conway
Garstone Croft
Kilworth Height
Kilworth Drive
Greyfriars
Greyfriars Crs
Carnoustie Close
Greenacres
Harris CP School
Wychnor
Somerset Pk
Manor Ct
Hoylake Cl
Muirfield Cl
Uplands Chase
Walker Lane
Sharoe Brook
Preston Grasshoppers Rugby Football Club
Lower Greenfield
Higher Greenfield
Mayfield Av
Boys Lane
Ridgeford Gdns
Kings Drive
St
Westgate
Southgate
Regent Drive
Regent Grove
Eastgate
Beacon Avenue
Beacon Grove
St Pius X Preparatory School
Nooklands
Newgate
Foregate
Our Ladys High School
St Theresa's
St Anthony's Crs
St Anthonys School
St Catherine's Dr
St Anthony's Dr
School
Stratford Dr
Berwick Dr
Dunbar Dr
Oxford Road
Banbury Drive
Edgehill Cl
Aubigny Dr
Woodside Av
The Triangle
York Av
Highgate Av
WATLING
National Football Museum
Post Gradu Medical
Higher
Lower
Eaves La
Hillpark Av
Alvern Av
Hillside Av
Savick Road
Causeway
Woodway
Pineway
Cleveleys Av
Rossall Dr
Thornton Av
Causeway Av
Beechwood Av
Cadley Av
Austin Crs
WOODPLUMPTON ROAD
B5411
Lythcoe Av
Millcroft
Mill Lane
Dunkirk Av
Laurel Bank Av
Banksfield Av
Filberts Cl
The Filberts
Links Fld
Links Gate
Under Saxon Hey
Cadley Dr
Cadley Av
Hollins Grove
Brook Cft
Doctors Surg
Athelstan Fold
Drakes Cft
Ansdell Gv
Seymour Road
Lytham St
Inkerman St
Howarth Rd
Hamer Av
Rose Av
Clovelly Av
Cintra Av
Balcarres Rd
Talbot St
Douglas Rd N
Brook Rd N
Harland St
Norris St
Robinson St
Douglas Rd
St Cuthbert's Cl
Lawrence St
Brook St
Rundle Rd
Linton Street
Derby Road
Lytham Rd
Blundell Rd
Ainslie Rd
Queen's Rd
Guild Community Healthcare NHS Trust
Moorbrook School
Symonds Rd
Balfour Rd
Lorraine Av
Holmes Ct
WOODPLUMPTON ROAD
Haslam Park
Bristow Av
Windsor Avenue
Fulshaw Rd
Parkfield Avenue
Shelley Rd
Lane End Trading Estate
Coniston Av
Oxhey Trading Estate
Parker St
School
De Lacy
Murdock Av
Lulworth Av
Inkerman
Ridley Rd
Balcarres Rd
Norris Street
Emmanuel Street
Widdman Street
Plungington Road
Eldon Street
School Street
Henderson Street
Brackenbury Road
Elliott St
Doctors Surgery
Doctors Surg
College
Preston
Doctors Surg
Stock
PO
Miles St

B4
1 Bedford Rd
2 Beechway
3 Devonshire Rd
4 Fairfield Rd
5 Lindale Rd
6 Lulworth Rd
7 Mason Hill Vw
8 Merryburn Cl
A3
1 The Coombes
2 Moorgate
A4
1 Allengate
2 Vicarage Cl
A2
1 Medway
2 Winton Av
A1
1 Craven Cl
2 Heaton Mount Av
3 Mickleden Av
4 Oakridge Cl
5 Sandwick Cl
C4
1 Ironside Cl
C5
1 Parkside
2 Sherbourne Crs
D1
1 Larchgate
2 Rowangate
D3
1 Bowlers Cl
2 Carloway Av
3 Kilmuir Cl
4 The Lodgings
5 Marybank Cl
6 Portree Cl
7 Waterford Cl
D4
1 Brookfield Av
2 Grasmere Cl
3 Highfield Av
4 Lucerne Rd
5 Rydal Cl
D5
1 Ash Holme
2 Holme Slack La
3 Lilac Gv
4 Primrose Gv
5 Primrose La
6 Primrose Rd
C3, D2
Street names for this grid square are listed at the back of the index
A
B
C
D
37
45
58
1
2
3
4
5
EASTWAY
B6241
Fulwood
St Peters Primary School
Primary School
St Clares RC School
A&E
Royal Preston Hospital
Archbishop Temple School
Preston College
Sharoe Green Hospital
Post Graduate Medical Centre
National Football Museum
Fulwood Hall Hosp
Golf Club
Savick Brook
Eaves Brook
WATLING STREET ROAD
B6242
BLACKPOOL ROAD
A5085
A6063
Moor Park
Sherburn School
Dental Health Centre
Holme Slack CP School
Primary School
Preston North End FC
Deepdale County Junior & Infant School
Preston College
Lancashire Co Council
Preston College Park School
Moor Park High School
Doctors Surgery
High School
Sharoe Green Lane
Tower Lane
Vincents Road
Fairways
Sherwood Way
Pittman Way
Midgery Lane
Longsands
Melrose Av
Coniston Road
Westway
Victoria Road
Chapman Road
Garrison Rd
Higher Bank Road
Lower Bank Road
Holme Slack Lane
Manor House Lane
1 grid square represents 500 metres

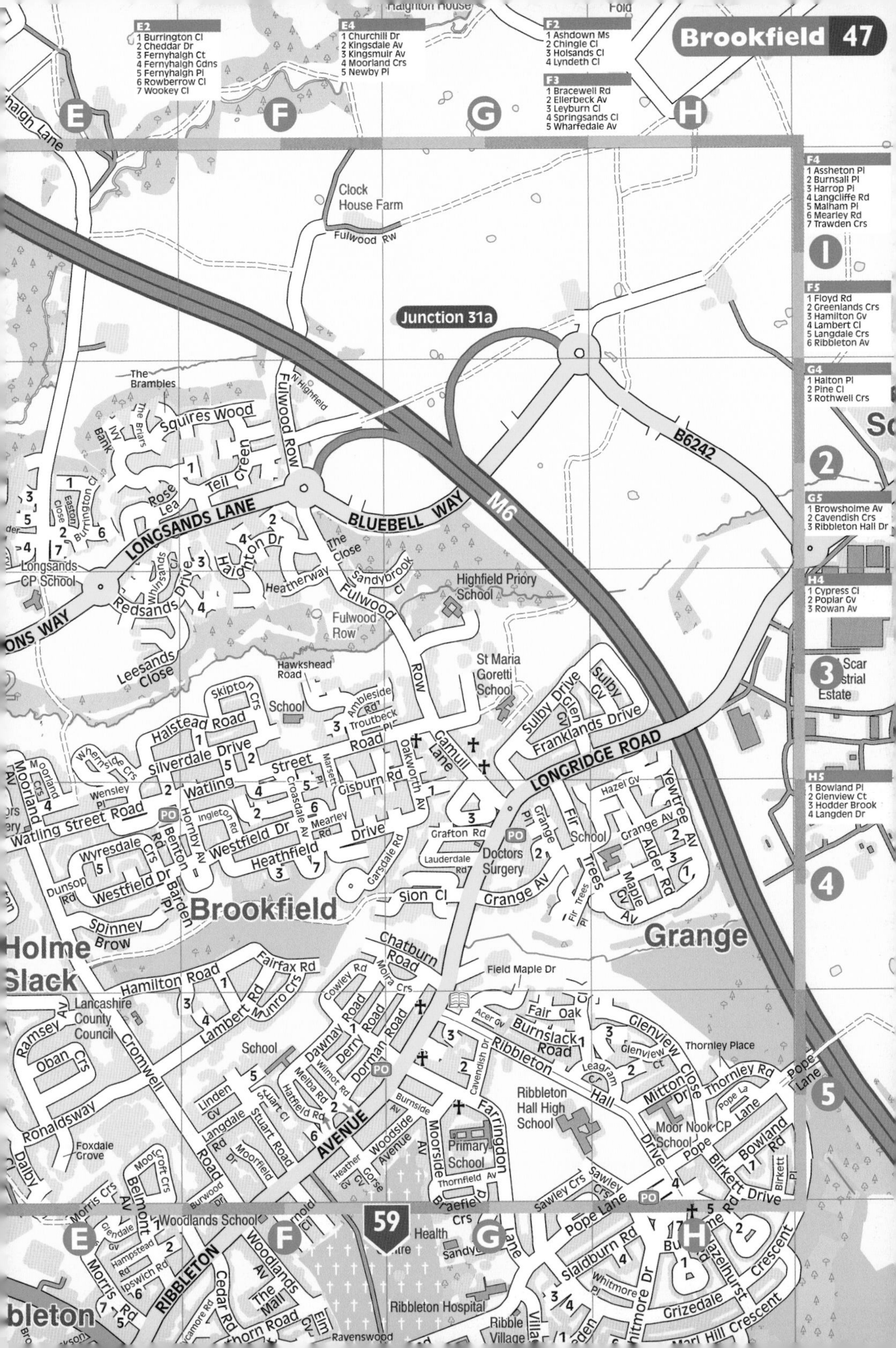
E2
1 Burrington Cl
2 Cheddar Dr
3 Fernyhalgh Ct
4 Fernyhalgh Gdns
5 Fernyhalgh Pl
6 Rowberrow Cl
7 Wookey Cl
E4
1 Churchill Dr
2 Kingsdale Av
3 Kingsmuir Av
4 Moorland Crs
5 Newby Pl
F2
1 Ashdown Ms
2 Chingle Cl
3 Holsands Cl
4 Lyndeth Cl
F3
1 Bracewell Rd
2 Ellerbeck Av
3 Leyburn Cl
4 Springsands Cl
5 Wharfedale Av
F4
1 Assheton Pl
2 Burnsall Pl
3 Harrop Pl
4 Langcliffe Rd
5 Malham Pl
6 Mearley Rd
7 Trawden Crs
F5
1 Floyd Rd
2 Greenlands Crs
3 Hamilton Gv
4 Lambert Cl
5 Langdale Crs
6 Ribbleton Av
G4
1 Halton Pl
2 Pine Cl
3 Rothwell Crs
G5
1 Browsholme Av
2 Cavendish Crs
3 Ribbleton Hall Dr
H4
1 Cypress Cl
2 Poplar Gv
3 Rowan Av
H5
1 Bowland Pl
2 Glenview Ct
3 Hodder Brook
4 Langden Dr
Clock House Farm
Fulwood Rw
Junction 31a
M6
B6242
Bluebell Way
Longsands Lane
Longsands CP School
The Brambles
Squires Wood
Teil Green
Rose Lea
Fulwood Row
Haighton Dr
Redsands Drive
Whinsands Cl
Heatherway
The Close
Sandybrook Cl
Highfield Priory School
Fulwood Row
Leesands Close
Hawkshead Road
School
Skipton Crs
Halstead Road
Ambleside Rd
Troutbeck Pl
St Maria Goretti School
Sulby Drive
Glen Gv
Sulby Gv
Franklands Drive
Longridge Road
Silverdale Drive
Watling Street Road
Gisburn Rd
Oakworth Av
Gamull Lane
Moorland Av
Wensley Pl
Hornby Av
Ingleton Rd
Croasdale Av
Mearley Rd
Westfield Dr
Heathfield
Drive
Garsdale Rd
Grafton Rd
Lauderdale Rd
Doctors Surgery
Grange Pl
Fir Trees
School
Hazel Gv
Yewtree Av
Grange Av
Alder Rd
Maple Gv
Wyresdale Crs
Benton Rd
Barden Pl
Dunsop Rd
Westfield Dr
Sion Cl
Brookfield
Spinney Brow
Grange
Holme Slack
Chatburn Road
Field Maple Dr
Fairfax Rd
Hamilton Road
Lambert Rd
Munro Crs
Cowley Rd
Moira Crs
Lancashire County Council
Ramsey Av
Oban Crs
Cromwell Road
School
Dawnay Road
Derry Road
Dorman Road
Fair Oak Cl
Burnslack Road
Acer Gv
Ribbleton Hall Drive
Cavendish Dr
Glenview Close
Glenview Ct
Thornley Place
Thornley Rd
Pope Lane
Leagram Cres
Mitton Dr
Ribbleton Hall High School
Moor Nook CP School
Bowland Rd
Birkett Drive
Birkett Pl
Linden Gv
Langdale Rd
Stuart Road
Stuart Cl
Moorfield Dr
Melba Rd
Wilmot Rd
Hatfield Rd
Avenue
Burnside Av
Woodside Avenue
Moorside Av
Farringdon Lane
Primary School
Thornfield Av
Braefield Crs
Ronaldsway
Foxdale Grove
Dalby
Belmont Av
Mooro Croft Crs
Burwood Dr
Heather Gv
Gorse Gv
Sawley Crs
Pope Lane
Morris Crs
Woodlands School
Glendale Gv
Hampstead Rd
Ipswich Rd
Ribbleton
Cedar Rd
Woodlands Av
The Mall
Health Centre
59
Ribbleton Hospital
Ribble Village
Slaidburn Rd
Whitmore Pl
Whitmore Dr
Hazelhurst
Crescent
Grizedale
Marl Hill Crescent
Ravenswood
bleton

D2
1 Beatty Cl
2 Jervis Cl
3 Kirkstone Rd
4 Raleigh Cl
5 Troutbeck Rd
C3
1 Avondale Rd
Blackpool Airport
D3
1 Press Rd
D4
1 Devonshire Rd
2 St George's Sq
D5
1 Douglas St
2 St Anne's Rd West
38
60
Starr Hills
CLIFTON DRIVE NORTH
A584
Sidmouth Rd
Salcombe Road
Kilgrimol Gdns
Seaton Crs
Highbury Road West
St Annes Old Links Golf Club
Duncan Cl
Anson Cl
Kendal Rd
Tudor Road
St David's Road
Barton Road
Dalton St
Myerscough Avenue
Caryl Road
Lime Grove
Norwood Road
Summerfields
Wyredale Rd
PO
Cavendish Rd
St Hilda's Rd
North Cross
Lancashire County C
Bentinck Rd
Lime Grove
St Leonard's Rd
Chatsworth Road
St Andrew's Road
Rowsley Road
Sandgate
North Promenade
Beach Road
Toy & Teddy Bear Museum
Hotel
Ribble St
Dove St
Todmorden Road
Salter's Bank
Fernlea Leisure
A B C D
1 2 3 4 5

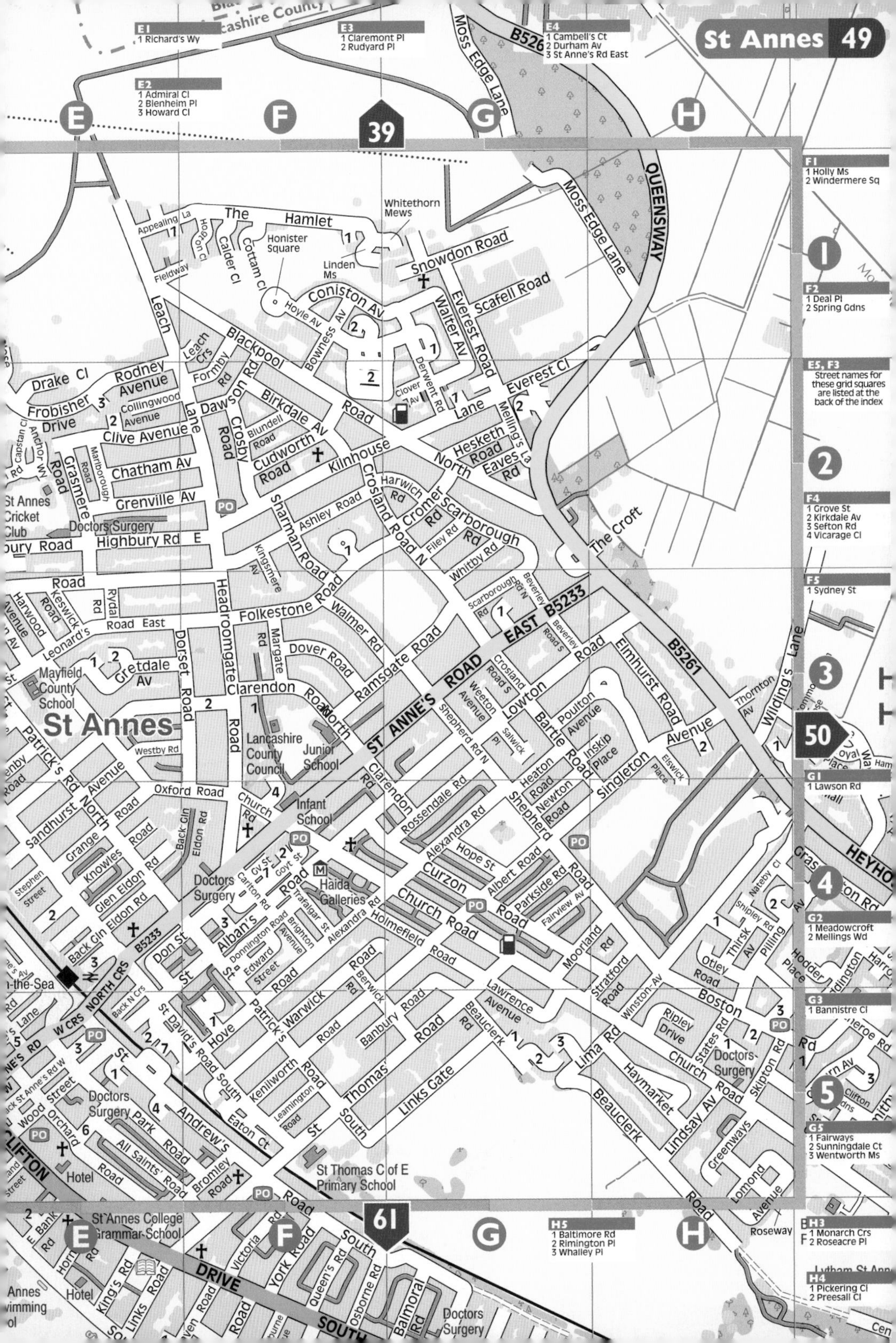

St Annes 49
E1
1 Richard's Wy
E2
1 Admiral Cl
2 Blenheim Pl
3 Howard Cl
E3
1 Claremont Pl
2 Rudyard Pl
E4
1 Cambell's Ct
2 Durham Av
3 St Anne's Rd East
F1
1 Holly Ms
2 Windermere Sq
F2
1 Deal Pl
2 Spring Gdns
E5, F3
Street names for these grid squares are listed at the back of the index
F4
1 Grove St
2 Kirkdale Av
3 Sefton Rd
4 Vicarage Cl
F5
1 Sydney St
G1
1 Lawson Rd
G2
1 Meadowcroft
2 Mellings Wd
G3
1 Bannistre Cl
G5
1 Fairways
2 Sunningdale Ct
3 Wentworth Ms
H3
1 Monarch Crs
2 Roseacre Pl
H4
1 Pickering Cl
2 Presall Cl
H5
1 Baltimore Rd
2 Rimington Pl
3 Whalley Pl
39
50
61
E
F
G
H
1
2
3
4
5
B5261
B5233
QUEENSWAY
Moss Edge Lane
The Hamlet
Whitethorn Mews
Honister Square
Linden Ms
Snowdon Road
Scafell Road
Everest Road
Everest Cl
Coniston Av
Walter Av
Bowness Av
Hoyle Av
Appealing La
Hogton Cl
Calder Cl
Cottam Cl
Fieldway
Leach Lane
Leach Crs
Formby Rd
Blackpool Road North
Drake Cl
Rodney Avenue
Frobisher Drive
Collingwood Avenue
Clive Avenue
Chatham Av
Grenville Av
Grasmere Road
Marlborough Road
Dawson Rd
Crosby Road
Birkdale Av
Blundell Road
Cudworth Road
Kilnhouse Lane
Clover Av
Derwent Rd
Melling's La
Hesketh Road
Eaves Rd
Crosland Road N
Harwich Rd
Cromer Rd
Scarborough Rd
Filey Rd
Whitby Rd
Ashley Road
Sharman Road
Kingsmere Av
Folkestone Road
Walmer Rd
Ramsgate Road
Beverley Rd N
Beverley Road S
The Croft
St Annes Cricket Club
Doctors Surgery
Highbury Rd E
Headroomgate Road
Rydal Rd
Keswick Rd
Harwood Av
Leonard's Road East
Dorset Road
Margate Rd
Dover Road
Gretdale Av
Mayfield County School
Clarendon Road North
Lancashire County Council
Junior School
Infant School
St Annes
ST ANNE'S ROAD EAST
Crosland Road S
Weeton Avenue
Lowton Road
Bartle Road
Poulton Avenue
Inskip Place
Elmhurst Road
Thornton Av
Wilding's Lane
Singleton Avenue
Elswick Place
Salwick Pl
Shepherd Rd N
Heaton Road
Newton Road
Shepherd Road
Westby Rd
Oxford Road
Patrick's Rd North
Sandhurst Avenue
Church Rd
Back Gln
Eldon Rd
Clarendon Rd
Rossendale Rd
Alexandra Rd
Hope St
Albert Road
Parkside Rd
Fairview Av
Curzon Road
Church Road
Holmefield Road
Moorland Rd
Stratford Road
Winston Av
Ripley Drive
Boston Road
Otley Road
Thirsk Av
Shipley Rd
Nateby Cl
Pilling Av
Hodder Place
Grange Road
Knowles Road
Glen Eldon Rd
Eldon Rd
Stephen Street
Gv St
Goyt St
Carlton Rd
Doctors Surgery
Haida Galleries
Trafalgar St
Brighton Avenue
Donnington Road
Alban's Road
Edward Street
Warwick Road
Berwick Rd
Banbury Road
Thomas Road
Patrick's Road
Lawrence Avenue
Beauclerk Rd
Lima Rd
Haymarket
Beauclerk
Church Road
States Rd
Doctors Surgery
Skipton Rd
Lindsay Av
Greenways
Lomond Avenue
Roseway
Don St
Hove St
St David's Road South
Kenilworth Road
Leamington Road
South St
Links Gate
Eaton Ct
St Andrew's Road
Park Road
All Saints' Road
Bromley Road
St Thomas C of E Primary School
Back Gln Eldon Rd
NORTH CRS
W CRS
Back N Crs
Wood Street
Orchard Road
Doctors Surgery
Hotel
CLIFTON
St Annes College Grammar School
Victoria Rd
York Road
Queen's Rd
Osborne Rd
Balmoral Rd
South Drive
DRIVE
SOUTH
King's Rd
Links Road
Hotel
Doctors Surgery
Lytham St Annes
HEYHOUSES
PO
-the-Sea

A4
1 Bowes Lyon Pl
2 Lunesdale Cl
A3
1 Britannia Wk
A5
1 Downham Pl
2 Fallowfield Rd
3 Ilkley Av
4 Kirton Crs
B5
1 Belgrave Cl
2 Knightsbridge Cl
3 Mayfair Cl
4 Twickenham Pl
C5
1 Hampstead Cl
40
49
62
Anna's Road
West Moss Lane
North Houses Lane
Moss Hall Lane
Moss Sluice
Lytham Moss
Hey Houses
FY8
Commonwealth Close
Jubilee Way
Royal Place
Hampton Ct
The Mall
Silverdale Road
South Moss Road
Arnside Av
Ulverston Crs
HEYHOUSES LANE
B5261
BLACKPOOL RD
Grassington Rd
Waddington Road
Harrogate Rd
Settle Place
Sabden Place
Bowland Pl
Hodder Place
School
Clitheroe Rd
Sawley Av
Edwinstowe Road
Sherwood Rd
Tuxford Rd
Gisburn Av
Clifton Gdns
Smithy Lane
Smithy Cft
South Hey
Brooklands Rd
Hilton Avenue
Shipley Rd
Thirsk Av
Pilling Av
Otley Road
Boston Rd
States Rd
Doctors Surgery
PO
Greenways
Lomond Avenue
Roseway
Regent Avenue
Islay Road
Kintour Road
Highgate Pl
Hall Park Drive
Kingston Dr
Audley Cl
Moss Hall Farm
Cemetery
Blackpool & Fylde College
Lytham St Annes High School
Ansdell CP School
Lytham Leisure Centre
Rufford Rd
Wellow Place
Albany Rd
Lansdowne Road
Fylde Road
Worsley Road
Greenwich Drive
Shaftesbury Close
Bexley Place
grid square represents 500 metres

E
F
41
G
H
Ballam Road
Lower Ballam
North Farm
I
Brays Road
Ivy Farm
LC
LYTHAM ROAD
2
Moss Side
Moss Side Station
Higher Ballam
3
52
Ballam Road
Peg's Lane
B5259
Cartmell Lane
4
SALTCOTES
Birks Farm
Eastham Hall
5
ROAD
Liggard Brook
63
E
F
G
H
Drive
Laburnum Avenue
Laurel Avenue
Lilac
Green Drive Golf Club
Saltcotes
Cem
Wicklow Av
Grampian
Cheviot Av
Cotswold Rd
1
4

A
B
C
D
Wrea Green
B5259
MOSS SIDE LANE
Bryning Lane
Bryning Avenue
North Farm
Willowmead Pk
B5259
ROAD
LC
Moss Side
Moss Side Station
New House Farm
Bryning Hall Lane
Wrea Brook
Bryning Hall Farm
51
Cartmell Lane
Huck Lane
Eastham Hall
Little Carr Side Farm
Lodge Lane
West End La
Warton Hall
64
A
B
C
D
1
2
3
4
5
Cotswold Rd
Wicklow Av
Industrial Estate
grid square represents 500 metres

F5
1 Maple Gv
G5
1 Church Gdns
2 Harbour Av
3 Sunnyside Av
4 Wordsworth Av
Lane
E
F
42
G
H
I
2
3
54
4
5
Prospect Farm
Hillock
Hillock Lane
Bryning
Bryning Lane
Kellamergh
Hillock Lane
Lane
Church Road
Ramsgate Cl
Dover Cl
Folkestone Close
Hastings Av
Canberra Way
Canberra Way
Moorhead Gdns
Harbour
Queensway
Tennyson Av
Keats Av
Byron Av
Windy Harbour Farm
Fir Grove
Marlborough Av
Chatsworth Av
Poplar Avenue
Beech Avenue
Elm Av
Olive Gv
Blenheim Dr
Inglewood Close
Drive
Ash
Clifton Avenue
Lane
Holy Family Primary School
Ribble View Close
Peg Way
Post Lane
The Orch
ROAD
Cedar Av
Highgate
Lane
Elder Close
Millfield Close
Westfield Drive
Mill La
Westway
Church Cl
Lamaleach Drive
Eastway
Rydal Av
Calder Av
Delany Drive
Larch Cl
Poplar Dr
Oak Dr
Beech Dr
Ash Dr
Willow
Woodlands
PO
65
St Pauls School
E
F
G
H
LYTHAM
Rake Lane
A584
Florence Av
Cardwell Cl
Ferrier Bank
Warton

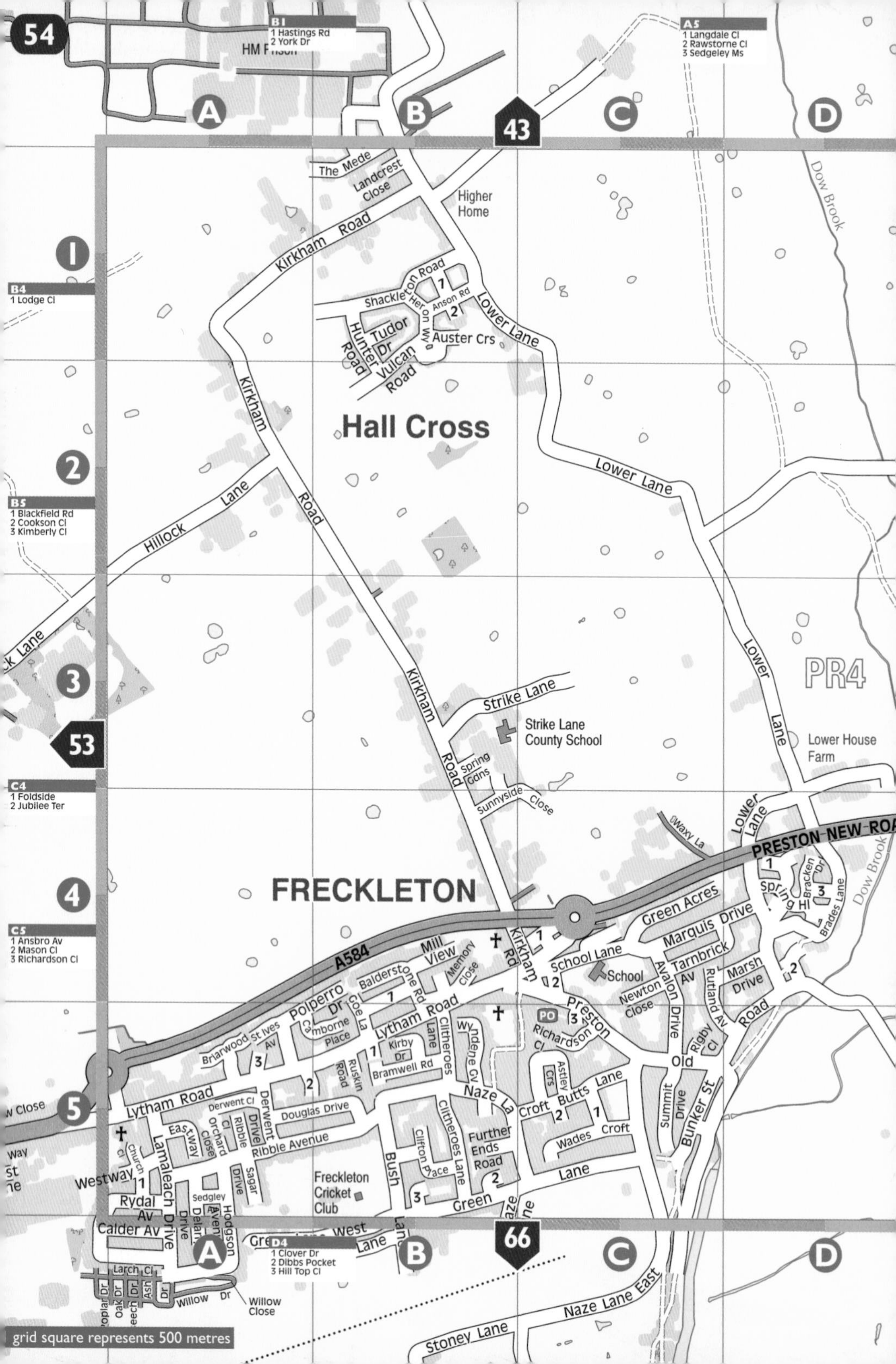
54
B1
1 Hastings Rd
2 York Dr
HM Prison
A5
1 Langdale Cl
2 Rawstorne Cl
3 Sedgeley Ms
43
B4
1 Lodge Cl
B5
1 Blackfield Rd
2 Cookson Cl
3 Kimberly Cl
C4
1 Foldside
2 Jubilee Ter
C5
1 Ansbro Av
2 Mason Cl
3 Richardson Cl
53
D4
1 Clover Dr
2 Dibbs Pocket
3 Hill Top Cl
66
Hall Cross
FRECKLETON
PR4
Dow Brook
The Mede
Landcrest Close
Higher Home
Kirkham Road
Shackleton Road
Heron Wy
Anson Rd
Tudor Dr
Hunter Road
Vulcan Road
Auster Crs
Lower Lane
Hillock Lane
Strike Lane
Strike Lane County School
Spring Gdns
Sunnyside Close
Lower House Farm
Waxy La
PRESTON NEW ROAD
A584
Mill View
Memory Close
Balderstone Rd
Polperro Dr
Goe La
Camborne Place
Lytham Road
Kirby Dr
Clitheroes Lane
Wyndene Gv
Briarwood
St Ives Av
Ruskin Road
Bramwell Rd
School Lane
School
Green Acres
Marquis Drive
Tarnbrick Av
Newton Close
Avalon Drive
Rutland Av
Marsh Drive
Rigby Cl
Spring Hl
Bracken Dr
Brades Lane
Preston Old Road
PO
Richardson Cl
Astley Crs
Butts Lane
Croft
Naze La
Derwent Cl
Derwent Drive
Douglas Drive
Eastway
Orchard Close
Ribble Cl
Ribble Avenue
Sagar Drive
Church Cl
Lamaleach Drive
Westway
Rydal Av
Calder Av
Sedgley Avenue
Delaney Drive
Hodgson Drive
Clifton Place
Clitheroes Lane
Further Ends Road
Bush Lane
Freckleton Cricket Club
Green Lane
Wades Croft
Summit Drive
Bunker St
Green Lane West
Larch Cl
Poplar Dr
Oak Dr
Beech Dr
Ash Dr
Willow Dr
Willow Close
Naze Lane East
Stoney Lane
w Close
grid square represents 500 metres

G1
1 Sunny Bank Av
Highgate Cl
Vicarage
E
F
G
H
Parrox
Hawthorne Av
Hornby Drive
Birch Av
Cedar Cl
Bryning Lane
Beech Dr
Blackthorn Cl
Hill Crs
Scale Hall La
Bluecoat Crs
Newton
with Scales
PO
Lowfield Close
Marsh View
Maple Cl
Alder Cl
Lane
School
Lane
Newton Bluecoat School
Oak Lane
Grange Lane
Street
Thames
BLACKPOOL ROAD
Madis
Leisu
A584
Newton Marsh
Freckleton Marsh
Clifton Farm
Grange Farm
67

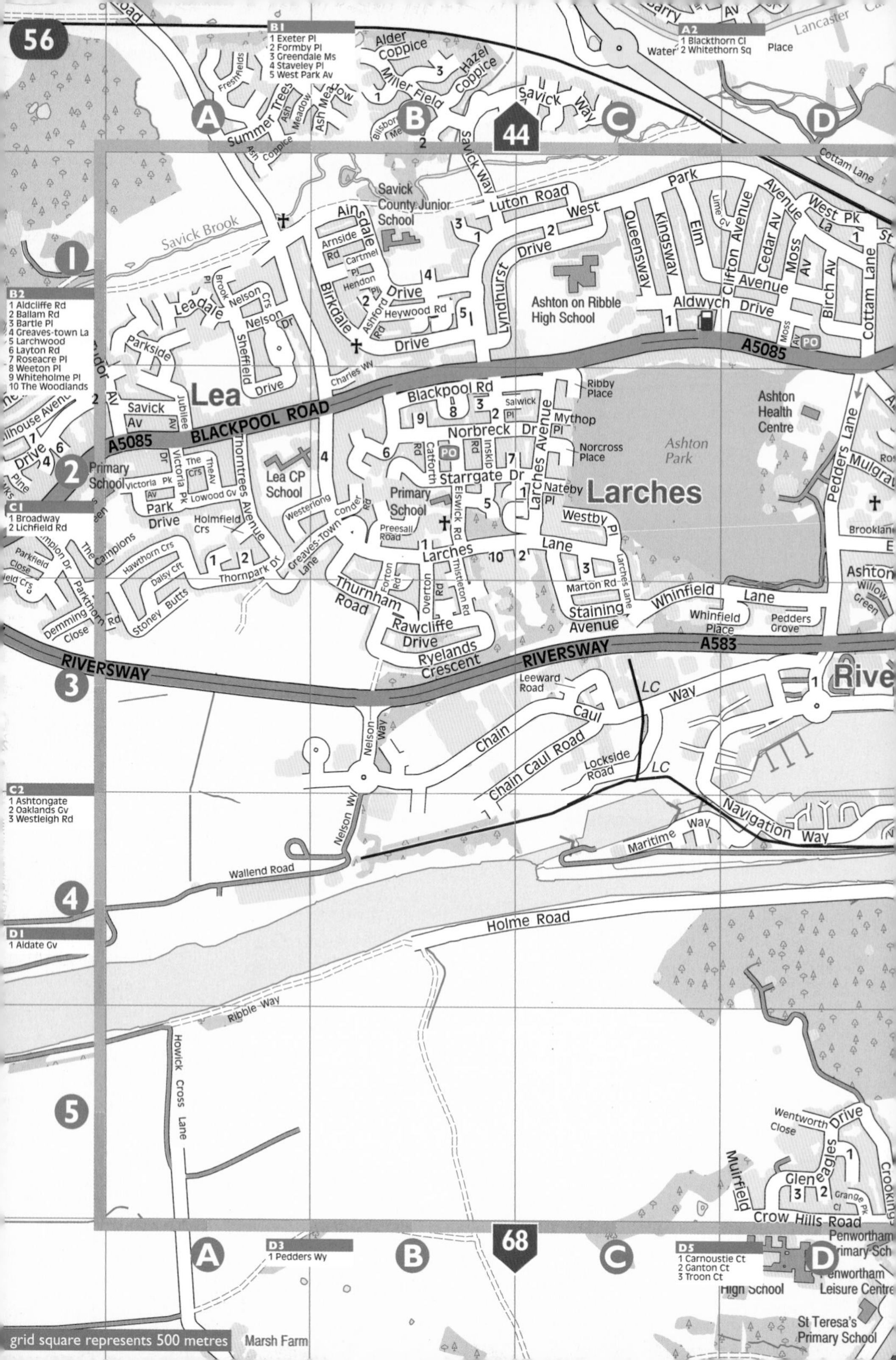
B1
1 Exeter Pl
2 Formby Pl
3 Greendale Ms
4 Staveley Pl
5 West Park Av
A2
1 Blackthorn Cl
2 Whitethorn Sq
B2
1 Aldcliffe Rd
2 Ballam Rd
3 Bartle Pl
4 Greaves-town La
5 Larchwood
6 Layton Rd
7 Roseacre Pl
8 Weeton Pl
9 Whiteholme Pl
10 The Woodlands
C1
1 Broadway
2 Lichfield Rd
C2
1 Ashtongate
2 Oaklands Gv
3 Westleigh Rd
D1
1 Aldate Gv
D3
1 Pedders Wy
D5
1 Carnoustie Ct
2 Ganton Ct
3 Troon Ct
44
68
Alder Coppice
Hazel Coppice
Miller Field
Savick Way
Summer Trees
Ash Meadow
Ash Coppice
Fresnfields
Lancaster
Place
Cottam Lane
Savick County Junior School
Savick Brook
Luton Road
West Park Avenue
Queensway
Kingsway
Elm
Lime Gv
Clifton Avenue
Cedar Av
Moss Av
Birch Av
West Pk La
Ainsdale Drive
Arnside Rd
Cartmel Pl
Hendon Pl
Ashford Rd
Heywood Rd
Birkdale Drive
Lyndhurst Drive
Ashton on Ribble High School
Aldwych Drive
PO
A5085
Leadale
Brook Pl
Nelson Crs
Nelson Dr
Sheffield Drive
Parkside
Tudor Av
Charles Wy
Lea
Savick Av
Jubilee Av
BLACKPOOL ROAD
Blackpool Rd
Salwick Pl
Ribby Place
Mythop Pl
Norbreck Dr
Norcross Place
Ashton Health Centre
Ashton Park
Pedders Lane
Mulgrave
Brookland
Larches
Larches Avenue
Nateby Pl
Westby Pl
Starrgate Dr
Catforth Rd
Inskip
Elswick Rd
Primary School
Lea CP School
Westerlong
Conder Rd
Greaves-Town Lane
Preesall Road
Thorntrees Avenue
Victoria Pk
The Crs
The Av
Lowood Gv
Park Drive
Holmfield Crs
Thornpark Dr
Hawthorn Crs
Daisy Cft
Stoney Butts
The Campions
Parkfield Close
Parkthorn Rd
Demming Close
Millhouse Avenue
Pine Drive
Thurnham Road
Forton Rd
Overton Rd
Thistleton Rd
Rawcliffe Drive
Ryelands Crescent
Larches Lane
Marton Rd
Staining Avenue
Whinfield Lane
Whinfield Place
Pedders Grove
Ashton
Willow Green
RIVERSWAY
A583
Leeward Road
LC
Chain Caul Way
Chain Caul Road
Lockside Road
Nelson Way
Nelson Wy
Navigation Way
Maritime Way
Wallend Road
Holme Road
Ribble Way
Howick Cross Lane
Wentworth Drive
Wentworth Close
Muirfield
Gleneagles
Grange Pk
Crookings
Crow Hills Road
Penwortham Primary School
Penwortham Leisure Centre
High School
St Teresa's Primary School
Marsh Farm
grid square represents 500 metres

E1
1 Armstrong St
2 Fairfield Dr
3 Park View Av
E2
1 Prospect Pl
E5
1 Princes Ct
F1, F2
Street names for these grid squares are listed at the back of the index
F3
1 Strand St West
G1
1 Greenbank Av
2 Haig Av
3 Havelock St
4 Oxheys St
5 Stanhope St
6 Villiers St
G2, G3, G4, H4
Street names for these grid squares are listed at the back of the index
G5
1 Ardee Rd
2 Beech St
3 Brixey St
4 Clifton St
5 Colman Ct
6 Tay St
7 Tyne St
8 Winckley Rd
H1
1 Bloomfield Ct
2 Cambridge St
3 Cambridge Wk
4 Elliott Cl
5 Elliott Wk
6 Hammond St
7 Havelock St
8 Henderson St
9 Moor Hall St
10 Otway St
11 Trafford St
H2
1 Barlow St
2 Berkeley St
3 Eastham St
4 Elliott St
5 Eversleigh St
6 Greenbank St
7 Hammond Ct
8 Hammond St
9 Harcourt St
10 Hawkins Cl
11 Hawkins St
12 Heysham St
H3
1 Bhailok St
2 Edward St
3 Gildow St
4 Cradwell St
5 Kirkham St
6 Moss St
7 Pollard St
8 Radnor St
9 St Peter's Sq
10 Stocks St
H5
1 Beech Ter
2 Hind St
3 North Cliff St
4 South Cliff St
5 Warton St
45
58
69
Haslam Park
Lane Ends Trading Estate
Oxhey Trading Estate
Preston Bowl
Starkie Industrial Estate
Parker St Industrial Estate
Aqueduct St Industrial Estate
Dewhurst Industrial Estate
Fylde Road Industrial Estate
Lancashire Co Council
Springfield Industrial Est
English Martyrs Junior School
Moorbrook School
Doctors Surgery
Preston College
Primary School
Sacred Heart RC School
Docklands Medical Centre
Docklands
Marina
UCI Cinema
Wellfield Business Park
University
Atlas Foundry Estate
Penwortham Holme Recreation Centre
Fishergate Hill Surg
St Stephens School
Preston Sports Club
Preston Cricket Club
Preston Stn
St Marys Health Centre
PR1
TULKETH BROW
TULKETH ROAD
WATERY LANE
FYLDE ROAD
A583
A5072 WEST STRAND
STRAND ROAD
JUNCTION RD
MARSH LANE
GUILD WAY
A59 GUILD WAY
LIVERPOOL ROAD
A59 LEYLAND ROAD
MOOR LANE
Navigation Way
Port Way
Channel Way
Holme Road
River Ribble
Blundell Lane
Shaftesbury Avenue
Kensington Avenue
Kingsway
Queensway
Highgate
Fishergate Hill
West Cliff
Victoria Street
Pedder Street
Maudland Road
Plungington Road
Brackenbury Road
Woodplumpton Road
Stocks Road
Lytham Rd
Seymour Road
Windsor Avenue
Bristow Av

58
A4
1 Back Starkie St
2 Chaddock St
3 Chapel Wks
4 Charnley St
5 Falkland St
6 Fleet St
7 Market St
8 New Cock Yd
9 Temple Ct
A1, A2, A3
Street names for these grid squares are listed at the back of the index
A5, B1, B2, B3
Street names for these grid squares are listed at the back of the index
B4, B5, C2, C5
Street names for these grid squares are listed at the back of the index
C1
1 Chatham Pl
2 Hawkhurst Rd
3 Penguin St
4 St George's Rd
5 Wren St
C3
1 Church St
2 Driscoll St
3 Newton St
4 Owen St
5 Ribbleton Pl
6 St Mary's Ct
7 St Mary's St N
8 Witton St
C4
1 Albyn Bank Rd
2 Albyn St East
3 Ashworth St
4 Dickson St
5 Duke St
6 Mellor Pl
7 Primrose Hl
8 Richmond St
D1
1 Church Ct
2 Clifton Crs
3 William Young Cl
D4
1 Alexandra St
2 Clara St
3 Clitheroe St
4 Darwen St
5 Ephraim St
6 Montjoly St
7 Thomas St
8 Trout St
9 Zetland St
46
57
70
A
B
C
D
1
2
3
4
5
A5085
A6063
B6242
B6243
A6
BLACKPOOL ROAD
DEEPDALE ROAD
NORTH ROAD A6
MOOR LANE
FYLDE RD
CORPORATION ST
FRIARGATE
RINGWAY
STANLEY STREET
RIBBLETON LANE B6243
NEW HALL LANE
LONDON ROAD A6
Preston College
Lancashire Co Council
Moor Park High School
Preston North End FC
Deepdale County Junior & Infant School
St Stephen's Rd
St Thomas' Road
St George's Road
Moor Park Av
Springfield Industrial Est
Moorbrook St
English Martyrs Junior
University of Central Lancashire
Preston Borough Council
Raza Mosque
Sedgwick St
Burrow Road
Argyll Rd
Essex St
Castleton
Porter St
Lincoln St
Deepdale Surg
Guild Trading Estate
Secondary School
West View Leisure Centre
Harrison Trading Estate
Guild Community Healthcare N H S Trust
Ribbleton Lane Trading Est
Lancashire County Mus Service
Queens Retail Park
Kaymar Industrial Estate
Police Court
Law Courts
Borough Council
St Johns Cen
Town Hall
Guildhall
Harris Mus & Art Gallery
Corn Exchange
Mkt Halls
St Georges Shopping Cen
Fishergate Shopping Cen
Preston Stn
Cardinal Newman College
Frenchwood CP School
Frenchwood Knoll
Southern Parade
Frenchwood Av
PRESTON
Frenchwood
Christ the King High School
Lancashire County Council
Ribble Way
Avenham Colonnade
Bank Parade
Ashworth Lane
Malvern Avenue
Lawrence Avenue
Boulevard
Preston Cricket Club
Riverside
South R Industrial Est
Warner
grid square represents 500 metres

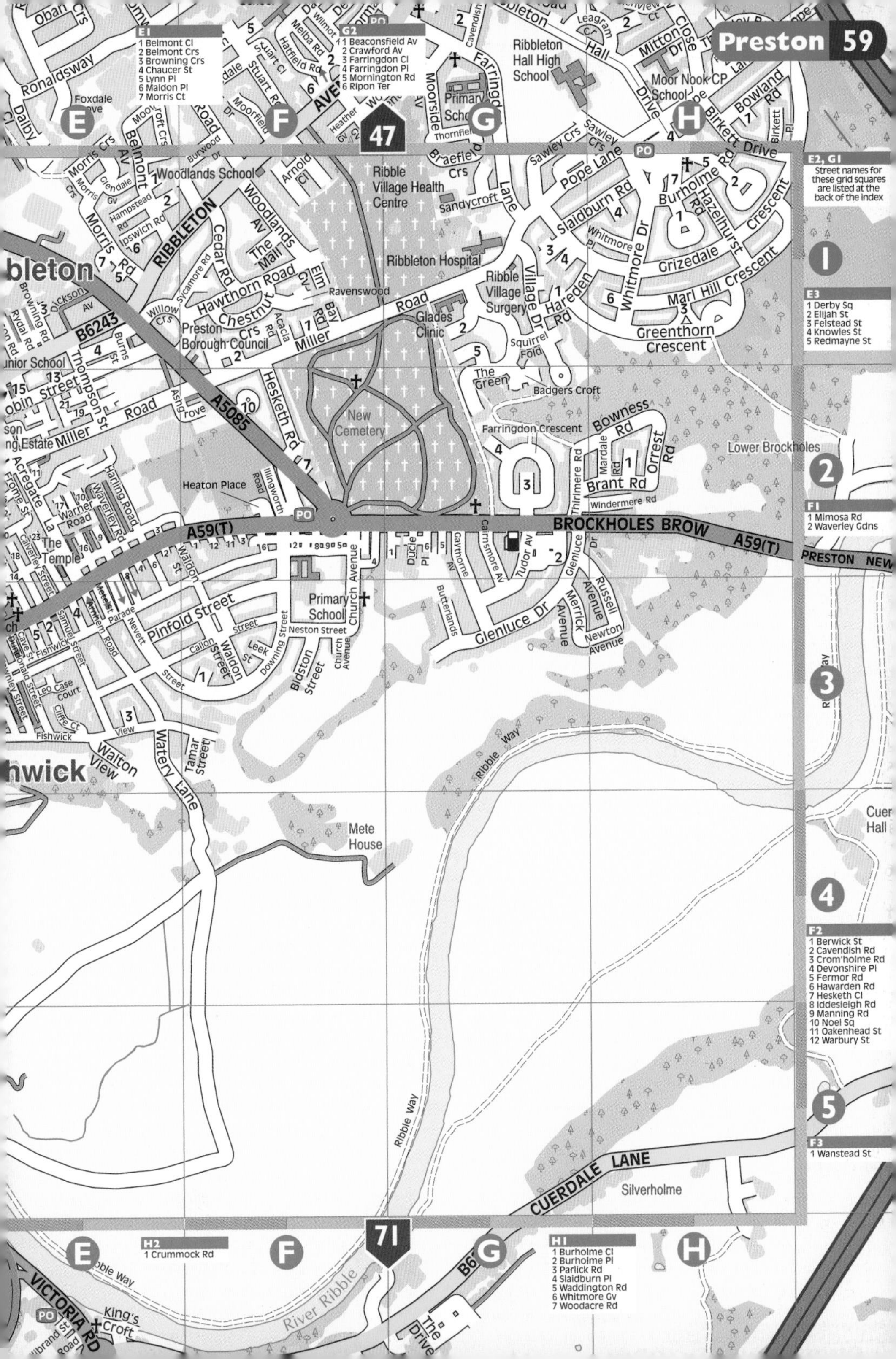
E1
1 Belmont Cl
2 Belmont Crs
3 Browning Crs
4 Chaucer St
5 Lynn Pl
6 Maldon Pl
7 Morris Ct
G2
1 Beaconsfield Av
2 Crawford Av
3 Farringdon Cl
4 Farringdon Pl
5 Mornington Rd
6 Ripon Ter
E2, G1
Street names for these grid squares are listed at the back of the index
E3
1 Derby Sq
2 Elijah St
3 Felstead St
4 Knowles St
5 Redmayne St
F1
1 Mimosa Rd
2 Waverley Gdns
F2
1 Berwick St
2 Cavendish Rd
3 Crom'holme Rd
4 Devonshire Pl
5 Fermor Rd
6 Hawarden Rd
7 Hesketh Cl
8 Iddesleigh Rd
9 Manning Rd
10 Noel Sq
11 Oakenhead St
12 Warbury St
F3
1 Wanstead St
H2
1 Crummock Rd
H1
1 Burholme Cl
2 Burholme Pl
3 Parlick Rd
4 Slaidburn Pl
5 Waddington Rd
6 Whitmore Gv
7 Woodacre Rd
47
71
Ronaldsway
Foxdale Grove
Ribbleton Hall High School
Moor Nook CP School
Woodlands School
Ribble Village Health Centre
Ribbleton Hospital
Ribble Village Surgery
Glades Clinic
Preston Borough Council
New Cemetery
Heaton Place
Ravenswood
Badgers Croft
Farringdon Crescent
Lower Brockholes
RIBBLETON
bbleton
B6243
A5085
A59(T)
BROCKHOLES BROW
PRESTON NEW
Miller Road
Hawthorn Road
Chestnut Crs
Pope Lane
Slaidburn Rd
Grizedale
Marl Hill Crescent
Greenthorn Crescent
Hazelhurst Crescent
Birkett Drive
Whitmore Dr
Village Dr
Hareden Rd
Squirrel Fold
The Green
Bowness Rd
Brant Rd
Orrest Rd
Windermere Rd
Thirlmere Rd
Glenluce Dr
Merrick Avenue
Russell Avenue
Newton Avenue
Butterlands
Primary School
Church Avenue
Neston Street
Pinfold Street
Waldon Street
Bidston Street
Downing Street
Leek St
Hesketh Rd
Illingworth Road
Thompson St
Robin Street
Acregate La
Harling Road
Waverley Rd
Warner Road
The Temple
Fishwick
Walton View
Watery Lane
Tamar Street
Leo Case Court
hwick
Mete House
Ribble Way
Cuer Hall
Silverholme
CUERDALE LANE
River Ribble
VICTORIA RD
King's Croft
The Drive
PO

Salter's Bank
48
A
B
C
D
1
2
3
4
5
orden Road
Dove St
Fernlea Leisure
grid square represents 500 metres

E1
1 Fairhaven La
2 Royds St
F1
1 Alexandria Dr
F2
1 Kintbury Rd
G1
1 Windsor Rd
H1
1 Pershore Rd
49
62
LYTHAM
ST ANNE'S
Doctors Surgery
St Annes College Grammar School
St Thomas' Primary School
Hotel
Queen Mary School
King Edward School
Blackpool & Fylde College
Ansdell
Wood Street
Orchard Road
Park Road
All Saints' Road
Andrew's Road
Bromley Road
Kenilworth Road
Leamington Road
Eaton Ct
St Thomas' Road
South
Links Gate
Clifton
St Anne's Rd W
Bank Rd
Hornby Rd
King's Rd
Links Road
Fairhaven Road
Victoria Rd
York Road
Queen's Rd
Osborne Rd
Balmoral Rd
Croyde Rd
Sandringham Road
Qu Mary Av
Evesham Rd
Drive South
A584
Derbe Road
Lightburne Avenue
Riley Avenue
Cartmell Road
Hungerford Rd
Laverton Road
Newbury Road
The Boulevard
Lancaster Avenue
Denford Av
Shalbourn Road
King Edward Avenue
Promenade
South Promenade
Rosebery Av
Arundel Road
Finsbury Av
Channing Rd
Kingsway
St Paul's Avenue
Myra Road
Cyprus Avenue
Eddington Road
Coronation Rd
Pollux Gate
Lindsay
Greenways
Lomond Avenue
Roseway
Smithy Cft
Lytham St Annes High School
Fairhaven Lake
St Annes Swimming Pool

A2
1 Miletas Pl
A1
1 Belmont Rd
2 Newlands Rd
B1
1 Blackpool Rd
2 Brompton Cl
3 Malvern Rd
4 Ollerton Rd
5 Rutland Ct
6 Walesby Pl
B2
1 Buckingham Rd
2 Gloucester Rd
3 Princes Rd
C2
Street names for this grid square are listed at the back of the index
D2
1 Larchwood Cl
2 Maplewood Cl
D3
1 The Leylands
50
61
Ansdell
Blackpool & Fylde College
Lytham St Annes High School
Ansdell CP School
Lytham Leisure Centre
Fylde Rugby Club
Fairhaven Golf Club
Lytham Hall
Ansdell & Fairhaven Station
Doctors Surgery
Fairhaven Lake
Hall Park CP School
Lytham Cricket Club
BLACKPOOL ROAD
CLIFTON DRIVE
A584
CHURCH RD
B5261
FAIRLAWN ROAD
Forest Drive
Broadwood Way
Commonside
Inner Promenade
Arundel Road
Kingsway
Central Drive
Seymour Rd
Woodlands
Windsor Road
Cambridge Road
Church Drive
WEST

E2
1 Nookfield Cl
E3
1 Ashton St
2 Beach St
3 Green St
4 Hastings Pl
5 Horsfall Av
6 Market Sq
7 Queen St
8 St Cuthbert's Cl
9 The Serpentine
E
F
G
H
51
64
ROAD
Liggard Brook
Laburnum Avenue
Laurel Avenue
Lilac Av
Green Drive Golf Club
Saltcotes
Green Drive
Doctors Surgery
Norfolk Road
St Peters RC School
East Holme
Tewkesbury Dr
Cotswold Rd
Grampian
Wicklow Av
Cem
Bredon Cl
Park View Road
Bellingham Rd
Talbot Road
Lytham C of E Primary School
Wykeham Rd
Mythop Cl
S Holme
St Bedes RC High School
Guardian Sports Club
MYTHOP ROAD B5259
Lytham
Lythall Avenue
Saltcotes Road
Saltcotes Pl
PRESTON RO
Graving Dock
Tennyson Av
Three Worlds Business Centre
F3
1 Bannister St
2 Bath Rd
3 Bath St
4 Chapel St
5 Clifton St
6 Dicconson Ter
7 George St
8 Pleasant St
9 Shepherd St
10 South Clifton St
11 Talbot Ter
G2
1 Copeland Pl
2 Gilderdale Ct
3 Kielder Ct
4 Rothbury Pl
Ring Dyke Way
Forest Drive
Calf Cft
Molyneux Pl
Southfold
Starfield Cl
Long Acre Place
Rogerley Close
Painley Cl
Moorfield Drive
Alder Gv
Gregory Place
Ballam Road
Lytham Station
Mythop Av
Bleasdale Rd
Pendle Pl
The Glades
Brook Rd
Badgers Walk East
PARK VW RD
STATION RD B5259
Lorne Street
South St
Preston Road
Lytham Hospital
Waterfront Business
Cleveland Road
Station Rd
Police Station
Westby St
Westby Street
Cecil St
E Cecil St
Agnew St
Westwood Ms
Doctors Surgery
School La
Park St
S Westby St
N Clifton St
St Peters RC School
Haven Road
North Warton Street
Freckleton St
Albert St
Trent St
Warton Street
South Warton Street
Lytham Posey Bowl
S Clifton Street
Henry St
Hotel
Lowther Ter
Gregson Street
Westwood Rd
Livesey St
Road
CENTRAL BEACH
EAST BEACH A584
A584
Lytham Windmill
G3
1 Birch St
2 East Cliffe
3 Grosvenor St
4 St John's St
5 South Warton St
6 Victoria St
7 West Cliffe
8 Wharf St
H1
1 The Belfry
2 Cheltenham Crs
3 Chiltern Cl
4 Howgill Wy
5 Saltcotes Rd
H2
1 Arnold Rd
2 Bedford Rd
3 Browning Av
4 Burns Av
5 Byron Av
6 Fairsnape Rd
7 Green Hey
8 Hamilton Cl
9 Oswald Rd
10 Ribchester Rd
11 Wellington St
12 Whitecotes Dr
13 Wordsworth Av
H3
1 Nelson St
1
2
3
4
5

A2
1 Meadow La
A1
1 Mendip Cl
A
B
C
D
52
Lodge Lane
West End La
Warton Hall
Lidun Park Industrial Estate
Boundary Road
Wicklow Av
Grampian
Cheviot Av
Cotswold Rd
Cem
Tewkesbury Dr
Bredon Cl
Mornington Road
PRESTON ROAD A584
LYTHAM ROAD A584
Saltcotes Pl
Graving Dock Road
Marine Business Centre
Worlds Business Centre
Dock Road
South St
Preston Road
Waterfront Marine Business Park
Wrea Brook
1
2
3
4
5
63

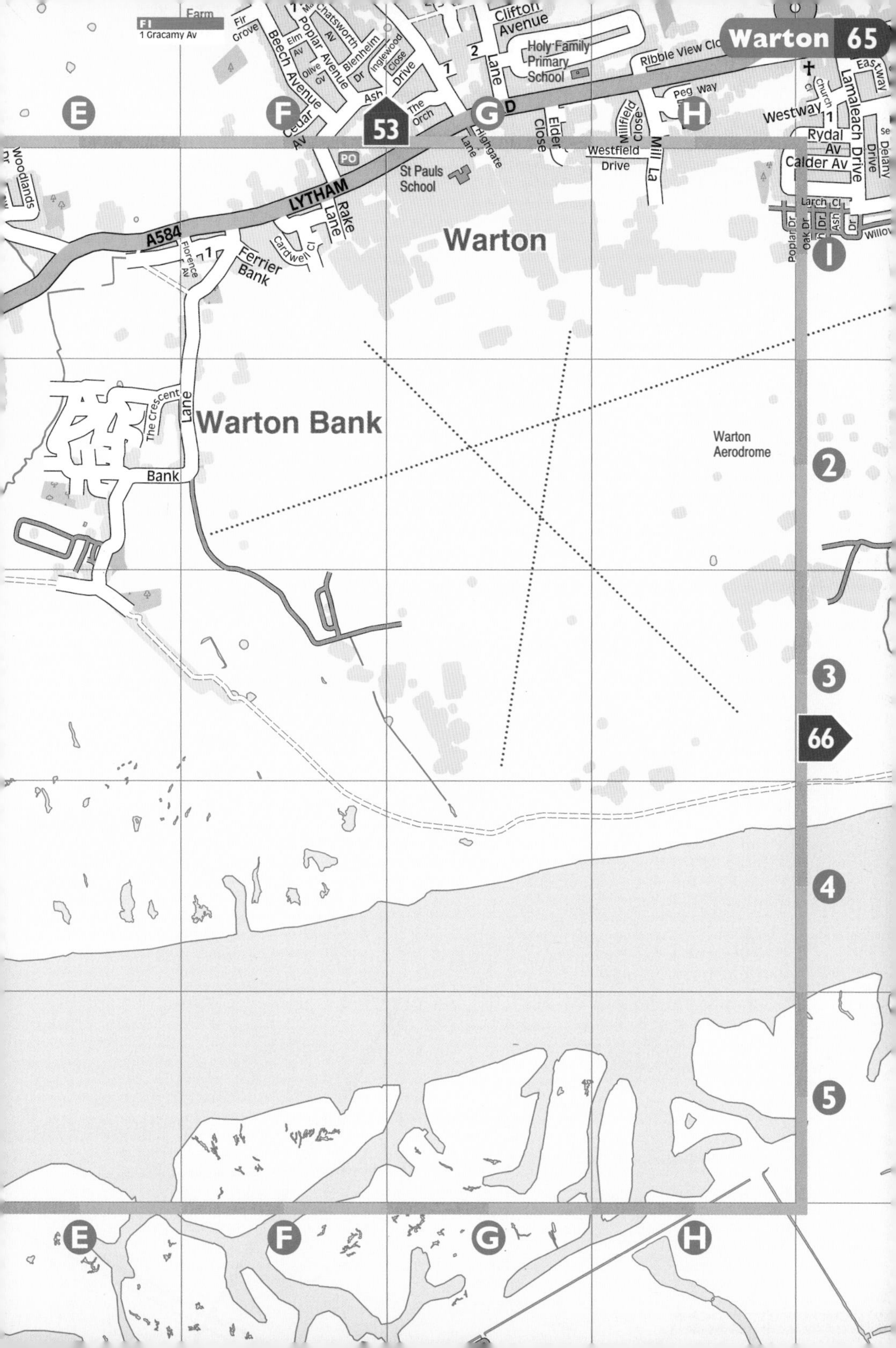
F1
1 Gracamy Av
Farm
Fir Grove
Beech Avenue
Elm Av
Olive Gv
Poplar Avenue
Chatsworth Av
Blenheim Dr
Inglewood Close
Ash Drive
The Orch
Cedar Av
Clifton Avenue
Lane
Holy Family Primary School
Ribble View Cl
Peg Way
Millfield Close
Elder Close
Mill La
Westfield Drive
Highgate Lane
St Pauls School
PO
LYTHAM
A584
Rake Lane
Cardwell Cl
Florence Av
Ferrier Bank
Woodlands Dr
Warton
Westway
Church Cl
Lamaleach Drive
Eastway
Rydal Av
Calder Av
Delany Drive
Larch Cl
Poplar Dr
Oak Dr
Ash Dr
Willow
The Crescent
Lane
Warton Bank
Bank
Warton Aerodrome
53
66
E
F
G
H
I
2
3
4
5

66
Lytham Road
Derwent Cl
Derwent
Douglas Drive
Bramwell
Ruskin Road
Naze La
Croft
Butts
Lane
2
1
Summit Drive
Bunker St
Eastway
Orchard Cl
Close
Ribble
Drive
Ribble Avenue
Clifton Place
Clitheroes Lane
Further Ends Road
Wades Croft
Church Cl
Lamaleach Drive
Westway
1
Sagar Drive
Sedgley Avenue
Freckleton Cricket Club
Bush Lane
Green
Lane
54
Naze Lane
A
B
C
D
Rydal Av
Calder Av
Delany Drive
Hodgson Avenue
Green Lane West
Green Lane West
Larch Cl
Poplar Dr
Oak Dr
Beech Dr
Ash Dr
Willow Dr
Willow Close
1
Naze Lane East
Stoney Lane
Bush Lane
Cherry Lane
Freckleton Pool
Warton Aerodrome
2
Lane
Pool
Naze Lane East
Naze Mount
Naze La East
3
65
River Ribble
Longton Sands
4
5
A
B
C
D
Hesketh Out Marsh
grid square represents 500 metres

E
F
55
G
H
Grange Farm
I
2
Hutton Sands
Hutton Marsh
3
4
Longton Marsh
Ribble Way
5
E
F
G
H

D3
1 Crabtree Av
D2
1 Brandwood
2 Danesway
3 Parklands Cl
4 Whitefield Rd W
5 Willow Cl
56
75
Crow Hills Road
Penwortham Primary Sch
Priory High School
Penwortham Leisure Centre
St Teresa's Primary School
Marsh Farm
Howick
Howick Cross
Howick Gallery
Howick Park Drive
Howick Park Avenue
Howick Pk Close
Liverpool Road
Cross Lane
Townley Lane
Stanley Grove
Blashaw Lane
Carlisle Avenue
Wilton Grove
Manor Grove
Parklands Av
Whitefield Rd
Moor Avenue
Central Drive
Tarn Cl
The Spinney
Mulberry Avenue
Mayflower Avenue
Primary School
Birch
Crownlee
Howick Moor Lane
All Hallows RC High School
Howick Primary School
LIVERPOOL ROAD
A59(T)
Ratten Lane
Fensway
Cardale
Walkdale
The Dellway
Stanley Avenue
Anchor Drive
The Greenacres
Hall Croft
Lindle Crescent
Lindle Close
Lindle Avenue
Lindle Lane
Hutton
Saunders' Lane
Tolsey Dr
Hutton Grammar School
Hutton Hall Avenue
Moor Lane
Westminster Place
Stiles Av
Top Acre
Stonefold
LONGTON BY-PASS
Windsor Av
Balmoral Road
Boundary Cl
The Cedars
Sandringham Pk Dr
Station
Chapel Lane
South Avenue
Brierfield
Shaftesbury Av
Dickson Hey
Spinney Cl
New Longton
Royalty

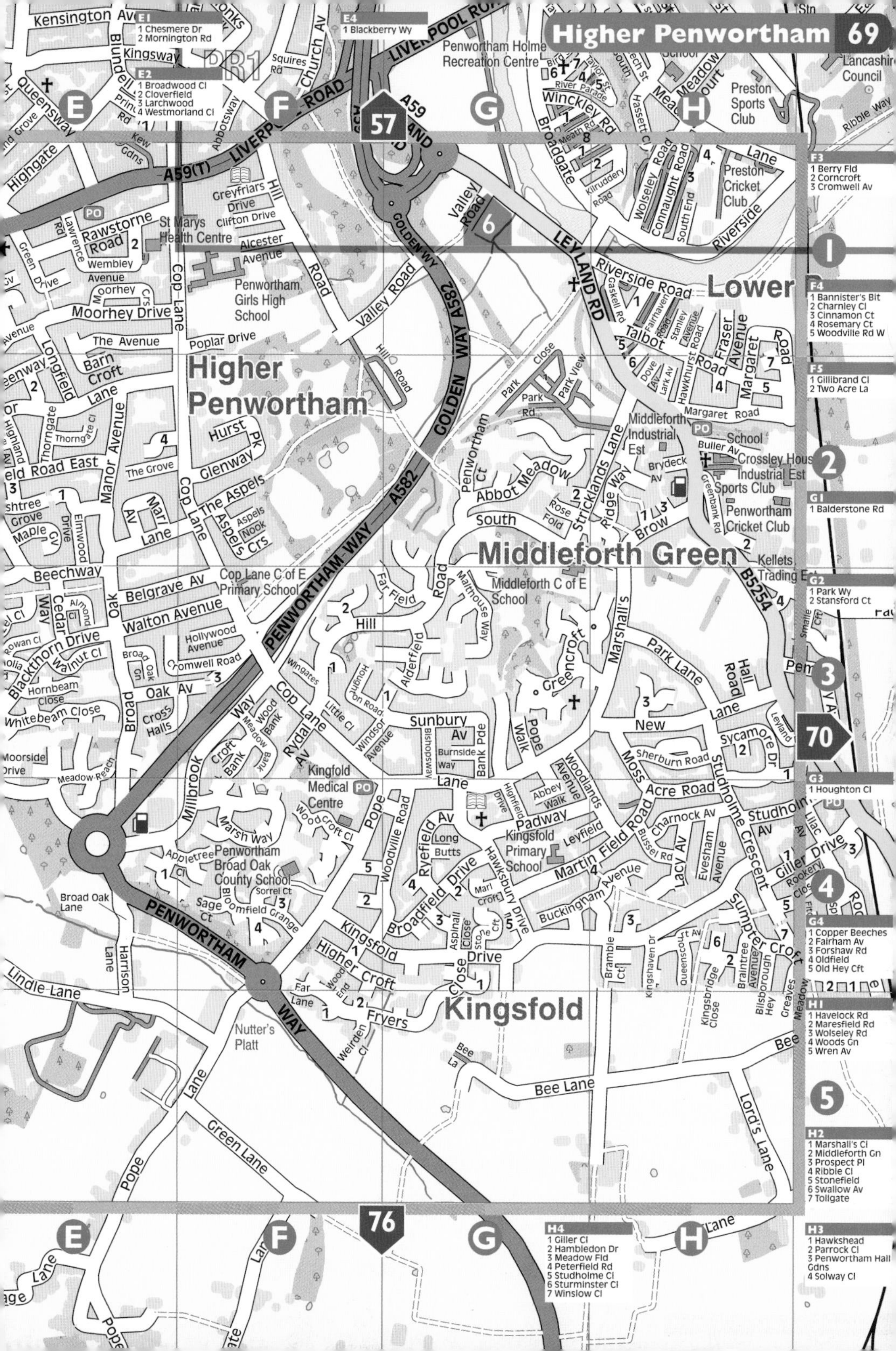
E1
1 Chesmere Dr
2 Mornington Rd
E2
1 Broadwood Cl
2 Cloverfield
3 Larchwood
4 Westmorland Cl
E4
1 Blackberry Wy
PR1
57
Penwortham Holme Recreation Centre
Preston Sports Club
Lancashire Council
F3
1 Berry Fld
2 Corncroft
3 Cromwell Av
F4
1 Bannister's Bit
2 Charnley Cl
3 Cinnamon Ct
4 Rosemary Ct
5 Woodville Rd W
F5
1 Gillibrand Cl
2 Two Acre La
G1
1 Balderstone Rd
G2
1 Park Wy
2 Stansford Ct
G3
1 Houghton Cl
G4
1 Copper Beeches
2 Fairham Av
3 Forshaw Rd
4 Oldfield
5 Old Hey Cft
H1
1 Havelock Rd
2 Maresfield Rd
3 Wolseley Rd
4 Woods Gn
5 Wren Av
H2
1 Marshall's Cl
2 Middleforth Gn
3 Prospect Pl
4 Ribble Cl
5 Stonefield
6 Swallow Av
7 Tollgate
H3
1 Hawkshead
2 Parrock Cl
3 Penwortham Hall Gdns
4 Solway Cl
H4
1 Giller Cl
2 Hambledon Dr
3 Meadow Fld
4 Peterfield Rd
5 Studholme Cl
6 Sturminster Cl
7 Winslow Cl
LIVERPOOL ROAD
A59(T)
LEYLAND RD
GOLDEN WAY A582
PENWORTHAM WAY
B5254
Preston Cricket Club
St Marys Health Centre
Penwortham Girls High School
Higher Penwortham
Lower P
Middleforth Industrial Est
Crossley House Industrial Est
Sports Club
Penwortham Cricket Club
Kellets Trading Est
Middleforth Green
Cop Lane C of E Primary School
Middleforth C of E School
Kingsfold Medical Centre
Penwortham Broad Oak County School
Kingsfold Primary School
Kingsfold
Nutter's Platt
70
76
Bee Lane
Lord's Lane
Green Lane
Lindle Lane
Broad Oak Lane
Harrison Lane
Pope Lane
Cop Lane
Hill Road
Valley Road
Riverside Road
Riverside
Park Lane
New Lane
Moss Acre Road
Studholme Crescent
Martin Field Road
Buckingham Avenue
Sunbury Av
Marshall's Brow
Strickland's Lane
Abbot Meadow
Greencroft
Hurst Pk
Glenway
The Aspels
Moorhey Drive
The Avenue
Poplar Drive
Longfield
Manor Avenue
Beechway
Belgrave Av
Walton Avenue
Blackthorn Drive
Broad Oak Av
Millbrook Way
Rydal Av
Woodville Road
Broadfield Drive
Hawksbury Drive
Higher Croft
Fryers
Kingsfold Drive

PRESTON
A5
1 Werneth Cl
A4
1 Burwood Cl
2 Chelford Cl
3 Giller Fold
4 Northleach Av
Frenchwood
Lancashire County Council
Christ the King High School
Preston Sports Club
Preston Cricket Club
58
7
Penwortham
B5
1 Fir Trees Rd
South Ribble Industrial Est
Warner Brothers Cinema
Winery Lane
Capitol Way
LONDON WAY
Walton
St Leonards C of E Primary School
Old Tram Road
Factory Lane
Walton-le-Dale
B6230 HENNEL LANE
Hennel Lane
Carrwood Road
Millwood Road
Todd Lane North
The Ferns
Kilngate
Fieldside Close
Badgers Way
Oakland Glen
Clough Avenue
Valley View Road
The Oaks
Springwood Cl
Simmons Av
Old Oak Gardens
Carrwood
Bellis Way
Summerfield Close
Leigh Brow
C3
1 Dovetree Cl
2 Jasmine Rd
Kellets Trading Est
B5254
Pembury Av
69
C5
1 Doodstone Cl
2 New Rd
Studholme Av
Lilac Av
Giller Drive
Rookery Close
Rookery Drive
Evesham Avenue
Fitchfield
Spring Gdns
Castle Fold
D2
1 Oakwood Av
Croft
Kingsbridge Close
Braintree Avenue
Bilsborough Hey
Greaves Meadow
Penwortham Lane
Pool Lane
Lyndale Grove
Lyndale Av
Highfield Gv
Highfield Avenue
Bee Lane
LEYLAND ROAD
Moorhey School
Round Acre
Far Cft
Marina Close
Marina Grove
Marina Dr
Mark Cl
Conway Av
Ampleforth Dr
St Cuthbert's Road
Mercer Road
St Gerrard's Rd
Lourdes Avenue
Doodstone Av
Doodstone Nook
Medway Close
Watering Pool
Linden Drive
Camwood Drive
Linden Cl
Lostock Hall CP School
Lostock Hall High School
Glendale Avenue
Glendale Crs
Green Drive
Southlands Av
Flag Lane
Lord's Lane
D3
1 Cherry Trees
2 Denby Cl
3 The Doultons
4 Forest Cl
77
Laburnum Av
North Gv
BROWNEDGE ROAD
Tardy Gate
Tardygate Trading Est
Half Acre
Bridge Close
Village Surg
Primary School
Marilyn Av
Prospect Av
Rosemeade Av
Mayfield Av
Bridge Rd
The Crs
Graham Av
grid square represents 500 metres

E1
1 Chapel Yd
2 Cooper Hill Cl
E2
1 Drakes Hollow
2 Heaton Cl
3 Walton Gn
E3
1 Balmoral Rd
2 Cavendish Pl
3 Kent Av
4 Rutland Av
E4
1 Duddle La
2 Lawrence Av
3 Wordsworth Pl
E5
1 Convent Cl
2 Langdale Cl
F1
1 Butcher Brow
2 Prince's Rd
3 Queen's Rd
F3
1 Beech Hill Cl
2 Crowell Wy
3 Kilsby Cl
4 Lowesby Cl
F4
1 Balshaw St
2 Buttermere Cl
3 Haydock St
4 Longworth St
5 Pear Tree Cl
6 Pear Tree St
7 Water St
F5
1 Clayton St
2 Countessway
3 Greenwood St
4 Hodson St
5 James St
6 John St
7 Oakland St
G4
1 Ashworth St
2 Whalley St
G5
1 Eaveswood Cl
2 Elm Dr
3 Lodge Cl
4 Tyne St
5 Yewlands Av
H4
1 Woodlands Av
59
72
78
Junction 3
M6
CUERDALE LANE
B6230
Silverholme
River Ribble
Ribble Way
VICTORIA RD
King's Croft
CHURCH BROW
Riverside Medical Cen
Mill Lane
A675
HIGHER WALTON ROAD
CANN BRIDGE ST
The Drive
Knot Lane
Ennerdale Drive
Kingsdale Close
Queensdale Cl
Darwen View
Lady Pl
School
Park Place
The Surgery
CHORLEY RD
Hotel
Regent Road
Warwick Rd
Allerton Road
Ambleway
Holland House Road
Devonport Close
Windsor Road
Cinnamon Hill South
Devon Cl
Hampshire Road
Hunters Lodge
B6258
CHORLEY ROAD
Charnley Fold Ind Estate
Charnley Fold
Charnley Fold La
School St
School Lane
Cottage Lane
Kittlingborne Brow
Brown La
Walton-le-Dale Sch Clinic
Bamber Bridge Clinc
Secondary School
Charnley Fold Industrial Est
Lancashire Co Council
Sollam's Close
Wynfield
Sylvan Grove
Brown Lane
Brindle Road
Collins Road North
The Crs
Skipton Cl
St Aidans Pk
Fourfields
Whitefield Meadow
Doctors Surg
Chestnut Close
Renshaw Drive
Crescent
Holland Av
Grasmere Close
Ambleside Cl
Coniston Drive
Pear Tree
Wellington Place
Milton Close
Masefield Place
Selkirk Drive
Albany Drive
Tennyson Place
Fairfax Place
Grenville Avenue
Lane
Duddle
Rydal Avenue
Kentmere Avenue
Longbrook Av
Dean St
Aspden St
School
Collins Road
Ash Grove
Poplar Avenue
Coppice School
Larch Grove
St Aidans School
Hazel Av
Hazel Gv
Hazel Cl
Avenue
Brindle Road
The Ryan Medical Cen
Maple Drive
Withy Gv Crescent
Trees
Poplar Close
Poplar Grove
Withy Trees
Withy Close
Withy Grove Close
Bamber Bridge (Withy Park) Leisure Centre
BAMBER BRIDGE
Primary School
B5257
BROWNEDGE LANE
BROWNEDGE ROAD
Danesway
Danes Drive
St Mary's Av
St Jude's Av
St Mary's Cl
Brownedge Cl
Saint Mary's Rd
Ellen Street
Teven St
Meanygate
Regentsway
Queen
Withy Gv Rd
Kingsway
Smith Street
Grove St
Moon St
Carr Street
Edward
Bamber Bridge Stn
Police Station
LC
Oxford Rd
Savick Cl
Holme Road
Outram
LONDON
Walton Summit
Moorhey Crescent
Bradkirk Lane
Brindle Close

M6
D2
1 Rossall Cl
2 Silverdale Cl
3 Winster Cl
A3
1 Lark Hl
A
B
C
D
Smithy House
Potter Lane
1
D3
1 Arnside Cl
2 Methuen Cl
Bannister Close
Bannister Hall Lane
Bannister Hall Drive
Bannister Hall Crs
Shop La
CAMBRIDGE STREET
2
D5
1 Appleby Cl
2 Hayfield Cl
3 Meadowside Dr
PO
River Darwent
Coup Green
Coupe Green
Grange Drive
Coupe Green
Lowick Close
Rusland Crs
Woodhall Dr
Coupe Green CP School
Thornton Dr
Cleveleys Rd
Cartmel Dr
Poulton Crescent
Holker Cl
Fox Lane
BLACKBURN RD
Bridge Street
Brook St
School
Church St
Brow
3
Rosewood Drive
Rosewood Avenue
Hawthorne Avenue
Primary School
Ashtree Court
HOGHTON LANE
A675
Hoghton Lane
Hall Lane
Higher Walton
71
Charles Crs
Gregson Lane
Four Lane Ends
Daub Bells
Central Avenue
Rhodesway
Lydric Avenue
Conway Court
Squires Close
Junction 30
M6
4
Shuttling Fields Lane
Aldersleigh Crs
Larch Gate
Alma Row
Gregson
Bank Head Lane
Alder Drive
Birch Crs
Willow Close
Hayfield Avenue
Hillpark Avenue
Westfield Drive
Primary School
Bournesfield
Bourne's Row
5
79
Moorhey Crescent
Bridle Road
Stephendale Av
Brindle Close
Greystock
Bank Head La
grid square represents 500 metres

Knight's Farm
Bottoms
Green L
G4
1 The Croft
2 Willow Field Cha
Dark Wd Lane
E
F
G
H
Firwood Lane
I
H4
1 Fowler Cl
Goose Foot Lane
Stanley Grange
2
Roach Road
Brook Lane
Cripple Gate Lane
Hollins Cl
Manor Close
3
Quaker
Lane
PO
Gib
Station Rd
LC
Brindle Lodge
Brookhouse Close
Brookhouse Drive
The Crossing
Fowler Cl
4
hapel
Hoghton
HOGHTON LANE
5
Hatchwood Farm
Oram
Road
Hill Hou
Lane
A675

A2
1 Bentley Park Rd
2 Townfield Cl
A1
1 Ash Gv
2 Brook Hey
A3
1 Tranmoor
B1
1 East Sq
2 Fengrove
3 West Sq
B2
1 The Coppice
B3
1 Meadowside
B4
1 Gill Nook
2 Hunters Fold
LONGTON
Walmer Bridge
Little Hoole Moss Houses
Longton Health Cen
Methodist School
The Beeches Medical Cen
Longton School
South Ribble Borough Council
Cemetery
Diamond Hall Farm
Light Industrial Est
Little Hoole CP School
Longton Business Park
LONGTON BY-PASS
A59(T)
Liverpool Road
Liverpool Old Rd
Hall Lane
Hall Carr Lane
Drumacre Lane West
Gill Lane
Knoll Lane
Dob Lane
Moss Lane
Chapel Lane
School Lane
Franklands
Birkdale Av
Formby Crescent
Dale Avenue
Mereside Cl
Briar Croft
Woodlands Way
Highfield Drive
Fairview Close
Tristan Av
School St
Old Ml Ct
Gower Grove
Walmer Green
Long Meadow
Marlfield
Oldfield
Acre Grove
Thornfield
Southfield
Critchley Close
Blackhurst Court
Poplar Avenue
Farmend Close
Thirlmere Close
Kentmere Drive
Intack Road
Avalwood Avenue
Chapel Park Road
Green Gate
Cross Field
Stonefield
grid square represents 500 metres

New Longton
Midge Hall
68
76
E
F
G
H
1
2
3
4
5
H1
1 Royalty Gdns
LONGTON BY-PASS
A59(T)
Saunders' Lane
Chapel Lane
Park Av
South Avenue
Brierfield
Amersham Close
Shaftesbury Av
Boundary Cl
The Cedars
Sandringham Pk Dr
Windsor Av
Balmoral Road
Royalty
Royalty Avenue
Lane
Station Road
Hey End
Dickson Hey
Spinney Cl
Chesham Drive
Latimer Drive
The Vinery
Churchside
Knot Acre
Moor Field
Woodside Av
Waverley Drive
Nursery Lane
Brownhill Lane
Wham Lane
Barn Lane
Hugh
Moss Lane
New Longton C of E School
Southfield Drive
Sheephill Lane
Wham Hey
Avenue
Orchard
Cathrow Drive
The Close
Hollings Way
Willow
Hawthorn Close
Brookdale
Hill Top
Oak Grove
Mossway
Ash Grove
Long Moss Lane
Sod Hall Lane
East
Thornton Barn
Wholesome Lane
Land Lane
Gill Lane
Midge Hall Lane
Singleton's Farm
LC
Jane Lane
Longme
Stati
Pleasant
Whi
Stal
Nook
Place

D5
1 Riversides Cl
Lord's La
Green Lane
Pope Lane
Lane
A
B
C
D
69
Royalty Avenue
Royalty Lane
Nib Lane
Cage Lane
Newgate Lane
1
White Stake
Pope Lane
PENWORTHAM WAY
Wham Lane
Chain House Lane
Chain House Lane
Brook Lane
2
Long Moss Lane
Lodge View
Parker Lane
Naptha Lane
LC
Naptha Cott
Brook Lane
Lodge Lane
Startley Nook
3
75
FLENSBURG WAY
A582 FLENSBURG WAY
Moss Lane
Moss Lane
Farington Moss
4
Murray Avenue
Mark's Av
Croston Road
B5253
Thornton Dr
Five Acres
Fylde Av
Bispham Av
5
WAY
Bannister Lane
Riverside Avenue
Croston Road
Brookside Cl
FLENSBURG
80
Jane Lane
Hugh Lane
gate
Lane

E2
1 Cheshire House Cl
F1
1 Barnfield
2 Great Meadow
3 Harold Ter
4 Orchard Cft
5 Sephton St
6 William St
F2
1 Brackenbury Cl
2 Chadwick Gdns
3 Constable Av
4 Gainsborough Av
G1
1 Cedar Av
2 Fern Cl
3 Lindley St
4 Maureen Av
5 Mossfield Cl
G2
1 Albrighton Cl
2 Birtwistle St
3 King St
4 Princess St
5 Queen St
H1
1 Baytree Cl
2 Blenheim Cl
3 Breeze Mt
4 Bridge End
5 Fellway Cl
6 Malvern Cl
7 Pastures New
8 The Pickerings
9 River Heights
10 Stonebridge Cl
11 Woodstock Cl
H5
1 St Judes Av
2 Woodside
70
78
81
Tardy Gate
Lostock Hall
Cuerden Green
PR5
FARINGTON ROAD
A582
A582 LOSTOCK LANE
BROWNEDGE ROAD B5257
WATKIN LANE
STANIFIELD LANE
A5083
LYDIATE LANE
Centurion Way
Centurion Industrial Estate
Fowler Lane
Fowler Avenue
Old School Lane
Stoney Lane
Croston Road
School Lane
Coote Lane
Tardygate Trading Est
Lostock Hall Station
Lostock Hall High School
St Gerrards School
Farington St Pauls C of E School
Carr Lane
Windermere Avenue
Kentmere Av
Grasmere

B1
1 Baldwin St
2 Bymbrig Cl
3 Cranbourne St
4 Earls Av
5 Hopwood St
6 Nelson St
7 Smithy St
A1
1 Kiddlington Cl
2 Regency Av
3 Riverway Cl
B2
1 East St
2 Spinners Sq
C1
1 Asland Cl
2 Brennand Cl
3 Brown St
4 Cambridge Rd
5 Douglas Cl
6 Dunsop Cl
7 Fell Cl
8 Hareden Cl
9 Hodder Cl
10 Jackson St
11 Mckenzie St
12 Montgomery St
13 Princess St
14 Sergeant St
C2
1 Hopwood St
D4
1 Mallards Wk
Bamber Bridge Football Club
Walton Summit
Bamber Bridge (Withy Park) Leisure Centre
Lancashire County Council
New Mill Industrial Estate
St Saviours C of E Primary School
Junction 1a
Junction 29a
Junction 29/1
Clayton Green
Clock House
Cuerden Hall
LONDON WAY
WIGAN ROAD
LOSTOCK LANE
BROWNEDGE ROAD
M6
M65
A6
A49
A5083
71
77
82
grid square represents 500 metres

E3 1 Little Banks Cl
F1 1 Hudson Ct
F2 1 Craigflower Ct
F3 1 Elmfield Dr
F5 1 The Heathers
72
83
Jack Green
Seed Lee
Junction 9/2
M61
M65
Pippin Street
Thorpe Green
Top of the
Bank Head Lane
Brindle Road
Greystock Close
Stephendale Av
Oakshott Place
Ranglet Road
Kellet Lane
Sceptre Way
Brindle Fold
Smithy Lane
Sandy Lane
B5256
Westwood Rd
Clayton Brook Road
Cough Lane
Clayton Brook County School
Clayton Brook Surgery
Westwood County Primary School
Clayton Green Business Park
Hotel
Preston Road
A6
Mill House
Oram
Back Bourne's Row
Holt Lane
Radburn Brow
The Beeches

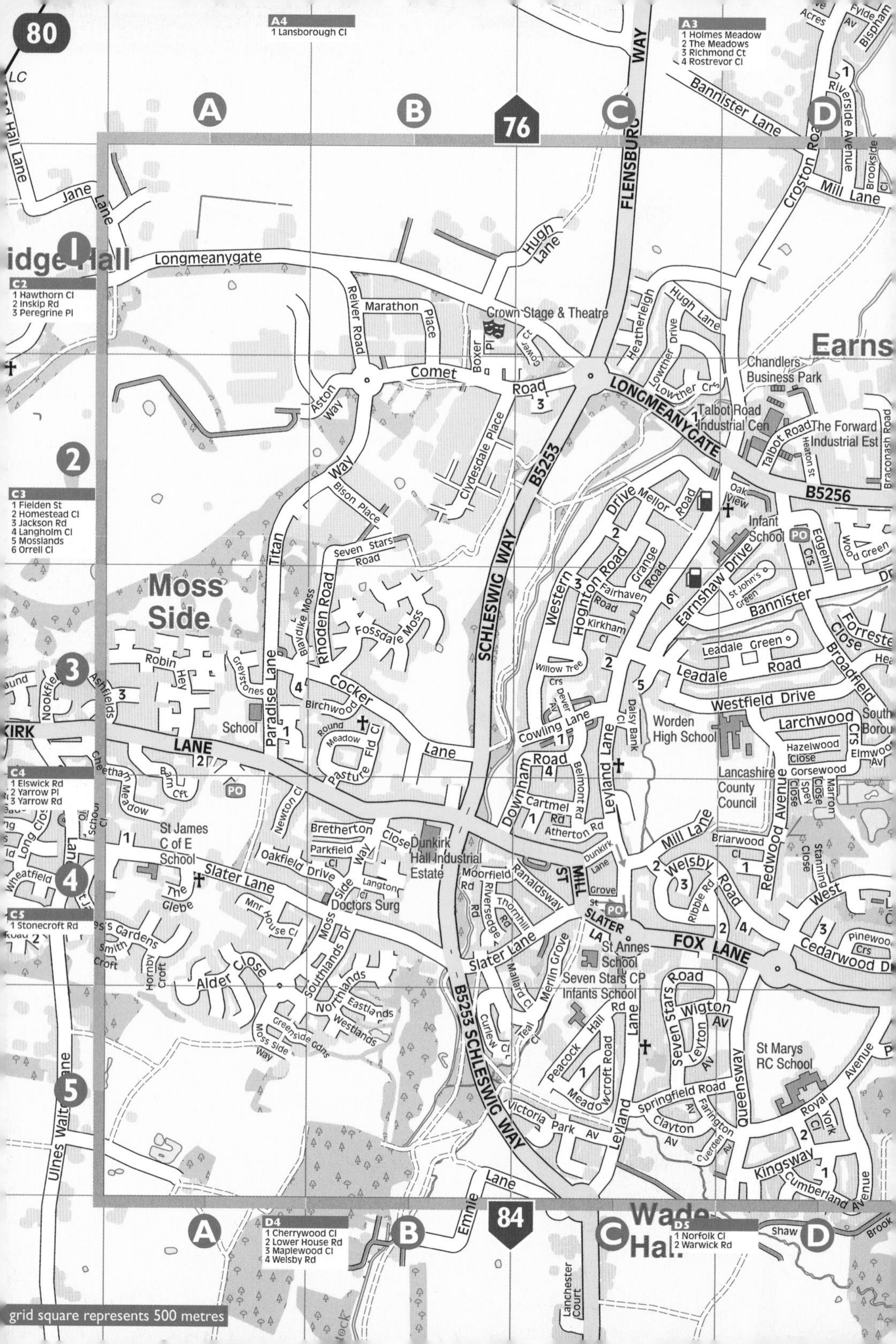

80
A4
1 Lansborough Cl
A3
1 Holmes Meadow
2 The Meadows
3 Richmond Ct
4 Rostrevor Cl
A
B
C
D
76
84
C2
1 Hawthorn Cl
2 Inskip Rd
3 Peregrine Pl
C3
1 Fielden St
2 Homestead Cl
3 Jackson Rd
4 Langholm Cl
5 Mosslands
6 Orrell Cl
C4
1 Elswick Rd
2 Yarrow Pl
3 Yarrow Rd
C5
1 Stonecroft Rd
D4
1 Cherrywood Cl
2 Lower House Rd
3 Maplewood Cl
4 Welsby Rd
D5
1 Norfolk Cl
2 Warwick Rd
1
2
3
4
5
Moss Side
Earns
Wade Hall
Longmeanygate
LONGMEANYGATE
FLENSBURG WAY
SCHLESWIG WAY
B5253 SCHLESWIG WAY
B5253
B5256
Bannister Lane
Croston Road
Riverside Avenue
Mill Lane
Brookside Cl
Hugh Lane
Marathon Place
Reiver Road
Comet Road
Crown Stage & Theatre
Boxer Pl
Gower Ct
Aston Way
Titan Way
Bison Place
Clydesdale Place
Seven Stars Road
Rhoden Road
Fossdale Moss
Blaydike Moss
Heatherleigh
Lowther Drive
Lowther Crs
Chandlers Business Park
Talbot Road Industrial Cen
Talbot Road
The Forward Industrial Est
Heaton St
Braconash Road
Mellor Road
Oak View
Infant School
Edgehill Crs
Wood Green
Earnshaw Drive
St John's Green
Western Drive
Hoghton Road
Grange Road
Fairhaven Road
Kirkham Cl
Bannister Dr
Forrester Close
Broadfield
Leadale Green
Leadale Road
Westfield Drive
Worden High School
Larchwood Crs
Hazelwood Close
Gorsewood Close
Spey Close
Marron Close
Elmwood
South Borough
Lancashire County Council
Redwood Avenue
Willow Tree Crs
Dever Av
Cowling Lane
Daisy Bank Cl
Leyland Lane
Downham Road
Belmont Rd
Cartmel Rd
Atherton Rd
Mill Lane
Briarwood Cl
Stanning Close
Welsby Road
Ribble Rd
West
Pinewood Crs
Cedarwood Dr
FOX LANE
Robin Hey
Greystones
Paradise Lane
Cocker Lane
Birchwood
Round Meadow
Pasture Fld Cl
School
LANE
KIRK
Ashfields
Nookfield
Cheetham Meadow
Barn Cft
St James C of E School
Newton Cl
Bretherton Close
Parkfield Cl
Oakfield Drive
Moss Side Way
Langton Cl
Dunkirk Hall Industrial Estate
Moorfield Rd
Riversedge Rd
Thornhill Rd
Ranaldsway
MILL ST
Dunkirk Lane
Grove St
SLATER LA
Slater Lane
The Glebe
Mnr House Cl
Doctors Surg
Southlands Dr
Northlands
Eastlands
Westlands
Greenside Gdns
Moss Side Way
Alder Close
Smith Croft
Hornby Croft
Long Close
Wheatfield
Ulnes Walton Lane
Hall Lane
Jane Lane
St Annes School
Seven Stars CP Infants School
Mallard Cl
Merlin Grove
Curlew Cl
Teal Cl
Peacock Hall Rd
Meadowcroft Road
Leyland Lane
Seven Stars Road
Wigton Av
Leyton Av
Queensway
St Marys RC School
Springfield Road
Clayton Av
Farington Av
Cuerden Av
Victoria Park Av
Royal Avenue
York Cl
Kingsway
Cumberland Avenue
Emnie Lane
Lanchester Court
Shaw
Brook
PO
LC
grid square represents 500 metres

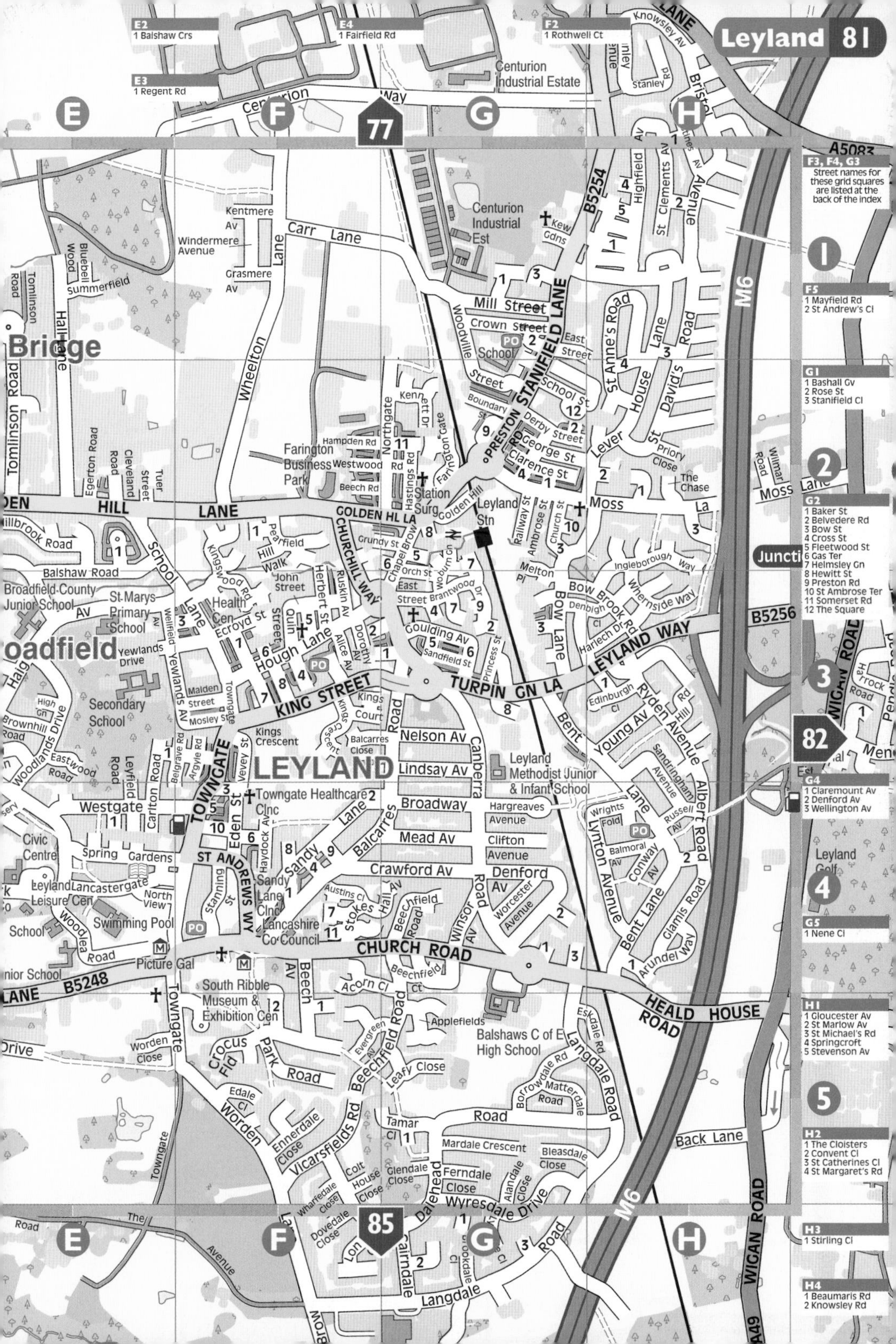

Leyland 81
E2
1 Balshaw Crs
E4
1 Fairfield Rd
F2
1 Rothwell Ct
E3
1 Regent Rd
F3, F4, G3
Street names for these grid squares are listed at the back of the index
F5
1 Mayfield Rd
2 St Andrew's Cl
G1
1 Bashall Gv
2 Rose St
3 Stanifield Cl
G2
1 Baker St
2 Belvedere Rd
3 Bow St
4 Cross St
5 Fleetwood St
6 Gas Ter
7 Helmsley Gn
8 Hewitt St
9 Preston Rd
10 St Ambrose Ter
11 Somerset Rd
12 The Square
G4
1 Claremount Av
2 Denford Av
3 Wellington Av
G5
1 Nene Cl
H1
1 Gloucester Av
2 St Marlow Av
3 St Michael's Rd
4 Springcroft
5 Stevenson Av
H2
1 The Cloisters
2 Convent Cl
3 St Catherines Cl
4 St Margaret's Rd
H3
1 Stirling Cl
H4
1 Beaumaris Rd
2 Knowsley Rd
77
82
85
Centurion Way
Centurion Industrial Estate
Centurion Industrial Est
Knowsley Av
Stanley Rd
Bristol Avenue
A5083
B5254
M6
Highfield Av
St Clements Av
Kentmere Av
Windermere Avenue
Grasmere Av
Carr Lane
Wheelton Lane
Bluebell Wood
Tomlinson Road
Summerfield
Hall Lane
Bridge
Kew Gdns
Mill Street
Crown Street
School
East Street
Woodville Street
Boundary St
School St
STANIFIELD LANE
PRESTON RD
St Anne's Road
House Lane
St David's Road
Lever House Lane
Priory Close
The Chase
Moss Lane
Derby Street
George St
Clarence St
Farington Business Park
Hampden Rd
Westwood Rd
Beech Rd
Northgate
Hastings Rd
Kennett Dr
Farington Gate
Station Surg
Golden Hill
Leyland Stn
Egerton Road
Cleveland Road
Tuer Street
GOLDEN HILL LANE
GOLDEN HL LA
CHURCHILL WAY
Railway St
Ambrose St
Church St
Moss La
Ingleborough Way
Whernside Way
Melton Pl
Bow Lane
Bow Brook Rd
Denbigh Cl
Harlech Dr
LEYLAND WAY
B5256
Junction
WIGAN ROAD
Harrock Road
Pendle Rd
Millbrook Road
School Lane
Balshaw Road
Broadfield County Junior School
St Marys Primary School
Broadfield
Pearfield
Hill Walk
Kingswood Rd
John Street
Herbert St
Ruskin Av
Grundy St
Chapel Brow
Orch St
East Street
Woburn Gn
Brantwood Dr
Health Cen
Ecroyd St
Wellfield
Quin Street
Hough Lane
Alice Av
Dorothy Av
Goulding Av
Sandfield St
Princess St
PO
Yewlands Drive
Yewlands Av
Malden Street
Mosley St
Towngate
KING STREET
Kings Court
Kings Crescent
Balcarres Close
TURPIN GN LA
Edinburgh Cl
Ryden Avenue
Hill Rd
Young Av
Bent Lane
Sandringham Avenue
Albert Road
High Gn
Brownhill Road
Haig
Woodlands Drive
Secondary School
Eastwood Road
Leyfield Road
Carlton Road
Belgrave Rd
Argyle Rd
Vevey St
TOWNGATE
LEYLAND
Nelson Av
Lindsay Av
Canberra Road
Leyland Methodist Junior & Infant School
Westgate
Towngate Healthcare Clnc
Broadway
Hargreaves Avenue
Wrights Fold
Russell Av
Lynton Avenue
Balmoral Av
Conway Av
Eden St
Haydock Av
Sandy Lane
Balcarres Road
Mead Av
Clifton Avenue
Leyland Golf
Civic Centre
Spring Gardens
ST ANDREWS WAY
Crawford Av
Denford Av
Leyland Leisure Cen
Lancastergate
North View
Stanning St
Sandy Lane Clnc
Austins Cl
Stokes Hall Av
Beechfield Road
Worcester Avenue
Glamis Road
Swimming Pool
Woodlea Road
Lancashire Co Council
Winsor Av
School
CHURCH ROAD
Arundel Way
Junior School
B5248
Picture Gal
Beech Av
Beechfield Ct
Acorn Cl
HEALD HOUSE ROAD
South Ribble Museum & Exhibition Cen
Applefields
Balshaws C of E High School
Eskdale Rd
Langdale Road
Worden Close
Crocus Fld
Park Road
Evergreen Av
Leafy Close
Borrowdale Rd
Matterdale Road
Drive
Edale Cl
Worden
Ennerdale Close
Vicarsfields Rd
Tamar Cl
Road
Mardale Crescent
Bleasdale Close
Back Lane
Colt House Close
Glendale Close
Dalehead
Ferndale Close
Alandale Close
Wyresdale Drive
Wharfedale Close
Dovedale Close
Cairndale
Brookdale Cl
Langdale
The Avenue
A49
E
F
G
H

82
B2
1 Azalea Cl
2 Rose Cl
3 Snowdrop Cl
A3
1 Chiltern Meadow
Clayton Green
78
Berkeley Dr
Nell Lane
A5083
WIGAN ROAD
Oaktree Av
West Drive
Elm Gv
Birch Av
Willow Crs
D1
1 Beechwood Cft
Shady Lane
Cuerden Valley Country Park
Dovecote
SHEEP HILL BROW
Glenmore
Clayton-le-Woods C of E Primary School
Back Lane
SHEEP HILL
SHEEP LANE
TOWN BROW
Camellia Dr
Magnolia Drive
Cypress Close
Petunia Close
Lune Dr
Clayton-Le-Woods
Moss Lane
Wilmar
Junction 28
LANCASTER LANE
B5256
Halton Av
Kent Drive
Levens Drive
Newby Drive
Caton Close
Lancaster Avenue
Spring Meadow
Kirkby Av
Claughton Avenue
Kellet Av
Stoney Holt
Ashurst Road
Pendle Road
Hampson Avenue
Harrock Road
Hunters Rd
School
Cunnery Meadow
A49 WIGAN ROAD
Mendip Road
Higher Meadow
81
Traceys Industrial Est
Albert Road
Lostock Meadow
Whitethorn Close
River Lostock
Leyland Golf Club
Lisieux Hall Hospital
HOUSE
B5248
DAWSON LANE
Back Lane
86
1 grid square represents 500 metres

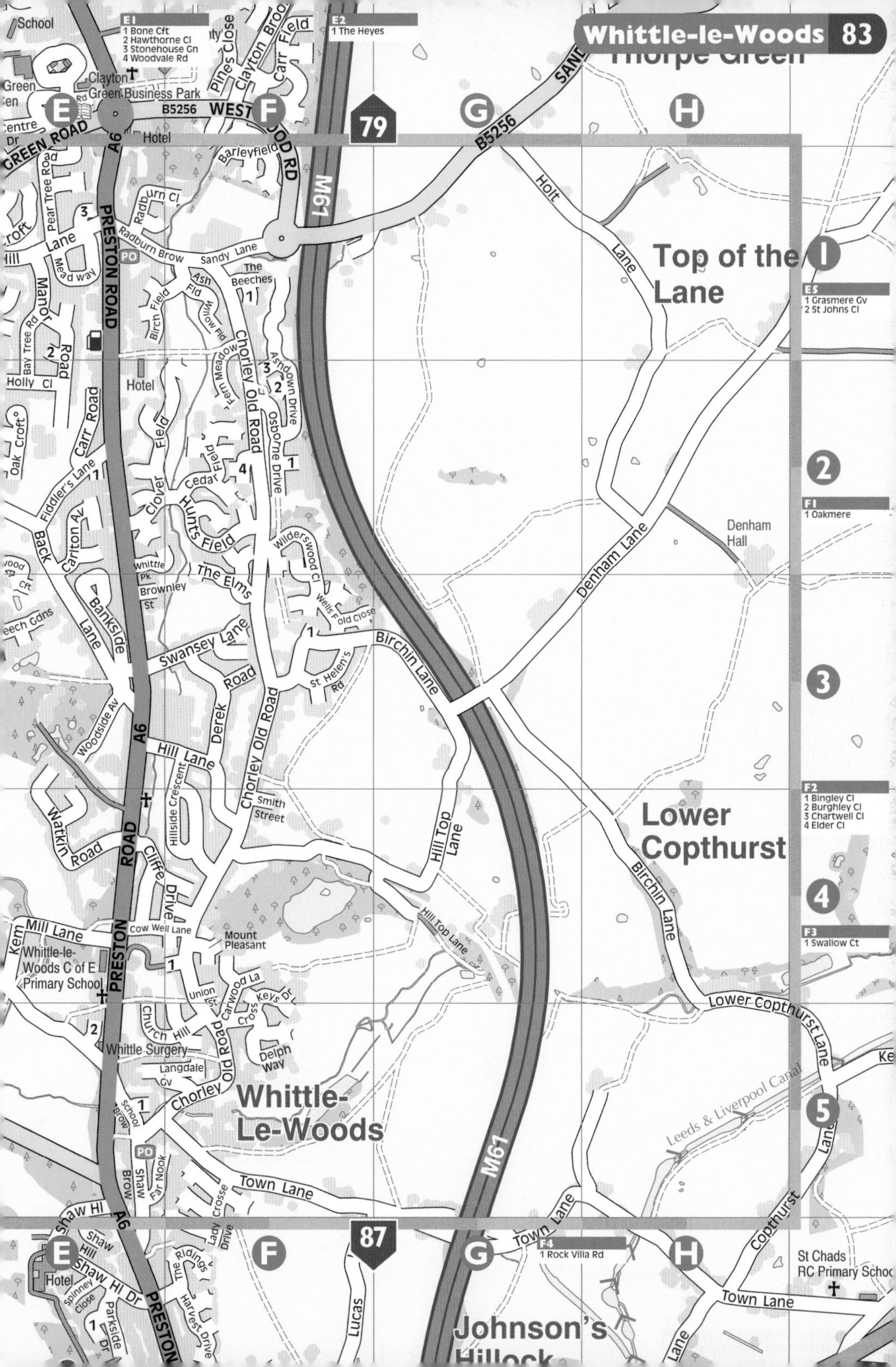
E1
1 Bone Cft
2 Hawthorne Cl
3 Stonehouse Gn
4 Woodvale Rd
E2
1 The Heyes
E5
1 Grasmere Gv
2 St Johns Cl
F1
1 Oakmere
F2
1 Bingley Cl
2 Burghley Cl
3 Chartwell Cl
4 Elder Cl
F3
1 Swallow Ct
F4
1 Rock Villa Rd
79
87
M61
A6
B5256
Top of the Lane
Lower Copthurst
Whittle-Le-Woods
Johnson's Hillock
Thorpe Green
Clayton Green Business Park
PRESTON ROAD
Chorley Old Road
Denham Lane
Birchin Lane
Holt Lane
Hill Top Lane
Lower Copthurst Lane
Town Lane
Leeds & Liverpool Canal
Denham Hall
Whittle-le-Woods C of E Primary School
Whittle Surgery
Mount Pleasant
St Chads RC Primary School
Hotel
School
Swansey Lane
Hill Lane
Derek Road
Mill Lane
Cliffe Drive
Cow Well Lane
Back Lane
Carr Road
Watkin Road
Hillside Crescent
Hunts Field
The Elms
Osborne Drive
Ashdown Drive
Radburn Brow
Sandy Lane
Smith Street
Union St
Church Hill
Delph Way
Langdale Gv
School Brow
Shaw Brow
Far Nook
Lady Crosse Drive
Shaw Hill
Shaw Hl Dr
The Ridings
Harvest Drive
Spinney Close
Parkside Dr
Lucas
Copthurst Lane

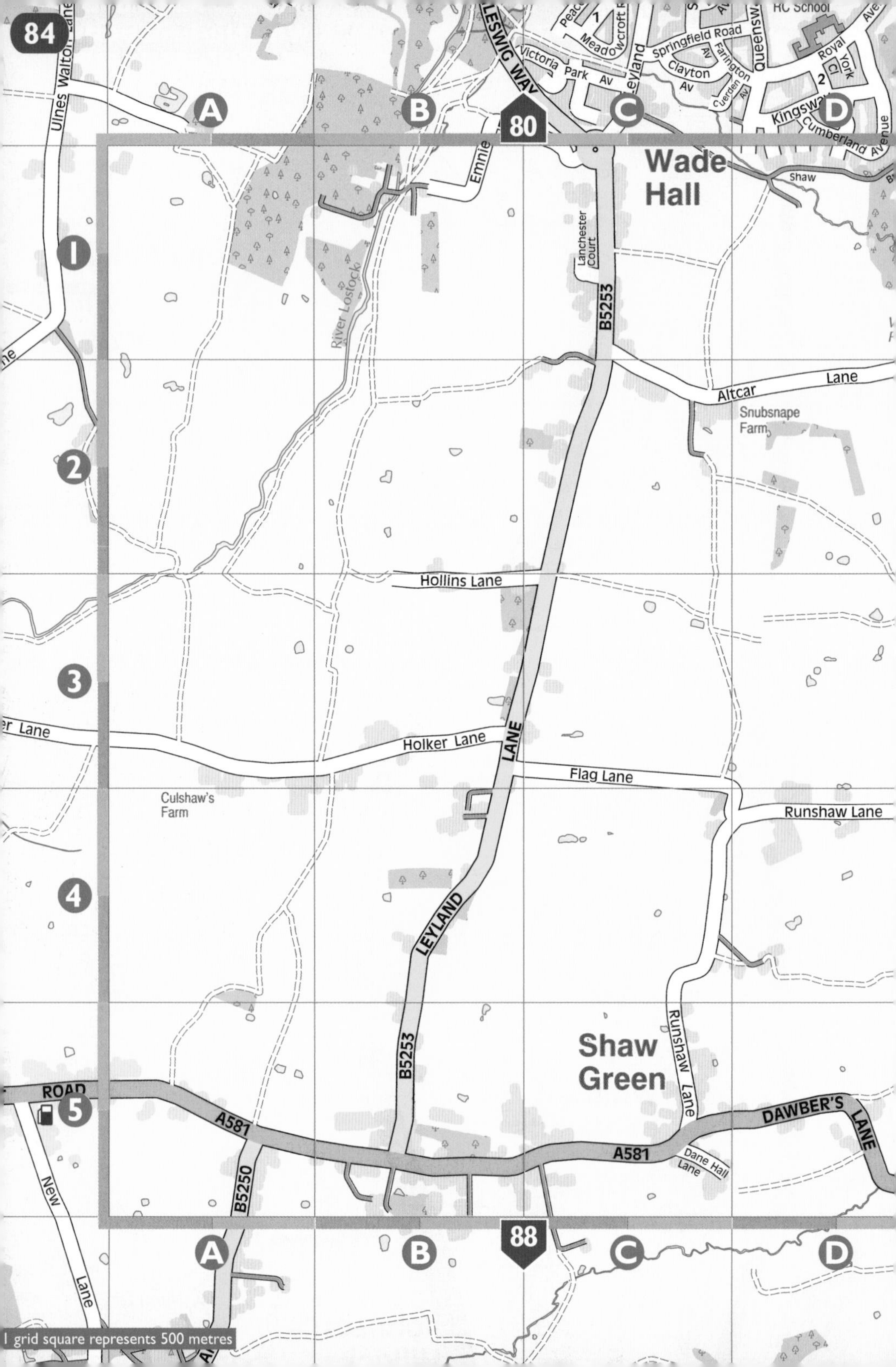
84
80
88
Wade Hall
Shaw Green
Ulnes Walton Lane
Meadowcroft
Springfield Road
Victoria Park Av
Clayton Av
Farington Av
Queensway
Royal York Cl
Kingsway
Cumberland Avenue
RC School
Leyland
Emnie
River Lostock
Lanchester Court
B5253
Shaw
Altcar Lane
Snubsnape Farm
Hollins Lane
Holker Lane
Flag Lane
Runshaw Lane
Culshaw's Farm
LEYLAND LANE
A581
B5250
DAWBER'S LANE
Dane Hall Lane
ROAD
New Lane
A
B
C
D
1
2
3
4
5
1 grid square represents 500 metres

G1
1 Kingsdale Cl
2 Silverdale Cl
3 Wasdale Cl
H3
1 Birch Av
H4
1 Boarded Barn
2 Northside
3 Southside
81
86
89
E
F
G
H
I
2
3
4
5
Road
Leafy Close
Edale Cl
Worden
Ennerdale Close
Vicarsfields Rd
Beech
Tamar Cl
Road
Mardale Crescent
Bleasdale Close
Back Lane
Towngate
Fern Close
Alandale Close
Wharfedale Close
Dovedale Close
Lonsdale Cl
Dalehead Dr
Wyresdale Drive
Cairndale
Brookdale Cl
Lyndale Cl
Road
Langdale
The Avenue
Road
Lane
Holt Brow
M6
WIGAN ROAD
A49
Runshaw College
Runshaw Lane
Runshaw Hall
Barn Lane
Nixon Hillock
Shawbrook Cl
Chestnut Av
Limes Av
Avenue
Wigan Rd
Grange Drive
Turnbury Close
Cedar
Briar Avenue
Yew Tree Av
Primrose Hill Rd
Poplar Av
Runshaw La
Euxton CP School
Beech Av
Laurel Avenue
Runshaw Lane
Runshaw Lane
PO
St Mary's Ga
WIGAN ROAD
Orchard Cl
Sycamore Avenue
Oak Av
School
West Ter
Glencroft
Barnside
Greenside
Woodside
Greenside
Crofters Gn
Village Cft
Meadowcroft
The Croft
Vicarage Cl
St Marys School
Euxton C of E Primary Sch
EUXTON
Firbank
Brookside
Casterton
Church Walk
Countess
Euxton Hall Gdns
Euxton Hall Hospital
BALSHAW
Anderton Rd
DAWBER'S LA
Old Dawber's La
A49
M6

86
A4
1 Old School La
A3
1 Mile Stone Meadow
Back Lane
WIGAN ROAD
A
B
82
C
D
DAWSON LANE
1
D4
1 Camomile Cl
2 Columbine Cl
2
D5
1 Banastre
2 Browns Hey
Mile Stone Meadow
Belfry Close
Turnbury Close
East
Ter
Wigan Rd
3
Avenue
South Terrace
West Ter
85
Euxton Lane
Orchard Cl
Lane
Lane
Euxton Lane
Woodcock Fold
St Mary's Ga
WIGAN ROAD
Sycamore Avenue
Tree
Mimosa
Chancery
4
Crofters Gn
Village Cft
Oak Av
School
Whinny
Pear
1
Vicarage Cl
A49
St Marys School
Euxton C of E Primary Sch
Brookside
Lane
Casterton
Washington Lane
5
Church Walk
Park Av
Earls Way
Empress Way
Princess Way
Countess Way
Barons Wy
Regents Wy
Talbot Dr
Queensway
Kingsway
WEST WAY
Clough Acre
Threlfall
Wymundsley
Judeland
Buckshaw CP School
Euxton Hall Gdns
Euxton Hall Hospital
BALSHAW LANE
PO
A
90
A581
SOUTHPORT RD
B
B5252
C
Chancery
D
Anderton Rd
Dale
Grasmere Cl
Highways Av
Bredon Av
Chiltern Av
Coniston Av
Cotswold Av
Conway Cl
Mallom Av
Long Copse
The Farthings
Merefield
Hawk
FOX
1 grid square represents 500 metres

Whittle-Le-Woods
Johnson's Hillock
Hartwood
cas Green
Junction 8
E1
1 The Walled Gdn
E5
1 Edgefield
2 Woodmancote
F1
1 Buckton Cl
F2
1 Catley Cl
2 Chysden Cl
3 Lingwell Cl
4 Mottram Cl
F4
1 The Spinney
G5
1 Bannerman Ter
2 Clayburn Cl
3 Cornflower Cl
4 Cowslip Wy
5 Garfield Ter
6 Milton Ter
7 Morrison St
H5
1 Chestnut Av
H4
1 Alpine Rd
83
91
St Chads RC Primary School
Chorley & District Hospital
A&E
Chorley North Business Park
St Michaels C of E High School
Highfield Industrial Est
St Peters C of E Junior School
Chorley Sports Centre
PRESTON ROAD
MOSS LANE
EUXTON LANE
BLACKBURN ROAD
BLACKBURN BROW
BOTANY BROW
HARPER'S LANE
WATER ST
Leeds and Liverpool Canal
Town Lane
Copthurst Lane
Dark Lane
Lucas Lane
Halliwell Lane
Moss Lane
Lea Road
Foxglove Drive
Dunham Drive
Royton Drive
Orchard Drive
Olive Cl
Stamford Dr
New Moss La
Hardacre Lane
Parkside Drive
Parkside South
Shaw Hl Dr
Spinney Close
Harvest Drive
The Ridings
Lady Crosse Drive
Honeysuckle Close
Lupin Cl
Bluebell Close
Spring Mews
Spring Crs
Gorse Cl
Preston Rd
Temple Wy
Oak Dr
Maple Gv
Linden Grove
Pine Gv
Laburnum Rd
Rowan Gv
Hazel Gv
Cherry Tree Grove
Hartwood Gn
Fern Bank
Long Cft
Meadow Close
Barn Close
Dutch Barn
Broadfields
Studfold
Foxcote
Fairway
Highfield Rd
Rookwood Av
The Grove
The Crs
North St
Harperley
Deerfold
Chorley Hall Rd
Shakespeare Ter
Springs Rd
Beaconsfield Ter
Wordsworth Ter
Thornhill Road
Birch Rd
Sycamore Rd
Coltsfoot Dr
Poppy Av
Northgate Dr
Larch Av
Cedar Rd
Elm Gv
Willow Rd
Daisy Fold
Mason Street
School
Knowley Brow
Bagganley Lane
Guildford Av
Epsom Close
Carleton
Ewell Cl
Dorking Road
Sutton
Redhill Gv
Melford Cl
Merton Gv
Millfield Road
Elmwood
Woodfall
Ravel Dr
Park Rd
Railway Rd
Old Br Wy
Corporation St
Geoffrey St
Curate St
Vicarage St
St Peter's St
Marlborough St
Smithills Cl
Moorfields
Dunscar Dr
Withnell Gv
Holcombe Gv
Bagganley La
Nab Rd
CHORLEY

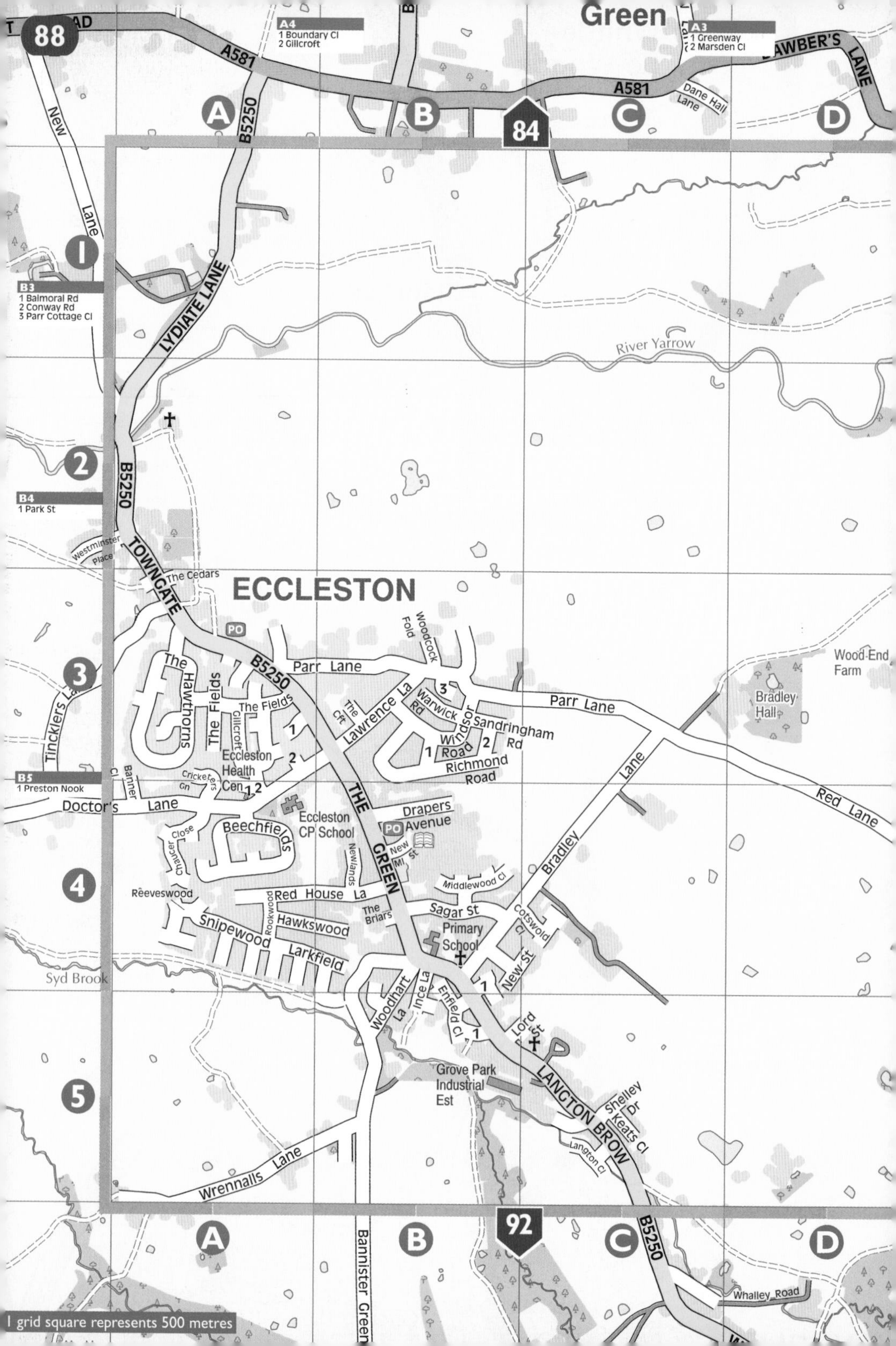
88
A4
1 Boundary Cl
2 Gillcroft
Green
A3
1 Greenway
2 Marsden Cl
A581
B5250
DAWBER'S LANE
Dane Hall Lane
84
New Lane
B3
1 Balmoral Rd
2 Conway Rd
3 Parr Cottage Cl
LYDIATE LANE
River Yarrow
B4
1 Park St
Westminster Place
TOWNGATE
The Cedars
ECCLESTON
PO
Woodcock Fold
Parr Lane
Wood End Farm
Bradley Hall
The Hawthorns
The Fields
Gillcroft
Eccleston Health Cen
Tincklers La
Lawrence La
The Cft
Warwick Rd
Windsor Road
Sandringham Rd
Richmond Road
Red Lane
Bradley Lane
B5
1 Preston Nook
Banner Cl
Cricketers Gn
Doctor's Lane
Beechfields
Chaucer Close
Eccleston CP School
THE GREEN
Drapers Avenue
New Mi St
Newlands
Middlewood Cl
Reeveswood
Red House La
Rookwood
Hawkswood
Snipewood
Larkfield
The Briars
Sagar St
Primary School
Cotswold Cl
New St
Syd Brook
Woodhart La
Ince La
Enfield Cl
Lord St
Grove Park Industrial Est
LANGTON BROW
Shelley Dr
Keats Cl
Langton Cl
Wrennalls Lane
Bannister Green
92
Whalley Road
1 grid square represents 500 metres

H1
1 Hillside Cl
E
F
G
H
85
Church Walk
Euxton Hall Gdns
Countess
Euxton Hall Hospital
BALSHAW
Anderton Rd
Pennine
DAWBER'S LANE
Old Dawber's La
Mill Lane
M6
A581
Fieldside Av
1
A49
Daisy Hill Fold
Pincock St
Pincock Brow
Pincock
2
German La
Back Lane
Mill Lane
SIBBERING BROW CROSS BROW
Bolton Green
3
90
Back Lane
Charnock Green
CHARNOCK BROW
4
Delph Lane
Old Hall Lane
Old Hall
5
93
PR7
PRESTON
Brook Lane
Park Hall Leisure Centre
PO
Church Lane

Church Walk
Park Av
Countess Way
D3
1 Heathrow Pl
Empress Way
Barons Wy
Regents Wy
Talbot Dr
Princess Way
Queensway
Kingsway
A
B
86
C
D
A1
1 Ambleside Av
WEST
Threlfall
Wymundsley
Jouland
Balshaw School
Euxton Hall Gdns
Euxton Hall Hospital
BALSHAW LANE
PO
A581 SOUTHPORT RD
Dale Av
Pennine Av
Anderton Rd
Highways Av
Grasmere Cl
Chiltern Av
Bredon Av
Coniston Av
Cotswold Av
Conway Cl
Mallom Av
Hawkshead Av
Bredon Av
B5252
Chancery
Long Copse
Merefield
The Farthings
FOXHOLE RD
Dunrobin Dr
Daisy Hill Fold
A49
D5
1 Arnold Pl
2 Brancker St
3 Green St
4 Jackson Rd
5 Lawnwood Av
6 Moor Rd
7 Swords Cross Cl
Ackhurst Business Park
Ackhurst Park Industrial Est
Chorley West Business Park
Foxhole Rd
Pincock Brow
Lancashire College for Adult Education
Lancashire Sc I C T Centre
Chorley West Business Park
German La
Lucas Av
Common Bank Lane
Ackhurst Road
Hornchurch Dr
Warton Pl
Binbrook Place
Copperwood Wy
Common Bank Industrial Estate
Primary School
Bolton Green
German Lane
Common Bank Employment Area
River Yarrow
Stansted Rd
Ringway
Woodford Copse
Yeadon Gv
Manston Gv
Lydd Gv
Hurn Gv
SIBBERING BROW CROSS BROW
CHARNOCK BROW
89
Rookery Cl
Gillibrand Hall
Delph Lane
Clover Road
Kingsley Dr
Longfield Mnr
Liptrott Rd
Southlands High School
Harestone Av
Lydgate
Charnock House
Delph Lane
94
B5251
Butterworth Brow
Birkacre Rd
Dob Brow
ROAD
Meadowlands
Alma Dr
Church
1 grid square represents 500 metres

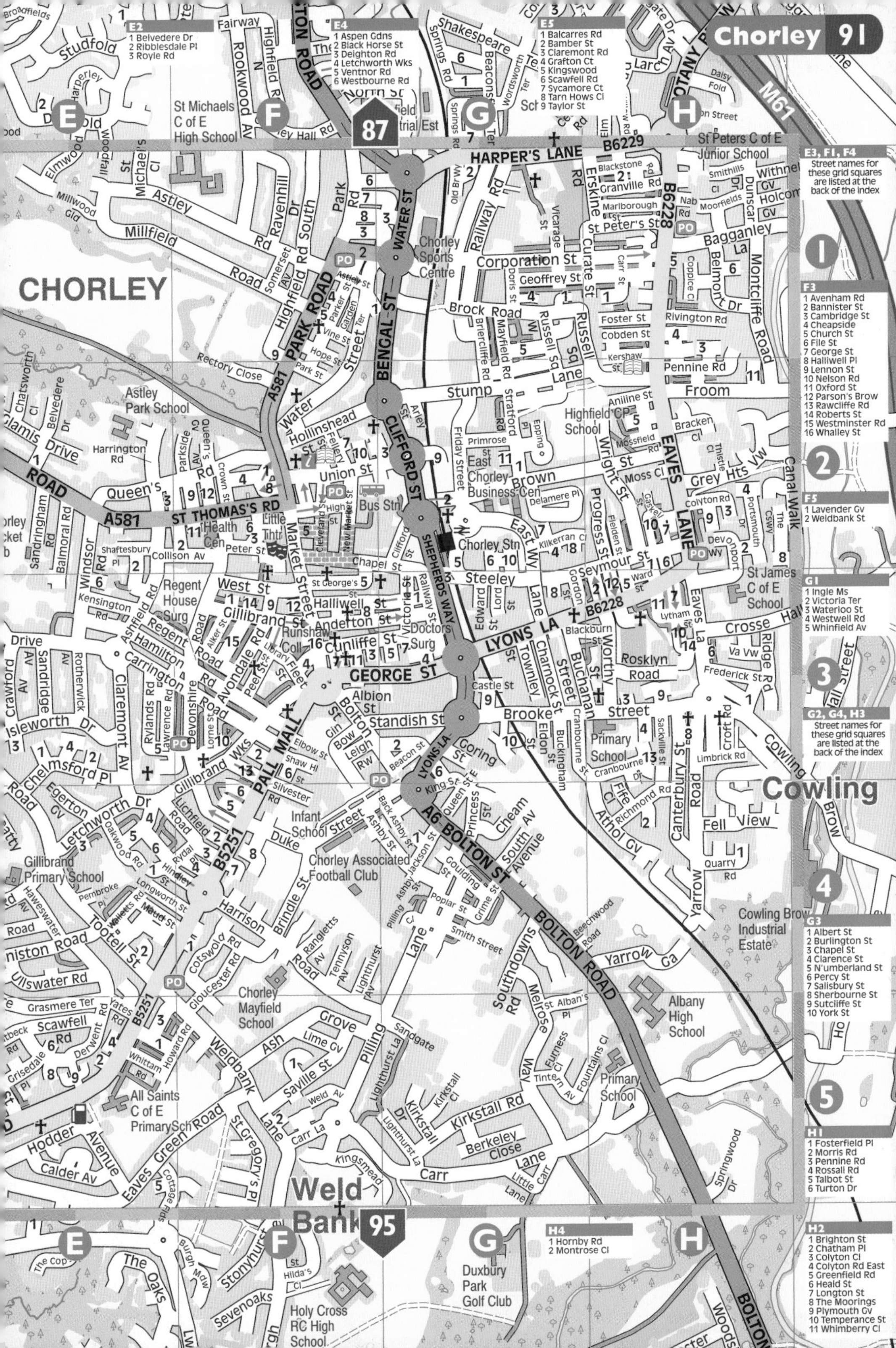

Chorley 91
E2
1 Belvedere Dr
2 Ribblesdale Pl
3 Royle Rd
E4
1 Aspen Gdns
2 Black Horse St
3 Deighton Rd
4 Letchworth Wks
5 Ventnor Rd
6 Westbourne Rd
E5
1 Balcarres Rd
2 Bamber St
3 Claremont Rd
4 Grafton Ct
5 Kingswood
6 Scawfell Rd
7 Sycamore Ct
8 Tarn Hows Cl
9 Taylor St
E3, F1, F4
Street names for these grid squares are listed at the back of the index
F3
1 Avenham Rd
2 Bannister St
3 Cambridge St
4 Cheapside
5 Church St
6 File St
7 George St
8 Halliwell Pl
9 Lennon St
10 Nelson Rd
11 Oxford St
12 Parson's Brow
13 Rawcliffe Rd
14 Roberts St
15 Westminster Rd
16 Whalley St
F5
1 Lavender Gv
2 Weldbank St
G1
1 Ingle Ms
2 Victoria Ter
3 Waterloo St
4 Westwell Rd
5 Whinfield Av
G2, G4, H3
Street names for these grid squares are listed at the back of the index
G3
1 Albert St
2 Burlington St
3 Chapel St
4 Clarence St
5 N'umberland St
6 Percy St
7 Salisbury St
8 Sherbourne St
9 Sutcliffe St
10 York St
H1
1 Fosterfield Pl
2 Morris Rd
3 Pennine Rd
4 Rossall Rd
5 Talbot St
6 Turton Dr
H4
1 Hornby Rd
2 Montrose Cl
H2
1 Brighton St
2 Chatham Pl
3 Colyton Cl
4 Colyton Rd East
5 Greenfield Rd
6 Heald St
7 Longton St
8 The Moorings
9 Plymouth Gv
10 Temperance St
11 Whimberry Cl
87
95
CHORLEY
Cowling
Weld Bank
M61
HARPER'S LANE B6229
ST THOMAS'S RD A581
PARK ROAD A581
BENGAL ST
WATER ST
CLIFFORD ST
SHEPHERDS WAY
LYONS LA B6228
EAVES LANE B6228
GEORGE ST
PALL MALL B5251
A6 BOLTON ST
BOLTON ROAD
St Michaels C of E High School
Astley Park School
Chorley Sports Centre
Highfield CP School
East Chorley Business Cen
Chorley Stn
Bus Stn
Health Cen
Little Thtr
Regent House Surg
Runshaw Coll
Doctors Surg
St James C of E School
St Peters C of E Junior School
Primary School
Infant School
Chorley Associated Football Club
Gillibrand Primary School
Chorley Mayfield School
All Saints C of E PrimarySch
Albany High School
Cowling Brow Industrial Estate
Duxbury Park Golf Club
Holy Cross RC High School

Grove Park
Industrial
Est
LANGTON BROW
Shelley
Dr
Keats Cl
Langton Cl
88
A
B
C
D
Wrennalls Lane
Bannister Green
B5250
Whalley Road
WOOD LANE
The Warings
Heskin
Old Hall
Heskin
Green
PH
1
2
3
4
5
Halfpenny
Lane
Bannister Gn
Town Lane
Heskin
Football
Club
PO
Withington
The Meadows
Barmskin Lane
Town Lane
Bentley Lane
Town
Lane
Barmskin
Lane
WOOD LANE
Cooper's
Lane
Smithy Brow
Church
Lane
Lane
Toogood
1 grid square represents 500 metres

E2
1 Yewlands Av
E
F
89
G
H
PR7
M6
PRESTON ROAD
Brook Lane
I
Church Lane
Park Hall
Leisure
Centre
Camelot
Hotel
Charnock
Richard
A49
Charter Lane
Charnock Richard
C of E
Primary School
Preston
Rd
Park Hall Road
Charnock Richard Service Area
2
Hotel
Mill
Lane
M6
A49
Chisnall
Lane
Chorley Lane
3
Croston Lane
PRESTON ROAD
94
Croston La
The
Foxwood
4
Lane
House
Carr
Town
Lane
Westend Av
Tansley Av
Burwell Avenue
St Oswalds RC
Primary School
5
Hill View
Drive
Wrightington
Bar
Lane
Town
PRESTON ROAD A49

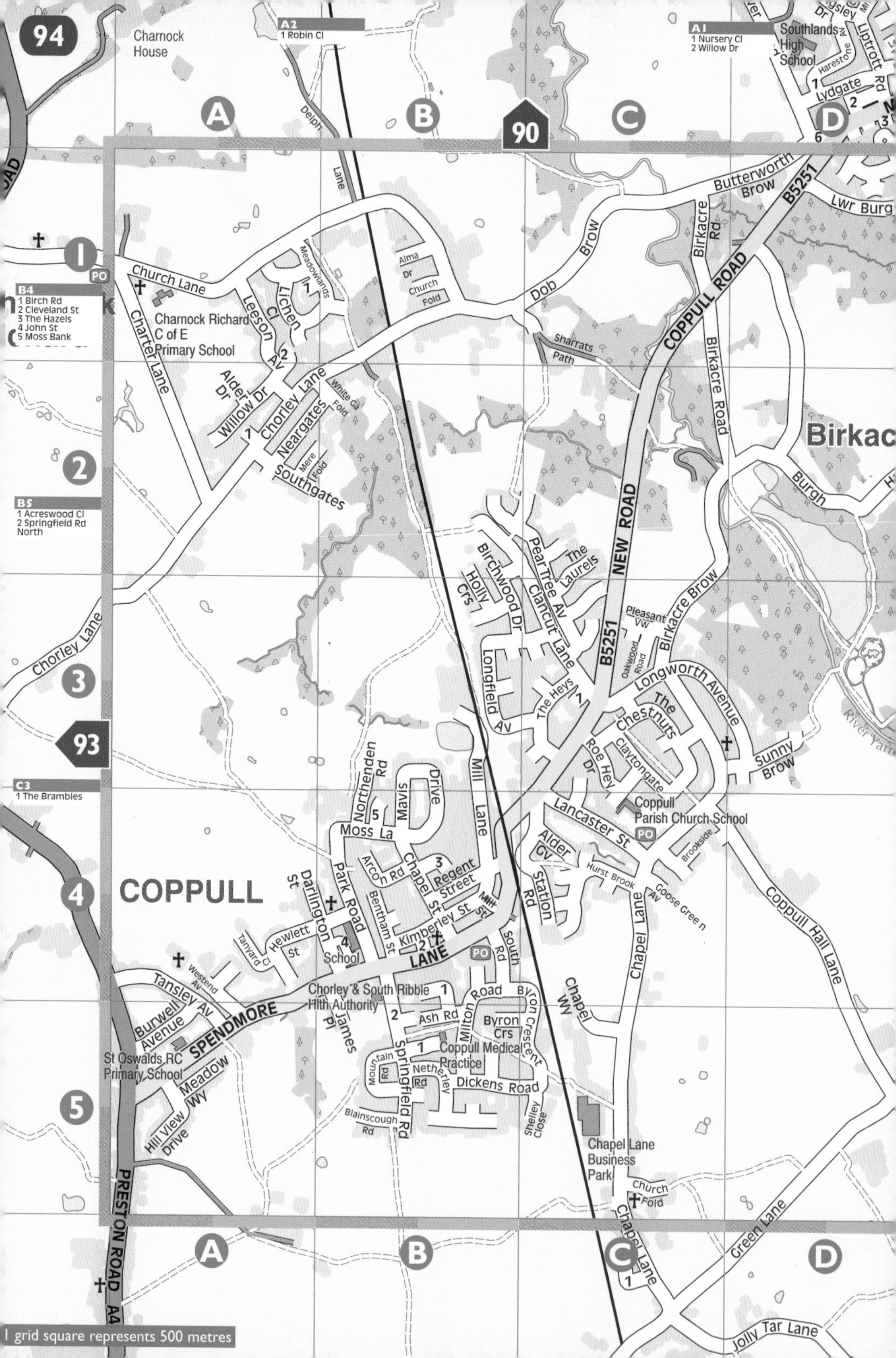
94
90
93
Charnock House
A2
1 Robin Cl
A1
1 Nursery Cl
2 Willow Dr
B4
1 Birch Rd
2 Cleveland St
3 The Hazels
4 John St
5 Moss Bank
B5
1 Acreswood Cl
2 Springfield Rd North
C3
1 The Brambles
Southlands High School
Charnock Richard C of E Primary School
Church Lane
Charter Lane
Chorley Lane
Dob Brow
Butterworth Brow
Birkacre Rd
Birkacre Road
Birkacre Brow
COPPULL ROAD
NEW ROAD
B5251
Sharrats Path
Birkac
Burgh
Longworth Avenue
Sunny Brow
Pear Tree Av
Clancut Lane
Birchwood Dr
Holly Crs
Longfield Av
The Heys
The Laurels
The Chestnuts
Pleasant Vw
Oakwood Road
Roe Hey Dr
Claytongate
Coppull Parish Church School
Lancaster St
Brookside
Alder Gv
Station Rd
Hurst Brook
Goose Green Av
Chapel Lane
Coppull Hall Lane
Mill Lane
Mavis Drive
Northenden Rd
Moss La
Arcon Rd
Chapel St
Regent Street
Kimberley St
Mill St
Bentham St
Park Road
Darlington St
Hewlett St
Tanyard Cl
School
COPPULL
SPENDMORE LANE
Westend Av
Tansley Av
Burwell Avenue
St Oswalds RC Primary School
Meadow Wy
Hill View Drive
Chorley & South Ribble Hlth Authority
James Pl
Ash Rd
Milton Road
Byron Crs
Byron Crescent
South Rd
Chapel Wy
Coppull Medical Practice
Springfield Rd
Mountain Rd
Netherley Rd
Dickens Road
Shelley Close
Blainscough Rd
Chapel Lane Business Park
Church Fold
Green Lane
Jolly Tar Lane
PRESTON ROAD
A4
Lichen Cl
Leeson Av
Alder Dr
Willow Dr
Neargates
Southgates
Meadowlands
Alma Dr
Church Fold
White Ga Fold
Mere Fold
Delph Lane
Lwr Burg
Lydgate Rd
Liptrott
Harestone Av
River Yarr
1 grid square represents 500 metres

E1
1 Oakwood Vw
E2
1 Yewtree Cl
91
Weld Bank
C of E PrimarySch
Hodder Avenue
Eaves Green Road
St Gregory's Pl
Lane
Saville St
Weld Av
Carr La
Kingsr
Lighthurst La
Lighthurst Dr
Kirkstall Dr
Kirkstall Cl
Kirkstall Rd
Berkeley Close
Carr Lane
Little Carr Lane
Springwood Dr
Cottage Flds
Burgh Mdw
The Copse
The Oaks
The Cedars
Stonyhurst
Sevenoaks
St Hilda's Cl
Burgh Lane
Holy Cross RC High School
Duxbury Park Golf Club
Lwr Burgh Way
Dale Vw
Woodlands Meadow
Saunders Ms
Firtree Cl
Yewtree Cl
Road
Burgh Hall
River Yarrow
Duxbury Park
Duxbury Hall Road
Chester Avenue
Winchester Av
Woodside
Worcester Pl
BOLTON RD
A5106
Martins Av
Heath Charnock
Gilbertson Road
WIGAN LANE
Rawlinson Lane
Leeds and Liverpool Canal
A6 WESTHOUGHTON ROAD
Grundy's Lane
South Burgh Lane
Coppull Hall Lane
E
F
G
H
I
1
2
3
4
5

Anchorsholme 21 F3
Ansdell 62 A1
Bamber Bridge 71 E5
Birkacre 94 D2
Bispham 24 B2
Blackpool 3 K5
Bolton Green 90 A3
Breedy Butts 26 B1
Broadfield 80 D3
Brookfield 47 F4
Broughton 36 C2
Bryning 53 E3
Burn Naze 17 H5
Cadley 45 F4
Carleton 25 H4
Charnock Green 89 G4
Charnock Richard 93 H1
Chorley 91 E1
Clayton Brook 78 D4
Clayton Green 78 D5
Clayton-le-Woods 82 A2
Cleveleys 20 B1
Cold Row 19 G4
Common Edge 39 F2
Coppull 94 A4
Cottam 44 B2
Coup Green 72 C2
Cowling 91 H4
Cuerden Green 77 H3
Dowbridge 43 H4
Earnshaw Bridge 80 D1
Eccleston 88 A3
Euxton 85 G5
Farington 76 D3
Farington Moss 76 B4
Fishwick 58 D3
Freckleton 54 A4
Fulwood 46 A3
Grange 47 H4
Great Marton 33 F2
Great Marton Moss 39 H4
Great Marton Moss Side 39 H1
Gregson Lane 72 D4
Haighton Top 37 G4
Hall Cross 54 B2
Hambleton 23 G3
Hambleton Moss Side 23 H2
Hardhorn 30 C2
Hartwood 87 F5
Hawes Side 5 K6
Heath Charnock 95 H3
Heskin Green 92 C2
Hey Houses 50 A3
Higher Ballam 51 E2
Higher Penwortham 69 F2
Higher Walton 72 B3
Hoghton 73 H4
Holme Slack 47 E4
Hoohill 28 D3
Howick Cross 68 C2
Ingol 44 D4
Jack Green 79 H1
Johnson's Hillock 87 G1
Kellamergh 53 F4
Kingsfold 69 G5
Kirkham 43 E2
Larches 56 C2
Layton 3 K2
Lea 56 A2
Leyland 81 F3
Little Bispham 20 B4
Little Carleton 29 F1
Little Layton 29 F2
Little Marton 34 B4
Little Poulton 27 E4
Little Thornton 22 C5
Longton 74 B1
Lostock Hall 77 F2
Lower Ballam 51 F1
Lower Bartle 44 A1
Lower Copthurst 83 H4
Lower Penwortham 69 H1
Lucas Green 87 E1
Lytham 63 H2
Lytham St Anne's 61 G3
Mereside 34 A4
Middleforth Green 69 G2
Moor End 19 G3
Moss Side 52 A2
Moss Side 80 A3
Mowbreck 43 F1
Mythop 35 E3
New Longton 75 H1
Newton 30 A4
Newton with Scales 55 E1
Nog Tow 44 C1
Norbreck 20 B5
Norcross 21 G5
Normoss 30 A3
North Shore 28 C2
Peel 40 D4
Peel Hill 40 C1
Penwortham Lane 70 A4
Pincock 89 H2
Pippin Street 79 H3
Poulton-le-Fylde 26 C5
Preesall 13 F1
Preesall Park 13 G5
Preston 7 K3
Pudding Pie Nook 37 F2
Queenstown 3 G1
Ribbleton 58 D1
Ribby 42 B4
Riverside Docklands 56 D3
Runshaw Moor 8
St Annes 4
Saltcotes 6
Scronkey 1
Seed Lee 7
Sharoe Green 4
Shaw Green 8
Singleton 3
Skippool 2
Smallwood Hey 1
South Shore
Sower Carr 1
Squires Gate 3
Staining 3
Stake Pool 1
Stalmine 1
Stanah 2
Staynall 1
Tanterton 4
Tardy Gate 7
Thornton 2
Thorpe Green 7
Top o'th' Lane 8
Treales 4
Trunnah 2
Wade Hall 8
Walmer Bridge 7
Walton-le-Dale 7
Walton Summit 7
Warbreck 2
Warton 6
Warton Bank 6
Weld Bank 9
Wesham 4
Whiteholme 2
White Stake 7
Whittle-le-Woods 8
Wrightington Bar 9

USING THE STREET INDEX

Street names are listed alphabetically. Each street name is followed by its postal town or area locality, the Postcode District, the page number, and the reference to the square in which the name is found.

Example: **Acreswood Cl** *CHLY/EC* PR7 .... **94** B5 1

Some entries are followed by a number in a blue box. This number indicates the location of the street within the referenced grid square. The full street name is listed at the side of the map page.

GENERAL ABBREVIATIONS

ACC ACCESS
ALY ALLEY
AP APPROACH
AR ARCADE
ASS ASSOCIATION
AV AVENUE
BCH BEACH
BLDS BUILDINGS
BND BEND
BNK BANK
BR BRIDGE
BRK BROOK
BTM BOTTOM
BUS BUSINESS
BVD BOULEVARD
BY BYPASS
CATH CATHEDRAL
CEM CEMETERY
CEN CENTRE
CFT CROFT
CH CHURCH
CHA CHASE
CHYD CHURCHYARD
CIR CIRCLE
CIRC CIRCUS
CL CLOSE
CLFS CLIFFS
CMP CAMP
CNR CORNER
CO COUNTY
COLL COLLEGE
COM COMMON
COMM COMMISSION
CON CONVENT
COT COTTAGE
COTS COTTAGES
CP CAPE
CPS COPSE
CR CREEK
CREM CREMATORIUM
CRS CRESCENT
CSWY CAUSEWAY
CT COURT
CTRL CENTRAL
CTS COURTS
CTYD COURTYARD
CUTT CUTTINGS
CV COVE
CYN CANYON
DEPT DEPARTMENT
DL DALE
DM DAM
DR DRIVE
DRO DROVE
DRY DRIVEWAY
DWGS DWELLINGS
E EAST
EMB EMBANKMENT
EMBY EMBASSY
ESP ESPLANADE
EST ESTATE
EX EXCHANGE
EXPY EXPRESSWAY
EXT EXTENSION
F/O FLYOVER
FC FOOTBALL CLUB
FK FORK
FLD FIELD
FLDS FIELDS
FLS FALLS
FLS FLATS
FM FARM
FT FORT
FWY FREEWAY
FY FERRY
GA GATE
GAL GALLERY
GDN GARDEN
GDNS GARDENS
GLD GLADE
GLN GLEN
GN GREEN
GND GROUND
GRA GRANGE
GRG GARAGE
GT GREAT
GTWY GATEWAY
GV GROVE
HGR HIGHER
HL HILL
HLS HILLS
HO HOUSE
HOL HOLLOW
HOSP HOSPITAL
HRB HARBOUR
HTH HEATH
HTS HEIGHTS
HVN HAVEN
HWY HIGHWAY
IMP IMPERIAL
IN INLET
IND EST INDUSTRIAL ESTATE
INF INFIRMARY
INFO INFORMATION
INT INTERCHANGE
IS ISLAND
JCT JUNCTION
JTY JETTY
KG KING
KNL KNOLL
L LAKE
LA LANE
LDG LODGE
LGT LIGHT
LK LOCK
LKS LAKES
LNDG LANDING
LTL LITTLE
LWR LOWER
MAG MAGISTRATE
MAN MANSIONS
MD MEAD
MDW MEADOWS
MEM MEMORIAL
MKT MARKET
MKTS MARKETS
ML MALL
ML MILL
MNR MANOR
MS MEW
MSN MISSI
MT MOU
MTN MOUNTA
MTS MOUNTAI
MUS MUSEU
MWY MOTORW
N NOR
NE NORTH EA
NW NORTH WE
O/P OVERPA
OFF OFFI
ORCH ORCHAR
OV OV
PAL PALA
PAS PASSA
PAV PAVILIC
PDE PARA
PH PUBLIC HOU
PK PA
PKWY PARKW
PL PLA
PLN PLA
PLNS PLAI
PLZ PLA
POL POLICE STATIC
PR PRIN
PREC PRECIN
PREP PREPARATO
PRIM PRIMA
PROM PROMENA
PRS PRINCE
PRT PO
PT POI
PTH PA
PZ PIAZ
QD QUADRA
QU QUEE
QY QU
R RIV
RBT ROUNDABO
RD ROA
RDG RID

...REPUBLIC
...RESERVOIR
...RUGBY FOOTBALL CLUB
...RISE
...RAMP
...ROW
...SOUTH
...SCHOOL
...SOUTH EAST
...SERVICE AREA
...SHORE
P ...SHOPPING
Y ...SKYWAY

SMT ...SUMMIT
SOC ...SOCIETY
SP ...SPUR
SPR ...SPRING
SQ ...SQUARE
ST ...STREET
STN ...STATION
STR ...STREAM
STRD ...STRAND
SW ...SOUTH WEST
TDG ...TRADING
TER ...TERRACE
THWY ...THROUGHWAY

TNL ...TUNNEL
TOLL ...TOLLWAY
TPK ...TURNPIKE
TR ...TRACK
TRL ...TRAIL
TWR ...TOWER
U/P ...UNDERPASS
UNI ...UNIVERSITY
UPR ...UPPER
V ...VALE
VA ...VALLEY
VIAD ...VIADUCT
VIL ...VILLA

VIS ...VISTA
VLG ...VILLAGE
VLS ...VILLAS
VW ...VIEW
W ...WEST
WD ...WOOD
WHF ...WHARF
WK ...WALK
WKS ...WALKS
WLS ...WELLS
WY ...WAY
YD ...YARD
YHA ...YOUTH HOSTEL

OSTCODE TOWNS AND AREA ABBREVIATIONS

OL ...Blackpool
 ...Bispham
OLE ...Blackpool east
OLS ...Blackpool south
/TH ...Cleveleys/Thornton

PLF/KEOS ...Poulton-le-Fylde/ Knott End-on-Sea
FTWD ...Fleetwood
LSTA ...Lytham St Anne's
PRES ...Preston

FUL/RIB ...Fulwood/Ribbleton
GAR/LONG ...Garstang/Longridge
KIRK/FR/WAR ...Kirkham/ Freckleton/Warton
LEY/BBR ...Leyland/Bamber Bridge

CHLYE ...Chorley east/ Adlington/Whittle-le-Woods
CHLY/EC ...Chorley/Eccleston
WGNNW/ST ...Wigan northwest/Standish

Index - streets

Aba - Ash

A

attoir Rd *BPOOL* FY1 ... 3 F1
bey Rd *BPOOLS* FY4 ... 38 C3
bey St *FUL/RIB* PR2 ... 6 D1
beyville *BPOOLS* FY4 ... 38 C2
bey Wk *PRES* PR1 ... 69 G4
bot Meadow *PRES* PR1 ... 69 G2
bots Cl *KIRK/FR/WA* PR4 ... 43 G4
botsford Rd *BPOOLE* FY3 ... 33 F2
botsway *PRES* PR1 ... 6 A6
bott Cft *KIRK/FR/WA* PR4 ... 44 D1
botts Wk *FTWD* FY7 ... 11 G1
ercorn Pl *BPOOLS* FY4 ... 38 A3
ercrombie Rd *FTWD* FY7 ... 11 F1
ngdon Dr *FUL/RIB* PR2 ... 56 D2
ngdon St *BPOOL* FY1 ... 2 C3
acia Rd *FUL/RIB* PR2 ... 59 F1
er Gv *FUL/RIB* PR2 ... 47 G5
churst Rd *CHLY/EC* PR7 ... 90 C2
orn Cl *LEY/BBR* PR5 ... 81 F4
orn Ms *BPOOLS* FY4 ... 34 B4
efield *LEY/BBR* PR5 ... 79 F5
e Ga *BPOOLS* FY4 ... 39 E1
egate La *PRES* PR1 ... 59 E2
es La *PLF/KEOS* FY6 ... 13 E3
eswood Cl *CHLY/EC* PR7 ... 94 B5 1
on Rd *BPOOLS* FY4 ... 5 J6
dison Crs *BPOOLE* FY3 ... 3 H2
dison Rd *FTWD* FY7 ... 11 F3
elaide Av *CLV/TH* FY5 ... 22 A4
elaide St *BPOOL* FY1 ... 2 D5
TWD FY7 ... 11 H1
RES PR1 ... 58 C3
elphi Pl *PRES* PR1 ... 7 G1
elphi St *BPOOL* FY1 ... 2 D5 1
RES PR1 ... 57 H2
miral Cl *LSTA* FY8 ... 49 E2 1
rian St *BPOOL* FY1 ... 4 C5
stone Av *BPOOLE* FY3 ... 29 F2
glebys Rd *PLF/KEOS* FY6 ... 12 D5
nes St *PRES* PR1 ... 7 J1
new Rd *FTWD* FY7 ... 11 F1
new St *LSTA* FY8 ... 63 E3
en Ct *KIRK/FR/WA* PR4 ... 43 E3 1
a Av *BPOOLE* FY3 ... 33 F3
sdale Av *BISP* FY2 ... 25 E2
CLV/TH FY5 ... 22 B3 1
TWD FY7 ... 16 D2
sdale Dr *FUL/RIB* PR2 ... 56 B1
slie Rd *FUL/RIB* PR2 ... 45 H5
tree Rd *BPOOLS* FY4 ... 5 F7
CLV/TH FY5 ... 21 H4
drie Pl *BISP* FY2 ... 25 E2
edale Av *BPOOLE* FY3 ... 5 K3
ndale Cl *LEY/BBR* PR5 ... 81 G5
any Av *BPOOLS* FY4 ... 38 C3
any Cl *PLF/KEOS* FY6 ... 30 C2 1
any Dr *LEY/BBR* PR5 ... 71 E4
any Rd *FTWD* FY7 ... 11 F2 1
STA FY8 ... 62 A1
atros St *PRES* PR1 ... 58 C1
ert Rd *BPOOL* FY1 ... 2 D6
FUL/RIB PR2 ... 46 A4
LEY/BBR PR5 ... 81 H3
STA FY8 ... 49 G4
PRES PR1 ... 58 A1 1
ert St *CHLY/EC* PR7 ... 91 G3 1
FTWD FY7 ... 11 H2
KIRK/FR/WA PR4 ... 42 D2

LSTA FY8 ... 63 G3
Albion Av *BPOOLE* FY3 ... 29 F4
Albion St *CHLY/EC* PR7 ... 91 F3
Albrighton Cl *LEY/BBR* PR5 ... 77 G2 1
Albrighton Crs *LEY/BBR* PR5 ... 77 G2
Albrighton Rd *LEY/BBR* PR5 ... 77 G2
Albyn Bank Rd *PRES* PR1 ... 58 C4 1
Albyn St East *PRES* PR1 ... 58 C4 2
Alcester Av *PRES* PR1 ... 6 A7
Alconbury Crs *CLV/TH* FY5 ... 20 C2
Aldate Gv *FUL/RIB* PR2 ... 56 D1 1
Aldcliffe Rd *FUL/RIB* PR2 ... 56 B2 1
Alder Cl *CLV/TH* FY5 ... 22 A3
KIRK/FR/WA PR4 ... 55 G1
LEY/BBR PR5 ... 80 A5
Alder Coppice *FUL/RIB* PR2 ... 44 B5
Alder Ct *FTWD* FY7 ... 10 C4
Alder Dr *CHLY/EC* PR7 ... 94 A2
LEY/BBR PR5 ... 72 C5
Alderfield *PRES* PR1 ... 69 G3
Alder Gv *BPOOLE* FY3 ... 29 E3 1
CHLY/EC PR7 ... 94 C4
LSTA FY8 ... 63 E3
PLF/KEOS FY6 ... 26 B5
Alderley Av *BPOOLS* FY4 ... 38 B3
Alder Rd *FUL/RIB* PR2 ... 47 H4
Aldersleigh Crs *LEY/BBR* PR5 ... 72 C5
Aldon Rd *PLF/KEOS* FY6 ... 26 D4
Aldwych Av *BPOOLE* FY3 ... 5 K2
Aldwych Dr *FUL/RIB* PR2 ... 56 C1
LEY/BBR PR5 ... 77 G2
Alert St *FUL/RIB* PR2 ... 57 F2
Alexandra Rd *BPOOL* FY1 ... 4 C5
CLV/TH FY5 ... 22 A4
KIRK/FR/WA PR4 ... 43 E2
LEY/BBR PR5 ... 70 D3
LSTA FY8 ... 49 F4
Alexandra St *PRES* PR1 ... 58 D4 1
Alexandria Dr *LSTA* FY8 ... 61 F1 1
Alford Fold *FUL/RIB* PR2 ... 45 G1
Alfred St *BPOOL* FY1 ... 2 E5
Alice Av *LEY/BBR* PR5 ... 81 F3
Alker La *CHLYE* PR6 ... 86 D4
Alker St *CHLY/EC* PR7 ... 91 F3
Allandale *BPOOLS* FY4 ... 38 C3
Allandale Av *CLV/TH* FY5 ... 17 F5
Allenbury Pl *BPOOLE* FY3 ... 33 G3 1
Allenby Av *FUL/RIB* PR2 ... 46 C4
Allenby Rd *LSTA* FY8 ... 49 E4
Allen Cl *CLV/TH* FY5 ... 20 D3
Allengate *FUL/RIB* PR2 ... 46 A4 1
Allen Wy *FTWD* FY7 ... 10 C4
Allerton Rd *LEY/BBR* PR5 ... 71 E3
All Hallows Rd *BISP* FY2 ... 24 D2
Allonby Av *CLV/TH* FY5 ... 17 E5
All Saints Rd *BISP* FY2 ... 24 D1
LSTA FY8 ... 49 E5
Alma Dr *CHLY/EC* PR7 ... 94 B1
Alma Rw *LEY/BBR* PR5 ... 72 D5
Alma St *PRES* PR1 ... 58 B2 1
Almond Cl *FUL/RIB* PR2 ... 46 D2 1
PRES PR1 ... 69 E3
Alpic Dr *CLV/TH* FY5 ... 20 C5
Alpine Av *BPOOLS* FY4 ... 39 E3 1
LEY/BBR PR5 ... 77 G2
Alpine Cl *LEY/BBR* PR5 ... 77 G2
Alpine Rd *CHLYE* PR6 ... 87 H4 1
Alsop St *PRES* PR1 ... 57 H1
Alston Av *CLV/TH* FY5 ... 16 D5
Alston Rd *BISP* FY2 ... 25 E5
Alston St *PRES* PR1 ... 59 E2 1
Altcar La *LEY/BBR* PR5 ... 84 C2

Althorp Cl *BPOOL* FY1 ... 3 F1
Alvern Av *FUL/RIB* PR2 ... 45 G4
Alvern Crs *FUL/RIB* PR2 ... 45 G4 1
Alwood Av *BPOOLE* FY3 ... 29 F4
Amberbanks Gv *BPOOL* FY1 ... 4 D4
Amber Ga *FUL/RIB* PR2 ... 44 C2
Amberwood *KIRK/FR/WA* PR4 ... 42 D3 1
Ambleside Av *CHLY/EC* PR7 ... 90 A1 1
Ambleside Cl *LEY/BBR* PR5 ... 71 F4
Ambleside Rd *BPOOLS* FY4 ... 34 B4
FUL/RIB PR2 ... 47 F3
Ambleway *LEY/BBR* PR5 ... 71 E2
Ambrose St *LEY/BBR* PR5 ... 81 G2
Amersham Cl *KIRK/FR/WA* PR4 ... 75 G1
Amounderness Wy *CLV/TH* FY5 ... 22 A5
FTWD FY7 ... 11 G4
Ampleforth Dr *LEY/BBR* PR5 ... 70 B5
Amy Johnson Wy *BPOOLS* FY4 ... 38 D3
Ancenis Ct *KIRK/FR/WA* PR4 ... 43 F3 1
Anchor Ct *PRES* PR1 ... 7 H3
Anchor Dr *KIRK/FR/WA* PR4 ... 68 A4
Anchorsholme La *CLV/TH* FY5 ... 21 F4
Anchorsholme La East *CLV/TH* FY5 ... 20 D3
Anchorsholme La West *CLV/TH* FY5 ... 20 C3
Anchor Wy *LSTA* FY8 ... 49 E2
Anderson St *BPOOL* FY1 ... 3 F7
Anderton Rd *CHLY/EC* PR7 ... 90 A1
Anderton St *CHLY/EC* PR7 ... 91 F3
Andertons Wy *FUL/RIB* PR2 ... 46 D3
Andrew St *PRES* PR1 ... 58 D2
Aniline St *CHLYE* PR6 ... 91 H2
Annan Crs *BPOOLS* FY4 ... 34 A4
Annaside Cl *BPOOLS* FY4 ... 39 E1 1
Anna's Rd *BPOOLS* FY4 ... 50 C1
Annesley Av *BPOOLE* FY3 ... 29 E2
Annis St *PRES* PR1 ... 58 D3
Ansbro Av *KIRK/FR/WA* PR4 ... 54 C5 1
Ansdell Gv *FUL/RIB* PR2 ... 45 F5
Ansdell Rd *BPOOL* FY1 ... 5 G4
Ansdell Rd North *LSTA* FY8 ... 62 B2
Ansdell Rd South *LSTA* FY8 ... 62 B3
Ansdell St *PRES* PR1 ... 58 D2 1
Anson Cl *LSTA* FY8 ... 48 D2
Anson Rd *KIRK/FR/WA* PR4 ... 54 B1
Antrim Rd *BISP* FY2 ... 28 C1
Appealing La *LSTA* FY8 ... 49 E1
Appleby Cl *LEY/BBR* PR5 ... 72 D5 1
Appleby Rd *BISP* FY2 ... 28 D1
Appleby St *PRES* PR1 ... 58 A2
Applefields *LEY/BBR* PR5 ... 81 G5
Appleton Cl *PLF/KEOS* FY6 ... 25 G5
Appletree Cl *PRES* PR1 ... 69 E4
Aqueduct St *FUL/RIB* PR2 ... 57 G2
Arcon Rd *CHLY/EC* PR7 ... 94 B4
Ardee Rd *PRES* PR1 ... 6 D6
Arden Gn *FTWD* FY7 ... 11 E2 1
Ardmore Rd *BISP* FY2 ... 24 D5
Argosy Av *BPOOLE* FY3 ... 29 F2
Argyle Rd *LEY/BBR* PR5 ... 81 F3
PLF/KEOS FY6 ... 26 C4
Argyll Rd *BISP* FY2 ... 28 C1
PRES PR1 ... 58 B2
Ariel Wy *FTWD* FY7 ... 11 E2
Arkholme Av *BPOOL* FY1 ... 5 G4
Arkwright Ct *BPOOLS* FY4 ... 40 A1
Arkwright Rd *PRES* PR1 ... 58 A1
Arley St *CHLY/EC* PR7 ... 91 G2
Arlington Av *BPOOLS* FY4 ... 38 B1 1
Armadale Rd *BISP* FY2 ... 29 E1
Armitstead Ct *FTWD* FY7 ... 11 F4 1

Armitstead Wy *FTWD* FY7 ... 11 F4
Armstrong St *FUL/RIB* PR2 ... 57 E1 1
Arndale Cl *FTWD* FY7 ... 10 C4 1
Arnhem Rd *PRES* PR1 ... 59 E3
Arnold Av *BPOOLS* FY4 ... 38 C1
Arnold Cl *FUL/RIB* PR2 ... 59 F1
Arnold Pl *CHLY/EC* PR7 ... 90 D5 1
Arnold Rd *LSTA* FY8 ... 63 H2 1
Arno St *PRES* PR1 ... 58 C4
Arnott Rd *BPOOLS* FY4 ... 5 J5
FUL/RIB PR2 ... 57 F1 1
Arnside Av *BPOOL* FY1 ... 5 G5
LSTA FY8 ... 50 A4
Arnside Cl *LEY/BBR* PR5 ... 72 D3 1
Arnside Rd *FUL/RIB* PR2 ... 56 B1
Arrowsmith Cl *LEY/BBR* PR5 ... 72 D4
Arrowsmith Dr *LEY/BBR* PR5 ... 72 D4
Arroyo Wy *FUL/RIB* PR2 ... 46 C4
Arthurs La *PLF/KEOS* FY6 ... 23 H2
Arthur St *FTWD* FY7 ... 11 H1
PRES PR1 ... 7 F3
Arundel Av *BISP* FY2 ... 24 B3 1
Arundel Dr *PLF/KEOS* FY6 ... 26 A1
Arundel Pl *PRES* PR1 ... 7 K4
Arundel Rd *LSTA* FY8 ... 61 H2
Arundel Wy *LEY/BBR* PR5 ... 81 H4
Ascot Rd *BPOOLE* FY3 ... 3 H3
CLV/TH FY5 ... 21 H4
Ash Av *KIRK/FR/WA* PR4 ... 43 E4
Ashbourne Crs *FUL/RIB* PR2 ... 44 D3
Ashburton Rd *BPOOL* FY1 ... 2 D1
Ashby St *CHLY/EC* PR7 ... 91 F4
Ashcombe Ga *CLV/TH* FY5 ... 22 B5 1
Ash Coppice *FUL/RIB* PR2 ... 44 A5
Ashdown Cl *PLF/KEOS* FY6 ... 25 H2 1
Ashdown Dr *CHLYE* PR6 ... 83 F1
Ashdown Ms *FUL/RIB* PR2 ... 47 F2 1
Ash Dr *CLV/TH* FY5 ... 22 A3
KIRK/FR/WA PR4 ... 53 F5
PLF/KEOS FY6 ... 26 B5
Asheldon St *PRES* PR1 ... 59 E2 2
Ash Fld *CHLYE* PR6 ... 83 F1
Ashfield *FUL/RIB* PR2 ... 36 D5
Ashfield Ct *FUL/RIB* PR2 ... 44 C2 1
Ashfield Rd *BISP* FY2 ... 25 E2
CHLY/EC PR7 ... 91 E3
Ashford Crs *GAR/LONG* PR3 ... 36 B2
Ashford Rd *FUL/RIB* PR2 ... 56 B1
Ash Gv *CHLY/EC* PR7 ... 91 F5
KIRK/FR/WA PR4 ... 43 F1
KIRK/FR/WA PR4 ... 74 A1 1
KIRK/FR/WA PR4 ... 75 G3
LEY/BBR PR5 ... 71 G5
Ashgrove *PRES* PR1 ... 59 E2
Ash Holme *PRES* PR1 ... 46 D5 1
Ash Lea Gv *PLF/KEOS* FY6 ... 19 G2
Ashleigh Ct *FUL/RIB* PR2 ... 46 B1
Ashleigh Ms *BPOOLE* FY3 ... 3 J7
Ashleigh St *PRES* PR1 ... 58 D4
Ashley Cl *BISP* FY2 ... 24 C5
CLV/TH FY5 ... 21 H5
Ashley Rd *LSTA* FY8 ... 49 F2
Ash Meadow *FUL/RIB* PR2 ... 44 B5
Ashmoor St *PRES* PR1 ... 57 H2
Ashmore Gv *CLV/TH* FY5 ... 20 D3
Ashness Cl *FUL/RIB* PR2 ... 37 E5
Ash Rd *CHLY/EC* PR7 ... 94 B5
Ash St *BPOOLS* FY4 ... 38 C2
FTWD FY7 ... 11 G2
Ashton Av *PLF/KEOS* FY6 ... 12 B1
Ashton Cl *FUL/RIB* PR2 ... 56 D2
Ashtongate *FUL/RIB* PR2 ... 56 C2 1

Ashton Rd *BPOOL* FY1 **5** F1
Ashton St *FUL/RIB* PR2 **6** D1
LSTA FY8 **63** E3 1
Ashtree Ct *LEY/BBR* PR5 **72** B3
Ashtree Gv *PRES* PR1 **69** E2
Ashurst Rd *LEY/BBR* PR5 **82** A3
Ashwell Pl *CLV/TH* FY5 **20** C5
Ashwood Cl *LSTA* FY8 **62** C2
Ashwood Rd *FUL/RIB* PR2 **45** G1
Ashworth Gv *PRES* PR1 **58** D5
Ashworth La *PRES* PR1 **58** C5
Ashworth Rd *BPOOLS* FY4 **34** A5
Ashworth St *LEY/BBR* PR5 **71** G4 1
PRES PR1 **58** C4 3
Askrigg Cl *BPOOLS* FY4 **39** G1
Asland Cl *LEY/BBR* PR5 **78** C1 1
Aspden St *LEY/BBR* PR5 **71** F5
Aspels Crs *PRES* PR1 **69** F2
Aspels Nook *PRES* PR1 **69** F2
The Aspels *PRES* PR1 **69** F2
Aspen Gdns *CHLY/EC* PR7 **91** E4 1
Aspinall Cl *PRES* PR1 **69** G4
Assheton Pl *FUL/RIB* PR2 **47** F4 1
Astland St *LSTA* FY8 **49** E5
Astley Crs *KIRK/FR/WA* PR4 **54** C5
Astley Rd *CHLY/EC* PR7 **91** E1
Astley St *CHLY/EC* PR7 **91** F1
Aston Av *CLV/TH* FY5 **21** G2
Aston Wy *LEY/BBR* PR5 **80** B2
Athelstan Fold *FUL/RIB* PR2 **45** F5
Atherton Rd *LEY/BBR* PR5 **80** C4
Athlone Av *BISP* FY2 **24** C5
Athol Gv *CHLYE* PR6 **91** H4
Atholl St *PRES* PR1 **6** D2
Aubigny Dr *FUL/RIB* PR2 **45** G4
Auburn Gv *BPOOL* FY1 **5** H3
Audenlea *CLV/TH* FY5 **21** F1
Audley Cl *LSTA* FY8 **62** B1
Aughton St *FTWD* FY7 **11** H1 1
Auster Crs *KIRK/FR/WA* PR4 **54** B1
Austin Crs *FUL/RIB* PR2 **45** E4
Austin Gv *BPOOL* FY1 **4** C5
Austins Cl *LEY/BBR* PR5 **81** F4
Austin Wy *BPOOLS* FY4 **41** E1
Avalon Dr *KIRK/FR/WA* PR4 **54** C4
Avalwood Av *KIRK/FR/WA* PR4 **74** C1
Avenham Colonnade *PRES* PR1 **7** J5
Avenham La *PRES* PR1 **7** J4
Avenham Pl *PRES* PR1 **7** K5 1
Avenham Rd *CHLY/EC* PR7 **91** F3 1
PRES PR1 **7** J4
Avenham St *PRES* PR1 **7** J3
Avenue Rd *BPOOLE* FY3 **29** H2
The Avenue *FUL/RIB* PR2 **44** D2
FUL/RIB PR2 **56** A2
LEY/BBR PR5 **85** E1
PLF/KEOS FY6 **26** A3
PRES PR1 **69** E1
Avon Av *FTWD* FY7 **16** D1
Avon Br *FUL/RIB* PR2 **36** B5
Avondale Crs *BPOOLS* FY4 **39** F1
Avondale Dr *LEY/BBR* PR5 **77** G1
Avondale Rd *CHLY/EC* PR7 **91** F3
LSTA FY8 **48** C3 1
Avon Gn *FTWD* FY7 **11** E2
Avon Pl *BPOOL* FY1 **28** C2 1
Avonside Av *CLV/TH* FY5 **21** G1
Avon St *LSTA* FY8 **49** E5 1
Avroe Crs *LSTA* FY8 **38** D4
Aylesbury Av *BPOOLS* FY4 **5** H6
Ayr Ct *FTWD* FY7 **17** E2 1
Ayrton Av *BPOOLS* FY4 **38** D1
Aysgarth Av *FUL/RIB* PR2 **46** A1
Aysgarth Ct *BPOOLS* FY4 **39** F1 1
Azalea Cl *FUL/RIB* PR2 **46** D2 2
LEY/BBR PR5 **82** B2 1

B

Babbacombe Av *BPOOLS* FY4 **38** B2 1
Back Ashburton Rd *BPOOL* FY1 **2** D1
Back Ashby St *CHLY/EC* PR7 **91** F4
Back Bourne's Rw *LEY/BBR* PR5 **72** D5
Back Church St *BPOOL* FY1 **2** C5
Back Clarendon Rd *BPOOL* FY1 **4** D3 1
Back Club St *LEY/BBR* PR5 **78** B2
Back Cookson St *BPOOL* FY1 **2** E4 1
Back Cop La *FTWD* FY7 **11** G2
Back Eaves St *BPOOL* FY1 **28** B3 2
Back Epsom Rd *CLV/TH* FY5 **21** F4 1
Back Glen Eldon Rd *LSTA* FY8 **49** F4
Back Grimshaw St *PRES* PR1 **7** K3 1
Back High St *BPOOL* FY1 **2** D2
Back La *CHLY/EC* PR7 **81** H5
CHLY/EC PR7 **89** E3
CHLYE PR6 **82** D2
PLF/KEOS FY6 **19** E1
Back Lord St *BPOOL* FY1 **2** D2
Back Moon Av *BPOOL* FY1 **4** D3 2
Back Mt *CHLY/EC* PR7 **91** F2 1
Back North Crs *LSTA* FY8 **49** E5
Back Pleasant St *BPOOL* FY1 **2** D1 1
Back Read's Rd *BPOOL* FY1 **2** E6
Back St Anne's Rd West
LSTA FY8 **49** E5
Back Seed St *PRES* PR1 **7** G2 1
Back Shannon St *BPOOL* FY1 **4** D1 1
Back Springfield Rd North
LSTA FY8 **49** E5 2
Back Starkie St *PRES* PR1 **7** H5 1
Back Warbreck Rd *BPOOL* FY1 **2** C2
Back Waterloo Rd *BPOOLS* FY4 **4** D6 1
Back West Crs *LSTA* FY8 **49** E5 3
Back Woodfield Rd *BPOOL* FY1 **4** D4 1
Badgers Cft *FUL/RIB* PR2 **59** G2
Badgers Wk East *LSTA* FY8 **63** G3
Badgers Wy *LEY/BBR* PR5 **70** C3
Bagganley La *CHLYE* PR6 **87** H5
Bagnold Rd *PRES* PR1 **59** E2 3
Bagot St *BPOOL* FY1 **4** D6
Bailey Ct *BPOOLE* FY3 **3** J3
Baines Av *BPOOLE* FY3 **29** F1
Bairstow St *BPOOL* FY1 **4** C1
PRES PR1 **7** H4
Bakers Ct *BPOOLS* FY4 **39** F1 2
Baker St *LEY/BBR* PR5 **81** G2 1
Balcarres Cl *LEY/BBR* PR5 **81** F3
Balcarres Pl *LEY/BBR* PR5 **81** F4 1
Balcarres Rd *CHLY/EC* PR7 **91** E5 1
FUL/RIB PR2 **45** F5
LEY/BBR PR5 **81** F4
Balderstone Rd *KIRK/FR/WA* PR4 **54** B4
PRES PR1 **6** D7
Baldwin Gv *BPOOL* FY1 **5** H3
Baldwin St *LEY/BBR* PR5 **78** B1 1
Balfour Cl *CLV/TH* FY5 **22** B5 2
Balfour Rd *FUL/RIB* PR2 **45** H5
Balfour St *LEY/BBR* PR5 **81** F3 1
Balham Av *BPOOLS* FY4 **39** E3
Ballam Rd *FUL/RIB* PR2 **56** B2 2
LSTA FY8 **51** E1
Ball St *BPOOL* FY1 **4** D5
PLF/KEOS FY6 **26** B4
Balmer Gv *BPOOL* FY1 **5** G1
Balmoral Av *LEY/BBR* PR5 **81** H4
Balmoral Pl *CLV/TH* FY5 **22** A4
Balmoral Rd *BPOOLS* FY4 **32** B5
CHLY/EC PR7 **88** B3 1
KIRK/FR/WA PR4 **68** D5
LEY/BBR PR5 **71** E3 1
LSTA FY8 **61** G1
Balmoral Ter *FTWD* FY7 **11** H1
Balniel Cl *CHLY/EC* PR7 **91** E3
Balshaw Crs *LEY/BBR* PR5 **81** E2 1
Balshaw La *CHLY/EC* PR7 **90** A1
Balshaw Rd *LEY/BBR* PR5 **81** E3
Balshaw St *LEY/BBR* PR5 **71** F4 1
Baltimore Rd *LSTA* FY8 **49** H5 1
Bamber Av *BISP* FY2 **24** C3
Bambers La *BPOOLS* FY4 **40** A2
Bamber St *CHLY/EC* PR7 **91** E5 2
Bamber's Wk *KIRK/FR/WA* PR4 **42** C1
Bamburgh Cl *BPOOLS* FY4 **39** G1 1
Bamton Av *BPOOLS* FY4 **38** C1
Banastre *CHLY/EC* PR7 **86** D5 1
Banbury Av *BISP* FY2 **28** D2
Banbury Dr *FUL/RIB* PR2 **45** H4
Banbury Rd *LSTA* FY8 **49** F5
Bancroft Av *CLV/TH* FY5 **21** H2
Bangor Av *BISP* FY2 **24** D3
Bank Cl *KIRK/FR/WA* PR4 **74** B1
Bank Cft *KIRK/FR/WA* PR4 **74** B1
Bankfield Ct *CLV/TH* FY5 **21** H4 1
Bankfield Gv *BPOOL* FY1 **5** J1
Bank Head La *LEY/BBR* PR5 **79** F1
Bank Hey St *BPOOL* FY1 **2** C6
Bank La *KIRK/FR/WA* PR4 **65** E2
Bank Pde *PRES* PR1 **7** J5
Bank Pl *FUL/RIB* PR2 **57** F2
Banksfield Av *FUL/RIB* PR2 **45** F5
Banksfield Pl *LEY/BBR* PR5 **78** C2
Bankside *CHLYE* PR6 **83** E3
Banks Rd *FUL/RIB* PR2 **45** F5 1
Banks St *BPOOL* FY1 **2** D3
Bank St *CHLY/EC* PR7 **91** F2 2
Banner Cl *CHLY/EC* PR7 **88** A3
Bannerman Ter *CHLYE* PR6 **87** G5 1
Bannister Cl *LEY/BBR* PR5 **72** A2
Bannister Dr *LEY/BBR* PR5 **80** D3
Bannister Gn *CHLY/EC* PR7 **92** B2
Bannister Hall Crs *LEY/BBR* PR5 **72** A2
Bannister Hall Dr *LEY/BBR* PR5 **72** A2
Bannister Hall La *LEY/BBR* PR5 **72** A2
Bannister La *LEY/BBR* PR5 **76** C5
Bannister's Bit *PRES* PR1 **69** F4 1
Bannister St *CHLY/EC* PR7 **91** F3 2
LSTA FY8 **63** F3 1
Bannistre Cl *LSTA* FY8 **49** G3 1
Barclay Av *BPOOLE* FY3 **33** F3
Barden Pl *FUL/RIB* PR2 **47** E4
Bardsea Pl *FUL/RIB* PR2 **44** C5 1
Bardsway *CLV/TH* FY5 **21** G1
Bardsway Av *BPOOLE* FY3 **3** K2
Barleyfield *CHLYE* PR6 **83** F1
Barlow Crs *BPOOLE* FY3 **3** J6
Barlow St *PRES* PR1 **57** H2 1
PRES PR1 **58** A1 2
Barmouth Av *BPOOLE* FY3 **33** G3
Barmskin La *CHLY/EC* PR7 **92** B4
Barnacre Cl *FUL/RIB* PR2 **37** F5
Barn Cft *LEY/BBR* PR5 **80** A3
PRES PR1 **69** E2
Barnfield *KIRK/FR/WA* PR4 **43** E3
LEY/BBR PR5 **77** F1 1
Barnfield Cl *CLV/TH* FY5 **17** F5 1
Barn Meadow *LEY/BBR* PR5 **79** E3
Barnsfold *FUL/RIB* PR2 **45** G2
Barnside *CHLY/EC* PR7 **85** H4
Baron Rd *BPOOL* FY1 **4** E5
Barons Wy *CHLY/EC* PR7 **86** A5
Barry Av *FUL/RIB* PR2 **44** C5
Bartle Pl *FUL/RIB* PR2 **56** B2 3
Bartle Rd *LSTA* FY8 **49** G3
Barton Av *BPOOL* FY1 **4** C3
PLF/KEOS FY6 **12** C1
Barton Rd *LSTA* FY8 **48** D3
Barton Sq *PLF/KEOS* FY6 **12** C1
Bashall Gv *LEY/BBR* PR5 **81** G1 1
Basil St *PRES* PR1 **58** D1
Bassenthwaite Rd
BPOOLE FY3 **34** A3 1
Bath Rd *LSTA* FY8 **63** F3 2
Bath St *BPOOLS* FY4 **4** C6
FUL/RIB PR2 **57** G2 1
LSTA FY8 **63** F3 3
Bathurst Av *BPOOLE* FY3 **29** G3
Bay Rd *FUL/RIB* PR2 **59** F1
Bayswater *BISP* FY2 **24** C3 1
The Bay *CLV/TH* FY5 **16** C4
Baytree Cl *LEY/BBR* PR5 **77** H1 1
Bay Tree Rd *CHLYE* PR6 **83** E2
Bazley Rd *LSTA* FY8 **62** B3
Beach Av *CLV/TH* FY5 **20** D1
LSTA FY8 **62** A3
Beachcomber Dr *CLV/TH* FY5 **20** C1 1
Beachley Rd *FUL/RIB* PR2 **44** D4 1
Beach Rd *CLV/TH* FY5 **20** C1
FTWD FY7 **11** E2
GAR/LONG PR3 **8** B4
LSTA FY8 **48** D4
Beach St *LSTA* FY8 **63** E3 2
Beacon Av *FUL/RIB* PR2 **45** G4
Beacon Gv *FUL/RIB* PR2 **45** G4
Beacon Rd *PLF/KEOS* FY6 **27** E4
Beaconsfield Av *PRES* PR1 **59** G2 1
Beaconsfield Ter *CHLYE* PR6 **87** G5
Beacon St *CHLY/EC* PR7 **91** G3
Beamont Dr *PRES* PR1 **6** C1
Bean Av *BPOOLS* FY4 **33** E5
Beardshaw Av *BPOOL* FY1 **5** H4
Bearswood Cft *CHLYE* PR6 **83** E2
Beattock Pl *BISP* FY2 **25** F2
Beatty Av *CHLY/EC* PR7 **91** E4
Beatty Cl *LSTA* FY8 **48** D2 1
Beauclerk Rd *LSTA* FY8 **49** G5
Beaufort Av *BISP* FY2 **24** C2
Beaumaris Rd *LEY/BBR* PR5 **81** H4 1
Beaumont Gdns
PLF/KEOS FY6 **25** H2 2
Beck Ct *FTWD* FY7 **10** D5
Beckdean Av *PLF/KEOS* FY6 **26** B5
Beck Gv *CLV/TH* FY5 **17** E5
Beckway Av *BPOOLE* FY3 **29** F3
Bedale Pl *CLV/TH* FY5 **21** E3
Bedford Av *CLV/TH* FY5 **16** D5
Bedford Rd *BPOOL* FY1 **28** C2
FUL/RIB PR2 **46** B4 1
LSTA FY8 **63** H2 2
Beech Av *BPOOLE* FY3 **3** J4
CHLY/EC PR7 **85** G4
KIRK/FR/WA PR4 **43** E4
KIRK/FR/WA PR4 **53** F5
LEY/BBR PR5 **81** F4
PLF/KEOS FY6 **26** B3
Beechcroft *CLV/TH* FY5 **16** C5 1
Beech Dr *FUL/RIB* PR2 **36** C5
KIRK/FR/WA PR4 **55** F1
KIRK/FR/WA PR4 **66** A1
PLF/KEOS FY6 **26** B5
The Beeches *CHLYE* PR6 **83** F1
PLF/KEOS FY6 **31** H1
Beechfield Av *BPOOLE* FY3 **5** J2
KIRK/FR/WA PR4 **42** A5
PLF/KEOS FY6 **13** E1
Beechfield Ct *LEY/BBR* PR5 **81** G4
Beechfield Rd *LEY/BBR* PR5 **81** G4
Beechfields *CHLY/EC* PR7 **88** A4
Beech Gdns *CHLYE* PR6 **83** E3
Beech Gv *FUL/RIB* PR2 **5**
Beech Hill Cl *LEY/BBR* PR5 **71**
Beech Rd *LEY/BBR* PR5 **8**
Beech St *PRES* PR1
Beech St South *PRES* PR1
Beech Ter *PRES* PR1
Beechway *FUL/RIB* PR2 **46** E
PRES PR1 **6**
Beechwood Av *FUL/RIB* PR2 **4**
LEY/BBR PR5 **7**
Beechwood Cft *CHLYE* PR6 **82** D
Beechwood Dr *CLV/TH* FY5 **2**
Beechwood Gv *BISP* FY2 **2**
Beechwood Rd *CHLY/EC* PR7 **9**
Bee La *PRES* PR1 **6**
Beenland St *PRES* PR1 **59** E
Beeston Av *PLF/KEOS* FY6 **2**
Beetham Pl *BPOOLE* FY3 **3**
Bela Gv *BPOOL* FY1 **5**
Belford Av *CLV/TH* FY5 **1**
Belfry Cl *CHLYE* PR6 **8**
The Belfry *LSTA* FY8 **63** H
Belgrave Av *KIRK/FR/WA* PR4 **4**
PRES PR1 **6**
Belgrave Cl *LSTA* FY8 **50** E
Belgrave Pl *PLF/KEOS* FY6 **25** H
Belgrave Rd *BPOOLS* FY4 **5**
LEY/BBR PR5 **8**
PLF/KEOS FY6 **25**
Bellingham Rd *LSTA* FY8 **63**
Bellis Wy *LEY/BBR* PR5 **70**
Bells La *LEY/BBR* PR5 **72**
Belmont Av *BPOOL* FY1 **4**
FUL/RIB PR2 **47**
PLF/KEOS FY6 **25**
Belmont Cl *FUL/RIB* PR2 **59** E
Belmont Crs *FUL/RIB* PR2 **59** E
Belmont Dr *CHLYE* PR6 **9**
Belmont Rd *FTWD* FY7 **1**
FUL/RIB PR2 **57** F
LEY/BBR PR5 **80**
LSTA FY8 **62** A
Belton Hl *FUL/RIB* PR2 **36**
Belvedere Dr *CHLY/EC* PR7 **91** E
Belvedere Rd *CLV/TH* FY5 **22**
LEY/BBR PR5 **81** C
Belverdale Gdns *BPOOLS* FY4 **39** F
Belvere Av *BPOOLS* FY4 **38**
Benbow Cl *LSTA* FY8 **48**
Bence Rd *PRES* PR1 **58**
Benenden Pl *CLV/TH* FY5 **21** C
Bengal St *CHLY/EC* PR7 **91** F
Bennett Av *BPOOL* FY1 **3**
Bennett Rd *CLV/TH* FY5 **21**
Bennett's La *BPOOLS* FY4 **39**
Benson Rd *BPOOLE* FY3 **29** E
Bentham Av *FTWD* FY7 **10**
Bentham St *CHLY/EC* PR7 **94**
Bentinck Av *BPOOLS* FY4 **38**
Bentinck Rd *LSTA* FY8 **48**
Bent La *LEY/BBR* PR5 **81**
Bentley Dr *BPOOLS* FY4 **41** E
KIRK/FR/WA PR4 **42**
Bentley Park Rd
KIRK/FR/WA PR4 **74** A
Benton Rd *FUL/RIB* PR2 **47**
Beresford St *BPOOL* FY1 **3**
Berkeley Cl *CHLY/EC* PR7 **91**
Berkeley Dr *LEY/BBR* PR5 **78**
Berkeley St *PRES* PR1 **57** H
Berkley Cl *KIRK/FR/WA* PR4 **42** C
Berry Fld *PRES* PR1 **69** F
Berry's La *PLF/KEOS* FY6 **26**
Berry St *LEY/BBR* PR5 **77**
PRES PR1 **7**
Bertrand Av *BPOOLE* FY3 **29**
Berwick Av *CLV/TH* FY5 **17**
Berwick Dr *FUL/RIB* PR2 **45**
Berwick Rd *BPOOLS* FY4 **38** D
LSTA FY8 **49**
PRES PR1 **7**
Berwick St *PRES* PR1 **59** F
Beryl Av *CLV/TH* FY5 **21**
Bescot Wy *CLV/TH* FY5 **21**
Bethel Av *BISP* FY2 **24**
Bethesda Rd *BPOOL* FY1 **2**
Beverley Av *PLF/KEOS* FY6 **30**
Beverley Cl *FUL/RIB* PR2 **57**
Beverley Gv *BPOOLS* FY4 **38**
Beverley Rd South *LSTA* FY8 **49**
Beverly Cl *CLV/TH* FY5 **21**
Bexhill Rd *FUL/RIB* PR2 **44**
Bexley Av *BPOOLE* FY3 **28**
Bexley Pl *LSTA* FY8 **62**
Bhailok St *PRES* PR1 **7**
Bibby Dr *BPOOLE* FY3 **34**
Bibby's La *BISP* FY2 **24**
Bickerstaffe St *BPOOL* FY1 **4** C
Bideford Av *BPOOLE* FY3 **29**
Bidston St *PRES* PR1 **59**

ington St KIRK/FR/WA PR4 .. 42 D2 1
ington St East
IRK/FR/WA PR4 ... 42 D2 2
sborough Hey PRES PR1 ... 69 H5
sborough Meadow
UL/RIB PR2 ... 44 B5
brook Pl CHLY/EC PR7 ... 90 D2
gley Av BPOOLE FY3 ... 29 F4 1
gley Cl CHLYE PR6 ... 83 F2 1
ch Av CHLY/EC PR7 ... 85 H3 1
LV/TH FY5 ... 21 E2
UL/RIB PR2 ... 56 D1
EY/BBR PR5 ... 82 B1
RES PR1 ... 68 D3
ch Crs LEY/BBR PR5 ... 72 D5
ch Fld CHLYE PR6 ... 83 E1
ch Gv PLF/KEOS FY6 ... 19 H2
chin La CHLYE PR6 ... 83 G3
chover Cl FUL/RIB PR2 ... 44 D3 1
ch Rd CHLY/EC PR7 ... 94 B4 1
HLYE PR6 ... 87 G5
ch St FTWD FY7 ... 11 G2
STA FY8 ... 63 G3 1
ch Tree Gdns BPOOLE FY3 ... 33 H3
ch Wy PLF/KEOS FY6 ... 26 A3
chway Av BPOOLE FY3 ... 3 J3
chwood LEY/BBR PR5 ... 80 A3
chwood Cl LSTA FY8 ... 62 C2 1
chwood Dr CHLY/EC PR7 ... 94 B2
UL/RIB PR2 ... 45 G1
LF/KEOS FY6 ... 23 G2
d St PRES PR1 ... 6 D6
kacre Brow CHLY/EC PR7 ... 94 C3
kacre Rd CHLY/EC PR7 ... 94 C1
kbeck Pl FTWD FY7 ... 10 D4 1
kdale Av BISP FY2 ... 25 E2
TWD FY7 ... 17 E2
IRK/FR/WA PR4 ... 74 A1
STA FY8 ... 49 F2
kdale Cl CLV/TH FY5 ... 22 B3
IRK/FR/WA PR4 ... 74 A1
kdale Dr FUL/RIB PR2 ... 56 B1
kett Dr FUL/RIB PR2 ... 47 H5
kett Pl FUL/RIB PR2 ... 47 H5
kside Wy BPOOLS FY4 ... 34 A4 1
k St PRES PR1 ... 6 E3
ey Bank PRES PR1 ... 58 D4
ey St BPOOL FY1 ... 2 C4
IRK/FR/WA PR4 ... 43 F3
RES PR1 ... 7 J3
ham Gn FTWD FY7 ... 11 E2 2
twistle St LEY/BBR PR5 ... 77 G2 2
hopgate PRES PR1 ... 7 J2
hopgate BPOOLE FY3 ... 29 H1
hopsway PRES PR1 ... 69 G3
on Pl LEY/BBR PR5 ... 80 B2
pham Av LEY/BBR PR5 ... 76 D5
pham Rd BISP FY2 ... 24 D3
ISP FY2 ... 29 E1
POOLE FY3 ... 29 E2
LV/TH FY5 ... 20 C2
pham St PRES PR1 ... 7 H1 1
tern Cl BPOOLE FY3 ... 29 H4
ckberry Wy PRES PR1 ... 69 E4 1
ck Bull La FUL/RIB PR2 ... 45 G4
ckburn Brow CHLYE PR6 ... 87 H5
ckburn Rd CHLYE PR6 ... 87 H2
EY/BBR PR5 ... 72 A2
ckburn St CHLYE PR6 ... 91 G3
ck Cft CHLYE PR6 ... 83 E1
ckfen Pl BISP FY2 ... 28 D2 1
ckfield Rd KIRK/FR/WA PR4 .. 54 B5 1
ck Horse St CHLY/EC PR7 ... 91 E4 2
ckhurst Ct KIRK/FR/WA PR4 ... 74 C1
ckpool Old Rd BPOOLE FY3 ... 25 G5
LF/KEOS FY6 ... 25 H5
ckpool Rd BISP FY2 ... 24 D3
UL/RIB PR2 ... 56 B2
IRK/FR/WA PR4 ... 42 A2
STA FY8 ... 49 H3
STA FY8 ... 62 B1 1
LF/KEOS FY6 ... 25 G3
RES PR1 ... 46 B5
ckpool Rd North LSTA FY8 ... 49 F1
ckstone Rd CHLYE PR6 ... 91 H1
ckthorn Cl CLV/TH FY5 ... 17 F4 1
UL/RIB PR2 ... 56 A2 1
IRK/FR/WA PR4 ... 55 F1
ckthorn Cft CHLYE PR6 ... 82 D2
ckthorn Dr PRES PR1 ... 68 D3
inscough Rd CHLY/EC PR7 ... 94 B5
irway Av BPOOLE FY3 ... 29 F4
ke Av LEY/BBR PR5 ... 77 F2
kiston St FTWD FY7 ... 11 G2
nche St FUL/RIB PR2 ... 57 F2 1
ndford Av CLV/TH FY5 ... 20 C3
shaw La PRES PR1 ... 68 D1
aydike Moss LEY/BBR PR5 ... 80 A3
aydon Av CLV/TH FY5 ... 17 E5
eachers Dr LEY/BBR PR5 ... 80 D3 1
Bleasdale Av BPOOLE FY3 ... 30 C5
CLV/TH FY5 ... 20 D3
KIRK/FR/WA PR4 ... 43 E2
PLF/KEOS FY6 ... 26 A5
Bleasdale Cl LEY/BBR PR5 ... 78 C1
LEY/BBR PR5 ... 81 G5
Bleasdale Rd LSTA FY8 ... 63 G2
PLF/KEOS FY6 ... 12 B1
Bleasdale St East PRES PR1 ... 58 C2 1
Belock St PRES PR1 ... 7 K3
Blenheim Av BPOOL FY1 ... 3 G7
KIRK/FR/WA PR4 ... 42 D3 2
Blenheim Cl LEY/BBR PR5 ... 77 H1 2
Blenheim Dr CLV/TH FY5 ... 22 A2
KIRK/FR/WA PR4 ... 53 F5
Blenheim Pl LSTA FY8 ... 49 E2 2
Bloomfield Ct PRES PR1 ... 57 H1 1
Bloomfield Gra PRES PR1 ... 69 F4
Bloomfield Rd BPOOL FY1 ... 4 D4
Blossom Av BPOOLS FY4 ... 39 F1
The Blossoms FUL/RIB PR2 ... 46 D2 3
Bluebell Cl CHLYE PR6 ... 87 E2
CLV/TH FY5 ... 17 F4
Blue Bell Pl PRES PR1 ... 7 K2
Bluebell Wy FUL/RIB PR2 ... 47 F2
Bluebell Wd LEY/BBR PR5 ... 81 E1
Bluecoat Crs KIRK/FR/WA PR4 ... 55 G1
Blundell La PRES PR1 ... 57 E5
Blundell Rd FUL/RIB PR2 ... 45 H5
LSTA FY8 ... 49 F2
Blundell St BPOOL FY1 ... 4 C2
Blythe Av CLV/TH FY5 ... 17 E4
Boarded Barn CHLY/EC PR7 ... 85 H4 1
Boardman Av BPOOL FY1 ... 5 H4
Bodmin St PRES PR1 ... 59 E2 5
Boegrave Av LEY/BBR PR5 ... 77 F1
Bold St FTWD FY7 ... 11 H1
PRES PR1 ... 57 G1
Bolton Av PLF/KEOS FY6 ... 26 A2
Bolton Rd CHLY/EC PR7 ... 91 G4
Boltons Ct PRES PR1 ... 7 J3
Bolton St BPOOL FY1 ... 4 C5
CHLY/EC PR7 ... 91 F3
Bond St BPOOLS FY4 ... 4 C7
Bone Cft CHLYE PR6 ... 83 E1 1
Bonney St CLV/TH FY5 ... 21 H1 1
Bonny St BPOOL FY1 ... 2 C7
Boome St BPOOLS FY4 ... 38 C2
Boothley Rd BPOOL FY1 ... 3 F2
Boothroyden BPOOL FY1 ... 28 B2
Bootle St PRES PR1 ... 58 D2
Borage Cl CLV/TH FY5 ... 17 G4 1
Borrowdale Av FTWD FY7 ... 11 E2
Borrowdale Rd BPOOLS FY4 ... 33 H4
LEY/BBR PR5 ... 81 G5
Boscombe Rd BPOOLS FY4 ... 38 B2
Bostock St PRES PR1 ... 7 J3 1
Boston Av BISP FY2 ... 24 D1
Boston Rd LSTA FY8 ... 49 H5
Bostonway BPOOLS FY4 ... 5 K7
Bosworth Pl BPOOLS FY4 ... 38 B4
Botany Brow CHLYE PR6 ... 87 H5
Boulevard PRES PR1 ... 70 C1
The Boulevard LSTA FY8 ... 61 G2
Boundary Cl CHLY/EC PR7 ... 88 A4 1
KIRK/FR/WA PR4 ... 75 G1
Boundary Rd FUL/RIB PR2 ... 45 G5 1
LSTA FY8 ... 64 A1
Boundary St LEY/BBR PR5 ... 81 G2
Bourble's La GAR/LONG PR3 ... 13 H3
Bourne May Rd PLF/KEOS FY6 ... 12 B1
Bournemouth Rd BPOOLS FY4 ... 38 B2
Bourne Rd CLV/TH FY5 ... 17 H4
Bournesfield LEY/BBR PR5 ... 72 D5
Bourne's Rw LEY/BBR PR5 ... 72 D5
Bourne Wy CLV/TH FY5 ... 17 F5
Bovington Av CLV/TH FY5 ... 21 F4
Bow Brook Rd LEY/BBR PR5 ... 81 G3
Bowes Lyon Pl LSTA FY8 ... 50 A4 1
Bowfell Cl BPOOLS FY4 ... 34 B4
Bowgreave Cl BPOOLS FY4 ... 39 F2
Bowland Av CHLYE PR6 ... 91 G2 1
FTWD FY7 ... 16 D1
Bowland Crs BPOOLE FY3 ... 29 G2
Bowland Pl FUL/RIB PR2 ... 47 H5 1
LSTA FY8 ... 50 A5
Bowland Rd FUL/RIB PR2 ... 47 H5
Bow La LEY/BBR PR5 ... 81 G3
PRES PR1 ... 6 E3
Bowlers Cl FUL/RIB PR2 ... 46 D3 1
Bowlingfield FUL/RIB PR2 ... 44 D2
Bowness Av BPOOLS FY4 ... 34 A5
CLV/TH FY5 ... 21 H2
LSTA FY8 ... 49 F2
Bowness Pl FTWD FY7 ... 10 C5
Bowness Rd PRES PR1 ... 59 H2
Bowood Ct BPOOLE FY3 ... 29 H3 1
Bowran St PRES PR1 ... 7 G2
Bow St LEY/BBR PR5 ... 81 G2 3
Boxer Pl LEY/BBR PR5 ... 80 B2
Boys La FUL/RIB PR2 ... 45 F3
Bracewell Av PLF/KEOS FY6 ... 27 E4
Bracewell Rd FUL/RIB PR2 ... 47 F3 1
Brackenbury Cl LEY/BBR PR5 ... 77 F2 1
Brackenbury Rd FUL/RIB PR2 ... 45 H5 1
Brackenbury St PRES PR1 ... 58 A1 3
Bracken Cl CHLYE PR6 ... 91 H2
Bracken Dr KIRK/FR/WA PR4 ... 54 D4
Braconash Rd LEY/BBR PR5 ... 80 D2
Braddon St PRES PR1 ... 59 E2 6
Brades Av CLV/TH FY5 ... 22 B2
Brades La KIRK/FR/WA PR4 ... 54 D4
Bradkirk La LEY/BBR PR5 ... 79 E1
Bradkirk Pl LEY/BBR PR5 ... 78 D2
Bradley La CHLY/EC PR7 ... 88 C4
Bradshaw La GAR/LONG PR3 ... 15 G4
Braefield Crs FUL/RIB PR2 ... 47 G5
Braemar Av CLV/TH FY5 ... 22 A5
Braemar Wk BISP FY2 ... 25 F1
Braintree Av PRES PR1 ... 69 H4
Braith Cl BPOOLS FY4 ... 33 F5
Braithwaite St BPOOL FY1 ... 2 C1
Bramble Cl KIRK/FR/WA PR4 ... 42 C2 1
Bramble Ct CLV/TH FY5 ... 21 G2
PRES PR1 ... 69 H4
Bramble Gdns PLF/KEOS FY6 ... 25 G5 1
The Brambles CHLY/EC PR7 ... 94 C3 1
FUL/RIB PR2 ... 47 E2
The Bramblings PLF/KEOS FY6 .. 25 H5 2
Bramley Av FTWD FY7 ... 11 E2
Brampton Av CLV/TH FY5 ... 17 F5
Brampton St FUL/RIB PR2 ... 57 F2 2
Bramwell Rd KIRK/FR/WA PR4 ... 54 B5
Brancker St CHLY/EC PR7 ... 90 D5 2
Brandiforth St LEY/BBR PR5 ... 71 F3
Brandwood PRES PR1 ... 68 D2 1
Branksome Av CLV/TH FY5 ... 21 F1
Branston Rd BPOOLS FY4 ... 5 K5
Branstree Rd BPOOLS FY4 ... 34 A4
Brant Ct FTWD FY7 ... 10 C5 1
Brant Rd PRES PR1 ... 59 G2
Brantwood Dr LEY/BBR PR5 ... 81 G3
Brathay Pl FTWD FY7 ... 10 D4 2
Brays Rd LSTA FY8 ... 51 F1
Bray St FUL/RIB PR2 ... 57 F2 3
Breck Cl PLF/KEOS FY6 ... 26 C2
Breck Dr PLF/KEOS FY6 ... 26 C2
Breck Rd BPOOLE FY3 ... 3 H6
PLF/KEOS FY6 ... 26 C2
Breckside Cl PLF/KEOS FY6 ... 26 C2
Brecon Cl BPOOL FY1 ... 5 H1
Bredon Av CHLY/EC PR7 ... 90 A1
Bredon Cl LSTA FY8 ... 63 H1
Breeze Cl CLV/TH FY5 ... 17 G5
Breeze Mt LEY/BBR PR5 ... 77 H1 3
Brennand Cl LEY/BBR PR5 ... 78 C1 2
Brentwood FTWD FY7 ... 11 E4 1
Brentwood Av CLV/TH FY5 ... 20 D3
PLF/KEOS FY6 ... 26 A4 1
Bretherton Cl LEY/BBR PR5 ... 80 B4
Bretherton Ter LEY/BBR PR5 ... 81 G3 1
Briar Av CHLY/EC PR7 ... 85 H3
Briar Bank Rw FUL/RIB PR2 ... 37 E5
Briar Cft KIRK/FR/WA PR4 ... 74 B2
Briar Fld BISP FY2 ... 25 F1
Briarfield Rd PLF/KEOS FY6 ... 25 H1
Briar Gv FUL/RIB PR2 ... 44 D4
Briar Ms CLV/TH FY5 ... 22 A3
Briar Rd CLV/TH FY5 ... 21 H3
The Briars CHLY/EC PR7 ... 88 B4
FUL/RIB PR2 ... 47 E2
Briarwood KIRK/FR/WA PR4 ... 54 A5
Briarwood Cl LEY/BBR PR5 ... 80 C4
Briarwood Ct CLV/TH FY5 ... 21 H5 1
Briarwood Dr BISP FY2 ... 25 E3 1
Brick House La PLF/KEOS FY6 ... 19 F5
Brickhouse La PLF/KEOS FY6 ... 19 G5
Bridge Bank LEY/BBR PR5 ... 58 D5 1
Bridge Cl LEY/BBR PR5 ... 77 F1
Bridge End LEY/BBR PR5 ... 77 H1 4
Bridge House Rd BPOOLS FY4 ... 33 F5
Bridge Rd FTWD FY7 ... 11 H2
FUL/RIB PR2 ... 57 F1
LEY/BBR PR5 ... 77 H1
LSTA FY8 ... 62 B2
Bridgeside LSTA FY8 ... 38 B4
Bridge St LEY/BBR PR5 ... 72 A3
LEY/BBR PR5 ... 78 B2
Bridge Ter LEY/BBR PR5 ... 58 D5 2
Bridgewater Av CLV/TH FY5 ... 21 F5 1
Bridgeway LEY/BBR PR5 ... 77 H1
Briercliffe Av BPOOLE FY3 ... 33 F3
Briercliffe Rd CHLYE PR6 ... 91 G1
Brierfield KIRK/FR/WA PR4 ... 75 G1
Brierley Av BPOOLE FY3 ... 3 J2
Brierley Rd LEY/BBR PR5 ... 78 D2
Brierley St PRES PR1 ... 57 G2 2
Briery Cl FUL/RIB PR2 ... 46 D4
Brieryfield Rd PRES PR1 ... 6 D2
Briery Hey LEY/BBR PR5 ... 79 F3
Briggs Rd FUL/RIB PR2 ... 57 F1
Brighton Av BPOOLS FY4 ... 32 B5 1
LSTA FY8 ... 49 F4
Brighton Crs FUL/RIB PR2 ... 44 D5
Brighton St CHLYE PR6 ... 91 H2 1
Bright St BPOOLS FY4 ... 4 C7
Brindle Cl LEY/BBR PR5 ... 79 E1
Brindle Fold LEY/BBR PR5 ... 79 F2
Brindle Rd CHLYE PR6 ... 79 G3
LEY/BBR PR5 ... 71 G4
Brindle St CHLY/EC PR7 ... 91 F4
PRES PR1 ... 58 D3
Brinwell Rd BPOOLS FY4 ... 33 H4
Brisbane Pl CLV/TH FY5 ... 21 F5
Bristol Av BISP FY2 ... 25 E3
FTWD FY7 ... 16 C1
LEY/BBR PR5 ... 77 H5
Bristow Av FUL/RIB PR2 ... 57 E1
Britannia Dr FUL/RIB PR2 ... 57 E3
Britannia Pl BPOOL FY1 ... 4 C6
Britannia Wk LSTA FY8 ... 50 A3 1
Brixey St PRES PR1 ... 6 D6
Brixham Pl BPOOLS FY4 ... 38 B2
Brixton Rd PRES PR1 ... 58 C5
Broadfield KIRK/FR/WA PR4 ... 36 A3
Broadfield Av BPOOLS FY4 ... 39 F3 2
PLF/KEOS FY6 ... 26 D4
Broadfield Dr LEY/BBR PR5 ... 80 D3
PRES PR1 ... 69 G4
Broadfields CHLY/EC PR7 ... 87 E5
Broadgate PRES PR1 ... 6 D6
Broadgreen Cl LEY/BBR PR5 ... 81 E3
Broadhurst Rd CLV/TH FY5 ... 21 E4
Broadlands Pl LSTA FY8 ... 62 D2
Broad Meadow LEY/BBR PR5 ... 77 F1
Broad Oak Gn PRES PR1 ... 69 E3
Broad Oak La BPOOLE FY3 ... 30 B5
KIRK/FR/WA PR4 ... 69 E4
PRES PR1 ... 69 E3
Broadpool La PLF/KEOS FY6 ... 23 G3
Broad Sq LEY/BBR PR5 ... 81 F4 2
Broad St LEY/BBR PR5 ... 81 F4 3
Broadwater Av FTWD FY7 ... 17 E1
Broadway BPOOLS FY4 ... 38 C1
FTWD FY7 ... 11 E4
FUL/RIB PR2 ... 45 G2
FUL/RIB PR2 ... 56 C1 1
LEY/BBR PR5 ... 81 G4
Broadwood Cl PRES PR1 ... 69 E2 1
Broadwood Dr FUL/RIB PR2 ... 45 H1
Broadwood Wy LSTA FY8 ... 62 C2
Brock Av FTWD FY7 ... 10 D4
Brockholes Brow PRES PR1 ... 59 G2
Brockholes Crs PLF/KEOS FY6 ... 26 C5
Brockholes Vw PRES PR1 ... 58 D4
Brocklewood Av PLF/KEOS FY6 ... 30 B2
Brock Rd CHLYE PR6 ... 91 G1
Brockway PLF/KEOS FY6 ... 26 B5
Brockway Av BPOOLE FY3 ... 29 F4
Broderick Av BISP FY2 ... 29 E1
Bromley Cl BISP FY2 ... 29 E1
Bromley Rd LSTA FY8 ... 49 F5
Bromley St PRES PR1 ... 6 D1 1
Brompton Cl LSTA FY8 ... 62 B1 2
Brompton Rd PLF/KEOS FY6 ... 30 B1
Bromsgrove Av BISP FY2 ... 24 C3
Brook Cft FUL/RIB PR2 ... 45 E5
Brookdale KIRK/FR/WA PR4 ... 75 H3
Brookdale Av CLV/TH FY5 ... 21 E4
Brookdale Cl LEY/BBR PR5 ... 85 G1
Brooke St CHLYE PR6 ... 91 G3
Brookfield Av BPOOLS FY4 ... 39 G2
CLV/TH FY5 ... 22 A2
FUL/RIB PR2 ... 46 D4 1
Brookfield Dr FUL/RIB PR2 ... 36 D5
Brookfield Pl LEY/BBR PR5 ... 78 D3
Brookfield Rd CLV/TH FY5 ... 22 A2
Brookfield St PRES PR1 ... 58 A2
Brook Gv CLV/TH FY5 ... 17 E5
Brook Hey KIRK/FR/WA PR4 ... 74 A1 2
Brookhouse Cl LEY/BBR PR5 ... 73 E4
Brookhouse Dr LEY/BBR PR5 ... 73 E4
Brookhouse St FUL/RIB PR2 ... 57 G2 3
Brooklands FUL/RIB PR2 ... 56 D2
Brooklands Av FUL/RIB PR2 ... 45 H1
KIRK/FR/WA PR4 ... 43 E3
Brooklands Rd LSTA FY8 ... 50 A5
Brook La CHLY/EC PR7 ... 93 G1
KIRK/FR/WA PR4 ... 76 C2
LEY/BBR PR5 ... 76 C3
Brooklyn Av BPOOLE FY3 ... 29 E2
Brook Meadow
KIRK/FR/WA PR4 ... 44 C1 1
Brook Pl FUL/RIB PR2 ... 56 A1
Brook Rd LSTA FY8 ... 63 G2
Brookside CHLY/EC PR7 ... 85 H5
CHLY/EC PR7 ... 94 C4
CLV/TH FY5 ... 22 A1
KIRK/FR/WA PR4 ... 42 D2 3
Brookside Cl LEY/BBR PR5 ... 80 D1

Brookside Rd FUL/RIB PR2 45 G1
Brook St BPOOLS FY4 5 J6
FTWD FY7 17 E1
FUL/RIB PR2 45 G5
KIRK/FR/WA PR4 42 D2
LEY/BBR PR5 72 A3
Brookview FUL/RIB PR2 46 C3
Brookway KIRK/FR/WA PR4 74 A1
Broomfield Mill St PRES PR1 58 A2 1
Broomfield Rd FTWD FY7 11 F3
Brough Av BISP FY2 25 E5
Broughton Av BPOOLE FY3 3 J1
Broughton St PRES PR1 45 H5
Broughton Tower Wy
FUL/RIB PR2 37 F5 1
Broughton Wy PLF/KEOS FY6 26 A1
Brow Hey LEY/BBR PR5 79 E3
Brownedge Cl LEY/BBR PR5 71 E5
Brownedge La LEY/BBR PR5 71 F5
Brownedge Rd LEY/BBR PR5 71 E5
Brownhill La KIRK/FR/WA PR4 75 E2
Brownhill Rd LEY/BBR PR5 81 E3
Browning Av CLV/TH FY5 21 G1
LSTA FY8 63 H2 3
Browning Crs PRES PR1 59 E1 3
Browning Rd PRES PR1 59 E1
Brown La LEY/BBR PR5 71 G4
Brownley St CHLYE PR6 83 E3
CHLYE PR6 91 H3 1
Browns Hey CHLY/EC PR7 86 D5 2
Brown's La KIRK/FR/WA PR4 42 B4
PLF/KEOS FY6 18 C2
Brown St CHLYE PR6 91 G2
CLV/TH FY5 21 H1
LEY/BBR PR5 78 C1 3
Browsholme Av FUL/RIB PR2 47 G5 1
Browsholme Cl PLF/KEOS FY6 29 H2 1
Brunel Wy BPOOLS FY4 40 A1
Brun Gv BPOOL FY1 5 J5
Brunswick Pl FUL/RIB PR2 57 F2 4
Brunswick St BPOOL FY1 2 C7
CHLY/EC PR7 91 G2 2
Bryan Rd BPOOLE FY3 3 H5
Brydeck Av PRES PR1 69 H2
Bryning Av BISP FY2 24 C3
Bryning Fern La
KIRK/FR/WA PR4 42 D4
Bryning Hall La KIRK/FR/WA PR4 52 B2
LSTA FY8 52 B3
Bryning La KIRK/FR/WA PR4 52 D2
Bryony Cl CLV/TH FY5 17 F4 2
Buchanan St BPOOL FY1 2 E3
CHLYE PR6 91 G3
Buckden Cl CLV/TH FY5 20 C2
Buckingham Av PRES PR1 69 G4
Buckingham Rd LSTA FY8 62 B2 1
Buckingham St CHLYE PR6 91 G3
Buckingham Wy PLF/KEOS FY6 26 A2
Bucklands Av FUL/RIB PR2 57 G1
Buckley Crs CLV/TH FY5 20 C5
Bucknell Pl CLV/TH FY5 21 E5
Buckshaw Hall Cl CHLY/EC PR7 87 E5
Buckton Cl CHLYE PR6 87 F1 1
Bude Cl KIRK/FR/WA PR4 44 C2 2
Buller Av PRES PR1 69 H2
Bullfinch St PRES PR1 58 C2 2
Bull Park La PLF/KEOS FY6 23 G4
Bulmer St FUL/RIB PR2 57 F1 3
Bunker St KIRK/FR/WA PR4 54 C5
Bunting Pl CLV/TH FY5 21 F3 1
Burbank Cl BPOOLS FY4 39 F3
Burford Cl BPOOLE FY3 29 G3 1
Burgate BPOOLS FY4 38 D3
Burgess Av BPOOLS FY4 39 E1 2
Burgh Hall Rd CHLY/EC PR7 94 D2
Burgh La CHLY/EC PR7 95 F1
Burgh La South CHLY/EC PR7 95 E3
Burghley Cl CHLYE PR6 83 F2 2
Burghley Ct LEY/BBR PR5 81 G3 2
Burgh Mdw CHLY/EC PR7 95 E1
Burholme Cl FUL/RIB PR2 59 H1 1
Burholme Pl FUL/RIB PR2 59 H1 2
Burholme Rd FUL/RIB PR2 59 H1
Burleigh Rd PRES PR1 6 E4 1
Burlington Rd BPOOLS FY4 38 B2
Burlington Rd West
BPOOLS FY4 38 A2 1
Burlington St CHLY/EC PR7 91 G3 2
Burnage Gdns BPOOLS FY4 38 D1
Burned House La PLF/KEOS FY6 13 G5
Burn Gv CLV/TH FY5 17 E5
Burnsall Av BPOOLE FY3 29 G1
Burnsall Pl FUL/RIB PR2 47 F4 2
Burns Av CLV/TH FY5 21 F2
LSTA FY8 63 H2 4
Burnside Av BPOOLS FY4 33 E5
FTWD FY7 10 C4
FUL/RIB PR2 47 G5
Burnside Wy PRES PR1 69 G3
Burnslack Rd FUL/RIB PR2 47 G5
Burns Pl BPOOLS FY4 33 F5 1
Burns Rd FTWD FY7 11 G1
Burns St PRES PR1 59 E1
Burrington Cl FUL/RIB PR2 47 E2 1
Burrow Rd PRES PR1 58 B2
Burrow's La PLF/KEOS FY6 18 D3
Burton Ct FTWD FY7 16 C1
Burton Rd BPOOLS FY4 33 F5
Burwell Av CHLY/EC PR7 94 A5
Burwood Cl PRES PR1 70 A4 1
Burwood Dr BPOOLE FY3 29 G4
FUL/RIB PR2 59 F1
Bushell Pl PRES PR1 7 J5 1
Bushell St PRES PR1 58 A2 2
Bush La KIRK/FR/WA PR4 66 B2
Bussel Rd PRES PR1 69 H4
Butcher Brow LEY/BBR PR5 71 F1 1
Bute Av BPOOL FY1 2 D1
Butler Pl PRES PR1 58 A1 4
Butler Rd BPOOL FY1 4 C2
Butler St BPOOL FY1 2 E3
PRES PR1 7 G4
Butterlands PRES PR1 59 G3
Buttermere Av CHLY/EC PR7 90 D4
FTWD FY7 10 C5
Buttermere Cl FUL/RIB PR2 46 D4
LEY/BBR PR5 71 F4 2
Buttermere Dr PLF/KEOS FY6 12 D1
Butterworth Brow CHLY/EC PR7 94 C1
Butterworth Cl KIRK/FR/WA PR4 43 E2
Butts Cl CLV/TH FY5 18 A5
Butts Rd CLV/TH FY5 17 H5
Buxton Av BISP FY2 24 D3
Byfield Av CLV/TH FY5 21 E5
Byland Cl BPOOLS FY4 38 C3 1
Bymbrig Cl LEY/BBR PR5 78 B1 2
Byron Av CLV/TH FY5 21 G1
KIRK/FR/WA PR4 53 G5
LSTA FY8 63 H2 5
Byron Crs CHLY/EC PR7 94 B5
Byron St BPOOLS FY4 4 D6
CHLY/EC PR7 91 G2 3
FTWD FY7 11 G2
BPOOLE FY3 33 F2 1

C

Cadby Av BPOOLE FY3 33 F3 1
Cadley Av FUL/RIB PR2 45 E5
Cadley Cswy FUL/RIB PR2 45 F4
Cadley Dr FUL/RIB PR2 45 E5
Cadogan Pl PRES PR1 7 J5
Cage La KIRK/FR/WA PR4 76 A1
Cairndale Dr LEY/BBR PR5 85 G1
Cairn Gv BPOOLS FY4 38 C4 1
Cairnsmore Av PRES PR1 59 G2
Calder Av CHLY/EC PR7 91 E5
CLV/TH FY5 21 F2
FTWD FY7 10 D4
FUL/RIB PR2 46 A2
KIRK/FR/WA PR4 65 H1
Calder Cl KIRK/FR/WA PR4 43 F3
LSTA FY8 49 F1
Calder Rd BISP FY2 28 C1
Calder St FUL/RIB PR2 6 A1
Caldervale Av PLF/KEOS FY6 26 A4
Caldicott Wy PLF/KEOS FY6 26 A1
Caledonian Av BPOOLE FY3 3 H1
Calf Croft Pl LSTA FY8 63 E2
Callon St PRES PR1 59 F3
Calverley St PRES PR1 59 E2
Calvert Pl BPOOLE FY3 29 G3 2
Cambell's Ct LSTA FY8 49 E4 1
Camborne Ct BPOOLE FY3 33 H3 1
Camborne Pl KIRK/FR/WA PR4 54 A5
Cambray Rd BPOOL FY1 28 C2
Cambridge Cl PRES PR1 57 H1
Cambridge Rd BPOOL FY1 3 G4
CLV/TH FY5 20 C1
FTWD FY7 11 E3
LEY/BBR PR5 78 C1 4
LSTA FY8 62 B2
Cambridge St CHLY/EC PR7 91 F3 3
PRES PR1 57 H1 2
Cambridge Wk PRES PR1 57 H1 3
Cam Cl LEY/BBR PR5 78 C1
Camden Pl PRES PR1 7 H4
Camden Rd BPOOLE FY3 3 J2
Camellia Dr LEY/BBR PR5 82 B2
Cameron Av BPOOLE FY3 3 J1
Cameron Cft CHLYE PR6 91 G2 4
Cam La LEY/BBR PR5 82 D1
Camomile Cl CHLY/EC PR7 86 D4 1
Campbell Av BPOOLE FY3 3 J1
Campbell St PRES PR1 58 C3
Campion Cl CLV/TH FY5 17 F4 3
Cam St PRES PR1 58 D1
Camwood LEY/BBR PR5 79 E5
Camwood Dr LEY/BBR PR5 70 C5
Cam Wood Fold CHLYE PR6 82 D1
Canada Crs BISP FY2 25 E4
Canal Wk CHLYE PR6 91 H2
Canberra Cl CLV/TH FY5 21 F5 2
Canberra Rd LEY/BBR PR5 81 G3
Canberra Wy KIRK/FR/WA PR4 53 G4
Cann Bridge St LEY/BBR PR5 71 H2
Cannock Av BPOOLE FY3 29 E2 2
Cannon Hl FUL/RIB PR2 57 F2 5
Cannon St PRES PR1 7 H3
Canterbury Av BPOOLE FY3 33 F2 2
Canterbury Cl PLF/KEOS FY6 26 A2 1
Canterbury St CHLYE PR6 91 H4
Cantsfield Av FUL/RIB PR2 45 E4
Canute St PRES PR1 58 B2
Capitol Wy LEY/BBR PR5 70 D1
Capstan Cl LSTA FY8 49 E2
Carcroft Av BISP FY2 24 D3
Cardale KIRK/FR/WA PR4 68 A4
Cardigan Pl BPOOLS FY4 38 A3 1
Cardigan St FUL/RIB PR2 57 G2
Cardinal Pl CLV/TH FY5 21 E1
Cardwell Cl KIRK/FR/WA PR4 65 F1
Carisbrooke Av BPOOLS FY4 39 G1 2
Carisbrooke Cl PLF/KEOS FY6 26 A1 1
Carleton Av BPOOLE FY3 29 F1
FUL/RIB PR2 47 E4
Carleton Dr PRES PR1 68 D2
Carleton Gdns PLF/KEOS FY6 25 H2
Carleton Ga PLF/KEOS FY6 26 A3
Carleton Rd CHLYE PR6 87 H3
Carleton Wy PLF/KEOS FY6 25 H2 3
Carlin Ga BISP FY2 24 B5
Carlisle Av FTWD FY7 10 D5
PRES PR1 68 D2
Carlisle Gv CLV/TH FY5 21 H2
Carlisle St PRES PR1 7 J2
Carloway Av FUL/RIB PR2 46 D3 2
Carlton Av CHLYE PR6 83 E2
Carlton Dr PRES PR1 58 C5
Carlton Gv BISP FY2 24 B3 2
Carlton Rd LEY/BBR PR5 81 E4
LSTA FY8 49 F4
Carlton St FUL/RIB PR2 6 D1
Carlyle Av BPOOLS FY4 38 B2
Carnarvon Rd PRES PR1 6 D4
Carnfield Pl LEY/BBR PR5 78 D1
Carnforth Av BISP FY2 25 E2
Carnoustie Cl FUL/RIB PR2 45 E1
Carnoustie Ct PRES PR1 56 D5 1
Caroline St BPOOL FY1 4 D1
PRES PR1 58 D2 2
Carr Barn Brow LEY/BBR PR5 79 F3
Carr Cl GAR/LONG PR3 15 E1
PLF/KEOS FY6 19 G5
Carr Dr KIRK/FR/WA PR4 42 C2
Carr End La PLF/KEOS FY6 19 G2
Carr Fld LEY/BBR PR5 79 F5
Carr Ga CLV/TH FY5 16 C5
Carr Head La PLF/KEOS FY6 26 C5
Carr House La WGNNW/ST WN6 93 E5
Carrington Rd CHLY/EC PR7 91 E3
Carr La CHLY/EC PR7 91 G5
GAR/LONG PR3 15 E2
KIRK/FR/WA PR4 43 H2
KIRK/FR/WA PR4 52 D5
LEY/BBR PR5 81 F1
PLF/KEOS FY6 23 G1
PLF/KEOS FY6 31 F1
Carr Meadow LEY/BBR PR5 79 F3
Carrol St PRES PR1 58 C2
Carr Pl LEY/BBR PR5 79 E2
Carr Rd CHLYE PR6 83 E2
CLV/TH FY5 24 D1
FTWD FY7 11 G1
KIRK/FR/WA PR4 43 F4
PLF/KEOS FY6 23 G2
Carr St CHLYE PR6 91 H1
LEY/BBR PR5 78 B1
PRES PR1 58 C4
Carrwood Dr KIRK/FR/WA PR4 43 F4 1
Carrwood Rd LEY/BBR PR5 70 C3
Carrwood Wy LEY/BBR PR5 70 C4
Carshalton Rd BPOOL FY1 28 B3
Carsluith Av BPOOLE FY3 5 K2
Carson Rd BPOOLS FY4 33 G4
Carter St BPOOL FY1 2 D5 2
Carterville Cl BPOOLS FY4 39 G1
Cart Ga PLF/KEOS FY6 13 F3
Cartmel Av FTWD FY7 10 C5
Cartmel Dr LEY/BBR PR5 72 D3
Cartmell La LSTA FY8 51 H4
Cartmell Rd BPOOLS FY4 34 B4
LSTA FY8 61 F2
Cartmel Pl FUL/RIB PR2 56 B1
Cartmel Rd LEY/BBR PR5 80 C4
Carwood La CHLYE PR6 83 F5
Caryl Rd LSTA FY8 48 C3
Casterton CHLY/EC PR7 85 H5
Castle Av PLF/KEOS FY6 25
Castle Fold PRES PR1 70
Castlegate BPOOL FY1 4
Castle La BPOOLE FY3 30
Castle Mt FUL/RIB PR2 46
Castlerigg Pl BPOOLS FY4 34
Castle St CHLY/EC PR7 91
PRES PR1 58 A
Castleton Rd PRES PR1 58
Castle Wk PRES PR1 6
Catforth Av BPOOLS FY4 33
Catforth Rd FUL/RIB PR2 56
Catherine Cl KIRK/FR/WA PR4 42 C
Catherine St CHLY/EC PR7 91 F
KIRK/FR/WA PR4 42
PRES PR1 58
Cathrow Dr KIRK/FR/WA PR4 75
Catley Cl CHLYE PR6 87 F
Caton Av FTWD FY7 10
Caton Cl LEY/BBR PR5 82
Caton Gv BPOOLE FY3 29 F
Catterall Cl BPOOL FY1 3
Caunce St BPOOL FY1 2
BPOOLE FY3 3
Causeway Av FUL/RIB PR2 45
The Causeway CHLYE PR6 91
Cavendish Crs FUL/RIB PR2 47 C
Cavendish Dr FUL/RIB PR2 47
Cavendish Pl LEY/BBR PR5 71 E
Cavendish Rd BISP FY2 24
LSTA FY8 48
PRES PR1 59 F
Cavendish St CHLYE PR6 91 H
Cave St PRES PR1 59
Caxton Av BISP FY2 24
Caxton Rd FUL/RIB PR2 37
Cecilia St PRES PR1 59 E
Cecil St BPOOL FY1 3
LSTA FY8 63
Cedar Av CHLY/EC PR7 85
CLV/TH FY5 21
FTWD FY7 17 E
FUL/RIB PR2 56
KIRK/FR/WA PR4 53
LEY/BBR PR5 77 G
PLF/KEOS FY6 13
PLF/KEOS FY6 30
Cedar Crs KIRK/FR/WA PR4 43
Cedar Fld CHLYE PR6 83
Cedar Rd CHLYE PR6 87
FUL/RIB PR2 59
Cedar Sq BPOOL FY1 2
The Cedars CHLY/EC PR7 88
CHLY/EC PR7 95
KIRK/FR/WA PR4 75
Cedar Wy PRES PR1 69
Cedarwood Cl LSTA FY8 62 C
Cedarwood Dr LEY/BBR PR5 80
Cedric Pl BISP FY2 24 C
Celandine Cl CLV/TH FY5 17
Cemetery La PLF/KEOS FY6 13
Cemetery Rd PRES PR1 58
Central Av KIRK/FR/WA PR4 42
LEY/BBR PR5 72
Central Av North CLV/TH FY5 21
Central Beach LSTA FY8 63
Central Dr BPOOL FY1 2
LSTA FY8 62
PRES PR1 68
Centre Dr LEY/BBR PR5 79
Centurion Wy LEY/BBR PR5 77
Chaddock St PRES PR1 7 H
Chadfield Rd BPOOL FY1 5
Chadwick Gdns LEY/BBR PR5 77 F
Chadwick St BPOOL FY1 4
Chaffinch Cl CLV/TH FY5 17
Chaffinch Ct BPOOLE FY3 29 H
Chain Caul Rd FUL/RIB PR2 56
Chain Caul Wy FUL/RIB PR2 56
Chain House La KIRK/FR/WA PR4 76
Chain La BPOOLE FY3 34 C
Chalfont Fld FUL/RIB PR2 45 F
Champagne Av BISP FY2 21
Chancery Rd CHLY/EC PR7 90
Chandler St PRES PR1 7 G
Channel Wy FUL/RIB PR2 6
Channing Rd LSTA FY8 62
Chapel Brow LEY/BBR PR5 81
Chapel Cl KIRK/FR/WA PR4 42
Chapel La CHLY/EC PR7 94
KIRK/FR/WA PR4 43
KIRK/FR/WA PR4 74
KIRK/FR/WA PR4 75
Chapel Meadow
KIRK/FR/WA PR4 74
Chapel Park Rd KIRK/FR/WA PR4 74
Chapel Rd BPOOLS FY4 39
FUL/RIB PR2 46
Chapel St BPOOL FY1 2
CHLY/EC PR7 91

HLY/EC PR7 91 G3 3
HLY/EC PR7 94 B4
STA FY8 63 F3 4
LF/KEOS FY6 26 B3
RES PR1 7 G3
pel Wks *KIRK/FR/WA* PR4 43 F4
RES PR1 7 H3 1
pel Wy *CHLY/EC* PR7 94 C4
pel Yd *LEY/BBR* PR5 71 E1 1
pman Rd *FUL/RIB* PR2 46 B5
rdonnay Crs *BISP* FY2 21 F5 3
rles Crs *LEY/BBR* PR5 72 B3
rles St *BPOOL* FY1 2 E4 2
rles Wy *FUL/RIB* PR2 56 B2
rlotte Pl *PRES* PR1 7 K4
rlotte St *PRES* PR1 7 K4
rnley Cl *PRES* PR1 69 F4 2
rnley Fold *LEY/BBR* PR5 71 G4
rnley Fold La *LEY/BBR* PR5 71 G3
rnley Rd *BPOOL* FY1 2 D6
rnley St *PRES* PR1 7 G3 1
rnock Av *PRES* PR1 69 H4
rnock Brow Preston Rd
HLY/EC PR7 89 H4
rnock Fold *PRES* PR1 58 B1 1
rnock St *CHLYE* PR6 91 G3
RK/FR/WA PR4 42 D2 4
EY/BBR PR5 81 F3 2
RES PR1 58 B1 2
rnwood Av *BPOOLE* FY3 29 G3 3
rter La *CHLY/EC* PR7 94 A1
rtwell Cl *CHLYE* PR6 83 F2 3
rtwell Ri *LEY/BBR* PR5 77 H1
Chase *CLV/TH* FY5 17 G5
EY/BBR PR5 81 H2
tburn Cl *PLF/KEOS* FY6 29 H2 2
tburn Rd *FUL/RIB* PR2 47 F4
tham Av *LSTA* FY8 49 E2
tham Pl *CHLYE* PR6 91 H2 2
RES PR1 58 C1 1
tsworth Av *BISP* FY2 24 C1
TWD FY7 10 C4
RK/FR/WA PR4 53 F5
tsworth Cl *CHLY/EC* PR7 91 E2
LV/TH FY5 22 B3 2
tsworth Rd *LEY/BBR* PR5 71 E3
EY/BBR PR5 81 F3 3
STA FY8 48 D4
tsworth St *PRES* PR1 58 D3
tteris Pl *CLV/TH* FY5 20 C3
ucer Av *CLV/TH* FY5 21 F1
ucer Cl *CHLY/EC* PR7 88 A4
ucer Rd *FTWD* FY7 11 G2
ucer St *PRES* PR1 59 E1 4
am Av *CHLY/EC* PR7 91 G4
apside *BPOOL* FY1 2 C4
HLY/EC PR7 91 F3 4
RES PR1 7 H3
ddar Av *BPOOLS* FY4 38 D2
ddar Dr *FUL/RIB* PR2 47 E2 2
lford Av *BPOOLE* FY3 29 E2 3
lford Cl *PRES* PR1 70 A4 2
lmsford Gv *CHLY/EC* PR7 91 E3 1
lmsford Pl *CHLY/EC* PR7 91 E4
lsea Av *BISP* FY2 29 E1
ltenham Crs *CLV/TH* FY5 22 B4 1
STA FY8 63 H1 2
ltenham Rd *BPOOL* FY1 28 B3
pstow Rd *BPOOLE* FY3 29 F2
riton Fld *FUL/RIB* PR2 45 F1
rry Cl *FUL/RIB* PR2 47 E2
RK/FR/WA PR4 42 C3
rrydale *BISP* FY2 24 D2 1
rry La *KIRK/FR/WA* PR4 66 A2
rry Tree Cl *GAR/LONG* PR3 15 G1
rry Tree Gdns *BPOOLS* FY4 33 G5
rry Tree Gv *CHLYE* PR6 87 F4
rry Tree Rd *BPOOLS* FY4 33 G4
rry Tree Rd North
POOLE FY3 33 G4
rry Trees *LEY/BBR* PR5 70 D3 1
rry Wd *PRES* PR1 68 D3
rrywood Av *CLV/TH* FY5 20 C3
STA FY8 62 C2 3
rrywood Cl *LEY/BBR* PR5 80 D4 1
ryl Dr *CLV/TH* FY5 21 H4
sham Dr *KIRK/FR/WA* PR4 75 G2
shire House Cl
EY/BBR PR5 77 E2 1
smere Dr *PRES* PR1 69 E1 1
ster Av *CHLY/EC* PR7 95 H1
LV/TH FY5 20 D2
LF/KEOS FY6 26 A4
sterfield Rd *BPOOL* FY1 28 B3
ster Rd *BPOOLE* FY3 3 H1
RES PR1 58 D2
stnut Av *BPOOLS* FY4 39 F3
HLY/EC PR7 85 H3
HLYE PR6 87 H5 1
RES PR1 68 D2

Chestnut Cl *LEY/BBR* PR5 71 F4
Chestnut Crs *FUL/RIB* PR2 59 F1
KIRK/FR/WA PR4 74 A1
Chestnut Dr *FUL/RIB* PR2 45 G1
The Chestnuts *CHLY/EC* PR7 94 C3
Cheviot Av *CLV/TH* FY5 17 F5
LSTA FY8 64 A1
Cheviot St *PRES* PR1 6 C1 1
Chichester Cl *CLV/TH* FY5 21 G2 2
Chiltern Av *BPOOLS* FY4 38 D1
CHLY/EC PR7 90 A1
PLF/KEOS FY6 26 A4
Chiltern Cl *LSTA* FY8 63 H1 3
Chiltern Meadow
LEY/BBR PR5 82 A3 1
The Chimes *KIRK/FR/WA* PR4 43 E4
Chindits Wy *FUL/RIB* PR2 46 C4
The Chines *FUL/RIB* PR2 45 H4 1
Chingle Cl *FUL/RIB* PR2 47 F2 2
Chipping Gv *BPOOLE* FY3 29 G2
Chislehurst Av *BPOOLS* FY4 5 G6
Chislehurst Pl *LSTA* FY8 50 B5
Chisnall La *CHLY/EC* PR7 93 E3
Chiswell Gv *CLV/TH* FY5 22 C4 1
Chiswick Gv *BPOOLE* FY3 33 H3
Chorley Hall Rd *CHLY/EC* PR7 87 F5
Chorley La *CHLY/EC* PR7 93 H3
Chorley Old Rd *CHLYE* PR6 83 F5
Chorley Rd *BPOOLE* FY3 25 F5
CHLY/EC PR7 95 G5
LEY/BBR PR5 71 E3
Christ Church St *PRES* PR1 6 E4
Christian Rd *PRES* PR1 7 F4
Church Av *PRES* PR1 6 B6
PRES PR1 59 F3
Church Brow *LEY/BBR* PR5 71 E1
Church Cl *KIRK/FR/WA* PR4 54 A5
Church Ct *PRES* PR1 58 D1 1
Church Dr *LSTA* FY8 62 D3
Churchfield *FUL/RIB* PR2 46 A2
Church Fold *CHLY/EC* PR7 94 B1
CHLY/EC PR7 94 C5
Church Gdns *KIRK/FR/WA* PR4 53 G5 1
Church Hl *CHLYE* PR6 83 E5
Churchill Cl *CLV/TH* FY5 21 H2 1
Churchill Dr *FUL/RIB* PR2 47 E4 1
Churchill Rd *FUL/RIB* PR2 46 D4
Churchill Wy *LEY/BBR* PR5 81 F2
Church La *CHLY/EC* PR7 94 A1
GAR/LONG PR3 36 C4
KIRK/FR/WA PR4 76 D2
PLF/KEOS FY6 23 H3
WGNNW/ST WN6 92 C5
Church Rd *CLV/TH* FY5 21 F2
KIRK/FR/WA PR4 42 D1
KIRK/FR/WA PR4 53 F4
LEY/BBR PR5 78 B2
LEY/BBR PR5 81 F4
LSTA FY8 49 F4
LSTA FY8 62 D3
Church Rw *PRES* PR1 7 J2
Churchside *KIRK/FR/WA* PR4 75 G1
Church St *BPOOL* FY1 2 D5
CHLY/EC PR7 91 F3 5
FTWD FY7 11 H2
KIRK/FR/WA PR4 43 F3
LEY/BBR PR5 72 A3
LEY/BBR PR5 81 G2
PLF/KEOS FY6 26 B4 1
PRES PR1 7 J3
PRES PR1 58 C3 1
Church Wk *CHLY/EC* PR7 85 H5
KIRK/FR/WA PR4 42 D1
Chysden Cl *CHLYE* PR6 87 F2 2
Cinnamon Ct *PRES* PR1 69 F4 3
Cinnamon Hill Dr North
LEY/BBR PR5 71 E3
Cinnamon Hill Dr South
LEY/BBR PR5 71 E3
Cintra Av *FUL/RIB* PR2 57 G1
Clairane Av *FUL/RIB* PR2 45 H2
Clancut La *CHLY/EC* PR7 94 C3
Clanfield *FUL/RIB* PR2 45 H1
Clara St *PRES* PR1 58 D4 2
Claremont Av *CHLY/EC* PR7 91 E3
Claremont Ct *BPOOL* FY1 28 C3 3
Claremont Pl *LSTA* FY8 49 E3 1
Claremont Rd *BPOOL* FY1 28 C3
CHLY/EC PR7 91 E5 3
Claremount Av *LEY/BBR* PR5 81 G4 1
Clarence Av *CLV/TH* FY5 20 D1
PLF/KEOS FY6 12 C1
Clarence St *CHLY/EC* PR7 91 G3 4
LEY/BBR PR5 81 G2
Clarendon Rd *BPOOL* FY1 4 D3
LSTA FY8 49 F3
Clarendon Rd North *LSTA* FY8 49 F3
Clarendon St *CHLYE* PR6 91 H3 3
PRES PR1 7 K5
Clare St *BPOOL* FY1 4 D5

Clark St *PLF/KEOS* FY6 26 D4
Claughton Av *LEY/BBR* PR5 82 B3
Clayburn Cl *CHLYE* PR6 87 G5 2
Clayton Av *LEY/BBR* PR5 80 C5
Clayton Brook Rd *LEY/BBR* PR5 79 F5
Clayton Crs *BPOOLS* FY4 38 D2
Claytongate *CHLY/EC* PR7 94 C3
Clayton Green Rd *CHLYE* PR6 83 E1
Clayton's Ga *PRES* PR1 7 G2 3
Clayton St *LEY/BBR* PR5 71 F5 1
Cleator Av *BISP* FY2 28 C1
Clegg Av *CLV/TH* FY5 20 C1
Clegg St *KIRK/FR/WA* PR4 43 E3 2
Clematis Cl *CHLY/EC* PR7 86 D4
Clevedon Rd *BPOOL* FY1 28 B3
FUL/RIB PR2 44 D4
Cleveland Av *FUL/RIB* PR2 46 D4
Cleveland Rd *LEY/BBR* PR5 81 E2
LSTA FY8 63 F3
Cleveland St *CHLY/EC* PR7 94 B4 2
Cleveleys Av *CLV/TH* FY5 16 D5
FUL/RIB PR2 45 F4
Cleveleys Rd *LEY/BBR* PR5 72 D3
Cliffe Ct *PRES* PR1 59 E3
Cliffe Dr *CHLYE* PR6 83 E4
Clifford Rd *BPOOL* FY1 2 D1
Clifford St *CHLY/EC* PR7 91 G2
Cliff Pl *BISP* FY2 24 B3
Cliff St *PRES* PR1 6 E5
Clifton Av *BPOOLE* FY3 34 A4
FUL/RIB PR2 56 D1
KIRK/FR/WA PR4 53 G5
LEY/BBR PR5 81 G4
Clifton Cl *CLV/TH* FY5 22 A3
Clifton Crs *BPOOLE* FY3 33 G3
PRES PR1 58 D1 2
Clifton Dr *BPOOLS* FY4 38 B3
LSTA FY8 62 A2
PRES PR1 6 A7
Clifton Dr North *LSTA* FY8 38 B5
Clifton Dr South *LSTA* FY8 49 E5
Clifton Gdns *LSTA* FY8 50 A5
Clifton Gv *CHLY/EC* PR7 91 E3 2
PRES PR1 46 D5
Clifton Pl *KIRK/FR/WA* PR4 54 B5
Clifton Rd *BPOOLS* FY4 34 B5
FTWD FY7 11 G3
Clifton St *BPOOL* FY1 2 C4
LSTA FY8 63 F3 5
PRES PR1 6 D6
Clinton Av *BPOOL* FY1 3 F7
Clitheroe Pl *BPOOLS* FY4 33 G5
Clitheroe Rd *LSTA* FY8 50 A5
Clitheroes La *KIRK/FR/WA* PR4 54 B5
Clitheroe St *PRES* PR1 58 D4 3
Clive Av *LSTA* FY8 49 E2
Clive Rd *PRES* PR1 57 E5
Clods Carr La *PLF/KEOS* FY6 12 D3
The Cloisters *BPOOLE* FY3 3 J4
LEY/BBR PR5 81 H2 1
The Close *CLV/TH* FY5 16 D5
CLV/TH FY5 20 D2 1
FUL/RIB PR2 47 F2
KIRK/FR/WA PR4 43 F4
KIRK/FR/WA PR4 75 H2
Clough Acre *CHLY/EC* PR7 86 D5
Clough Av *LEY/BBR* PR5 70 C3
The Clough *CHLYE* PR6 82 D1
Clovelly Av *BISP* FY2 24 C1
FUL/RIB PR2 45 G5
Clovelly Dr *PRES* PR1 68 D1
Clover Av *LSTA* FY8 49 G2
Clover Ct *BISP* FY2 25 F1
Clover Dr *KIRK/FR/WA* PR4 54 D4 1
Clover Fld *CHLYE* PR6 83 E2
Cloverfield *PRES* PR1 69 E2 2
Clover Ms *BPOOLE* FY3 3 J2
Clover Rd *CHLY/EC* PR7 90 D5
Club St *LEY/BBR* PR5 78 B2
Clydesdale Pl *LEY/BBR* PR5 80 B2
Clyde St *BPOOL* FY1 2 D1
FUL/RIB PR2 6 A1
Cobden St *CHLYE* PR6 91 H1
Cocker Av *PLF/KEOS* FY6 27 E5
Cocker La *LEY/BBR* PR5 80 B3
Cocker Rd *LEY/BBR* PR5 78 D2
Cocker Sq *BPOOL* FY1 2 C2 1
Cocker St *BPOOL* FY1 2 C2
Codale Av *BISP* FY2 24 D2
Colchester Rd *BPOOLE* FY3 33 F2
Cold Bath St *PRES* PR1 7 F1
Colebatch *FUL/RIB* PR2 45 G3 1
Colenso Rd *FUL/RIB* PR2 57 F1 4
Coleridge Av *CLV/TH* FY5 21 F1
Coleridge Rd *BPOOL* FY1 3 G2
Colesville Av *CLV/TH* FY5 21 H3
College Av *CLV/TH* FY5 20 C3
College Ct *PRES* PR1 57 H1
College Ga *CLV/TH* FY5 16 C4
Collingwood Av *BPOOLE* FY3 3 J3

LSTA FY8 49 E2
Collingwood Pl *BPOOLE* FY3 3 J2
Collingwood Rd *CHLY/EC* PR7 90 D3
Collins Av *BISP* FY2 25 E4
Collinson St *PRES* PR1 58 D2 3
Collins Rd *LEY/BBR* PR5 71 G5
Collins Rd North *LEY/BBR* PR5 71 G4
Collison Av *CHLY/EC* PR7 91 E2
Collyhurst Av *BPOOLS* FY4 39 E2
Colman Ct *PRES* PR1 6 D5
Colt House Cl *LEY/BBR* PR5 81 F5
Coltsfoot Dr *CHLYE* PR6 87 G5
Columbine Cl *CHLY/EC* PR7 86 D4 2
Colville Av *BPOOLS* FY4 38 C3 2
Colwyn Av *BPOOLS* FY4 5 K6
Colwyn Pl *FUL/RIB* PR2 44 D5
Colyton Cl *CHLYE* PR6 91 H2 3
Colyton Rd *CHLYE* PR6 91 H2
Colyton Rd East *CHLYE* PR6 91 H2 4
Comet Rd *LEY/BBR* PR5 80 B2
Commercial Rd *CHLY/EC* PR7 91 F1 2
Commercial St *BPOOLS* FY4 4 C6 1
Common Bank La *CHLY/EC* PR7 90 B3
Common Edge Rd *BPOOLS* FY4 39 G4
Commonside *LSTA* FY8 62 B2
Commonwealth Cl *LSTA* FY8 50 A3
Compley Av *PLF/KEOS* FY6 26 A5
Compley Gn *PLF/KEOS* FY6 26 A5
Compton Cl *PLF/KEOS* FY6 26 A2
Compton Gn *FUL/RIB* PR2 45 F1
Conder Av *CLV/TH* FY5 21 F2
Conder Rd *FUL/RIB* PR2 56 B2
Condor Gv *BPOOL* FY1 5 G3
LSTA FY8 48 D3
Congleton Cl *BPOOLS* FY4 33 H4
Congress St *CHLY/EC* PR7 91 F1 3
The Conifers *KIRK/FR/WA* PR4 43 F3
PLF/KEOS FY6 23 F2
Coniston Av *CHLY/EC* PR7 90 A1
CLV/TH FY5 21 H2
FTWD FY7 11 E2
FUL/RIB PR2 57 G1
LSTA FY8 49 F1
PLF/KEOS FY6 23 G2
PLF/KEOS FY6 25 H3
Coniston Dr *LEY/BBR* PR5 71 F4
Coniston Rd *BPOOLS* FY4 32 C5
CHLY/EC PR7 91 E4
FUL/RIB PR2 46 D4
Connaught Rd *PRES* PR1 6 E7
Consett Av *CLV/TH* FY5 17 E4
Constable Av *LEY/BBR* PR5 77 F2 3
Constable St *PRES* PR1 7 K1
Convent Cl *LEY/BBR* PR5 71 E5 1
LEY/BBR PR5 81 H2 2
Convent Crs *BPOOLE* FY3 29 G2
Conway Av *BPOOLE* FY3 29 H3
CLV/TH FY5 20 D2
LEY/BBR PR5 70 A5
LEY/BBR PR5 81 H4
Conway Cl *CHLY/EC* PR7 90 B1
Conway Ct *LEY/BBR* PR5 72 C4
Conway Dr *FUL/RIB* PR2 45 F2
Conway Rd *CHLY/EC* PR7 88 B3 2
Cookson Cl *KIRK/FR/WA* PR4 54 B5 2
Cookson Rd *CLV/TH* FY5 21 G1
Cookson St *BPOOL* FY1 2 E3
The Coombes *FUL/RIB* PR2 46 A3 1
Co-operative St *LEY/BBR* PR5 78 B1
Cooper Hill Cl *LEY/BBR* PR5 71 E1 2
Cooper Hill Dr *LEY/BBR* PR5 71 E1
Cooper Rd *PRES* PR1 6 D3
Cooper's La *CHLY/EC* PR7 92 A5
Cooper's Wy *BPOOL* FY1 3 G1
Coop St *BPOOL* FY1 2 D7
Coote La *KIRK/FR/WA* PR4 77 E2
Copeland Pl *LSTA* FY8 63 G2 1
Cop La *FTWD* FY7 11 G2
PRES PR1 69 E1
Copper Beeches *PRES* PR1 69 G4 1
Copperwood Wy *CHLY/EC* PR7 90 C3
Coppice Cl *CHLYE* PR6 91 H1
The Coppice *FUL/RIB* PR2 44 D4
KIRK/FR/WA PR4 43 E2
KIRK/FR/WA PR4 74 B2 1
Coppins Gn *PLF/KEOS* FY6 30 C1
Coppull Hall La *CHLY/EC* PR7 94 D4
Coppull Rd *CHLY/EC* PR7 94 C1
Copse Rd *FTWD* FY7 11 G3
The Copse *CHLY/EC* PR7 95 E1
Copthurst La *CHLYE* PR6 87 H1
Coral Cl *BPOOLS* FY4 33 G4
Corbridge Cl *BPOOLS* FY4 39 G1 3
PLF/KEOS FY6 26 A2
Corcas La *PLF/KEOS* FY6 18 D1
Corncroft *PRES* PR1 69 F3 2
The Corners *CLV/TH* FY5 16 C5
Cornfield *KIRK/FR/WA* PR4 44 B2 1
Cornflower Cl *CHLYE* PR6 87 G5 3
Cornford Rd *BPOOLS* FY4 33 H5

Cornthwaite Rd *FUL/RIB* PR2 45 H5 2
Cornwall Av *BISP* FY2 24 C5
CLV/TH FY5 17 E5
Cornwall Pl *BPOOLE* FY3 33 H3
Coronation Crs *PRES* PR1 58 C4
Coronation Rd *CLV/TH* FY5 20 C2
KIRK/FR/WA PR4 43 E3
LSTA FY8 62 A3
Coronation St *BPOOL* FY1 2 D5 3
Corporation St *BPOOL* FY1 2 C4
CHLYE PR6 91 G1
PRES PR1 7 G4
Corrib Rd *BISP* FY2 24 D5
Cotswold Av *CHLY/EC* PR7 90 A1
Cotswold Cl *CHLY/EC* PR7 88 B4
Cotswold Rd *BISP* FY2 28 D1
CHLY/EC PR7 91 F4
LSTA FY8 63 H1
Cottage Flds *CHLY/EC* PR7 91 E5
Cottage La *LEY/BBR* PR5 71 G4
Cottage St *PRES* PR1 7 J2 1
Cottam Av *FUL/RIB* PR2 44 C4
Cottam Cl *LSTA* FY8 49 F1
Cottam Gn *KIRK/FR/WA* PR4 44 B2
Cottam Hall La *FUL/RIB* PR2 44 C3
KIRK/FR/WA PR4 44 B3 1
Cottam La *FUL/RIB* PR2 44 D5
KIRK/FR/WA PR4 74 D3
Cottam Pl *PLF/KEOS* FY6 26 A5 1
Cottam St *CHLY/EC* PR7 91 F4 2
Cottam Wy *KIRK/FR/WA* PR4 44 B4
Cotton Ct *PRES* PR1 7 K2
Coulston Av *BISP* FY2 24 B4
Countess Cl *KIRK/FR/WA* PR4 43 E1 1
Countess Crs *BISP* FY2 24 C4
Countess Wy *CHLY/EC* PR7 86 A5
Countessway *LEY/BBR* PR5 71 F5 2
Coupe Gn *LEY/BBR* PR5 72 D2
Courtfield Av *BISP* FY2 28 D2
The Court *FUL/RIB* PR2 45 F1
Coventry St *CHLY/EC* PR7 91 F4 3
The Covert *CLV/TH* FY5 17 F5
The Cove *CLV/TH* FY5 16 C5
Coveway Av *BPOOLE* FY3 3 J3
Cowley Rd *BPOOLS* FY4 33 F5
FUL/RIB PR2 47 F5
Cowling Brow *CHLYE* PR6 91 H3
Cowling La *LEY/BBR* PR5 80 C3
Cowslip Wy *CHLYE* PR6 87 G5 4
Cow Well La *CHLYE* PR6 83 E4
Crabtree Av *PRES* PR1 68 D3 1
Crabtree Orch *CLV/TH* FY5 21 H1 2
Crabtree Rd *CLV/TH* FY5 21 H1
Cragg St *BPOOL* FY1 2 C7
Craigflower Ct *LEY/BBR* PR5 79 F2 1
Crake Av *FTWD* FY7 10 C4
Cranborne St *PRES* PR1 58 D4
Cranbourne Dr *CHLYE* PR6 91 H3
Cranbourne Gv *CLV/TH* FY5 22 C5 1
Cranbourne St *CHLYE* PR6 91 G3
LEY/BBR PR5 78 B1 3
Cranbrook Av *BISP* FY2 24 D2
Cranleigh Av *BISP* FY2 24 C4
Cranwell Ct *KIRK/FR/WA* PR4 42 D3
Craven Cl *FUL/RIB* PR2 46 A1 1
Crawford Av *BISP* FY2 24 D2
CHLY/EC PR7 91 E3
LEY/BBR PR5 81 F4
PRES PR1 59 G2 2
Crescent Rd *PLF/KEOS* FY6 26 C3 1
Crescent St *PRES* PR1 58 D2 4
The Crescent *BPOOLS* FY4 38 B1
CHLY/EC PR7 87 F5
FTWD FY7 17 E1
FUL/RIB PR2 56 A2
FUL/RIB PR2 56 D1
KIRK/FR/WA PR4 65 E2
LEY/BBR PR5 71 G4
LEY/BBR PR5 77 H1
PLF/KEOS FY6 13 F2
PLF/KEOS FY6 26 A3
Cresswood Av *CLV/TH* FY5 20 D3
Crestway *BPOOLE* FY3 29 F4
Creswell Av *FUL/RIB* PR2 44 C5
Crichton Pl *BPOOLS* FY4 38 B3
Cricketers Gn *CHLY/EC* PR7 88 A3
Cripple Gate La *LEY/BBR* PR5 73 H2
Croasdale Av *FUL/RIB* PR2 47 F3
Croasdale Dr *CLV/TH* FY5 21 F1
Crocus Fld *LEY/BBR* PR5 81 F5
Croft Bank *PRES* PR1 69 F3
Croft Butts La *KIRK/FR/WA* PR4 54 C5
Crofters Gn *CHLY/EC* PR7 85 H4
PRES PR1 57 H1
Crofters Ms *BPOOL* FY1 2 E1
Croftgate *FUL/RIB* PR2 46 A3
Croft Meadow *LEY/BBR* PR5 79 F3
Crofton Av *BISP* FY2 24 D2
Croft Rd *CHLYE* PR6 91 H3
Crofts Cl *KIRK/FR/WA* PR4 43 G3
Croft St *PRES* PR1 6 D2 1
The Croft *CHLY/EC* PR7 85 G4
CHLY/EC PR7 88 B3
CLV/TH FY5 20 D2 2
FTWD FY7 10 D4
LEY/BBR PR5 73 G4 1
LSTA FY8 49 H2
PLF/KEOS FY6 26 B5 1
Croft Wy *CLV/TH* FY5 22 A4
Crombleholme Rd *PRES* PR1 59 F2 3
Cromer Pl *FUL/RIB* PR2 44 D4 2
Cromer Rd *BISP* FY2 25 E3
LSTA FY8 49 G2
Cromford Wk *PRES* PR1 58 D3 1
Crompton Av *BPOOLS* FY4 39 E1
Crompton St *PRES* PR1 58 D2
Cromwell Av *PRES* PR1 69 F3 3
Cromwell Rd *BPOOL* FY1 28 C2
FUL/RIB PR2 47 E5
PRES PR1 69 E3
Cromwell St *PRES* PR1 58 B2 2
Crookall Cl *FTWD* FY7 11 F4 2
Crook Dale La *PLF/KEOS* FY6 19 H2
Crooked La *PRES* PR1 7 J2 2
Crookings La *PRES* PR1 56 D5
Crook St *CHLY/EC* PR7 91 E5
PRES PR1 58 C3
Cropper Rd *BPOOLS* FY4 39 H1
Crosby Gv *BPOOLE* FY3 33 F2 3
Crosby Pl *FUL/RIB* PR2 44 D4
Crosby Rd *LSTA* FY8 49 F2
Crosier Wk *KIRK/FR/WA* PR4 44 B3 2
Crosland Rd North *LSTA* FY8 49 F2
Crosland Rd South *LSTA* FY8 49 G3
Cross Brow Preston Rd
CHLY/EC PR7 89 H2
Crosse Hall La *CHLYE* PR6 91 H3
Cross Green Rd *FUL/RIB* PR2 45 H2 1
Cross Halls *PRES* PR1 69 E3
The Crossing *LEY/BBR* PR5 73 G4
Cross Keys Dr *CHLYE* PR6 83 F5
Crossland Rd *BPOOLS* FY4 5 K6
Cross St *BPOOL* FY1 2 D1
CHLY/EC PR7 91 F1 4
FTWD FY7 11 H1 2
LEY/BBR PR5 81 G2 4
LSTA FY8 48 D3
PRES PR1 7 H4
Cross Wy *CLV/TH* FY5 16 D5
Croston La *CHLY/EC* PR7 93 G4
Croston Rd *LEY/BBR* PR5 77 E3
Crowder Av *CLV/TH* FY5 21 H2 2
Crowell Wy *LEY/BBR* PR5 71 F3 2
Crow Hills Rd *PRES* PR1 56 D5
Crowle St *PRES* PR1 59 E2 8
Crown La *FTWD* FY7 11 H2
Crownlee *PRES* PR1 68 D3
Crown St *CHLY/EC* PR7 91 F2
LEY/BBR PR5 81 G1
PRES PR1 7 H1
Croyde Rd *LSTA* FY8 61 G1
Croydon Rd *BPOOLE* FY3 29 E3 4
Crummock Pl *BPOOLS* FY4 34 A4 2
Crummock Rd *PRES* PR1 59 H2 1
Crystal Gv *LSTA* FY8 49 E3
Crystal Rd *BPOOL* FY1 4 C5
CLV/TH FY5 17 H4
Cudworth Rd *LSTA* FY8 49 F2
Cuerdale La *LEY/BBR* PR5 71 G1
Cuerden Av *LEY/BBR* PR5 80 C5
Cuerden Cl *LEY/BBR* PR5 78 B5
Cuerden Ri *LEY/BBR* PR5 77 H2
Cuerden St *CHLYE* PR6 91 H3 4
Cuerden Wy *LEY/BBR* PR5 78 A1
Culbeck La *CHLY/EC* PR7 85 E4
Culham Cl *CLV/TH* FY5 21 G2 3
Cumberland Av *BPOOL* FY1 5 G1
CLV/TH FY5 16 D5
LEY/BBR PR5 80 D5
Cumbrian Av *BPOOLE* FY3 3 J1
Cunliffe Rd *BPOOL* FY1 5 H3
Cunliffe St *CHLY/EC* PR7 91 F3
PRES PR1 7 K1
Cunnery Meadow *LEY/BBR* PR5 82 B3
Cunningham Av *CHLY/EC* PR7 90 D4
Curate St *CHLYE* PR6 91 G1
Curlew Cl *CLV/TH* FY5 17 F5
LEY/BBR PR5 80 B5
Curtis Dr *FTWD* FY7 10 D3 1
Curwen St *PRES* PR1 58 D2 5
Curzon Rd *LSTA* FY8 49 G4
PLF/KEOS FY6 26 C4
Custom House La *FTWD* FY7 12 A1 1
Customs Wy *FUL/RIB* PR2 6 A1
Cypress Av *CLV/TH* FY5 21 E2
Cypress Cl *FUL/RIB* PR2 47 H4 1
LEY/BBR PR5 82 B2
Cypress Gv *BPOOLE* FY3 3 H1
LEY/BBR PR5 77 G1
Cyprus Av *LSTA* FY8 61 H2

D

Daggers Hall La *BPOOLS* FY4 5 K7
Daggers La *PLF/KEOS* FY6 13 F3
Daisy Bank Cl *LEY/BBR* PR5 80 C3
Daisy Cft *FUL/RIB* PR2 56 A3
Daisyfields *KIRK/FR/WA* PR4 44 C1 2
Daisy Fold *CHLYE* PR6 87 H5
Daisy Hill Fold *CHLY/EC* PR7 90 A1
Daisy La *PRES* PR1 46 D5
Daisy Meadow *LEY/BBR* PR5 79 E4
Dalby Cl *CLV/TH* FY5 21 F5 4
PRES PR1 47 E5
Dale Av *CHLY/EC* PR7 90 A1
Dalegarth Cl *BPOOLS* FY4 34 A4 3
Dalehead Rd *LEY/BBR* PR5 85 G1
Dale Ms *BPOOL* FY1 4 C1
Dalesford Cl *CLV/TH* FY5 22 A4 1
Dale St *BPOOL* FY1 4 C1
PRES PR1 58 C3
Dale Vw *CHLY/EC* PR7 95 F1
Dalewood Av *BPOOLS* FY4 5 J5
Dalkeith Av *BPOOLE* FY3 33 G3
Dallas St *PRES* PR1 45 H5
Dalmore Rd *FUL/RIB* PR2 44 D5
Dalton Av *BPOOLS* FY4 38 D3
Dalton St *LSTA* FY8 48 D3
Dane Hall La *CHLY/EC* PR7 84 C5
Danesbury Pl *BPOOL* FY1 3 F4
Danes Cl *KIRK/FR/WA* PR4 43 G3
Danes Dr *LEY/BBR* PR5 71 E5
Danesway *LEY/BBR* PR5 71 E5
PRES PR1 68 D2 2
Danewerke St *PRES* PR1 7 K1 1
Danson Gdns *BISP* FY2 28 D2 2
Darbishire Rd *FTWD* FY7 11 F1
Dark La *CHLYE* PR6 87 H1
Darley Av *BPOOLS* FY4 38 D1
Darlington St *CHLY/EC* PR7 94 A4
Dartmouth Cl
KIRK/FR/WA PR4 42 D3 3
Dart St *FUL/RIB* PR2 6 A1
Darwen St *PRES* PR1 58 D4 4
Darwen Vw *LEY/BBR* PR5 71 F1
Daub Hall La *LEY/BBR* PR5 72 D4
Dauntesey Av *BPOOLE* FY3 29 G4
Davenport Av *BISP* FY2 24 C2
Daventry Av *BISP* FY2 24 B3 3
Dawber's La *CHLY/EC* PR7 84 D5
Dawlish Av *BPOOLE* FY3 29 F2
Dawlish Pl *FUL/RIB* PR2 44 D5 1
Dawnay Rd *FUL/RIB* PR2 47 F5
Dawson La *CHLYE* PR6 82 B5
Dawson Pl *LEY/BBR* PR5 78 D2
Dawson Rd *LSTA* FY8 49 F2
Dayton Pl *BPOOLS* FY4 38 C2 1
Deal Pl *LSTA* FY8 49 F2 1
Dean Ct *FTWD* FY7 16 D1
Deansgate *BPOOL* FY1 2 D4
Dean St *BPOOLS* FY4 4 C7
LEY/BBR PR5 71 F5
Deborah Av *FUL/RIB* PR2 46 B1
Deepdale Av *PLF/KEOS* FY6 25 H2
Deepdale Mill St *PRES* PR1 58 C2 3
Deepdale Rd *BPOOLS* FY4 34 A5
FTWD FY7 11 G3 1
PRES PR1 46 C5
Deepdale St *PRES* PR1 58 C3
Deerfold *CHLY/EC* PR7 87 E5
Deerhurst Rd *CLV/TH* FY5 21 E5
Deeside *BPOOLS* FY4 38 D3
Dee St *LSTA* FY8 49 E5 4
Deighton Av *LEY/BBR* PR5 81 F4 4
Deighton Rd *CHLY/EC* PR7 91 E4 3
De Lacy St *FUL/RIB* PR2 57 G1
Delamere Pl *CHLYE* PR6 91 G2
Delany Dr *KIRK/FR/WA* PR4 54 A5
Delaware Rd *BPOOLE* FY3 29 E1
Delaware St *PRES* PR1 58 D2
The Dell *FUL/RIB* PR2 45 G1
The Dellway *KIRK/FR/WA* PR4 68 A3
Delphene Av *BISP* FY2 24 D1
CLV/TH FY5 20 D5 1
Delph La *CHLY/EC* PR7 90 A4
Delph Wy *CHLYE* PR6 83 F5
Delta La *FTWD* FY7 11 G2 1
Denbigh Av *CLV/TH* FY5 21 E3
Denbigh Cl *LEY/BBR* PR5 81 G3
Denby Cl *LEY/BBR* PR5 70 D3 2
Denebank *BISP* FY2 24 D2 2
Deneway Av *BPOOLE* FY3 29 F4
Denford Av *LEY/BBR* PR5 81 G4 2
LSTA FY8 61 G2
Denham La *CHLYE* PR6 83 H3
Denham Wy *FTWD* FY7 11 F4
Denholme Gv *BISP* FY2 25 E2 1
Denmark Rd *LSTA* FY8 62 B1
Denstone Av *BISP* FY2 24 D3
Denville Av *CLV/TH* FY5 2
Denville Rd *PRES* PR1 58
Depot Rd *BPOOLE* FY3 2
Derbe Rd *LSTA* FY8 6
Derby Rd *BPOOL* FY1 2
CLV/TH FY5 2
FUL/RIB PR2 4
KIRK/FR/WA PR4 4
LSTA FY8 6
PLF/KEOS FY6 2
Derby Sq *PRES* PR1 59
Derby St *LEY/BBR* PR5 8
PRES PR1
Derek Rd *CHLYE* PR6 8
Derry Rd *FUL/RIB* PR2 4
Derwent Av *FTWD* FY7 1
Derwent Cl *KIRK/FR/WA* PR4 5
Derwent Dr *KIRK/FR/WA* PR4 5
Derwent Pl *CLV/TH* FY5 20
PLF/KEOS FY6 30
Derwent Rd *CHLY/EC* PR7 9
LSTA FY8 4
Derwentwater Pl *PRES* PR1 58
Dever Av *LEY/BBR* PR5 8
Devona Av *BPOOLS* FY4 33
Devon Av *FTWD* FY7 1
Devon Cl *LEY/BBR* PR5 7
Devonport Cl *LEY/BBR* PR5 7
Devonport Wy *CHLYE* PR6 9
Devonshire Av *CLV/TH* FY5 2
Devonshire Ms *CLV/TH* FY5 21
Devonshire Pl *PRES* PR1 59
Devonshire Rd *BISP* FY2 2
BPOOLE FY3 2
CHLY/EC PR7 9
FUL/RIB PR2 46
LSTA FY8 48
Devonshire Sq *BPOOL* FY1
Devon St *BPOOLS* FY4 5
Dewhurst Av *BPOOLS* FY4 3
Dewhurst Rw *LEY/BBR* PR5 7
Dewhurst St *PRES* PR1 57
Dianne Rd *CLV/TH* FY5 2
Dibbs Pocket *KIRK/FR/WA* PR4 54
Dicconson Ter *LSTA* FY8 63
Dickens Rd *CHLY/EC* PR7 9
Dickie's La *BPOOLS* FY4 3
Dickie's La South *BPOOLS* FY4 3
Dickson Av *PRES* PR1 5
Dickson Hey *KIRK/FR/WA* PR4 7
Dickson Rd *BPOOL* FY1
Dickson St *PRES* PR1 58
Digham Av *BISP* FY2 2
Dinckley Gv *BPOOL* FY1
Dingle Av *BPOOLE* FY3 2
The Dingle *FUL/RIB* PR2 4
Dinmore Av *BPOOLE* FY3 2
Dinmore Pl *BPOOLE* FY3 29
Division La *BPOOLS* FY4 3
Dob Brow *CHLY/EC* PR7 9
Dob La *KIRK/FR/WA* PR4 7
Dobson Av *LSTA* FY8 4
Dock Av *FTWD* FY7 1
Dock Rd *LSTA* FY8 6
Dock St *FTWD* FY7 11
Dodd Wy *LEY/BBR* PR5 7
Dodgeons Cl *PLF/KEOS* FY6 26
Dodgson Pl *PRES* PR1 5
Dodgson Rd *PRES* PR1 5
Dodson Rd *BPOOLE* FY3 2
Dole La *CHLY/EC* PR7 91
Doncaster Rd *BPOOLE* FY3 3
Donnington Rd *LSTA* FY8 4
PLF/KEOS FY6 2
Don St *LSTA* FY8 4
Doodstone Av *LEY/BBR* PR5 7
Doodstone Cl *LEY/BBR* PR5 70
Doodstone Nook *LEY/BBR* PR5 7
Dorchester Cl *CLV/TH* FY5 22
Dorchester Rd *BPOOL* FY1 2
Doris St *CHLYE* PR6 9
Dorman Rd *FUL/RIB* PR2 4
Dorothy Av *LEY/BBR* PR5 8
Dorritt Rd *BPOOLS* FY4 3
Dorset Av *CLV/TH* FY5 1
Dorset Rd *LSTA* FY8 4
PRES PR1 58
Dorset St *BPOOLS* FY4
Douglas Av *BPOOLE* FY3
PLF/KEOS FY6 1
Douglas Cl *LEY/BBR* PR5 78
Douglas Ct *FUL/RIB* PR2 45
Douglas Dr *KIRK/FR/WA* PR4 5
Douglas Pl *FTWD* FY7 1
Douglas Rd *FUL/RIB* PR2 4
Douglas Rd North *FUL/RIB* PR2 4
Douglas St *FUL/RIB* PR2 5
LSTA FY8 48
The Doultons *LEY/BBR* PR5 70
Dove Av *PRES* PR1 6

e Cl CLV/TH FY5 21 F3
ecote CHLYE PR6 82 D1
edale Av BPOOLE FY3 34 A3 2
/TH FY5 21 G1
L/RIB PR2 44 D4
edale Cl FUL/RIB PR2 44 D4
Y/BBR PR5 85 F1
er Cl KIRK/FR/WA PR4 53 G4
er Ct BPOOL FY1 5 J4
er Gdns PLF/KEOS FY6 25 H2
er Rd BPOOL FY1 5 H5
TA FY8 49 F3
e St LSTA FY8 48 D5
ES PR1 58 C2
etree Cl PRES PR1 70 C3 1
bridge KIRK/FR/WA PR4 43 G4
bridge Wy KIRK/FR/WA PR4 43 F3
nham Pl BPOOLS FY4 38 B4 1
TA FY8 50 A5 1
nham Rd LEY/BBR PR5 80 B4
ning Ct GAR/LONG PR3 36 B2
ning St PRES PR1 59 F3
Downs PLF/KEOS FY6 26 B3
e Cl LSTA FY8 49 E2
elowe Av BPOOLS FY4 39 F2
es Cft FUL/RIB PR2 45 F5
es Hollow LEY/BBR PR5 71 E2 1
ers Av CHLY/EC PR7 88 B4
cot Av BPOOLE FY3 29 G2 1
coll St PRES PR1 58 C3 2
Drive FUL/RIB PR2 46 B4
RK/FR/WA PR4 74 B1
Y/BBR PR5 71 G1
sfield Rd FTWD FY7 11 F1
nacre La East
RK/FR/WA PR4 74 D3
nacre La West
RK/FR/WA PR4 74 B3
mmond Av BPOOLE FY3 3 J1
burgh Av BPOOLE FY3 33 F2
den Rd FTWD FY7 11 G2
hess Dr BISP FY2 24 B4
ny Av FUL/RIB PR2 46 C4
e Pl PRES PR1 59 G2
k St GAR/LONG PR3 9 G4
dle La LEY/BBR PR5 71 E4 1
don Av FTWD FY7 10 D5
ey Av BISP FY2 28 D1
dale Ct BPOOLS FY4 39 F3 3
es Meadow FUL/RIB PR2 44 D3
e St BPOOL FY1 4 D5
LY/EC PR7 91 F4
Y/BBR PR5 78 B2
RES PR1 58 C4 5
barton Cl BPOOLS FY4 39 G2 1
fries Cl BISP FY2 25 F2
bar Cl BPOOLS FY4 39 G2
bar Dr FUL/RIB PR2 45 G4
bar Rd FUL/RIB PR2 44 C5
can Av BISP FY2 24 C1
can Cl LSTA FY8 48 D1
can Pl FTWD FY7 11 E2 3
donald St PRES PR1 59 E3
elt Rd BPOOL FY1 5 G4
es Av BPOOLS FY4 38 B3
ham Dr CHLYE PR6 87 F2
kirk Av FUL/RIB PR2 45 F4
kirk La LEY/BBR PR5 80 C4
lin Cl CLV/TH FY5 17 G4 2
mail Av BPOOLE FY3 33 F3 2
more St PRES PR1 58 C3
oon Cl FUL/RIB PR2 44 C4
robin Dr CHLY/EC PR7 90 A1
scar Dr CHLYE PR6 91 H1
sop Cl BPOOL FY1 5 H5
Y/BBR PR5 78 C1 6
sop Rd FUL/RIB PR2 47 E4
vegan Cl BPOOLS FY4 39 G2 2
nam Av CLV/TH FY5 21 E1
TA FY8 49 E4 2
nam Rd BPOOL FY1 3 G4
ey Rd BPOOL FY1 5 F4
ton La FUL/RIB PR2 37 G4
AR/LONG PR3 36 D4
ch Barn Cl CHLY/EC PR7 87 E5
ton Rd BPOOLE FY3 3 H3
bury Hall Rd CHLY/EC PR7 95 G1
r St KIRK/FR/WA PR4 42 D3
nock Rd PRES PR1 59 E2 9
nock Rd North PRES PR1 59 E2 10

E

Eagles PLF/KEOS FY6 26 C2
ont Pl FTWD FY7 10 D4
s Av LEY/BBR PR5 78 B1 4
St PRES PR1 7 H2
sway BPOOLE FY3 30 B5
Earls Wy CHLY/EC PR7 86 A5
Earnshaw Dr LEY/BBR PR5 80 C3
Easington Crs BPOOLE FY3 29 G2
Eastbank Av BPOOLS FY4 39 G1
East Bank Rd LSTA FY8 61 E1
East Beach LSTA FY8 63 G3
East Boothroyden BPOOL FY1 28 B2 1
Eastbourne Cl FUL/RIB PR2 44 C3 1
Eastbourne Rd BPOOLS FY4 38 B2
East Cecil St LSTA FY8 63 E3
East Cliff PRES PR1 7 G5
East Cliffe LSTA FY8 63 G3 2
East Cliff Rd PRES PR1 7 G5
East Ct CLV/TH FY5 16 D4
Eastgate FUL/RIB PR2 45 G3
Eastham St PRES PR1 57 H2 3
East Holme LSTA FY8 63 G1
Eastlands LEY/BBR PR5 80 B5
East Md BPOOLE FY3 5 K2
Easton Cl FUL/RIB PR2 47 E2
East Park Dr BPOOLE FY3 33 F2
Eastpines Dr CLV/TH FY5 21 E4
East Rd FUL/RIB PR2 46 B4
Eastside BPOOLS FY4 33 F5
East Sq KIRK/FR/WA PR4 74 B1 1
East St LEY/BBR PR5 78 B2 1
LEY/BBR PR5 81 G1
PRES PR1 7 K1
East Ter CHLYE PR6 86 B3
East Topping St BPOOL FY1 2 D4
East Vw LEY/BBR PR5 58 D5
PRES PR1 58 B2
East Wy CHLYE PR6 91 G2
Eastway FUL/RIB PR2 37 F5
GAR/LONG PR3 36 B5
KIRK/FR/WA PR4 54 A5
Eastwood Av BPOOLE FY3 29 E2 4
FTWD FY7 11 F3 1
Eastwood Rd LEY/BBR PR5 81 E3
Eaton Av BPOOL FY1 5 F5
Eaton Ct LSTA FY8 49 F5
Eaton Pl KIRK/FR/WA PR4 42 D3
Eaton Wy PLF/KEOS FY6 30 C2
Eaves Green Rd CHLY/EC PR7 91 E5
Eaves La CHLYE PR6 91 H3
FUL/RIB PR2 45 H5
Eaves Rd LSTA FY8 49 G2
Eaves St BPOOL FY1 2 C1
Eaveswood Cl LEY/BBR PR5 71 G5 1
Ecclesgate Rd BPOOLS FY4 39 F3
Eccles St PRES PR1 58 D2 7
Eccleston Rd BPOOL FY1 5 H5
Ecroyd Rd FUL/RIB PR2 57 F1 5
Ecroyd St LEY/BBR PR5 81 F3
Edale Cl LEY/BBR PR5 81 F5
Eddington Rd LSTA FY8 61 H2
Eddleston Cl BPOOLE FY3 30 B5
Edelston Rd BPOOL FY1 2 E2
Eden Av FTWD FY7 10 D4
LSTA FY8 62 C3
Edenfield Av PLF/KEOS FY6 26 D5
Eden St BPOOL FY1 2 E3
LEY/BBR PR5 81 F4
Edenvale Av BISP FY2 24 B3
Edenway FUL/RIB PR2 45 G1
Edgefield CHLY/EC PR7 87 E5 1
Edgehill Cl FUL/RIB PR2 45 G4
Edgehill Crs LEY/BBR PR5 80 D2
Edgehill Dr FUL/RIB PR2 45 G4 2
Edgeway Pl CLV/TH FY5 22 A3 1
Edgeway Rd BPOOLS FY4 39 E2
Edinburgh Cl LEY/BBR PR5 81 H3
Edmondsen Pl FTWD FY7 11 F4 3
Edmonton Pl BISP FY2 25 F4 1
Edmund St PRES PR1 58 C3
Edward St BPOOL FY1 2 D4
CHLYE PR6 91 G3
CLV/TH FY5 17 H5
LEY/BBR PR5 70 D1
LEY/BBR PR5 78 B1
LEY/BBR PR5 81 F4 5
LSTA FY8 49 F4
PRES PR1 7 G2
Edwell Av BPOOLS FY4 5 G7
Edwinstowe Rd LSTA FY8 50 A5
Egan St PRES PR1 7 K1 2
Egbert St PRES PR1 58 B2
Egerton Gv CHLY/EC PR7 91 E4
Egerton Rd BPOOL FY1 28 B3
FUL/RIB PR2 56 D2
LEY/BBR PR5 81 E2
Egremont Av CLV/TH FY5 16 D4
Eider Cl CLV/TH FY5 17 F4
Eildon Dr PLF/KEOS FY6 30 B1
Elaine Av BPOOLS FY4 33 F4
Elbow St CHLY/EC PR7 91 F3
Elcho St PRES PR1 58 B1
Elderberry Cl CLV/TH FY5 17 F4 4
Elder Cl CHLYE PR6 83 F2 4
FUL/RIB PR2 47 E2
KIRK/FR/WA PR4 53 G5
Elderwood Av CLV/TH FY5 21 H5
Eldon St CHLYE PR6 91 G3
PRES PR1 57 H1
Elgin Pl BPOOLE FY3 29 G2 2
Elgin St PRES PR1 58 B1
Elijah St PRES PR1 59 E3 2
Elizabeth Cl BPOOLE FY3 30 B5
Elizabeth Ct PLF/KEOS FY6 26 B4 2
Elizabeth St BPOOL FY1 3 F3
FTWD FY7 11 H1
PRES PR1 7 H1
Elkfield Dr BPOOLE FY3 29 G1
Elland Pl BPOOL FY1 4 D4
Ellen Ct PRES PR1 58 A1
Ellen St LEY/BBR PR5 71 F5
PRES PR1 57 H2
Ellerbeck Av FUL/RIB PR2 47 F3 2
Ellerbeck Rd CLV/TH FY5 20 C2
Ellerslie Rd FUL/RIB PR2 57 E2
Ellesmere Av CLV/TH FY5 22 B3
Ellesmere Rd BPOOLS FY4 5 J6
Elletson St PLF/KEOS FY6 26 B3
Elliott Cl PRES PR1 57 H1 4
Elliott St PRES PR1 57 H2 4
Elliott Wk PRES PR1 57 H1 5
Ellisland BPOOLS FY4 34 A4
Elm Av BPOOLE FY3 3 J5
FUL/RIB PR2 56 C1
KIRK/FR/WA PR4 53 F5
PLF/KEOS FY6 26 B4
Elmbank Av CLV/TH FY5 20 C5
Elm Dr LEY/BBR PR5 71 G5 2
Elmfield Dr LEY/BBR PR5 79 F3 1
Elm Gv CHLYE PR6 87 H5
FUL/RIB PR2 59 F1
KIRK/FR/WA PR4 43 F1
LEY/BBR PR5 82 A1
Elmhurst Rd LSTA FY8 49 H3
Elmridge Crs BISP FY2 25 F4 2
Elms Av CLV/TH FY5 21 E2
LSTA FY8 62 C3
Elmside Cl CLV/TH FY5 22 B2 1
Elmsley St PRES PR1 45 H5
The Elms CHLYE PR6 83 F2
Elm St FTWD FY7 11 G2
Elmswood Cl LSTA FY8 62 D2
Elmwood CHLY/EC PR7 91 E1
Elmwood Av LEY/BBR PR5 80 D3
PLF/KEOS FY6 13 F2
Elmwood Dr CLV/TH FY5 22 A3 2
PRES PR1 69 E2
Elsby Av CLV/TH FY5 22 A4
Elsinore Cl FTWD FY7 11 F1 1
Elston Av BPOOLE FY3 29 G2 3
Elswick Pl BPOOLS FY4 39 E3 2
LSTA FY8 49 H3
Elswick Rd FUL/RIB PR2 56 B2
LEY/BBR PR5 80 C4 1
Elterwater PLF/KEOS FY6 12 C1 1
Elterwater Pl BPOOLE FY3 34 A3
Elton St FUL/RIB PR2 57 F2 6
Elvaston Wy PLF/KEOS FY6 26 A2
Emerald Cl CLV/TH FY5 21 F5
Emerson Av BPOOLS FY4 38 D1
Emerson Rd PRES PR1 59 E1
Emily St LEY/BBR PR5 77 F1
Emmanuel St PRES PR1 57 G1
Emmett St PRES PR1 58 A2 4
Emnie La LEY/BBR PR5 84 B1
Empire Gv BPOOLE FY3 3 G1
Empress Av FUL/RIB PR2 45 H4 2
Empress Dr BISP FY2 28 B1
Empress Wy CHLY/EC PR7 86 B5
Endeavour Cl FUL/RIB PR2 57 E4
Enderley Ct CLV/TH FY5 22 A3
Endsleigh Gdns BPOOLS FY4 38 D2
Enfield Cl CHLY/EC PR7 88 B4
Enfield Rd BPOOL FY1 28 C3
England Av BISP FY2 24 C3
English Martyrs' Pl PRES PR1 58 A1 6
Ennerdale Av FTWD FY7 10 C5
Ennerdale Cl LEY/BBR PR5 81 F5
Ennerdale Dr LEY/BBR PR5 71 F1
Ennerdale Rd BPOOLS FY4 34 A4
CHLY/EC PR7 90 D4
Enterprise Wy FTWD FY7 17 G3
Ephraim St PRES PR1 58 D4 5
Epping Cl BISP FY2 25 E2
Epping Pl CHLYE PR6 91 G2
Epsom Rd CLV/TH FY5 21 F4
Erdington Rd BPOOL FY1 4 E1
Erith Gv BISP FY2 24 C2
Erskine Rd CHLYE PR6 91 H1
Esher Pond FUL/RIB PR2 45 F2
Esk Av FTWD FY7 10 D4
Eskdale Av FTWD FY7 10 D5
Eskdale Cl BPOOLS FY4 33 F4
FUL/RIB PR2 37 E5
Eskdale Dr KIRK/FR/WA PR4 43 E1
Eskdale Rd LEY/BBR PR5 81 G5
Eskham Cl KIRK/FR/WA PR4 42 C2
Esplanade PLF/KEOS FY6 12 B1
PRES PR1 70 C1
The Esplanade FTWD FY7 11 G1
Essex Pl BISP FY2 25 F5
Essex St PRES PR1 58 B2
Eton Pk FUL/RIB PR2 46 D3
Ettrick Av FTWD FY7 10 D3
Euston St PRES PR1 6 D3
Euxton Hall Gdns CHLY/EC PR7 85 H5
Euxton La CHLY/EC PR7 86 A3
Evans St FUL/RIB PR2 57 G2
Everest Cl LSTA FY8 49 G2
Everest Dr BISP FY2 24 C1
Everest Rd LSTA FY8 49 G1
Evergreen Av LEY/BBR PR5 81 F5
The Evergreens
KIRK/FR/WA PR4 44 B4 1
Eversleigh Av CLV/TH FY5 21 F1
Eversleigh St PRES PR1 57 H2 5
Everton Rd BPOOLS FY4 38 C2 2
Evesham Av PRES PR1 69 H4
Evesham Cl CLV/TH FY5 21 E5 1
Evesham Rd BPOOLE FY3 29 H3 2
LSTA FY8 61 G1
Exchange St BPOOL FY1 2 D2
Exe St PRES PR1 58 C1
Exeter Dr CLV/TH FY5 21 G2
Exeter Pl FUL/RIB PR2 56 B1 1
Exeter St BPOOLS FY4 5 F6

F

Factory La PRES PR1 70 A3
Fairclough Rd CLV/TH FY5 17 G5
Fairfax Av BISP FY2 25 E1
Fairfax Pl LEY/BBR PR5 71 E4
Fairfax Rd FUL/RIB PR2 47 F4
Fairfield Av BPOOLE FY3 29 H3
PLF/KEOS FY6 26 B4
Fairfield Ct FTWD FY7 11 F4
Fairfield Dr FUL/RIB PR2 57 E1 2
Fairfield Rd BPOOL FY1 28 C2
FUL/RIB PR2 46 B4 4
LEY/BBR PR5 81 E4 1
PLF/KEOS FY6 30 D3
Fairfield St LEY/BBR PR5 77 G2
Fairham Av PRES PR1 69 G4 2
Fairhaven Av FTWD FY7 16 D2
Fairhaven Cl CLV/TH FY5 22 B3 3
Fairhaven La LSTA FY8 61 E1 1
Fairhaven Rd LEY/BBR PR5 80 C3
LSTA FY8 61 E1
PRES PR1 69 H1
Fairholmes Cl CLV/TH FY5 21 H1 3
Fairholmes Wy CLV/TH FY5 21 G1
Fairhurst St BPOOL FY1 3 F3
Fairlawn Rd LSTA FY8 62 C4
Fairmont Dr PLF/KEOS FY6 23 H2
Fair Oak Cl FUL/RIB PR2 47 G5
Fairsnape Rd LSTA FY8 63 H2 6
Fairview Av LSTA FY8 49 G4
Fairview Cl KIRK/FR/WA PR4 74 A4
Fair Wy PLF/KEOS FY6 19 G2
Fairway BPOOLE FY3 25 G5
CHLY/EC PR7 87 F5
FTWD FY7 10 C5
PRES PR1 57 E5
Fairway Gdns PLF/KEOS FY6 12 B1
Fairway Rd BPOOLS FY4 5 K7
Fairways FUL/RIB PR2 46 B2
LSTA FY8 49 G5 1
Fairways Av GAR/LONG PR3 36 B2
Falcon Dr PLF/KEOS FY6 25 H5
Falcon St PRES PR1 58 C1
Falkirk Av BISP FY2 24 C1
Falkland Av BPOOLS FY4 33 F3
Falkland St PRES PR1 7 F3
Fallowfield Cl KIRK/FR/WA PR4 42 C2 2
Fallowfield Rd LSTA FY8 50 A5 2
Falmouth Av FTWD FY7 16 C1
Falmouth Rd BPOOL FY1 5 F4
Faraday Dr FUL/RIB PR2 46 D1
Faraday Wy BISP FY2 25 F2
PLF/KEOS FY6 25 F3
Far Cft LEY/BBR PR5 70 B5
Far Fld PRES PR1 69 F3
Faringdon Av BPOOLS FY4 39 E3
Farington Av LEY/BBR PR5 80 C5
Farington Ga LEY/BBR PR5 81 G2
Farington Rd LEY/BBR PR5 77 E3
Far La PRES PR1 69 F4
Farm Cl CLV/TH FY5 21 H2
Farmend Cl KIRK/FR/WA PR4 74 C1
Farnell Pl BPOOLS FY4 38 D2
Farnham Wy PLF/KEOS FY6 26 A2
Far Nook CHLYE PR6 83 E5

Farnworth Rd CLV/TH FY5 22 A3
Farringdon Cl PRES PR1 59 G2 3
Farringdon Crs FUL/RIB PR2 59 G2
Farringdon La FUL/RIB PR2 47 G5
Farringdon Pl PRES PR1 59 G2 4
Farrington St CHLY/EC PR7 91 F2 6
The Farthings CHLY/EC PR7 90 C1
Fayles Gv BPOOLS FY4 33 G3
Fazackerley St FUL/RIB PR2 57 F2 7
Fazakerley St CHLY/EC PR7 91 F2 5
Felgate Brow BPOOLE FY3 3 J4
Fell Cl LEY/BBR PR5 78 C1 7
Fellery St CHLY/EC PR7 91 F2
Fell Vw CHLYE PR6 91 H4
Fell Wy PLF/KEOS FY6 19 H2
Fellway Cl LEY/BBR PR5 77 H1 5
Felstead St PRES PR1 59 E3 3
Fenber Av BPOOLS FY4 38 C1
Fengrove KIRK/FR/WA PR4 74 B1 2
Fensway KIRK/FR/WA PR4 68 A4
Fenton Rd BPOOL FY1 3 F2
FUL/RIB PR2 46 D4
Ferguson Rd BPOOL FY1 5 J3
Fermor Rd PRES PR1 59 F2 5
Fern Bank CHLYE PR6 87 G4
Fern Cl LEY/BBR PR5 77 G1 2
Fern Ct FTWD FY7 10 C5
Ferndale Av BPOOLS FY4 38 D1
Ferndale Cl CLV/TH FY5 22 A2 1
LEY/BBR PR5 81 G5
Fern Gv BPOOL FY1 5 F1
Fernhurst Av BPOOLS FY4 5 H6
Fernleigh Cl BISP FY2 24 D2
Fern Meadow CHLYE PR6 83 F2
The Ferns FUL/RIB PR2 57 F1
LEY/BBR PR5 70 C3
Fernwood Av CLV/TH FY5 21 H5
Fernwood Cl LSTA FY8 62 C2 4
Fernyhalgh Ct FUL/RIB PR2 47 E2 3
Fernyhalgh Gdns FUL/RIB PR2 47 E2 4
Fernyhalgh Pl FUL/RIB PR2 47 E2 5
Ferrier Bank KIRK/FR/WA PR4 65 F1
Fiddler's La CHLYE PR6 83 E2
Fidler La LEY/BBR PR5 77 E3
Fielden St CHLYE PR6 91 H2
LEY/BBR PR5 80 C3 1
Fieldfare Cl CLV/TH FY5 17 G4 3
Fieldhouse Av CLV/TH FY5 22 B2
Fielding Rd BISP FY2 28 D2
Field Maple Dr FUL/RIB PR2 47 G4
Fieldside Av CHLY/EC PR7 89 H2
Fieldside Cl LEY/BBR PR5 70 D3
The Fields CHLY/EC PR7 88 A3
Field St BPOOL FY1 4 E3
Fieldway LSTA FY8 49 E1
Fife Cl CHLYE PR6 91 H4
Fifth Av BPOOLS FY4 38 C1
Filberts Cl FUL/RIB PR2 45 F4
The Filberts FUL/RIB PR2 45 F5
File St CHLY/EC PR7 91 F3 6
Filey Pl BPOOL FY1 2 C3
FUL/RIB PR2 44 D4
Filey Rd LSTA FY8 49 G2
The Finches PLF/KEOS FY6 25 H5
Finchley Rd BPOOL FY1 28 B2
Finsbury Av BPOOL FY1 5 G4
LSTA FY8 61 H2
Firbank CHLY/EC PR7 85 H5
Fir Cl FTWD FY7 10 C4
Firfield Cl KIRK/FR/WA PR4 42 C3
Fir Gv BPOOL FY1 5 J4
KIRK/FR/WA PR4 53 F5
Firshill Cl CLV/TH FY5 21 H4
First Av BPOOLS FY4 38 C1
FUL/RIB PR2 56 D1
PLF/KEOS FY6 26 C4
Firswood Cl LSTA FY8 62 C2 5
Fir Tree Av FUL/RIB PR2 45 E4 1
Firtree Cl CHLY/EC PR7 95 F2
Fir Tree Pl CLV/TH FY5 21 F4
Fir Trees Av FUL/RIB PR2 47 G4
KIRK/FR/WA PR4 70 A5
Fir Trees Crs LEY/BBR PR5 70 B5
Fir Trees Pl FUL/RIB PR2 47 G4
Fir Trees Rd LEY/BBR PR5 70 B5 1
Firwood La LEY/BBR PR5 73 G1
Fishergate PRES PR1 7 F4
Fishergate Hl PRES PR1 6 D5 1
Fisher's La BPOOLS FY4 39 F3
Fisher St BPOOL FY1 3 F3
Fish St PRES PR1 58 A2 5
Fishwick Pde PRES PR1 59 E3
Fishwick Rd PRES PR1 58 D3
Fishwick Vw PRES PR1 59 E3
Fitchfield PRES PR1 70 A4
Fitzgerald St PRES PR1 58 D2 3
Fitzroy Rd BISP FY2 24 D4
Fitzroy St PRES PR1 6 D3
Five Acres LEY/BBR PR5 76 D5
Flag La LEY/BBR PR5 84 C3
PRES PR1 70 A5
Flakefleet Av FTWD FY7 11 E5
Flaxfield Wy KIRK/FR/WA PR4 43 E3
Fleet St BPOOL FY1 2 E6
CHLY/EC PR7 91 F3
LSTA FY8 48 D4
PRES PR1 7 G3
Fleetwood Rd CLV/TH FY5 20 D4 2
CLV/TH FY5 24 D1
FTWD FY7 11 E4
PLF/KEOS FY6 25 H1
Fleetwood Rd North CLV/TH FY5 17 G4
Fleetwood Rd South CLV/TH FY5 21 H4
Fleetwood St FUL/RIB PR2 57 G2
LEY/BBR PR5 81 G2 5
Flensburg Wy LEY/BBR PR5 76 D3
Fletcher Rd PRES PR1 58 C2
Flett St FUL/RIB PR2 57 F2 8
Flintoff Wy PRES PR1 46 C5
Florence Av KIRK/FR/WA PR4 65 F1
Florence St BPOOLS FY4 39 G2 3
Flowerfield KIRK/FR/WA PR4 44 B2 2
Floyd Rd FUL/RIB PR2 47 F5 1
Floyer St PRES PR1 58 C4
Fluke Hall La GAR/LONG PR3 9 H3
Foldside KIRK/FR/WA PR4 54 C4 1
Folkestone Cl CLV/TH FY5 17 F5 2
KIRK/FR/WA PR4 53 G4
Folkestone Rd LSTA FY8 49 F3
Fordstone Av PLF/KEOS FY6 13 E2
Fordway Av BPOOLE FY3 3 K3
Foregate FUL/RIB PR2 45 H4
Forest Cl LEY/BBR PR5 70 D3 4
Forest Dr LSTA FY8 62 C2
Forest Ga BPOOLE FY3 3 H5
Forest Wy FUL/RIB PR2 46 A3
Forestway LEY/BBR PR5 81 E4
Formby Av FTWD FY7 16 D2
Formby Crs KIRK/FR/WA PR4 74 A2
Formby Pl FUL/RIB PR2 56 B1 2
Formby Rd LSTA FY8 49 F2
Forrester Cl LEY/BBR PR5 80 D3
Forshaw Av BPOOLE FY3 29 F2
LSTA FY8 48 D3
Forshaw Cl FTWD FY7 11 F4 4
Forshaw Rd PRES PR1 69 G4 3
Forton Rd FUL/RIB PR2 56 B3
Fossdale Moss LEY/BBR PR5 80 B3
Foster Cft PRES PR1 6 A5
Fosterfield Pl CHLYE PR6 91 H1 1
Foster St CHLYE PR6 91 H1
Fouldrey Av PLF/KEOS FY6 26 D2
Foundry St CHLY/EC PR7 91 F2 6
Fountains Cl CHLY/EC PR7 91 G5
Fourfields LEY/BBR PR5 71 F5
Four Lane Ends LEY/BBR PR5 72 C4
Four Oaks Rd LEY/BBR PR5 78 D3
Fourth Av BPOOLS FY4 38 C1
Fowler Av LEY/BBR PR5 77 G3
Fowler Cl LEY/BBR PR5 73 H4 1
Fowler La LEY/BBR PR5 77 F3
Fowler St FUL/RIB PR2 45 G5 3
Foxcote CHLY/EC PR7 87 E5
Foxdale Av BPOOLE FY3 28 D3
Foxdale Gv PRES PR1 47 E5
Foxglove Dr CHLYE PR6 87 E2
Foxhall Rd BPOOL FY1 4 C1
Foxhall Sq BPOOL FY1 4 C2
Foxhole Rd CHLY/EC PR7 90 C2
Fox La LEY/BBR PR5 72 D3
LEY/BBR PR5 80 D5
Fox St PRES PR1 7 G3
Foxwood Dr KIRK/FR/WA PR4 42 C3
The Foxwood CHLY/EC PR7 93 H4
Francis St BPOOL FY1 2 C2
FUL/RIB PR2 57 F2 9
Franklands Dr FUL/RIB PR2 47 G3
Franklands Fold
KIRK/FR/WA PR4 74 B1
Frank St PRES PR1 58 A2
Fraser Av PRES PR1 69 H2
Frazer Gv BPOOLS FY4 4 C6 2
Freckleton Rd KIRK/FR/WA PR4 43 F5
Freckleton St BPOOL FY1 3 F7
LSTA FY8 63 G3
Frederick St BPOOLS FY4 5 G6
CHLYE PR6 91 H3
Fredora Av BPOOLE FY3 33 G3
Freemantle Av BPOOLS FY4 38 A4
Frenchwood Av LSTA FY8 62 D2
PRES PR1 58 C5
Frenchwood St PRES PR1 7 K5 2
Freshfields FUL/RIB PR2 44 A5
Friargate PRES PR1 7 H3
The Friars FUL/RIB PR2 45 H4 3
Friary Cl KIRK/FR/WA PR4 43 G4
Friday St CHLY/EC PR7 91 G2 5
CHLYE PR6 91 G2
Frinton Gv BISP FY2 25 E1
Friths Av LEY/BBR PR5 72 D5
Frobisher Dr LSTA FY8 49 E2
Frome St PRES PR1 59 E2
Froom St CHLYE PR6 91 H2
Fryers Cl PRES PR1 69 F5
The Fulmars PLF/KEOS FY6 25 H5 3
Fulshaw Rd FUL/RIB PR2 57 E1
Fulwood Av BPOOLE FY3 29 F2 1
Fulwood Hall La FUL/RIB PR2 46 C4
Fulwood Hts FUL/RIB PR2 46 D3
Fulwood Rw FUL/RIB PR2 47 F1
Furlong Crs BPOOLE FY3 29 G1 1
Furlong La PLF/KEOS FY6 26 B3
Furness Av BPOOLE FY3 29 G2
FTWD FY7 10 D5
Furness Cl CHLY/EC PR7 91 G5
Furness Dr PLF/KEOS FY6 26 D4
Further Ends Rd
KIRK/FR/WA PR4 54 B5
Fylde Av LEY/BBR PR5 76 D5
Fylde Rd FUL/RIB PR2 57 G2
LSTA FY8 62 B1
PLF/KEOS FY6 26 C3
Fylde St KIRK/FR/WA PR4 43 E4
PRES PR1 7 F1
Fylde View Cl PLF/KEOS FY6 26 B5

G

The Gables KIRK/FR/WA PR4 44 B4
Gadsby St BPOOL FY1 4 C4
Gainsborough Av
LEY/BBR PR5 77 F2 4
Gainsborough Rd BPOOL FY1 3 G6
Galloway Crs BISP FY2 25 F2
Galloway Rd FTWD FY7 11 F1
Galway Av BISP FY2 24 D4
Gamble Rd CLV/TH FY5 17 H5
Gamull La FUL/RIB PR2 47 G3
Ganton Ct PRES PR1 56 D5 2
Gardeners Ms BPOOL FY1 2 E1
Garden St KIRK/FR/WA PR4 43 E4 1
LSTA FY8 49 E5 5
PRES PR1 7 G4
Garden Ter BPOOLS FY4 4 D6
CHLY/EC PR7 91 F1
Garden Wk CLV/TH FY5 16 D4
FUL/RIB PR2 57 E2
Gardner St PRES PR1 7 H1
Garfield St FTWD FY7 11 H1 3
Garfield Ter CHLYE PR6 87 G5 5
Garland Gv FTWD FY7 10 D3 2
Garrick Gv BPOOLE FY3 29 E3 6
Garrison Rd FUL/RIB PR2 46 C5
Garsdale Cl LEY/BBR PR5 71 F1
Garsdale Rd FUL/RIB PR2 47 F4
Garstang Cl PLF/KEOS FY6 26 A4 2
Garstang Rd FUL/RIB PR2 36 C5
GAR/LONG PR3 36 C5
PLF/KEOS FY6 27 F4
Garstang Rd East PLF/KEOS FY6 26 C4
Garstang Rd North
KIRK/FR/WA PR4 42 D1
Garstang Rd South
KIRK/FR/WA PR4 42 D2
Garstang Rd West BPOOLE FY3 29 G1
PLF/KEOS FY6 26 A5
Garstone Cft FUL/RIB PR2 45 F2
Garton Av BPOOLS FY4 38 C2
Gaskell Crs CLV/TH FY5 21 G2
Gaskell Rd PRES PR1 69 H1
Gaskell St CHLYE PR6 91 H2
Gas Ter LEY/BBR PR5 81 G2 6
Gatesgarth Av FUL/RIB PR2 46 A1
Gateside Dr BPOOLE FY3 29 F2
Gateway Cl CLV/TH FY5 22 B5
Gathurst Rd FUL/RIB PR2 57 F1 6
Gaulter's La PLF/KEOS FY6 13 G2
Gaydon Wy CLV/TH FY5 21 E5
Gaythorne Av PRES PR1 59 G2
Geldof Dr BPOOL FY1 28 C2
General St BPOOL FY1 2 C2
Geneva Rd FUL/RIB PR2 46 D4
Geoffrey St CHLYE PR6 91 G1
PRES PR1 58 D2
George Av BPOOLS FY4 33 F4
George's Rd PRES PR1 7 G3
George St BPOOL FY1 2 E4
CHLY/EC PR7 91 F3 7
LEY/BBR PR5 81 G2
LSTA FY8 63 F3 7
PRES PR1 58 C4
German La CHLY/EC PR7 90 A2
Gerrard's Ter PLF/KEOS FY6 26 A3
Gerrard St PRES PR1 6 D3
Gib La LEY/BBR PR5 73 H3
Gilbertson Rd CHLY/EC PR7 95 H3
Gilbert St CHLY/EC PR7 91 F4 4
Gildabrook Rd BPOOLS FY4 38 D3
Gilderdale Ct LSTA FY8 63
Gildow St PRES PR1
Gillcroft CHLY/EC PR7 88
Giller Cl PRES PR1 69
Giller Dr PRES PR1 6
Giller Fold PRES PR1 70
Gillett St PRES PR1 58
Gillibrand Cl PRES PR1 69
Gillibrand St CHLY/EC PR7 9
LEY/BBR PR5 7
Gillibrand Wks CHLY/EC PR7 9
Gill La KIRK/FR/WA PR4 7
Gill Nook KIRK/FR/WA PR4 74
Gillow Rd KIRK/FR/WA PR4 4
Gin Bow CHLY/EC PR7 91
Gisburn Av LSTA FY8 5
Gisburn Gv BPOOLE FY3 29
Gisburn Rd FUL/RIB PR2 4
The Glades LSTA FY8 6
Gladeway CLV/TH FY5 2
Gladstone St BPOOLS FY4
Gladstone Wy CLV/TH FY5 21
Glamis Dr CHLY/EC PR7 9
Glamis Rd LEY/BBR PR5 8
Glastonbury Av BPOOL FY1
Glebe Cl FUL/RIB PR2 4
Glebe La KIRK/FR/WA PR4 43
The Glebe LEY/BBR PR5 8
Glenapp Av BPOOLS FY4 3
Glenarden Av CLV/TH FY5 2
Glencoe Av BPOOLE FY3 2
Glencourse Dr FUL/RIB PR2 4
Glencroft CHLY/EC PR7 8
Glencross Pl BPOOLS FY4 3
Glendale Av LEY/BBR PR5 7
Glendale Cl BISP FY2 2
LEY/BBR PR5 8
PLF/KEOS FY6 2
Glendale Crs LEY/BBR PR5 7
Glendale Gv FUL/RIB PR2 5
Gleneagles Ct
KIRK/FR/WA PR4 43
Gleneagles Dr FUL/RIB PR2 4
PRES PR1 5
Glen Eldon Rd LSTA FY8 4
Glenfield Av BISP FY2 2
Glen Gv FUL/RIB PR2 4
Glenholme Gdns
PLF/KEOS FY6 26
Glenluce Dr PRES PR1 5
Glenmere Crs CLV/TH FY5 2
Glenmore CHLYE PR6 8
Glenmore Av CLV/TH FY5 2
Glenroyd Cl BPOOLE FY3
Glen St BPOOLE FY3
The Glen FUL/RIB PR2 59
PLF/KEOS FY6 1
Glenview Cl FUL/RIB PR2 4
Glenview Ct FUL/RIB PR2 47
Glenway PRES PR1 6
Glenwood St BPOOLE FY3
Glossop Cl BISP FY2 2
Gloucester Av BPOOL FY1
CLV/TH FY5 1
LEY/BBR PR5 81
Gloucester Rd CHLY/EC PR7 9
LSTA FY8 62
Glover's Ct PRES PR1
Glover St PRES PR1
Godwin Av BPOOLE FY3 5
Goe La KIRK/FR/WA PR4 5
Golbourne St PRES PR1 58
Goldburn Cl FUL/RIB PR2 4
Golden Hl LEY/BBR PR5 8
Golden Hill La LEY/BBR PR5 8
Golden Wy PRES PR1
Goldfinch St PRES PR1 5
Goldsboro Av BPOOLE FY3 33
Goldstone Dr CLV/TH FY5 2
Golf Vw FUL/RIB PR2 44
Good St PRES PR1
Goodwood Av BISP FY2 2
FUL/RIB PR2 4
Goose Foot La LEY/BBR PR5 7
Goose Green Av CHLY/EC PR7 9
Gordale Cl BPOOLS FY4 33
Gordon Av CLV/TH FY5 2
Gordon Rd FTWD FY7 1
LSTA FY8 6
Gordonstoun Pl CLV/TH FY5 21
Gordon St BPOOLS FY4 4
CHLYE PR6 9
PRES PR1 5
Goring St CHLY/EC PR7 9
Gorse Av CLV/TH FY5 2
Gorse Cl CHLYE PR6 8
Gorse Gv FUL/RIB PR2 4
Gorse Rd BPOOLE FY3
Gorsewood LEY/BBR PR5 8
Gorton St BPOOL FY1

'orth Rd *BISP* FY2 28 C1
gh La *LEY/BBR* PR5 79 E4
ding Av *LEY/BBR* PR5 81 G3
ding St *CHLY/EC* PR7 91 G4
er Ct *LEY/BBR* PR5 80 C2
er Gv *KIRK/FR/WA* PR4 74 B5
: St *LSTA* FY8 49 F4
amy Av *KIRK/FR/WA* PR4 65 F1 1
well St *PRES* PR1 6 E2
ton Ct *CHLY/EC* PR7 91 E5 4
ton Rd *FUL/RIB* PR2 47 G4
ton St *BPOOL* FY1 3 F1
RES PR1 6 E5
am Av *LEY/BBR* PR5 77 H1
am St *PRES* PR1 58 C2
npian Wy *LSTA* FY8 63 H1
nby Av *BPOOLE* FY3 29 E2
nge Av *CLV/TH* FY5 21 H2
IL/RIB PR2 47 G4
nge Dr *CHLYE* PR6 85 H3
Y/BBR PR5 72 C2
nge Gdns *PLF/KEOS* FY6 26 B5
nge La *KIRK/FR/WA* PR4 55 F1
F/KEOS FY6 19 E2
nge Park Cl *PRES* PR1 56 D5
nge Pl *FUL/RIB* PR2 47 G4
nge Rd *FTWD* FY7 10 D3
IL/RIB PR2 45 F5 2
Y/BBR PR5 80 C3
TA FY8 49 E4
F/KEOS FY6 23 H3
Grange *KIRK/FR/WA* PR4 44 B3
Granings *KIRK/FR/WA* PR4 44 A2
nt Dr *KIRK/FR/WA* PR4 74 B4
ntham Rd *BPOOL* FY1 28 C3 7
RK/FR/WA PR4 31 H4
nville Rd *BPOOL* FY1 3 G4
POOLE FY3 3 H3
HLYE PR6 91 H1
smere Av *CLV/TH* FY5 21 H2 3
TWD FY7 11 E2
Y/BBR PR5 81 F1
smere Cl *CHLY/EC* PR7 90 A1
IL/RIB PR2 46 D4 2
Y/BBR PR5 71 E4
smere Gv *CHLYE* PR6 83 E5 1
smere Rd *BPOOL* FY1 4 E1 1
TA FY8 49 E2
smere Ter *CHLY/EC* PR7 91 E5
ssington Pl *CLV/TH* FY5 21 F4
ssington Rd *LSTA* FY8 49 H4
ving Dock Rd *LSTA* FY8 63 H2
at Avenham St *PRES* PR1 7 J5
at George St *PRES* PR1 58 B2
at Gill *KIRK/FR/WA* PR4 74 B4
at Greens La *LEY/BBR* PR5 79 E4
at Hanover St *PRES* PR1 58 B2
at Meadow *CHLY/EC* PR7 86 D5
Y/BBR PR5 77 F1 2
at Shaw St *PRES* PR1 7 G2
at Townley St *PRES* PR1 59 E3
at Tunstead *KIRK/FR/WA* PR4 74 B2
aves Meadow *PRES* PR1 69 H5
aves St *PRES* PR1 7 K3 2
aves-town La *FUL/RIB* PR2 56 B2 4
be Cl *BPOOLE* FY3 29 H3 3
enacres *FUL/RIB* PR2 45 E1
en Acres *KIRK/FR/WA* PR4 54 C4
enacres Av *KIRK/FR/WA* PR4 43 E4
Greenacres *KIRK/FR/WA* PR4 68 A4
en Av *BPOOLS* FY4 38 C2
enbank *PLF/KEOS* FY6 26 C4 1
enbank Av *PRES* PR1 57 G1 1
enbank Rd *PRES* PR1 69 H2
enbanks *BISP* FY2 25 F4
enbank St *PRES* PR1 57 H2 6
enbriar Cl *BPOOLE* FY3 29 F1
encroft *PRES* PR1 69 G3
endale Cl *FTWD* FY7 10 C4 2
endale Ms *FUL/RIB* PR2 56 B1 3
en Dick's La *GAR/LONG* PR3 14 A1
en Dr *CLV/TH* FY5 16 C5
UL/RIB PR2 45 H1
EY/BBR PR5 70 D5
STA FY8 63 E1
LF/KEOS FY6 30 C2
RES PR1 69 E1
enfield Cl *FTWD* FY7 11 F4 5
enfield Dr *LEY/BBR* PR5 77 F1
enfield Rd *CHLYE* PR6 91 H2 5
LV/TH FY5 21 E4
TWD FY7 11 F4
enfields Crs
IRK/FR/WA PR4 42 C2 3
enfield Wy *FUL/RIB* PR2 45 E3
enfinch Ct *BPOOLE* FY3 29 H4 2
en Ga *FUL/RIB* PR2 45 F5 3
en Hey *LSTA* FY8 63 H2 7
enhill Av *KIRK/FR/WA* PR4 43 E2
enhill Pl *BPOOL* FY1 3 F2

Greenlands Crs *FUL/RIB* PR2 47 F5 2
Green La *KIRK/FR/WA* PR4 54 B5
KIRK/FR/WA PR4 69 F5
LEY/BBR PR5 76 D2
PLF/KEOS FY6 13 G4
Green La West *KIRK/FR/WA* PR4 66 A1
Greenmead Cl
KIRK/FR/WA PR4 44 B3 3
Green Meadow La *PLF/KEOS* FY6 23 F4
Greenmount Av *CLV/TH* FY5 21 G1 1
KIRK/FR/WA PR4 43 E3 3
Green Oak Pl *CLV/TH* FY5 21 G4 1
Green Pl *LEY/BBR* PR5 78 D3
Greenside *CHLY/EC* PR7 85 H4
Greenside Gdns *LEY/BBR* PR5 80 A5
Green St *CHLY/EC* PR7 90 D5 3
LSTA FY8 63 E3 3
Greensway *GAR/LONG* PR3 36 B2 1
The Green *CHLY/EC* PR7 88 B4
FUL/RIB PR2 59 G1 2
Greenthorn Crs *FUL/RIB* PR2 59 H1
Green Wy *BPOOLS* FY4 39 F1
Greenway *CHLY/EC* PR7 88 A3 1
FUL/RIB PR2 45 G1
PRES PR1 69 E2
Greenways *LSTA* FY8 49 H5
Greenwich Dr *LSTA* FY8 62 B1
Greenwood *LEY/BBR* PR5 79 E5
Greenwood Av *BPOOL* FY1 5 J4
Greenwood Cl *LSTA* FY8 62 C2 6
Greenwood St *LEY/BBR* PR5 71 F5 3
PRES PR1 58 C4
Gregory Av *BISP* FY2 24 C2
Gregory Pl *LSTA* FY8 63 E3
Gregson Cl *BPOOLS* FY4 39 F1 3
Gregson Dr *FTWD* FY7 11 F4 6
Gregson La *LEY/BBR* PR5 72 D4
Gregson St *LSTA* FY8 63 E3
Gregson Wy *FUL/RIB* PR2 46 C3
Grenfell Av *BPOOLE* FY3 29 E3
Grenville Av *LEY/BBR* PR5 71 E4
LSTA FY8 49 E2
Gresham Rd *CLV/TH* FY5 20 D3
Gresley Pl *BISP* FY2 25 E5 1
Greta Pl *FTWD* FY7 10 D4
Gretdale Av *LSTA* FY8 49 E3
Gretna Crs *CLV/TH* FY5 20 D4
Greyfriars Av *FUL/RIB* PR2 45 G3 2
Greyfriars Crs *FUL/RIB* PR2 45 G3
Greyfriars Dr *PRES* PR1 6 A7
Grey Heights Vw *CHLYE* PR6 91 H2
Greystock Av *FUL/RIB* PR2 45 H2
Greystock Cl *LEY/BBR* PR5 79 E1
Greystoke Pl *BPOOLS* FY4 38 B3
Greystones *LEY/BBR* PR5 80 A3
Grime St *CHLY/EC* PR7 91 G4
Grimsargh St *PRES* PR1 59 E2 11
Grimshaw St *PRES* PR1 7 K3
Grindleton Cl *BPOOLE* FY3 29 H2 3
Grisedale Pl *CHLY/EC* PR7 91 E5
Grizedale Av *PLF/KEOS* FY6 26 A4
Grizedale Cl *FUL/RIB* PR2 59 G1 3
Grizedale Crs *FUL/RIB* PR2 59 H1
Grizedale Pl *FUL/RIB* PR2 59 G1 4
Grizedale Rd *BPOOLS* FY4 34 A4
Grosvenor Pl *FUL/RIB* PR2 57 E1
Grosvenor Rd *CHLY/EC* PR7 90 D4
Grosvenor St *BPOOL* FY1 2 E4
LSTA FY8 63 G3 3
PRES PR1 58 C4
Grove Av *KIRK/FR/WA* PR4 74 A1
Grove Rd *LEY/BBR* PR5 58 D5
Grove St *LEY/BBR* PR5 78 C1
LEY/BBR PR5 80 C4
LSTA FY8 49 F4 1
The Grove *CHLYE* PR6 87 F5
CLV/TH FY5 21 E1
PRES PR1 69 E2
Grundy Ms *BPOOLS* FY4 38 C1
Grundy's La *CHLY/EC* PR7 95 F4
Grundy St *LEY/BBR* PR5 81 F2
Guildford Av *BISP* FY2 24 C1
Guildford Rd *PRES* PR1 7 J4
Guildford Wy *PLF/KEOS* FY6 26 A1
Guildhall St *PRES* PR1 7 H4
Guild Rw *PRES* PR1 7 J3
Guild Wy *FUL/RIB* PR2 6 C4
Gynn Av *BPOOL* FY1 28 B2

H

Hackensall Rd *PLF/KEOS* FY6 12 C2
Haddon Pl *FUL/RIB* PR2 45 G5 4
Haddon Rd *BISP* FY2 24 C2
Hadleigh Rd *PLF/KEOS* FY6 26 A1 2
Haig Av *FUL/RIB* PR2 57 G1 2
LEY/BBR PR5 81 E3
Haigh Cl *CHLY/EC* PR7 90 D3
Haigh Crs *CHLY/EC* PR7 90 D3
Haighton Ct *FUL/RIB* PR2 46 B1
Haighton Dr *FUL/RIB* PR2 47 F2
Haig Rd *BPOOL* FY1 4 C5
Half Acre *LEY/BBR* PR5 77 F1
Halford Pl *CLV/TH* FY5 21 E5
Halfpenny La *CHLY/EC* PR7 92 A2
Halifax St *BPOOLE* FY3 33 F3 3
Hall Av *BPOOLS* FY4 5 F6
Hall Cft *KIRK/FR/WA* PR4 68 A4
Hall Ga *CHLY/EC* PR7 90 D1
Hall Gate La *PLF/KEOS* FY6 19 G1
Halliwell La *CHLYE* PR6 87 F3
Halliwell Pl *CHLY/EC* PR7 91 F3 3
Halliwell St *CHLY/EC* PR7 91 F3
Hall La *LEY/BBR* PR5 81 E1
Hall Park Dr *LSTA* FY8 50 B5
Hall Rd *FUL/RIB* PR2 45 H3
PRES PR1 69 H3
Hall St *FUL/RIB* PR2 57 F2
Hallwood Rd *CHLY/EC* PR7 90 D5
Halstead Rd *FUL/RIB* PR2 47 E3
Halton Av *CLV/TH* FY5 17 E5
LEY/BBR PR5 82 A2
Halton Gdns *BPOOLS* FY4 33 F5
Halton Pl *FUL/RIB* PR2 47 G4 1
Hambledon Dr *PRES* PR1 69 H4 2
Hamer Rd *FUL/RIB* PR2 45 G5
Hamilton Cl *LSTA* FY8 63 H2 8
Hamilton Gv *FUL/RIB* PR2 47 F5 3
Hamilton Rd *CHLY/EC* PR7 91 E3
FUL/RIB PR2 47 E5
Hamlet Rd *FTWD* FY7 11 E2
The Hamlet *LSTA* FY8 49 F1
Hammerton Pl *BPOOLE* FY3 29 G2 4
Hammond Ct *PRES* PR1 57 H2 7
Hammond's Rw *PRES* PR1 7 K3
Hammond St *PRES* PR1 57 H1 6
PRES PR1 57 H2 8
PRES PR1 58 A1 7
Hampden Rd *LEY/BBR* PR5 81 F2
Hampshire Pl *BPOOLS* FY4 39 F2
Hampshire Rd *LEY/BBR* PR5 71 E3
Hampson Av *LEY/BBR* PR5 82 A3
Hampson Gv *PLF/KEOS* FY6 13 E2 1
Hampstead Cl *LSTA* FY8 50 C5 1
Hampstead Ms *BPOOL* FY1 28 C3 8
Hampstead Rd *FUL/RIB* PR2 59 E1
Hampton Cl *CHLY/EC* PR7 91 E2
Hampton Ct *LSTA* FY8 50 A3
Hampton Pl *CLV/TH* FY5 21 E1
Hampton Rd *BPOOLS* FY4 32 B5
Hampton St *FUL/RIB* PR2 57 F1 7
Hanbury St *FUL/RIB* PR2 57 F2 10
The Handbridge *FUL/RIB* PR2 45 H3 1
Handley Rd *BPOOL* FY1 3 F2
Handsworth Ct *BPOOL* FY1 28 C3 9
Handsworth Rd *BPOOL* FY1 28 C3
Hanley Cl *PLF/KEOS* FY6 19 G2
Hanover Crs *BISP* FY2 24 C1
Hanover St *PRES* PR1 58 A2 6
Hapton St *CLV/TH* FY5 17 H5 1
Harbour Av *KIRK/FR/WA* PR4 53 G5 2
Harbour Cl *FTWD* FY7 11 F4
Harbour La *KIRK/FR/WA* PR4 53 G4
Harcourt Rd *BPOOLS* FY4 5 G7
Harcourt St *PRES* PR1 57 H2 9
Hardacre La *CHLYE* PR6 87 E2
Hardcastle Rd *FUL/RIB* PR2 45 H5 3
Hardhorn Rd *PLF/KEOS* FY6 26 B5
Hardhorn Wy *PLF/KEOS* FY6 26 B5
Hardman St *BPOOL* FY1 3 F2
Hardwicke St *PRES* PR1 7 J1 1
Hardy Dr *CHLY/EC* PR7 90 D3
Hareden Cl *LEY/BBR* PR5 78 C1 8
Hareden Rd *FUL/RIB* PR2 59 G1
Harestone Av *CHLY/EC* PR7 90 D5
Harewood Av *BPOOLE* FY3 29 G1
Harewood Cl *PLF/KEOS* FY6 26 A2
Harewood Rd *PRES* PR1 58 C1
Hargate Rd *CLV/TH* FY5 22 A2
Hargreaves Av *LEY/BBR* PR5 81 G4
Hargreaves Ct *FUL/RIB* PR2 44 C4 1
Hargreaves St *CLV/TH* FY5 21 H1
Harland St *FUL/RIB* PR2 45 G5
Harlech Av *BPOOL* FY1 5 G5
Harlech Dr *LEY/BBR* PR5 81 G3
Harley Rd *BPOOLE* FY3 3 J6
Harling Rd *PRES* PR1 59 E2
Harold Av *BPOOLS* FY4 39 G2
Harold Ter *LEY/BBR* PR5 77 F1 3
Harperley *CHLY/EC* PR7 87 E5
Harper's La *CHLY/EC* PR7 91 G1
Harrington Av *BPOOLS* FY4 38 B3
Harrington Rd *CHLY/EC* PR7 91 E2
Harrington St *PRES* PR1 7 F1
Harris Av *BPOOL* FY1 5 H5
Harrison Av *CLV/TH* FY5 21 H2
Harrison La *KIRK/FR/WA* PR4 69 E4
Harrison Rd *CHLY/EC* PR7 91 F4
FUL/RIB PR2 45 H3
Harrison St *BPOOL* FY1 5 F1
Harris St *FTWD* FY7 11 G2
PRES PR1 7 J3
Harrock Rd *LEY/BBR* PR5 82 A3
Harrogate Rd *LSTA* FY8 50 A4
Harrop Pl *FUL/RIB* PR2 47 F4 3
Harrow Av *FTWD* FY7 11 F2
Harrow Pl *BPOOLS* FY4 38 A3
LSTA FY8 62 B1
Harrowside *BPOOLS* FY4 38 B3
Harrowside West *BPOOLS* FY4 38 A3 2
Hartford Av *BPOOL* FY1 5 H3
Hartington Rd *PRES* PR1 6 D4
Hartwood Gn *CHLYE* PR6 87 F4
Harvest Dr *CHLYE* PR6 87 F1
Harwich Rd *LSTA* FY8 49 F2
Harwood Av *LSTA* FY8 49 E3
Harwood Cl *PLF/KEOS* FY6 19 G2
Haslemere Av *BPOOLE* FY3 5 K2
Haslow Pl *BPOOLE* FY3 29 F3
Hassett Cl *PRES* PR1 6 E6
Hastings Av *BISP* FY2 25 E2
KIRK/FR/WA PR4 53 G4
Hastings Cl *CLV/TH* FY5 22 A3
Hastings Pl *LSTA* FY8 63 E3 4
Hastings Rd *CLV/TH* FY5 22 A3
FUL/RIB PR2 57 E2
KIRK/FR/WA PR4 54 B1 1
LEY/BBR PR5 81 G2
Hatfield Av *FTWD* FY7 11 E4
Hatfield Cl *CLV/TH* FY5 22 A2
Hatfield Gdns *FTWD* FY7 11 E4 2
Hatfield Ms *FTWD* FY7 11 F4 7
Hatfield Rd *FUL/RIB* PR2 47 F5
Hatfield Wk *FTWD* FY7 11 E4 3
Hathaway *BPOOLS* FY4 33 E5
Hathaway Rd *FTWD* FY7 11 E2
Havelock Rd *LEY/BBR* PR5 78 B2
PRES PR1 69 H1 1
Havelock St *BPOOL* FY1 2 D7
PRES PR1 57 G1 3
PRES PR1 57 H1 7
PRES PR1 58 A1 8
Haven Rd *LSTA* FY8 63 F3
Hawarden Rd *PRES* PR1 59 F2 6
Hawes Side La *BPOOLS* FY4 5 J6
Haweswater Av *CHLY/EC* PR7 91 E4
Hawkhurst Av *FUL/RIB* PR2 45 G2
Hawkhurst Crs *FUL/RIB* PR2 45 G2 1
Hawkhurst Rd *PRES* PR1 58 C1 2
PRES PR1 69 H2
Hawking Pl *BISP* FY2 25 F2 1
Hawkins Cl *PRES* PR1 57 H2 10
Hawkins St *PRES* PR1 57 H2 11
Hawksbury Dr *PRES* PR1 69 G4
Hawkshead *PRES* PR1 69 H3 1
Hawkshead Av *CHLY/EC* PR7 90 A1
Hawkshead Rd *FUL/RIB* PR2 47 F3
Hawkshead Ter *BPOOLS* FY4 34 B5
Hawkstone Cl *CLV/TH* FY5 22 B4
Hawkswood *CHLY/EC* PR7 88 A4
Hawthorn Av *FTWD* FY7 17 E1
Hawthorn Cl *KIRK/FR/WA* PR4 42 C2 4
KIRK/FR/WA PR4 75 H2
LEY/BBR PR5 80 C2 1
Hawthorn Crs *FUL/RIB* PR2 56 A2
Hawthorne Av *LEY/BBR* PR5 72 B3
Hawthorne Cl *CHLYE* PR6 83 E1 2
Hawthorne Gv *PLF/KEOS* FY6 25 G2
Hawthorne Rd *CLV/TH* FY5 21 H4
Hawthorn Rd *BPOOL* FY1 2 E1
FUL/RIB PR2 59 F1
The Hawthorns *CHLY/EC* PR7 88 A3
FUL/RIB PR2 46 A2
Haydock Av *LEY/BBR* PR5 81 F4
Haydock St *LEY/BBR* PR5 71 F4 3
Haydon Av *LEY/BBR* PR5 77 F2
Hayfield Av *BISP* FY2 25 E5 2
LEY/BBR PR5 72 D5
PLF/KEOS FY6 26 C4
Hayfield Cl *LEY/BBR* PR5 72 D5 2
Hayling Pl *FUL/RIB* PR2 44 D4 3
Haymarket *LSTA* FY8 49 H5
Haysworth St *PRES* PR1 58 A1 9
Haywood Cl *FUL/RIB* PR2 37 F5
Hazel Av *FTWD* FY7 17 F1 1
LEY/BBR PR5 71 H5
Hazel Cl *LEY/BBR* PR5 71 G5
PRES PR1 69 E3
Hazel Coppice *FUL/RIB* PR2 44 B5
Hazeldene Rd *FTWD* FY7 11 E4
Hazel Gv *BPOOLE* FY3 3 J5
CHLYE PR6 87 F4
FUL/RIB PR2 47 H4
LEY/BBR PR5 71 G5
Hazelhurst Rd *FUL/RIB* PR2 59 H1
Hazelmere Rd *FUL/RIB* PR2 36 C5 1
FUL/RIB PR2 56 D2 1
The Hazels *CHLY/EC* PR7 94 B4 3

Hazelwood Cl LEY/BBR PR5 80 D3
Hazlewood Cl CLV/TH FY5 21 G2
Head Dyke La GAR/LONG PR3 15 E3
PLF/KEOS FY6 14 B3
Headfort Cl BISP FY2 24 D5
Headley Rd LEY/BBR PR5 80 D3
Headroomgate Back Rd
LSTA FY8 49 F3 1
Headroomgate Rd LSTA FY8 49 F3
Heald House Rd LEY/BBR PR5 81 H5
Heald St BPOOLE FY3 3 G2
CHLYE PR6 91 H2 6
Healey St BPOOLE FY3 3 H1
Heather Cl CLV/TH FY5 21 H3 2
Heather Gv FUL/RIB PR2 47 F5
Heatherleigh LEY/BBR PR5 80 C2
The Heathers LEY/BBR PR5 79 F5 1
Heatherway FUL/RIB PR2 47 F3
Heathfield Dr FUL/RIB PR2 47 F4
Heathfield Rd FTWD FY7 11 E4
Heathrow Pl CHLY/EC PR7 90 D3 1
Heathway FUL/RIB PR2 46 A2
Heathway Av BPOOLE FY3 3 K3
Heatley St PRES PR1 7 G2
Heaton Cl LEY/BBR PR5 71 E2 2
PLF/KEOS FY6 26 A2
Heaton Mount Av
FUL/RIB PR2 46 A1 2
Heaton Pl PRES PR1 59 F2
Heaton Rd LSTA FY8 49 G4
Heaton St LEY/BBR PR5 80 D2
Hebden Av BPOOL FY1 5 G5
Heeley Rd LSTA FY8 48 D3
Helen's Cl BPOOLS FY4 39 E2
Hellifield FUL/RIB PR2 45 H1
Helmsdale Rd BPOOLS FY4 39 F1
Helmsley Gn LEY/BBR PR5 81 G2 7
Hemingway BPOOLS FY4 5 G7
Henderson Rd FTWD FY7 11 F4 8
Henderson St FUL/RIB PR2 45 H5
PRES PR1 57 H1 8
Hendon Pl FUL/RIB PR2 56 B1
Henley Av CLV/TH FY5 20 D2
Henley Ct BISP FY2 29 E1 1
Hennel La LEY/BBR PR5 70 D3
Henrietta St PRES PR1 58 C3
Henry St BPOOL FY1 4 E3
LSTA FY8 63 E3
Henson Av BPOOLS FY4 39 E2
Henthorne St BPOOL FY1 3 F2
Herbert St LEY/BBR PR5 81 F2
PRES PR1 58 C2 5
Hereford Av BPOOLE FY3 5 K2
Heriot Cl CLV/TH FY5 21 F3
Heritage Wy CLV/TH FY5 21 F3
The Hermitage CLV/TH FY5 21 F2
Hermon Rd CLV/TH FY5 21 E3
Hermon St PRES PR1 59 E2 12
Hern Av LEY/BBR PR5 77 F1
Heron Cl CLV/TH FY5 17 F4
Heron Wy BPOOLE FY3 29 H3
KIRK/FR/WA PR4 54 B1
Herschell St PRES PR1 7 K5
Hesketh Av BISP FY2 24 B3
Hesketh Cl PRES PR1 59 F2 7
Hesketh Pl FTWD FY7 11 H1
Hesketh Rd FUL/RIB PR2 59 F2
LSTA FY8 49 G2
Hesketh St FUL/RIB PR2 57 F2
Hetherington Pl BISP FY2 25 E5 3
Heversham Av FUL/RIB PR2 46 A1
Hewitt St LEY/BBR PR5 81 G2 8
Hewlett St CHLY/EC PR7 94 A4
Hexham Av CLV/TH FY5 17 E5
Hey End KIRK/FR/WA PR4 75 G1
The Heyes CHLYE PR6 83 E2 1
Heyhouses La LSTA FY8 50 A4
Heysham St PRES PR1 57 H2 12
Heys St CLV/TH FY5 21 H1
The Heys CHLY/EC PR7 94 C3
Heywood Rd FUL/RIB PR2 56 B1
Higham Gv BPOOLE FY3 33 F3 4
Highbank Av BPOOLS FY4 33 G5
Highbury Av BPOOLE FY3 29 E2
FTWD FY7 11 F3
Highbury Rd LSTA FY8 48 D2
Highbury Rd East LSTA FY8 49 E2
Highbury Rd West LSTA FY8 48 D2
Highcroft Av BISP FY2 25 E2
Highcross Av PLF/KEOS FY6 30 B2
Highcross Hl PLF/KEOS FY6 30 B2
Highcross Rd PLF/KEOS FY6 30 B2 1
Higher Bank Rd FUL/RIB PR2 46 A5
Higher Cft PRES PR1 69 F4
Higher Furlong KIRK/FR/WA PR4 74 A3
Higher Gn PLF/KEOS FY6 26 B4
Higher Greenfield FUL/RIB PR2 45 E3
Higher Meadow LEY/BBR PR5 82 B3
Higher Moor Rd BPOOLE FY3 25 G5
Higher Walton Rd LEY/BBR PR5 71 F2
Highfield Av FUL/RIB PR2 46 D4 3
LEY/BBR PR5 70 D5
LEY/BBR PR5 81 H1
Highfield Dr FUL/RIB PR2 36 D5
KIRK/FR/WA PR4 74 A3
PRES PR1 69 G4
Highfield Gv LEY/BBR PR5 70 D5
Highfield Rd BPOOLS FY4 38 C2
Highfield Rd North CHLY/EC PR7 87 F5
Highfield Rd South CHLY/EC PR7 91 F1
Highgale Gdns LEY/BBR PR5 77 H2
Highgate BPOOLS FY4 38 D3
High Ga FTWD FY7 10 D3
Highgate PRES PR1 69 E1
Highgate Av FUL/RIB PR2 45 H4
Highgate Cl FUL/RIB PR2 46 A4
Highgate La KIRK/FR/WA PR4 53 G5
High Gate La PLF/KEOS FY6 19 E4
Highgate Pl LSTA FY8 50 B5
High Gn LEY/BBR PR5 81 E3
Highgrove Av CHLY/EC PR7 93 E1
Highland Av PRES PR1 69 E2
Highrigg Dr GAR/LONG PR3 37 E4
High St BPOOL FY1 2 D2
CHLY/EC PR7 91 F2
FTWD FY7 11 H2
PRES PR1 7 J1
Highways Av CHLY/EC PR7 90 A1
Hilary Av BISP FY2 24 C2
Hillbrook Rd LEY/BBR PR5 81 E2
Hill Crs KIRK/FR/WA PR4 55 G1
Hill Crest Av FUL/RIB PR2 36 D5 1
Hillcrest Av FUL/RIB PR2 44 D4
Hillcrest Rd BPOOLS FY4 38 B4
Hillcroft FUL/RIB PR2 45 F1
Hill La CHLYE PR6 83 E3
Hillock La KIRK/FR/WA PR4 53 F4
Hillpark Av FUL/RIB PR2 45 G4
LEY/BBR PR5 72 C5
Hill Rd LEY/BBR PR5 81 H3
PRES PR1 6 A7
Hill Rd South PRES PR1 69 F3
Hillside Av FUL/RIB PR2 45 G4
KIRK/FR/WA PR4 43 G3
LEY/BBR PR5 77 E2
PLF/KEOS FY6 13 F2
Hillside Cl BPOOLE FY3 3 J3
CHLY/EC PR7 89 H1 1
CLV/TH FY5 22 B4
Hillside Crs CHLYE PR6 83 F4
Hillside Dr PLF/KEOS FY6 19 G2
Hillside Rd PRES PR1 58 D5 3
Hill St BPOOLS FY4 4 D6
PRES PR1 7 G2
Hill Top KIRK/FR/WA PR4 75 H3
Hill Top Cl KIRK/FR/WA PR4 54 D4 3
Hill Top La CHLYE PR6 83 G4
Hill View Dr CHLY/EC PR7 94 A5
Hillview Rd KIRK/FR/WA PR4 43 E2
Hill Wk LEY/BBR PR5 81 F2
Hillylaid Rd CLV/TH FY5 22 A2
Hilstone La BISP FY2 28 D1
Hilton Av BPOOLS FY4 4 D6
LSTA FY8 50 A5
Hindley Cl FUL/RIB PR2 46 D1
Hindley St CHLY/EC PR7 91 E4
Hind St PRES PR1 6 E5
Hobart Pl CLV/TH FY5 21 F4
Hockley Pl BPOOLE FY3 29 F3 2
Hodder Av BPOOL FY1 5 G5
CHLY/EC PR7 91 E5
FTWD FY7 10 D4
Hodder Brook FUL/RIB PR2 47 H5 3
Hodder Cl LEY/BBR PR5 78 C1 9
Hodder Pl LSTA FY8 49 H4
Hodder Wy PLF/KEOS FY6 26 B5
Hodgson Av KIRK/FR/WA PR4 54 A5
Hodgson Pl PLF/KEOS FY6 26 B5 2
Hodgson Rd BPOOL FY1 28 B1
Hodson St LEY/BBR PR5 71 F5 4
Hoghton Cl LSTA FY8 49 F1
Hoghton La LEY/BBR PR5 72 C3
Hoghton Rd LEY/BBR PR5 80 C3
Hoghton St LEY/BBR PR5 77 F1
Hoghton Vw PRES PR1 58 D5 4
Holbeck Av BPOOLS FY4 33 F5
Holcombe Gv CHLYE PR6 91 H1
Holcombe Rd BISP FY2 29 E1 2
Holcroft Pl LSTA FY8 62 D2
Holgate BPOOLS FY4 39 F1
Holker Cl LEY/BBR PR5 72 D3
Holland Av LEY/BBR PR5 71 F4
Holland House Rd LEY/BBR PR5 71 F3
Holland Rd FUL/RIB PR2 57 F2 11
Hollings KIRK/FR/WA PR4 75 G2
Hollinhead Crs FUL/RIB PR2 45 E4
Hollinhurst Av PRES PR1 6 A6
Hollins Cl LEY/BBR PR5 73 H3
Hollins Gv FUL/RIB PR2 45 E5
Hollinshead St CHLY/EC PR7 91 F2
Hollins La LEY/BBR PR5 84 B3
Hollins Rd PRES PR1 46 C5
Hollybank Cl FUL/RIB PR2 44 C3
Holly Cl CHLYE PR6 83 E2
CLV/TH FY5 22 A1
Holly Crs CHLY/EC PR7 94 B2
Holly Ms LSTA FY8 49 F1 1
Holly Pl LEY/BBR PR5 79 E3
Holly Rd BPOOL FY1 28 C1
CLV/TH FY5 21 H1
Hollywood Av BPOOLE FY3 3 J4
PRES PR1 69 F3
Hollywood Gv FTWD FY7 11 F2
Holman St PRES PR1 58 D2 10
Holme Av FTWD FY7 16 D1
Holmefield Av CLV/TH FY5 21 E2
Holmefield Cl CLV/TH FY5 21 E2
Holmefield Rd LSTA FY8 49 F4
PLF/KEOS FY6 12 C1
Holme Rd LEY/BBR PR5 78 A1
PRES PR1 6 C4
Holmes Ct PRES PR1 45 H5
Holme Slack La PRES PR1 46 D5 2
Holmes Meadow
LEY/BBR PR5 80 A3 1
Holmes Rd CLV/TH FY5 21 G1
Holmeswood KIRK/FR/WA PR4 43 E3 4
Holmfield Crs FUL/RIB PR2 56 A2
Holmfield Rd BISP FY2 28 B1
FUL/RIB PR2 46 B4
Holmrook Rd PRES PR1 58 C2
Holsands Cl FUL/RIB PR2 47 F2 3
Holstein St PRES PR1 7 K1
Holt Brow LEY/BBR PR5 85 F1
Holt La CHLYE PR6 83 G1
Holts La PLF/KEOS FY6 26 D4
Holyoake Av BISP FY2 29 E1
Homestead LEY/BBR PR5 79 E5
Homestead Cl LEY/BBR PR5 80 C3 2
Homestead Dr FTWD FY7 11 E5
Homestead Wy FTWD FY7 11 E5
Honeypot La PLF/KEOS FY6 27 H3
Honeysuckle Cl CHLYE PR6 87 E2
Honeysuckle Pl BISP FY2 25 F1 1
Honister Av BPOOLE FY3 5 K3
Honister Cl FTWD FY7 10 D4 3
Honister Sq LSTA FY8 49 F1
Honiton Wy KIRK/FR/WA PR4 44 C2
Hools La GAR/LONG PR3 14 C1
Hope St CHLY/EC PR7 91 F1
LSTA FY8 49 G4
PRES PR1 7 G2
Hopton Rd BPOOL FY1 4 C3
Hopwood St LEY/BBR PR5 78 B1 5
LEY/BBR PR5 78 C2 1
PRES PR1 7 K1
Hornbeam Cl PRES PR1 69 E3
Hornby Av FTWD FY7 16 D1 1
FUL/RIB PR2 47 F4
Hornby Ct KIRK/FR/WA PR4 43 F4
Hornby Cft LEY/BBR PR5 80 A5
Hornby Rd BPOOL FY1 3 F6
CHLYE PR6 91 H4 1
LSTA FY8 61 E1
Hornchurch Dr CHLY/EC PR7 90 D2
Horncliffe Rd BPOOLS FY4 38 B2
Hornsea Cl FUL/RIB PR2 44 D4
Hornsey Av LSTA FY8 38 B4
Horsebridge Rd BPOOLE FY3 29 H2
Horsfall Av LSTA FY8 63 E3 3
Hough La LEY/BBR PR5 81 F3
Houghton Av BPOOLS FY4 5 G7
Houghton Cl PRES PR1 69 G3 1
Houghton Rd PRES PR1 69 F3
Houghton St CHLYE PR6 91 G2 6
Houldsworth Rd FUL/RIB PR2 45 H5 4
Houseman Pl BPOOLS FY4 39 E1
Hove Av FTWD FY7 16 C1
Hove Rd LSTA FY8 49 F5
Howard Cl LSTA FY8 49 E2 3
Howard Rd CHLY/EC PR7 91 E5
Howard St BPOOL FY1 2 E2
Howarth Crs PLF/KEOS FY6 26 C4
Howarth Rd FUL/RIB PR2 45 F5
Howe Gv CHLY/EC PR7 90 D3
The Howgills FUL/RIB PR2 46 B1
Howgill Wy LSTA FY8 63 H1 4
Howick Cross La PRES PR1 56 A5
Howick Moor La PRES PR1 68 C3
Howick Park Av PRES PR1 68 C2
Howick Park Cl PRES PR1 68 C2
Howick Park Dr PRES PR1 68 C2
Hoylake Cl FUL/RIB PR2 45 E2
Hoyle Av LSTA FY8 49 F1
Hoyle's La KIRK/FR/WA PR4 44 C2
Huck La LSTA FY8 52 A4
Hudson Ct LEY/BBR PR5 79 F1 1
Hudson Rd BPOOL FY1 5 G4
Hudson St PRES PR1 7 K4
Hugh Barn La KIRK/FR/WA PR4 75 F2
Hughes Gv BISP FY2
Hugh La LEY/BBR PR5
Hull Rd BPOOL FY1
Hull St FUL/RIB PR2
Hulme Av CLV/TH FY5
Humber Av BPOOLE FY3 29
Hungerford Rd LSTA FY8
Hunter Rd KIRK/FR/WA PR4
Hunters Fold KIRK/FR/WA PR4 74
Hunters Ldg LEY/BBR PR5
Hunters Rd LEY/BBR PR5
Huntingdon Rd CLV/TH FY5
Huntley Av BPOOLE FY3 29
Hunts Fld CHLYE PR6
Hunt St PRES PR1 6
Hurn Gv CHLY/EC PR7
Hurst Brook CHLY/EC PR7
Hurstmere Av BPOOLS FY4
Hurst Pk PRES PR1
Hurstway FUL/RIB PR2
Hurstway Cl FUL/RIB PR2 45
Hyde Rd BPOOL FY1

I

Iddesleigh Rd PRES PR1 59
Idlewood Pl CLV/TH FY5 21
Ilford Rd BPOOLS FY4
Ilkley Av LSTA FY8 50
Ilkley Gv CLV/TH FY5
The Illawalla CLV/TH FY5
Illingworth Rd PRES PR1
Ilway LEY/BBR PR5
Imperial St BPOOL FY1 28
Ince La CHLY/EC PR7
Ingleborough Wy LEY/BBR PR5
Ingleby Cl CLV/TH FY5
Ingle Head FUL/RIB PR2
Ingle Ms CHLYE PR6 91
Inglenook Cl CLV/TH FY5 21
Ingleton Av BISP FY2
Ingleton Rd FUL/RIB PR2
Ingleway CLV/TH FY5
Ingleway Av BPOOLE FY3
Inglewood Cl FTWD FY7
KIRK/FR/WA PR4
Inglewood Gv BISP FY2 25
Ingol Gv PLF/KEOS FY6
Ingol La PLF/KEOS FY6
Ingot St PRES PR1
Ingthorpe Av BISP FY2
Inkerman St FUL/RIB PR2
Inner Prom LSTA FY8
Inskip Pl BPOOLS FY4 39
LSTA FY8
Inskip Rd FUL/RIB PR2
LEY/BBR PR5 80
Intack Rd KIRK/FR/WA PR4
Inver Rd BISP FY2
Ipswich Pl CLV/TH FY5
Ipswich Rd FUL/RIB PR2
Irongate LEY/BBR PR5
Ironside Cl FUL/RIB PR2 46
Irving Cl BISP FY2
Irvin St PRES PR1
Isherwood St PRES PR1 58
Islay Rd LSTA FY8
Isleworth Dr CHLY/EC PR7
Ivy Av BPOOLS FY4
Ivy Bank FUL/RIB PR2

J

Jackson Rd CHLY/EC PR7 90
LEY/BBR PR5 80
Jackson St BPOOLE FY3
CHLY/EC PR7
LEY/BBR PR5 78 C
Jacson St PRES PR1
James Av BPOOLS FY4
Jameson Rd FTWD FY7
Jameson St BPOOL FY1
James Pl CHLY/EC PR7
James St LEY/BBR PR5 71
PRES PR1
Janice Dr FUL/RIB PR2
Jasmine Rd PRES PR1 70
Jeffrey Sq BPOOL FY1
Jellicoe Cl LSTA FY8
Jem Ga CLV/TH FY5
Jemmett St FUL/RIB PR2
Jenny La BPOOLS FY4
Jensen Dr BPOOLS FY4
Jepson Wy BPOOLS FY4
Jersey Av BISP FY2

's Cl LSTA FY8 48 D2 2
nond Av BPOOLS FY4 38 B1
Hill St BPOOLS FY4 33 F3 5
son Rd BPOOLS FY4 33 F3
spool FUL/RIB PR2 45 F2 1
St BPOOL FY1 4 D4 2
LY/EC PR7 94 B4 4
V/TH FY5 17 H5
Y/BBR PR5 71 F5 6
Y/BBR PR5 81 F3
sville Av BPOOLS FY4 39 E1
William St PRES PR1 58 D3 2
e Av BPOOLE FY3 33 F3
lee Av FUL/RIB PR2 56 A2
F/KEOS FY6 13 E2
lee Dr CLV/TH FY5 20 C1
lee La BPOOLS FY4 39 H2
lee La North BPOOLS FY4 39 G1
lee Rd LEY/BBR PR5 77 F2
lee Ter KIRK/FR/WA PR4 54 C4 2
lee Wy LSTA FY8 50 A3
land CHLY/EC PR7 86 D5
ction Rd PRES PR1 6 C3
Av BPOOLS FY4 33 G4
e's Wk KIRK/FR/WA PR4 74 A4
per Cl PLF/KEOS FY6 13 E1 1
per Cft CHLYE PR6 82 D3
and St PRES PR1 7 K1

K

nryan Cl BISP FY2 25 F2
e St FUL/RIB PR2 57 F2 12
St BPOOL FY1 2 D7
RES PR1 6 E3 1
sden Av BPOOLS FY4 38 D1
ting Ct FTWD FY7 11 F3 2
ts Av KIRK/FR/WA PR4 53 G5
ts Cl CHLY/EC PR7 88 C5
V/TH FY5 21 G2
ts Wy KIRK/FR/WA PR4 44 A4
e Cl CLV/TH FY5 21 G2
per's Hey CLV/TH FY5 17 G5 1
h Gv CLV/TH FY5 20 D3
et Acre LEY/BBR PR5 77 F2
et Av LEY/BBR PR5 82 A3
et La LEY/BBR PR5 79 E3
ett St CHLY/EC PR7 91 F2 7
marsh Cl BPOOLE FY3 33 H3 2
o Av CLV/TH FY5 20 D3
ons Av CLV/TH FY5 22 A2
verdale Rd CLV/TH FY5 21 F4
vin Rd CLV/TH FY5 24 D1
Mill La CHLYE PR6 83 E4
np St FTWD FY7 11 H2 1
npton Av BPOOLE FY3 5 K1
dal Av BPOOLE FY3 29 F1
V/TH FY5 16 D5
dal Rd LSTA FY8 48 D2
dal St PRES PR1 7 F1 1
ilworth Av FTWD FY7 11 E3
ilworth Gdns BPOOLS FY4 38 B1
ilworth Rd LSTA FY8 49 F5
mure Pl PRES PR1 58 A1 10
net Dr FUL/RIB PR2 37 E5
nett Dr LEY/BBR PR5 81 G2
nington Rd FUL/RIB PR2 46 B4
sington Av PRES PR1 57 E5
sington Rd BPOOLE FY3 3 H6
HLY/EC PR7 91 E3
V/TH FY5 20 C1 2
STA FY8 62 B2
t Av CLV/TH FY5 17 E5
EY/BBR PR5 71 E3 3
t Dr LEY/BBR PR5 82 A2
tmere Av LEY/BBR PR5 71 E4
EY/BBR PR5 81 F1
tmere Dr BPOOLS FY4 34 A4
RK/FR/WA PR4 74 C1
t Rd BPOOL FY1 4 E1
t's Cl KIRK/FR/WA PR4 42 C1
t St FTWD FY7 11 H1
RES PR1 58 A1
wyn Av BPOOLE FY3 5 J1
r Pl PRES PR1 6 B1
shaw St CHLYE PR6 91 H2
slea Av PLF/KEOS FY6 30 B2
ton Gv BPOOLS FY4 38 C3 3
trel Cl CLV/TH FY5 17 F4
wick Gv PLF/KEOS FY6 12 D1 1
wick Rd BPOOL FY1 5 F1
STA FY8 49 E3
vin Av PLF/KEOS FY6 26 D2
v Gdns LEY/BBR PR5 81 G1
RES PR1 57 E5
v Gv CLV/TH FY5 20 D3
brooke Av BPOOLS FY4 38 B4

Kiddlington Cl LEY/BBR PR5 78 A1 1
Kidsgrove FUL/RIB PR2 44 C3
Kielder Ct LSTA FY8 63 G2 3
Kilbane St FTWD FY7 11 F5 1
Kildare Av CLV/TH FY5 17 G5
Kildare Rd BISP FY2 24 D4
Kilgrimol Gdns LSTA FY8 48 C3
Kilkerran Cl CHLYE PR6 91 G2
Kilmory Pl BISP FY2 25 F2
Kilmuir Cl FUL/RIB PR2 46 D3 3
Kiln Cft CHLYE PR6 82 D1
Kilngate LEY/BBR PR5 70 D3
Kilnhouse La LSTA FY8 49 F2
Kiln La PLF/KEOS FY6 23 F2
Kilruddery Rd PRES PR1 6 D7
Kilsby Cl LEY/BBR PR5 71 F3 3
Kilshaw St PRES PR1 58 A2 7
Kilworth Height FUL/RIB PR2 45 G3
Kimberley Av BPOOLS FY4 38 D3
Kimberley Rd FUL/RIB PR2 57 F1 8
Kimberley St CHLY/EC PR7 94 B4
Kimberly Cl KIRK/FR/WA PR4 54 B5 3
Kincardine Av BPOOLS FY4 39 G2
Kincrag Pl BISP FY2 25 F1
Kincraig Rd BISP FY2 25 F1
King Edward Av BISP FY2 28 B1
LSTA FY8 61 G2
Kingfisher Dr PLF/KEOS FY6 25 H5
Kingfisher St PRES PR1 58 C1
King George Av BISP FY2 28 B1
Kingsbridge Cl PRES PR1 69 H5
Kings Cl BPOOLE FY3 30 C5
PLF/KEOS FY6 26 C4
Kingscote Dr BPOOLE FY3 3 K1
Kings Ct LEY/BBR PR5 81 F3
Kings Crs LEY/BBR PR5 81 F3
King's Cft LEY/BBR PR5 71 E1
Kingsdale Av FUL/RIB PR2 47 E4 2
Kingsdale Cl LEY/BBR PR5 71 G1
LEY/BBR PR5 85 G1 1
Kings Dr FUL/RIB PR2 45 G3
Kingsfold Dr PRES PR1 69 F4
Kingshaven Dr PRES PR1 69 H5
Kingsland Gv BPOOL FY1 5 H3
Kingsley Cl CLV/TH FY5 21 G1
Kingsley Dr CHLY/EC PR7 90 D5
Kingsley Rd BPOOLE FY3 33 H3 3
KIRK/FR/WA PR4 44 B2
Kingsmead CHLY/EC PR7 91 F5
Kingsmede BPOOLS FY4 39 E2
Kingsmere Av LSTA FY8 49 F2
Kingsmuir Av FUL/RIB PR2 47 E4 3
Kings Rd CLV/TH FY5 20 C2 1
LSTA FY8 61 E1
King's Sq BPOOL FY1 2 E5
Kingston Av BPOOLS FY4 38 C3
Kingston Dr LSTA FY8 50 B5
King St BPOOL FY1 2 E4
CHLY/EC PR7 91 G4
FTWD FY7 11 G2
LEY/BBR PR5 77 G2 3
LEY/BBR PR5 81 F3
King's Wk CLV/TH FY5 16 D4
Kingsway BPOOLS FY4 38 C1
CHLY/EC PR7 86 B5
CLV/TH FY5 20 C2
FUL/RIB PR2 56 C1
LEY/BBR PR5 78 B1
LEY/BBR PR5 80 D5
LSTA FY8 62 A2
PRES PR1 57 E5
Kingsway Av GAR/LONG PR3 36 B2
Kingsway West PRES PR1 68 D1
Kingswood CHLY/EC PR7 91 E5 5
Kingswood Cl LSTA FY8 62 C2 7
Kingswood Rd LEY/BBR PR5 81 F2
Kingswood St PRES PR1 6 E3 2
Kinnerton Pl CLV/TH FY5 21 F4
Kinross Crs BPOOLS FY4 33 G4 1
Kintbury Rd LSTA FY8 61 F2 1
Kintour Rd LSTA FY8 50 C5
Kintyre Cl BPOOLS FY4 39 F1
Kipling Dr BPOOLE FY3 33 H3
Kirby Dr KIRK/FR/WA PR4 54 B5
Kirby Rd BPOOL FY1 4 D3
Kirkby Av CLV/TH FY5 17 E5
LEY/BBR PR5 82 B3
Kirkdale Av LSTA FY8 49 F4 2
Kirkgate KIRK/FR/WA PR4 43 F3
Kirkham Av BPOOL FY1 5 J3
Kirkham By-pass
KIRK/FR/WA PR4 43 E4
Kirkham Cl LEY/BBR PR5 80 C3
Kirkham Rd KIRK/FR/WA PR4 43 H2
Kirkham St PRES PR1 7 F1
Kirkstall Av BPOOL FY1 5 K4
Kirkstall Cl CHLY/EC PR7 91 G5
Kirkstall Dr CHLY/EC PR7 91 G5
Kirkstall Rd CHLY/EC PR7 91 G5
Kirkstone Av FTWD FY7 10 D5
Kirkstone Dr CLV/TH FY5 24 C1
Kirkstone Rd LSTA FY8 48 D2 3
Kirton Crs LSTA FY8 50 A5 4
Kirton Pl CLV/TH FY5 21 E3
Kittiwake Cl CLV/TH FY5 21 F3 4
Kittlingborne Brow
LEY/BBR PR5 71 H3
Kitty La BPOOLS FY4 39 H4
Knaresboro Av BPOOLE FY3 33 F2 5
Knaresborough Cl
PLF/KEOS FY6 26 A2 2
Knightsbrdige Cl
KIRK/FR/WA PR4 42 C2 5
Knightsbridge Av BPOOLS FY4 38 D2 1
Knightsbridge Cl LSTA FY8 50 B5 2
Knights Cl CLV/TH FY5 21 F3
Knoll La KIRK/FR/WA PR4 74 A5
Knot Acre KIRK/FR/WA PR4 75 H1
Knot La LEY/BBR PR5 71 F1
Knowle Av BISP FY2 28 C1
CLV/TH FY5 21 E3
Knowles Rd LSTA FY8 49 E4
Knowles St CHLY/EC PR7 91 F4 5
PRES PR1 59 E3 4
The Knowle BISP FY2 24 C5
Knowley Brow CHLYE PR6 87 H5
Knowsley Av BPOOLE FY3 5 J1
LEY/BBR PR5 77 H5
Knowsley Cl LEY/BBR PR5 72 D4
Knowsley Crs CLV/TH FY5 22 A2
Knowsley Dr LEY/BBR PR5 73 E4
Knowsley Ga FTWD FY7 10 D2
Knowsley Rd LEY/BBR PR5 81 H4 2
Knowsley St PRES PR1 7 K4 1
Knox Gv BPOOL FY1 5 G2
Knutsford Rd BPOOLE FY3 33 H3 4
Korea Rd FUL/RIB PR2 46 C3
Kumara Crs BPOOLS FY4 33 H4
Kylemore Av BISP FY2 24 D5
Kyston Cl BPOOL FY1 3 G1

L

Laburnum Av LEY/BBR PR5 77 G1
LSTA FY8 63 F1
Laburnum Cl PRES PR1 46 D5
Laburnum Dr FUL/RIB PR2 36 C5 2
Laburnum Rd CHLYE PR6 87 G4
Laburnum St BPOOLE FY3 3 H1 1
Lacy Av PRES PR1 69 H4
Lady Crosse Dr CHLYE PR6 87 F1
Ladyman St PRES PR1 6 E3
Lady Pl LEY/BBR PR5 71 F2
Ladysmith Rd FUL/RIB PR2 57 F1 9
Lady St PRES PR1 7 H1
Lady Well Dr FUL/RIB PR2 46 D1
Ladywell St PRES PR1 7 F2
Laidley's Wk FTWD FY7 11 E1
Lakeland Gdns CHLY/EC PR7 90 D5
Lake Rd LSTA FY8 62 A3
Lake Rd North LSTA FY8 62 A2
Lakeway BPOOLE FY3 29 F4
Lakewood Av CLV/TH FY5 20 D3 1
Lamaleach Dr KIRK/FR/WA PR4 54 A5
Lambert Cl FUL/RIB PR2 47 F5 4
Lambert Rd FUL/RIB PR2 47 F5
Lambs Hill Cl CLV/TH FY5 22 B3 4
Lamb's La GAR/LONG PR3 14 C2
Lambs Rd CLV/TH FY5 22 B4
Lanark Av BISP FY2 24 C1 1
Lancaster Av CLV/TH FY5 22 A2
LEY/BBR PR5 82 B3
LSTA FY8 61 F2
Lancaster Cl PLF/KEOS FY6 12 D1
Lancaster Ga FTWD FY7 10 D3
Lancastergate LEY/BBR PR5 81 E4
Lancaster La LEY/BBR PR5 82 A3
Lancaster Rd BPOOLE FY3 33 G3
GAR/LONG PR3 15 G1
PLF/KEOS FY6 13 G3
PRES PR1 7 H1 2
Lancaster Rd North PRES PR1 58 A2
Lancaster St CHLY/EC PR7 94 C4
Lanchester Ct LEY/BBR PR5 84 C1
Lancia Crs BPOOLS FY4 41 E2 2
Landcrest Cl KIRK/FR/WA PR4 54 B1
Land La KIRK/FR/WA PR4 75 E3
Landseer Av BISP FY2 24 C3
Landseer St PRES PR1 58 D2 11
Lanefield Dr CLV/TH FY5 16 D5
Langcliffe Rd FUL/RIB PR2 47 F4 4
Langdale Cl CLV/TH FY5 21 H2
KIRK/FR/WA PR4 54 A5 1
LEY/BBR PR5 71 E5 2
Langdale Crs FUL/RIB PR2 47 F5 5
Langdale Gv CHLYE PR6 83 E5
Langdale Pl BPOOLS FY4 34 A4 4
Langdale Rd BPOOLS FY4 33 H4
FUL/RIB PR2 47 F5
LEY/BBR PR5 85 G1
LSTA FY8 48 D3
Langden Crs LEY/BBR PR5 78 C2
Langden Dr FUL/RIB PR2 47 H5 4
Langdon Wy BISP FY2 25 E5
Langfield Av BPOOLS FY4 38 C3
Langfield Cl FUL/RIB PR2 37 E5 1
Langholm Cl LEY/BBR PR5 80 C3 4
Langholme Rd PRES PR1 68 D2
Langport Cl FUL/RIB PR2 37 E5
Lang St BPOOL FY1 2 E2
Langton Brow CHLY/EC PR7 88 C5
Langton Cl CHLY/EC PR7 88 C5
LEY/BBR PR5 80 B4
Langton Rd KIRK/FR/WA PR4 43 E3
Langton St PRES PR1 6 D4
Langwood FTWD FY7 11 E4 4
Lansborough Cl LEY/BBR PR5 80 A4 1
Lansdowne Pl BPOOL FY1 2 C2 2
Lansdowne Rd KIRK/FR/WA PR4 42 D1
LSTA FY8 62 B1
Lansdown Hl FUL/RIB PR2 45 F1
The Lanterns PLF/KEOS FY6 26 B3 1
Lappet Gv KIRK/FR/WA PR4 44 B3 4
The Lapwings PLF/KEOS FY6 25 H5 4
Larbreck Rd BPOOLE FY3 3 J1
Larch Av CHLYE PR6 87 H5
Larch Cl KIRK/FR/WA PR4 66 A1
PLF/KEOS FY6 13 E1
Larches Av FUL/RIB PR2 56 C2
Larches La FUL/RIB PR2 56 B2
Larchgate FUL/RIB PR2 46 D1 1
Larch Ga LEY/BBR PR5 72 D4
Larch Gv LEY/BBR PR5 71 G5
Larchwood FUL/RIB PR2 56 B2 5
PRES PR1 69 E2 3
Larchwood Cl LSTA FY8 62 D2 1
Larchwood Crs LEY/BBR PR5 80 D3
Lark Av PRES PR1 69 H2
Lark Ct FTWD FY7 10 D5
Larkfield CHLY/EC PR7 88 A4
Lark Hl LEY/BBR PR5 72 A3 1
Larkhill Rd PRES PR1 58 C4
Larkhill St BPOOL FY1 2 E3
PRES PR1 58 C4
Larkholme Av FTWD FY7 11 E5
Larkholme La FTWD FY7 11 E5
Larkholme Pde FTWD FY7 10 D5
Latham Av BPOOLE FY3 5 K2
Latham St PRES PR1 7 J5
Latimer Dr KIRK/FR/WA PR4 75 G1
Lauderdale Av CLV/TH FY5 20 D3
Lauderdale Rd FUL/RIB PR2 47 G4
Lauderdale St PRES PR1 6 E5
Laundry Rd North
BPOOLS FY4 39 G3 1
Laurel Av BPOOL FY1 5 J4
CHLY/EC PR7 85 G4
FTWD FY7 17 F1
LSTA FY8 63 F1
Laurel Bank Av FUL/RIB PR2 45 F5
Laurel Dr CLV/TH FY5 21 H4
The Laurels CHLY/EC PR7 94 C2
Laurel St PRES PR1 7 K3
Laurier Av BPOOLS FY4 38 C2
Lauriston Cl BPOOLS FY4 39 G2 4
Lavender Cl FUL/RIB PR2 46 D2
Lavender Gv CHLY/EC PR7 91 F5 1
Laverton Rd LSTA FY8 61 F1
Lawnswood Av PLF/KEOS FY6 25 H5
Lawnswood Crs BPOOLE FY3 34 A3
Lawn Tennis Ct BPOOLS FY4 38 D3
Lawnwood Av CHLY/EC PR7 90 D5 5
Lawrence Av LEY/BBR PR5 71 E4 2
LSTA FY8 49 G4
PRES PR1 70 C1
Lawrence La CHLY/EC PR7 88 B3
Lawrence Rd CHLY/EC PR7 91 E3
PRES PR1 69 E1
Lawrence St BPOOLS FY4 4 C6 4
FUL/RIB PR2 45 G5
Lawson Rd BPOOLE FY3 33 G2
LSTA FY8 49 G1 1
Lawsons Ct CLV/TH FY5 22 A3
Lawsons Rd CLV/TH FY5 22 A3
Lawson St CHLYE PR6 91 H3 5
PRES PR1 7 H1
Laxey Gv PRES PR1 47 E5
Laycock Ga BPOOLE FY3 3 H2
Layton Rd BPOOLE FY3 3 J2
FUL/RIB PR2 56 B2 6
Lazenby Av FTWD FY7 10 C4
Leach Crs LSTA FY8 49 F1
Leach La LSTA FY8 49 E1
Leach Pl LEY/BBR PR5 79 E1
Leadale FUL/RIB PR2 56 A1
Leadale Gn LEY/BBR PR5 80 C3
Leadale Rd LEY/BBR PR5 80 C3
Leaford Av BPOOLE FY3 29 E2

Leafy Cl LEY/BBR PR5 81 G5
Leagram Crs FUL/RIB PR2 47 G5
Leamington Rd BPOOL FY1 3 F5
LSTA FY8 49 F5
Leander Av PLF/KEOS FY6 26 B5
Lea Rd CHLYE PR6 87 F2
Leavesley Rd BPOOL FY1 28 C2
Lea Way Cl CLV/TH FY5 22 B5
Leckhampton Rd BPOOL FY1 28 B2
Ledbury Rd BPOOLE FY3 29 G3
Leeds Rd BPOOL FY1 3 G5
Leehouse Dr PLF/KEOS FY6 30 B2 2
Leek St PRES PR1 59 F3
Lee Rd BPOOLS FY4 33 H5
Leesands Cl FUL/RIB PR2 47 E3
Leeson Av CHLY/EC PR7 94 A1
Leeward Rd FUL/RIB PR2 56 C3
Leicester Av CLV/TH FY5 20 D1
Leicester Ga CLV/TH FY5 21 E1 1
Leicester Rd BPOOL FY1 3 G5
PRES PR1 58 A2
Leigh Brow PRES PR1 70 C4
Leigh Rw CHLY/EC PR7 91 F3
Leighton Av FTWD FY7 10 D3
Leighton St PRES PR1 6 E1
Leith Av CLV/TH FY5 20 D2
Lennon St CHLY/EC PR7 91 F3 9
Lennox Ct BPOOLS FY4 38 D1
Lennox Ga BPOOLS FY4 38 D1
Lennox St PRES PR1 7 J4
Lentworth Av BISP FY2 24 D2
Leo Case Ct PRES PR1 59 E3
Leopold Gv BPOOL FY1 2 D5 4
Leslie Av CLV/TH FY5 22 A2
Letchworth Dr CHLY/EC PR7 91 E4
Letchworth Wks CHLY/EC PR7 91 E4 4
Leven Av FTWD FY7 10 D3 3
Levens Cl PLF/KEOS FY6 30 B2
Levens Dr LEY/BBR PR5 82 A2
PLF/KEOS FY6 30 B1
Levensgarth Av FUL/RIB PR2 37 E5
Levens Gv BPOOL FY1 5 F3
Levens St PRES PR1 59 E2 13
Lever House La LEY/BBR PR5 81 H2
Lever St BPOOLE FY3 3 J6
Levine Av BPOOLS FY4 33 G4
Lewtas St BPOOL FY1 2 D2
Lex St PRES PR1 58 D3
Leyburn Av BISP FY2 24 C2
FTWD FY7 11 E4
Leyburn Cl FUL/RIB PR2 47 F3 3
Leyfield PRES PR1 69 G4
Leyfield Cl BPOOLE FY3 29 G1
Leyfield Rd LEY/BBR PR5 81 E3
Leyland La LEY/BBR PR5 80 C5
Leyland Rd PRES PR1 6 C6
The Leylands LSTA FY8 62 D3 1
Leyland Wy LEY/BBR PR5 81 H3
Leys Rd BISP FY2 28 D1
Leyton Av LEY/BBR PR5 80 C5
Library Rd CHLYE PR6 79 E5
Library St CHLY/EC PR7 91 F3
PRES PR1 7 J3
Lichen Cl CHLY/EC PR7 94 A1
Lichfield Rd BPOOL FY1 28 C2
CHLY/EC PR7 91 E4
FUL/RIB PR2 56 C1 2
Liege Rd LEY/BBR PR5 81 F4 6
Lightbown Av BPOOLE FY3 5 J2
Lightburne Av LSTA FY8 61 F1
Lightfoot Cl GAR/LONG PR3 36 C5
Lightfoot Green La
KIRK/FR/WA PR4 36 A5
Lightfoot La FUL/RIB PR2 36 C5
KIRK/FR/WA PR4 44 C1
Lighthurst Av CHLY/EC PR7 91 F4
Lighthurst La CHLY/EC PR7 91 F5
Lightwood Av BPOOLS FY4 5 F7
LSTA FY8 62 B3
Lilac Av BPOOL FY1 5 G3
LSTA FY8 63 F1
PRES PR1 70 A4
Lilac Gv PRES PR1 46 D5 3
Lily Gv PRES PR1 46 D5
Lily St BPOOL FY1 3 F4
Lima Rd LSTA FY8 49 G5
Limbrick Rd CHLYE PR6 91 H3
Lime Av KIRK/FR/WA PR4 43 E4
Limebrest Av CLV/TH FY5 22 B4
Lime Cha GAR/LONG PR3 36 B5
Limechase Cl BPOOLS FY4 39 G2 5
Lime Cl PRES PR1 68 D2
Lime Gv BISP FY2 25 E5
CHLY/EC PR7 91 F5
CLV/TH FY5 22 A3
FUL/RIB PR2 56 C1
LSTA FY8 48 D3
PLF/KEOS FY6 26 C5
Limerick Rd BISP FY2 24 D4
Limes Av CHLY/EC PR7 85 H3
Linadale Av CLV/TH FY5 21 H2 4
Lincoln Av CLV/TH FY5 21 E1
FTWD FY7 11 E3
Lincoln Rd BPOOL FY1 3 F5
Lincoln St PRES PR1 58 C2
Lindale Rd FUL/RIB PR2 46 B4 5
Lindbeck Rd BPOOLS FY4 34 A4
Lindel La PLF/KEOS FY6 13 F4
Lindel Rd FTWD FY7 11 E4
Linden Av CLV/TH FY5 21 F1
Linden Cl CLV/TH FY5 21 F2
LEY/BBR PR5 70 C5
Linden Dr LEY/BBR PR5 70 C5
Linden Gn CLV/TH FY5 21 F1
Linden Gv CHLYE PR6 87 G4
FUL/RIB PR2 47 F5
Linden Ms LSTA FY8 49 F1
Linden Pl BISP FY2 25 E4
Lindle Av KIRK/FR/WA PR4 68 B4
Lindle Cl KIRK/FR/WA PR4 68 B4
Lindle Crs KIRK/FR/WA PR4 68 B4
Lindle La KIRK/FR/WA PR4 68 B4
Lindley St LEY/BBR PR5 77 G1 3
Lindsay Av BPOOLE FY3 5 K2
LEY/BBR PR5 81 G3
LSTA FY8 49 H5
PLF/KEOS FY6 26 B5
Lindsay Dr CHLY/EC PR7 90 D3
Linfield Ter BPOOLS FY4 38 D2
Lingfield Rd FTWD FY7 11 E5
Lingwell Cl CHLYE PR6 87 F2 3
Links Fld FUL/RIB PR2 45 F5
Links Ga CLV/TH FY5 22 B5
FUL/RIB PR2 45 F5
LSTA FY8 49 G5
Links Rd BPOOL FY1 28 C1
LSTA FY8 61 E1
PLF/KEOS FY6 12 B1
PRES PR1 57 E5
The Links CLV/TH FY5 20 C1
Links Vw LSTA FY8 62 A1
Linnet Cl BPOOLE FY3 29 H4
Linnet St PRES PR1 58 C1
Linton Gv PRES PR1 69 E1
Linton St FUL/RIB PR2 45 G5
Liptrott Rd CHLY/EC PR7 90 D5
Little Acre CLV/TH FY5 22 B4
KIRK/FR/WA PR4 74 B1
Little Banks Cl LEY/BBR PR5 79 E3 1
Little Carr La CHLY/EC PR7 91 G5
Little Cl PRES PR1 69 F3
Little Poulton La PLF/KEOS FY6 26 D4
Little Tongues La PLF/KEOS FY6 13 F2
Little Twining KIRK/FR/WA PR4 74 B2
Liverpool New Rd
KIRK/FR/WA PR4 74 A5
Liverpool Old Rd
KIRK/FR/WA PR4 74 A3
Liverpool Rd BPOOL FY1 3 G5
KIRK/FR/WA PR4 68 B3
PRES PR1 6 C6
Livesey St LSTA FY8 63 E3
PRES PR1 58 C4
Livet Av BPOOLS FY4 38 D1
Livingstone Rd BPOOL FY1 2 E7
Lochinch Cl BPOOLS FY4 39 G2
Lockerbie Av CLV/TH FY5 20 D4
Lockhart Rd PRES PR1 58 A1 11
Lockhurst Av CLV/TH FY5 21 F4 3
Lockside Rd FUL/RIB PR2 56 C3
Lockwood Av PLF/KEOS FY6 26 B3
Lodge Cl CLV/TH FY5 20 C5 1
KIRK/FR/WA PR4 54 B4 1
LEY/BBR PR5 71 G5 3
Lodge Ct BPOOLE FY3 30 B5
Lodge La KIRK/FR/WA PR4 64 B1
LEY/BBR PR5 76 D3
PLF/KEOS FY6 27 H5
Lodge St PRES PR1 6 E2
Lodge Vw KIRK/FR/WA PR4 76 D2
The Lodgings FUL/RIB PR2 46 D3 4
Lodore Rd BPOOLS FY4 38 C2
Loftos Av BPOOLS FY4 32 D5
Lomond Av BPOOLE FY3 33 F3
LSTA FY8 61 H1
London Rd BPOOLE FY3 3 H3
PRES PR1 58 C4
London St FTWD FY7 11 G1
London Wy LEY/BBR PR5 70 D3
Long Acre LEY/BBR PR5 79 F4
Long Acre Pl LSTA FY8 63 E2
Longbrook Av LEY/BBR PR5 71 F4
Long Butts PRES PR1 69 G4
Long Copse CHLY/EC PR7 90 C1
Long Croft Meadow
CHLY/EC PR7 87 E5
Longfield FUL/RIB PR2 37 E5 2
PRES PR1 69 E1
Longfield Av CHLY/EC PR7 94 B3
PLF/KEOS FY6 26 B3
Longfield Mnr CHLY/EC PR7 90 D5
Longfield Pl PLF/KEOS FY6 26 B3 2
Longford Av BISP FY2 25 E2
Longhouse La PLF/KEOS FY6 30 B2
Longley Cl FUL/RIB PR2 37 E5
Long Meadow CHLY/EC PR7 90 D5
KIRK/FR/WA PR4 42 C3
KIRK/FR/WA PR4 74 A5
Longmeadow La CLV/TH FY5 22 A1
Longmeanygate LEY/BBR PR5 80 A1
Long Moss La KIRK/FR/WA PR4 75 F3
Longridge Av BPOOLS FY4 39 E3
Longridge Rd FUL/RIB PR2 47 G4
Longsands La FUL/RIB PR2 46 D3
Longton Av CLV/TH FY5 21 H2
Longton By-pass
KIRK/FR/WA PR4 74 B5
Longton Rd BPOOL FY1 3 F5
Longton St CHLYE PR6 91 H2 7
Longway BPOOLS FY4 33 F5
Longworth Av CHLY/EC PR7 94 C3
Longworth St CHLY/EC PR7 91 E4
LEY/BBR PR5 71 F4 4
PRES PR1 58 D2
Lonsdale Av FTWD FY7 11 E3
Lonsdale Cl LEY/BBR PR5 85 F1
Lonsdale Crs FTWD FY7 11 E3 1
Lonsdale Rd BPOOL FY1 4 D3
PRES PR1 58 D2 12
Lord's Av LEY/BBR PR5 77 G2
Lords Cft CHLYE PR6 82 D2
Lord's La PRES PR1 69 H5
Lord St BPOOL FY1 2 D2
CHLY/EC PR7 88 B5
CHLYE PR6 91 G3
FTWD FY7 11 H2
LSTA FY8 48 D4
PRES PR1 7 J2
Lord's Wk PRES PR1 7 K2
Lorne Rd BISP FY2 24 D5
Lorne St CHLY/EC PR7 91 F3
LSTA FY8 63 G2
Lorraine Av FUL/RIB PR2 45 H5
Lorton Cl FUL/RIB PR2 46 A2
Lostock Gdns BPOOLS FY4 38 D2
Lostock La LEY/BBR PR5 77 H2
Lostock Meadow CHLYE PR6 82 D3
Lostock Sq LEY/BBR PR5 77 G2
Lostock Vw LEY/BBR PR5 77 F2
Lothian Av FTWD FY7 10 D3
Lothian Pl BISP FY2 25 E2
Lotus Dr BPOOLS FY4 41 E2 3
Loughrigg Ter BPOOLS FY4 34 A4
Louise St BPOOL FY1 4 D1
Lourdes Av LEY/BBR PR5 70 B5
Lovat Rd PRES PR1 58 A1
Lowcroft KIRK/FR/WA PR4 36 A2
Lowcross Rd PLF/KEOS FY6 26 C5
Lower Bank Rd FUL/RIB PR2 46 A5
Lower Burgh Wy CHLY/EC PR7 94 D1
Lower Copthurst La CHLYE PR6 83 H5
Lower Fld LEY/BBR PR5 77 E3
Lower Gn PLF/KEOS FY6 26 C4
Lower Greenfield FUL/RIB PR2 45 E4
Lower House Rd LEY/BBR PR5 80 D4 2
Lower La KIRK/FR/WA PR4 54 B1
Lower Lune St FTWD FY7 11 H1 4
Lower Wk CLV/TH FY5 20 C5
Lowesby Cl LEY/BBR PR5 71 F3 4
Lowesway BPOOLS FY4 33 F5
CLV/TH FY5 21 H1 4
Lowfield Cl KIRK/FR/WA PR4 55 F1
Lowfield Rd BPOOLS FY4 39 F1
Low Gn LEY/BBR PR5 81 E3
Lowick Cl LEY/BBR PR5 72 D2
Lowick Dr PLF/KEOS FY6 30 B1
Lowland Wy BISP FY2 25 F1
Low Moor Rd BISP FY2 25 E4
Lowood Gv FUL/RIB PR2 56 A2
Lowrey Ter BPOOL FY1 4 D4
Lowry Cl LEY/BBR PR5 77 F2
Lowther Av BISP FY2 24 B5
Lowther Crs LEY/BBR PR5 80 C2
Lowther Dr LEY/BBR PR5 80 C2
Lowther Rd FTWD FY7 11 F2
Lowther St FUL/RIB PR2 57 F2
Lowther Ter LSTA FY8 63 E3
Lowthian St PRES PR1 7 H2
Lowthorpe Crs PRES PR1 58 C1
Lowthorpe Rd PRES PR1 58 C1
Lowton Rd LSTA FY8 49 G3
Loxham Gdns BPOOLS FY4 38 D2 2
Loxley Gn FUL/RIB PR2 46 D2
Loxley Pl CLV/TH FY5 21 E5
Loxley Pl East CLV/TH FY5 21 E5
Lucas Av CHLY/EC PR7 90 A2
Lucas La CHLYE PR6 87 F1
Lucerne Rd FUL/RIB PR2 46 D4 4
Ludlow Gv BISP FY2 25 F5
Lulworth Av BPOOLE FY3 33 G3
FUL/RIB PR2 5
Lulworth Pl LEY/BBR PR5 7
Lulworth Rd FUL/RIB PR2 46
Lund St PRES PR1
Lune Cl KIRK/FR/WA PR4 4
Lunedale Av BPOOL FY1
Lune Dr LEY/BBR PR5 8
Lune Gv BPOOL FY1
Lune Rd FTWD FY7 1
Lunesdale Cl LSTA FY8 50
Lunesdale Rd KIRK/FR/WA PR4 4
Lune St PRES PR1
Lune Vw PLF/KEOS FY6 1
Lupin Cl CHLYE PR6 8
Lupton St CHLY/EC PR7 91
Luton Rd CLV/TH FY5 2
FUL/RIB PR2 5
Lutwidge Av PRES PR1 5
Lyceum Av BPOOLE FY3
Lychfield LEY/BBR PR5 7
Lyddesdale Av CLV/TH FY5 2
Lydd Gv CHLY/EC PR7 9
Lydgate CHLY/EC PR7 9
Lydiate La CHLY/EC PR7 8
LEY/BBR PR5 7
Lydric Av LEY/BBR PR5 7
Lyme Gv PLF/KEOS FY6 1
Lyncroft Crs BPOOLE FY3 2
Lyndale Av LEY/BBR PR5 7
Lyndale Cl LEY/BBR PR5 8
Lyndale Gv LEY/BBR PR5 7
Lyndeth Cl FUL/RIB PR2 47
Lyndhurst Av BPOOLS FY4
Lyndhurst Dr FUL/RIB PR2 5
Lynn Gv BPOOL FY1 2
Lynn Pl FUL/RIB PR2 59
Lynton Av BPOOLS FY4 3
LEY/BBR PR5 8
Lynton Ct FTWD FY7 16
Lynwood Av BPOOLE FY3 2
Lynwood Dr PLF/KEOS FY6 1
Lyons La CHLY/EC PR7 9
CHLYE PR6 9
Lythall Av LSTA FY8 6
Lytham Rd BPOOL FY1
BPOOLS FY4 3
FUL/RIB PR2 4
KIRK/FR/WA PR4 5
LSTA FY8 5
Lytham St CHLYE PR6 9
Lythcoe Av FUL/RIB PR2 4

M

Macauley Av BPOOLS FY4 3
Macbeth Rd FTWD FY7 1
Mackay Cft CHLYE PR6 91
Mackenzie Cl CHLYE PR6 91
Maclaren Cl BPOOLE FY3 30
Maddy St PRES PR1
Madison Av BISP FY2 2
Mafeking Rd FUL/RIB PR2 57
Magdalen Av CLV/TH FY5 2
Magnolia Cl FUL/RIB PR2 46
Magnolia Dr LEY/BBR PR5 8
Magnolia Rd PRES PR1 6
Maida V CLV/TH FY5 2
Main Dr PLF/KEOS FY6 2
Mains La PLF/KEOS FY6 2
Main Sprit Weind PRES PR1
Maitland Av CLV/TH FY5 2
Maitland Cl PRES PR1 58
Maitland St PRES PR1 58
PRES PR1 59
Malcolm Pl FTWD FY7 11
Malcolm St PRES PR1 59
Malden St LEY/BBR PR5 8
Maldern Av PLF/KEOS FY6 26
Maldon Pl FUL/RIB PR2 59
Malham Av BPOOLS FY4
Malham Pl FUL/RIB PR2 47
Mallard Cl CLV/TH FY5 1
LEY/BBR PR5 8
Mallard Ct BPOOLE FY3 2
Mallards Wk LEY/BBR PR5 78
Mallom Av CHLY/EC PR7 9
The Mall FUL/RIB PR2 5
LSTA FY8 5
Maltby Pl BPOOLS FY4 33
Malthouse Ct FUL/RIB PR2 57
Malthouse Wy PRES PR1 6
The Maltings CLV/TH FY5 1
KIRK/FR/WA PR4 7
Malton Dr LEY/BBR PR5 7
Malvern Av BPOOL FY1
PLF/KEOS FY6 1
PRES PR1 58
Malvern Cl LEY/BBR PR5 77

vern Rd LSTA FY8 62 B1 3
ES PR1 58 C5 1
vern St PRES PR1 70 C1
by Cl LEY/BBR PR5 73 E3
chester Rd BPOOLE FY3 3 H3
ES PR1 7 K3
ning Rd PRES PR1 59 F2 8
or Av FUL/RIB PR2 46 C4
ES PR1 69 E2
or Cl LEY/BBR PR5 73 E3
or Ct FUL/RIB PR2 45 E1
orcroft KIRK/FR/WA PR4 74 A1
or Dr CLV/TH FY5 20 D1
RK/FR/WA PR4 43 G4
or Gv PRES PR1 68 D2
or House Cl LEY/BBR PR5 80 A4
or House Crs PRES PR1 46 C5
or House La PRES PR1 46 C5
or La PRES PR1 69 E2
or Pk PRES PR1 46 D5
or Rd BPOOL FY1 3 G6
HLYE PR6 83 E1
WD FY7 11 E1
or Wd FTWD FY7 11 E2 5
RK/FR/WA PR4 43 F1
sfield Dr LEY/BBR PR5 72 D3
sfield Rd BPOOLE FY3 28 D2
ston Gv CHLY/EC PR7 90 D3
le Av BPOOLE FY3 3 H5
V/TH FY5 22 A4 3
WD FY7 17 F1 2
le Cl KIRK/FR/WA PR4 55 F1
le Dr LEY/BBR PR5 71 G5
LF/KEOS FY6 26 B5
le Gv CHLYE PR6 87 G4
JL/RIB PR2 47 H4
RK/FR/WA PR4 53 F5 1
ES PR1 69 E2
lewood Av PLF/KEOS FY6 13 E1
lewood Cl LEY/BBR PR5 80 D4 3
TA FY8 62 D2 2
lewood Dr CLV/TH FY5 20 C4
athon Pl LEY/BBR PR5 80 B1
chwood Rd BPOOLE FY3 29 H2
croft Av BPOOLS FY4 39 E1
dale Av BPOOLS FY4 34 A4
dale Crs LEY/BBR PR5 81 G5
dale Rd PRES PR1 59 H2
esfield Rd PRES PR1 6 D7
ewood CHLY/EC PR7 87 E5
garet Rd PRES PR1 69 H2
garet St PRES PR1 7 J1
gate Av BPOOLS FY4 39 E2 1
gate Rd FUL/RIB PR2 44 D4
STA FY8 49 F3
ilyn Av LEY/BBR PR5 77 G1
ina Av BPOOL FY1 5 G3
POOLE FY3 30 B2
ina Cl LEY/BBR PR5 70 B5
ina Dr FUL/RIB PR2 45 H1
EY/BBR PR5 70 B5
ina Gv LEY/BBR PR5 70 B5
ine Dr LSTA FY8 62 A3
ine Pde FTWD FY7 10 C5
iners Cl FTWD FY7 11 E5
iners Wy FUL/RIB PR2 56 D3
ino Cl CLV/TH FY5 22 B4
itime St FTWD FY7 11 F4
itime Wy FUL/RIB PR2 56 C4
k Cl PRES PR1 70 A5
ket Pl PLF/KEOS FY6 26 B4 3
ket Sq LSTA FY8 63 E3 6
ket St BPOOL FY1 2 C4
HLY/EC PR7 91 F2
IRK/FR/WA PR4 42 C2
LF/KEOS FY6 23 G2
RES PR1 7 H2
ket St West PRES PR1 7 G2
kham St FUL/RIB PR2 57 F2 13
kland St PRES PR1 6 E3 3
k's Av LEY/BBR PR5 76 D4
l Av PRES PR1 69 E2
lboro Rd BPOOLE FY3 3 H6
lborough Av CLV/TH FY5 16 C4
IRK/FR/WA PR4 53 F5
lborough Dr FUL/RIB PR2 36 C5
EY/BBR PR5 70 D2
lborough Rd LSTA FY8 49 E2
lborough St CHLYE PR6 91 H1
l Cft PRES PR1 69 G4
lfield KIRK/FR/WA PR4 74 A5
lfield Cl FUL/RIB PR2 44 C2
l Hill Crs FUL/RIB PR2 59 H1
lhill Rd BPOOLE FY3 29 G2
quis Dr KIRK/FR/WA PR4 54 C4
quis St KIRK/FR/WA PR4 42 D3
ron Cl LEY/BBR PR5 80 D3
sden Cl CHLY/EC PR7 88 A3 2
sden Rd BPOOLS FY4 5 G7
sden St KIRK/FR/WA PR4 43 F3

Marsett Pl *FUL/RIB* PR2 47 F3
Marshall Gv *FUL/RIB* PR2 44 D4
Marshall's Brow *PRES* PR1 69 H3
Marshall's Cl *PRES* PR1 69 H2 1
Marshdale Rd *BPOOLS* FY4 39 F1 4
Marsh Dr *KIRK/FR/WA* PR4 54 D4
Marsh La *PLF/KEOS* FY6 23 G3
PRES PR1 6 E2
Marsh Rd *CLV/TH* FY5 21 G2
Marsh Vw *KIRK/FR/WA* PR4 55 F1
Marsh Wy *PRES* PR1 69 F4
Marston Cl *FUL/RIB* PR2 45 F1
Marston Moor *FUL/RIB* PR2 45 F1
Martin Av *LSTA* FY8 38 C4 2
Martinfield *FUL/RIB* PR2 37 E5
Martin Field Rd *PRES* PR1 69 G4
Martins Av *CHLY/EC* PR7 95 H3
Marton Dr *BPOOLS* FY4 32 D5
Marton Rd *FUL/RIB* PR2 56 C3
Marybank Cl *FUL/RIB* PR2 46 D3 5
Masefield Av *CLV/TH* FY5 21 F1
Masefield Pl *LEY/BBR* PR5 71 E4
Mason Cl *KIRK/FR/WA* PR4 54 C5 2
Masonfield *LEY/BBR* PR5 79 E4
Mason Hill Vw *FUL/RIB* PR2 46 B4 7
Mason House Crs *FUL/RIB* PR2 44 D3 2
Mason St *CHLYE* PR6 87 H5
Masonwood *FUL/RIB* PR2 46 B2
Mather St *BPOOLE* FY3 3 H1
Matlock Pl *FUL/RIB* PR2 44 D3 3
Matterdale Rd *LEY/BBR* PR5 81 G5
Matthews Ct *BPOOLS* FY4 38 D1 1
Maudland Rd *BPOOL* FY1 4 E4
PRES PR1 7 F1
Maud St *CHLY/EC* PR7 91 E4
Maureen Av *LEY/BBR* PR5 77 G1 4
Maurice Gv *BISP* FY2 25 E5
Mavis Dr *CHLY/EC* PR7 94 B4
Maxwell Gv *BISP* FY2 25 E5
May Bell Av *CLV/TH* FY5 21 F1
Maycroft Av *PLF/KEOS* FY6 26 A2
Mayfair Cl *LSTA* FY8 50 B5 3
Mayfair Dr *CLV/TH* FY5 22 A4
Mayfair Gdns *CLV/TH* FY5 22 A3 3
Mayfair Rd *BPOOL* FY1 5 J4
Mayfield Av *BPOOLS* FY4 38 C2
CLV/TH FY5 17 G5
FUL/RIB PR2 44 D3 4
KIRK/FR/WA PR4 42 D3
LEY/BBR PR5 77 H1
Mayfield Rd *CHLYE* PR6 91 G1
FUL/RIB PR2 57 E2
LEY/BBR PR5 81 F5 1
LSTA FY8 49 F3 2
Mayflower Av *PRES* PR1 68 D2
Maynard St *FUL/RIB* PR2 57 G1
Mayor Av *BPOOL* FY1 5 F3
Maypark *LEY/BBR* PR5 78 D4
Mckenzie St *LEY/BBR* PR5 78 C1 11
Mead Av *LEY/BBR* PR5 81 G4
Meadow Av *FTWD* FY7 17 E1
PLF/KEOS FY6 8 A5
Meadoway *KIRK/FR/WA* PR4 74 A1
Meadow Bank *PRES* PR1 69 F3
Meadowbarn Cl *KIRK/FR/WA* PR4 44 B3
Meadowbrook *BPOOLE* FY3 34 A3
Meadow Ct *PRES* PR1 6 E6
Meadow Crs *PLF/KEOS* FY6 25 G4
Meadowcroft *CHLY/EC* PR7 85 G4
LSTA FY8 49 G2 1
Meadowcroft Av *CLV/TH* FY5 21 E2
PLF/KEOS FY6 23 G3
Meadowcroft Rd *LEY/BBR* PR5 80 C5
Meadow Dr *KIRK/FR/WA* PR4 65 E1
Meadowfield *FUL/RIB* PR2 46 A1
Meadow Fld *PRES* PR1 69 H4 3
Meadow Head La
KIRK/FR/WA PR4 74 A2
Meadowlands *CHLY/EC* PR7 94 A1
Meadow La *LEY/BBR* PR5 79 E5
LSTA FY8 64 A2 1
PLF/KEOS FY6 12 D2
Meadow Pk *BPOOLE* FY3 30 B5
KIRK/FR/WA PR4 42 C2
Meadow Reach *PRES* PR1 69 E4
Meadows Av *CLV/TH* FY5 21 F1
Meadowside *KIRK/FR/WA* PR4 74 B3 1
Meadowside Dr *LEY/BBR* PR5 72 D5 3
The Meadows *CHLY/EC* PR7 92 C3
CLV/TH FY5 21 F2
LEY/BBR PR5 80 A3 2
Meadow St *LEY/BBR* PR5 81 F3 4
PRES PR1 7 K1
Meadow Wy *CHLY/EC* PR7 94 A5
Meads Rd *FUL/RIB* PR2 57 E2
Meadway *BPOOLS* FY4 33 F4 1
CHLYE PR6 83 E1
PRES PR1 68 D1
Mealhouse La *CHLY/EC* PR7 91 F2 8
Meanwood Av *BPOOLS* FY4 39 F1

Meanygate *LEY/BBR* PR5 78 B1
Mearley Rd *FUL/RIB* PR2 47 F4 6
Meath Rd *PRES* PR1 6 D7
The Mede *KIRK/FR/WA* PR4 54 B1
Medlar Cl *KIRK/FR/WA* PR4 42 C2
Medlar Ct *KIRK/FR/WA* PR4 43 E2
Medlar Ga *KIRK/FR/WA* PR4 43 E2 1
Medlock Av *FTWD* FY7 10 C3
Medway *FUL/RIB* PR2 46 A2 1
Medway Av *FTWD* FY7 16 D1 2
Medway Cl *LEY/BBR* PR5 70 C5
Melba Rd *FUL/RIB* PR2 47 F5
Melbert Av *FUL/RIB* PR2 45 F5 4
Melbourne Av *CLV/TH* FY5 21 F5
FTWD FY7 16 D1
Melbourne St *PRES* PR1 7 H1 3
Melford Cl *CHLYE* PR6 87 H4
Mellings *PRES* PR1 58 D5
Mellings Fold *PRES* PR1 58 D5 5
Melling's La *LSTA* FY8 49 G2
Melling St *PRES* PR1 7 H1
Mellings Wd *LSTA* FY8 49 G2 2
Mellor Pl *PRES* PR1 58 C4 6
Mellor Rd *KIRK/FR/WA* PR4 43 E3
LEY/BBR PR5 80 C2
Mellwood Av *BPOOLE* FY3 29 F1 1
Melrose Av *BPOOLE* FY3 29 F2
FUL/RIB PR2 46 D3
Melrose Wy *CHLY/EC* PR7 91 G4
Melton Gv *LSTA* FY8 62 C3
Melton Pl *CLV/TH* FY5 20 C4 1
LEY/BBR PR5 81 G2
Melville Rd *BISP* FY2 24 C3 3
Memory Cl *KIRK/FR/WA* PR4 54 B4
Menai Dr *FUL/RIB* PR2 45 G1
Mendip Cl *LSTA* FY8 64 A1 1
Mendip Rd *LEY/BBR* PR5 82 A3
Mercer Rd *LEY/BBR* PR5 70 B5
Mercer St *PRES* PR1 58 D3
Mere Av *FTWD* FY7 10 D5
Mere Cl *GAR/LONG* PR3 36 B2 2
Merefield *CHLY/EC* PR7 90 D1
Mere Fold *CHLY/EC* PR7 94 A2
Mereland Rd *BPOOLE* FY3 33 G3
Mere Park Ct *BPOOLE* FY3 33 G2
Mere Rd *BPOOLE* FY3 3 H5
Mereside Cl *KIRK/FR/WA* PR4 74 A2
Merlin Gv *LEY/BBR* PR5 80 C5
Merlyn Rd *CLV/TH* FY5 21 E3
Merrick Av *PRES* PR1 59 G3
Merryburn Cl *FUL/RIB* PR2 46 B4 8
Merry Trees La *KIRK/FR/WA* PR4 44 B3
Mersey Rd *BPOOLS* FY4 32 B5
FTWD FY7 11 E2
Mersey St *FUL/RIB* PR2 6 A1
Merton Av *FUL/RIB* PR2 46 A2
Merton Gv *CHLYE* PR6 87 H4
Mete St *PRES* PR1 59 E3
Methuen Av *FUL/RIB* PR2 45 H2
LEY/BBR PR5 72 D3
Methuen Cl *LEY/BBR* PR5 72 D3 2
Methuen Dr *LEY/BBR* PR5 73 E3
Metropolitan Dr *BPOOLE* FY3 33 H3
Mexford Av *BISP* FY2 28 D1
Meyler Av *BPOOLE* FY3 29 E2
Mickleden Av *FUL/RIB* PR2 46 A1 3
Mickleden Rd *BPOOLS* FY4 34 A4
Micklegate *CLV/TH* FY5 20 C5 2
Middleforth Gn *PRES* PR1 69 H2 2
Middle St *BPOOL* FY1 4 D1
Middleton Av *FTWD* FY7 10 D5
Middlewood Cl *CHLY/EC* PR7 88 B4
Midge Hall La *KIRK/FR/WA* PR4 75 G5
Midgeland Rd *BPOOLS* FY4 39 G1
Midgery La *FUL/RIB* PR2 37 F5
Milbanke Av *KIRK/FR/WA* PR4 43 E2
Milbourne St *BPOOL* FY1 2 E4 3
Milburn Av *CLV/TH* FY5 17 F4
Mildred Cl *CLV/TH* FY5 21 G1
Miles St *PRES* PR1 58 A1
Mile Stone Meadow
CHLYE PR6 86 A3 1
Miletas Pl *LSTA* FY8 62 A2 1
Milford Av *BISP* FY2 28 D1 1
Millbank *FUL/RIB* PR2 45 F5 5
Millbrook Wy *PRES* PR1 69 F4
Millcroft *FUL/RIB* PR2 45 F4
Milldyke Cl *BPOOLS* FY4 39 F2 1
Miller Fld *FUL/RIB* PR2 44 B5
Miller La *KIRK/FR/WA* PR4 44 B3
Miller Rd *FUL/RIB* PR2 59 F1
PRES PR1 59 E2
Millersdale Cl *CLV/TH* FY5 22 C5 2
Millersgate *KIRK/FR/WA* PR4 44 B4
Miller St *BPOOL* FY1 4 C5
PRES PR1 58 D3
Millfield Cl *KIRK/FR/WA* PR4 53 H5
Millfield Rd *BPOOLS* FY4 39 F2 2
CHLY/EC PR7 91 E1
Mill Ga *FUL/RIB* PR2 45 G5 5

Mill Hvn *FUL/RIB* PR2 45 G5 6
Mill Hey Av *PLF/KEOS* FY6 30 C1
Mill Hl *PRES* PR1 7 F1
Mill House La *LEY/BBR* PR5 79 H1
Millington Av *BPOOLS* FY4 5 J7
Mill La *BPOOLE* FY3 30 B5
CHLY/EC PR7 89 F1
CHLY/EC PR7 93 F3
CHLY/EC PR7 94 B3
FTWD FY7 11 H2
FUL/RIB PR2 45 F4
KIRK/FR/WA PR4 53 H5
LEY/BBR PR5 71 E1
LEY/BBR PR5 80 C4
LEY/BBR PR5 80 D1
PLF/KEOS FY6 19 G2
Millom Av *BISP* FY2 24 D3 1
Millom Cl *FTWD* FY7 16 C1
Mill St *CHLY/EC* PR7 94 B4
KIRK/FR/WA PR4 43 E3
LEY/BBR PR5 80 C4
LEY/BBR PR5 81 G1
PLF/KEOS FY6 13 F3
PRES PR1 6 D2 2
Mill Vw *KIRK/FR/WA* PR4 54 B4
Millwood Gld *CHLY/EC* PR7 91 E1
Millwood Rd *LEY/BBR* PR5 70 C3
Milner Rd *LSTA* FY8 62 B2
Milner St *PRES* PR1 58 A1
Milnthorpe Av *CLV/TH* FY5 16 D4
Milton Av *BPOOLE* FY3 3 K4
CLV/TH FY5 21 G1
Milton Cl *LEY/BBR* PR5 71 E4
Milton Crs *KIRK/FR/WA* PR4 43 E3
PLF/KEOS FY6 30 B2
Milton Rd *CHLY/EC* PR7 94 B5
Milton St *FTWD* FY7 11 G1
Milton Ter *CHLYE* PR6 87 G5 6
Mimosa Cl *CHLY/EC* PR7 86 D4
Mimosa Rd *FUL/RIB* PR2 59 F1 1
Minster Pk *KIRK/FR/WA* PR4 44 B3 5
Minstrel Wk *PLF/KEOS* FY6 26 B3
Mintholme Av *LEY/BBR* PR5 72 D4
Mirfield Gv *BPOOLS* FY4 5 H6
Mitcham Rd *BPOOLS* FY4 33 H5
Mitton Dr *FUL/RIB* PR2 47 H5
Moira Crs *FUL/RIB* PR2 47 F4
Molyneux Dr *BPOOLS* FY4 38 D1
Molyneux Pl *LSTA* FY8 63 E2
Mona Pl *PRES* PR1 6 E2
Monarch Crs *LSTA* FY8 49 H3 1
Monk's La *PLF/KEOS* FY6 13 E5
Monks Wk *PRES* PR1 6 A5
Monroe Dr *FTWD* FY7 10 D3 4
Montague St *BPOOLS* FY4 4 C7
Montcliffe Rd *CHLYE* PR6 91 H1
Montgomery St
LEY/BBR PR5 78 C1 12
Montjoly St *PRES* PR1 58 D4 6
Montpelier Av *BISP* FY2 24 C2
Montreal Av *BPOOL* FY1 3 G6
Montrose Av *BPOOL* FY1 4 E1
Montrose Cl *CHLYE* PR6 91 H4 2
Moon Av *BPOOL* FY1 4 D4
Moon St *LEY/BBR* PR5 78 B1
Moor Av *PRES* PR1 68 C2
Moorbrook St *PRES* PR1 57 H2
Moorcroft *KIRK/FR/WA* PR4 36 A3
Moorcroft Crs *FUL/RIB* PR2 47 E5
Moore St *BPOOLS* FY4 4 D6
PRES PR1 58 D4
Moore Tree Dr *BPOOLS* FY4 33 G5
Moor Fld *KIRK/FR/WA* PR4 75 G2
Moorfield Av *BPOOLE* FY3 3 J3
PLF/KEOS FY6 25 H2
Moorfield Cl *FUL/RIB* PR2 36 D5
Moorfield Dr *FUL/RIB* PR2 47 F5
LSTA FY8 63 E2
Moorfield Rd *LEY/BBR* PR5 80 B4
Moorfields *CHLYE* PR6 91 H1
PLF/KEOS FY6 25 F3
Moorfields Av *FUL/RIB* PR2 36 D5
Moorgate *BPOOLS* FY4 39 F2 5
FUL/RIB PR2 46 A3 2
Moor Hall St *PRES* PR1 57 H1 9
Moorhead Gdns *KIRK/FR/WA* PR4 53 G4
Moorhen Pl *CLV/TH* FY5 21 F3 5
Moorhey Crs *LEY/BBR* PR5 78 D1
PRES PR1 69 E1
Moorhey Dr *PRES* PR1 69 E1
Moorhouse St *BPOOL* FY1 28 B3 8
The Moorings *CHLYE* PR6 91 H2 8
Moorland Av *FUL/RIB* PR2 47 E3
PLF/KEOS FY6 26 C3
Moorland Crs *FUL/RIB* PR2 47 E4 4
Moorland Gdns *PLF/KEOS* FY6 26 C3
Moorland Rd *LSTA* FY8 49 G4
PLF/KEOS FY6 26 C3
Moor La *KIRK/FR/WA* PR4 68 A5
Moor Park Av *BISP* FY2 25 E4

PRES PR1 58 B1
Moor Rd *CHLY/EC* PR7 90 D5 6
Moorside Av *FUL/RIB* PR2 47 G5
Moorside Dr *PRES* PR1 69 E3
Moor St *KIRK/FR/WA* PR4 43 E3
Moorview Ct *BPOOLS* FY4 39 F1 5
Moorway *PLF/KEOS* FY6 26 D3
Moresby Av *BPOOLE* FY3 29 H3 4
Moreton Dr *BPOOLE* FY3 30 B5
PLF/KEOS FY6 26 B5
Morland Av *KIRK/FR/WA* PR4 42 D1
LEY/BBR PR5 77 F2
Morley Rd *BPOOLS* FY4 5 K7
Mornington Rd *LSTA* FY8 64 A2
PRES PR1 59 G2 5
PRES PR1 69 E1 2
Morris Cl *LEY/BBR* PR5 81 F4 7
Morris Ct *FUL/RIB* PR2 59 E1 7
Morris Crs *FUL/RIB* PR2 59 E1
Morrison St *CHLYE* PR6 87 G5 7
Morris Rd *CHLYE* PR6 91 H1 2
FUL/RIB PR2 59 E1
Morston Av *BISP* FY2 25 E5
Mosley St *LEY/BBR* PR5 81 F3
PRES PR1 58 D3
Moss Acre Rd *PRES* PR1 69 H3
Moss Av *FUL/RIB* PR2 56 D1
Moss Bank *CHLY/EC* PR7 94 B4 5
Moss Bank Pl *BPOOLS* FY4 33 F5 2
Mossbourne Rd *PLF/KEOS* FY6 26 A5
Moss Bridge Pk *LEY/BBR* PR5 77 G1
Mossbrook Dr *KIRK/FR/WA* PR4 44 B3
Moss Cl *CHLYE* PR6 91 H2
Moss Edge La *LSTA* FY8 39 G5
Mossfield Cl *LEY/BBR* PR5 77 G1 5
Mossfield Rd *CHLYE* PR6 91 H2
Moss Hall La *LSTA* FY8 50 C3
Moss House La *GAR/LONG* PR3 15 H2
KIRK/FR/WA PR4 41 F1
PLF/KEOS FY6 13 G5
Moss House Rd *BPOOLS* FY4 39 G2
KIRK/FR/WA PR4 36 A3
Mosslands *LEY/BBR* PR5 80 C3 5
Moss La *CHLY/EC* PR7 94 B4
CHLYE PR6 87 G2
KIRK/FR/WA PR4 74 C5
KIRK/FR/WA PR4 75 F2
LEY/BBR PR5 76 C4
LEY/BBR PR5 77 G1
LEY/BBR PR5 81 H2
PLF/KEOS FY6 23 H3
Mossom La *CLV/TH* FY5 20 C5
Moss Side La *KIRK/FR/WA* PR4 52 B1
PLF/KEOS FY6 19 H2
Moss Side Wy *LEY/BBR* PR5 80 B4
Moss St *LEY/BBR* PR5 77 G1
PRES PR1 7 F1 2
Moss Wy *BPOOLS* FY4 39 F1 6
Mossway *KIRK/FR/WA* PR4 75 G3
Mottram Cl *CHLYE* PR6 87 F2 4
Mounsey Rd *LEY/BBR* PR5 78 C1
Mountain Rd *CHLY/EC* PR7 94 B5
Mountbatten Rd *CHLY/EC* PR7 90 D4
Mount Pleasant *CHLYE* PR6 83 F4
Mount Rd *FTWD* FY7 11 G1
Mount St *BPOOL* FY1 2 C2
FTWD FY7 11 G2
PRES PR1 7 G4
Mowbray Dr *BPOOLE* FY3 29 E1
Mowbray Rd *FTWD* FY7 11 E2
Mowbreck Ct *KIRK/FR/WA* PR4 43 E2 2
Mowbreck La *KIRK/FR/WA* PR4 42 D1
Muirfield *PRES* PR1 56 D5
Muirfield Cl *FUL/RIB* PR2 45 E2
Mulberry Av *PRES* PR1 68 D3
Mulberry Ms *BISP* FY2 25 F1 2
Mulgrave Av *FUL/RIB* PR2 56 D2
Muncaster Rd *PRES* PR1 58 A1
Munro Crs *FUL/RIB* PR2 47 F5
Munster Av *BISP* FY2 24 D4
Murchison Gv *CLV/TH* FY5 21 E3 1
Murdock Av *FUL/RIB* PR2 57 G1
Murray Av *LEY/BBR* PR5 76 D4
Murray St *LEY/BBR* PR5 81 G3 3
PRES PR1 57 H2
Myerscough Av *BPOOLS* FY4 39 F3 4
LSTA FY8 48 D3
Myra Rd *LSTA* FY8 61 H2
Myrtle Av *BPOOLE* FY3 3 H5
CLV/TH FY5 17 F4
PLF/KEOS FY6 26 C2
Myrtle Dr *KIRK/FR/WA* PR4 43 G4
Mythop Av *LSTA* FY8 63 G2
Mythop Cl *LSTA* FY8 63 F2
Mythop Pl *FUL/RIB* PR2 56 C2
Mythop Rd *BPOOLE* FY3 34 B3
LSTA FY8 63 G2

N

Nab Rd *CHLYE* PR6 91 H1
Nairn Cl *BPOOLS* FY4 39 G1 4
Nansen Rd *FTWD* FY7 11 F3
Napier Av *BPOOLS* FY4 38 B2
Napier Cl *LSTA* FY8 48 D2
Naptha La *LEY/BBR* PR5 76 B3
Nares St *FUL/RIB* PR2 57 F2 14
Nateby Av *BPOOLS* FY4 39 E3
Nateby Cl *LSTA* FY8 49 H4
Nateby Pl *FUL/RIB* PR2 56 C2
Navena Av *FTWD* FY7 10 D4
Navigation Wy *FUL/RIB* PR2 56 D4
Naze La *KIRK/FR/WA* PR4 54 B5
Naze La East *KIRK/FR/WA* PR4 66 C3
Neargates *CHLY/EC* PR7 94 A2
Ned's La *GAR/LONG* PR3 14 C1
PLF/KEOS FY6 19 H4
Nell La *LEY/BBR* PR5 78 A5
Nelson Av *LEY/BBR* PR5 81 G3
Nelson Crs *FUL/RIB* PR2 56 A1
Nelson Dr *FUL/RIB* PR2 56 A1
Nelson Rd *BPOOL* FY1 4 C4
CHLY/EC PR7 91 F3 10
FTWD FY7 11 F3
Nelson St *KIRK/FR/WA* PR4 42 D3
LEY/BBR PR5 78 B1 6
LSTA FY8 63 H3 1
Nelson Ter *PRES* PR1 6 D2 3
Nelson Wy *FUL/RIB* PR2 56 B4
Nene Cl *LEY/BBR* PR5 81 G5 1
Nesswood Av *BPOOLS* FY4 39 E2
Neston St *PRES* PR1 59 F3
Netherley Rd *CHLY/EC* PR7 94 B5
Nethway Av *BPOOLE* FY3 29 F4
Nevett St *PRES* PR1 59 E3
Neville Av *CLV/TH* FY5 21 E4
Neville Dr *CLV/TH* FY5 21 H4
Newark Pl *FUL/RIB* PR2 36 C5
New Bonny St *BPOOL* FY1 2 C6
Newbury Av *BPOOLS* FY4 5 G6
Newbury Cl *FUL/RIB* PR2 36 B5 1
Newbury Gn *FUL/RIB* PR2 36 B5 2
Newbury Rd *LSTA* FY8 61 F2
Newby Av *FTWD* FY7 10 D5
PLF/KEOS FY6 30 B1 2
Newby Dr *LEY/BBR* PR5 82 A2
Newby Pl *BPOOLS* FY4 33 H4
FUL/RIB PR2 47 E4 5
Newcastle Av *BPOOLE* FY3 3 H6
CLV/TH FY5 17 E5
New Cock Yd *PRES* PR1 7 H4
Newfield Rd *LEY/BBR* PR5 78 D2
Newgate *FUL/RIB* PR2 45 H4
Newgate La *KIRK/FR/WA* PR4 76 B1
New Hall Av *BPOOLS* FY4 39 H2
New Hall Av North *BPOOLS* FY4 39 H2
New Hall La *PRES* PR1 58 C3
New Hey La *KIRK/FR/WA* PR4 43 H4
Newhouse Rd *BPOOLS* FY4 33 F4
Newlands *CHLY/EC* PR7 88 B4
Newlands Av *BPOOLE* FY3 5 K3
PRES PR1 68 D2
Newlands Rd *LSTA* FY8 62 A1 2
Newlands Wy *PLF/KEOS* FY6 30 A1
New La *PRES* PR1 69 H3
New Links Av *FUL/RIB* PR2 44 D1
Newlyn Av *BPOOLS* FY4 39 E3
Newlyn Pl *FUL/RIB* PR2 44 C4 2
Newman Rd *BPOOL* FY1 28 D2 3
New Market St *CHLY/EC* PR7 91 F2
New Mill St *CHLY/EC* PR7 88 B4
New Moss La *CHLYE* PR6 87 F2
New Rd *CHLY/EC* PR7 94 C2
CLV/TH FY5 22 A5
LEY/BBR PR5 70 C5 2
LSTA FY8 38 B4
PLF/KEOS FY6 19 E5
New Rough Hey *FUL/RIB* PR2 44 C2
Newsham St *FUL/RIB* PR2 57 G2 6
Newsome St *LEY/BBR* PR5 81 F3 5
New St *CHLY/EC* PR7 88 B4
Newton Av *PLF/KEOS* FY6 26 A5
PRES PR1 59 G3
Newton Cl *KIRK/FR/WA* PR4 54 C5
LEY/BBR PR5 80 A4
Newton Dr *BPOOLE* FY3 29 G4
Newton Dr East *BPOOLE* FY3 29 H3
Newton Gv *CLV/TH* FY5 21 H5
Newton Pl *BPOOLE* FY3 29 G3
Newton Rd *FUL/RIB* PR2 57 E1
LSTA FY8 49 G4
Newton St *PRES* PR1 58 C3 3
Nib La *PRES* PR1 76 D1
Nichol St *CHLY/EC* PR7 91 F1 5
Nicksons La *PLF/KEOS* FY6 13 F2
Nightingale Dr *PLF/KEOS* FY6 25 H5
Nimes St *PRES* PR1 59 E3
Nine Elms *FUL/RIB* PR2 45 F2
Nithside *BPOOLS* FY4 34 A4
Noblett Ct *FTWD* FY7 11 F4 9
Noel Sq *FUL/RIB* PR2 59 F2 10
Nookfield Cl *LSTA* FY8 63 E2 1
Nooklands *FUL/RIB* PR2 45 H4
Nook La *LEY/BBR* PR5 78 A3
The Nook *BPOOLE* FY3 30 B5
Noor St *PRES* PR1 58 B2
Norbreck Dr *FUL/RIB* PR2 56 B2
Norbreck Rd *BISP* FY2 24 C1
Norcliffe Rd *BISP* FY2 24 C2
Norcross La *CLV/TH* FY5 21 G5
Norcross Pl *FUL/RIB* PR2 56 C2
Norfolk Av *BISP* FY2 24 B4
CLV/TH FY5 21 E1
Norfolk Cl *LEY/BBR* PR5 80 D5 1
Norfolk Rd *BPOOLE* FY3 33 G3
LEY/BBR PR5 71 E2
LSTA FY8 63 F1
PRES PR1 58 B2 4
Norkeed Rd *CLV/TH* FY5 20 C5
Norman Cl *CLV/TH* FY5 21 F3 6
Normandie Av *BISP* FY2 24 D4 1
Normandy Rd *KIRK/FR/WA* PR4 36 A2
Normoss Av *BPOOLE* FY3 29 G3
Normoss Rd *BPOOLE* FY3 29 H3
Norris St *CHLY/EC* PR7 91 F4 7
FUL/RIB PR2 45 G5
PRES PR1 57 G1
North Albert St *FTWD* FY7 11 H1 5
North Albion St *FTWD* FY7 11 G2 3
North Av *BPOOLE* FY3 28 D3
Northbrook Rd *LEY/BBR* PR5 80 D2
North Church St *FTWD* FY7 11 H1 6
North Cliff St *PRES* PR1 6 E5
North Clifton St *LSTA* FY8 63 F3
Northcote Rd *PRES* PR1 6 D4
Northcote St *LEY/BBR* PR5 81 F3 6
North Ct *CLV/TH* FY5 16 D4
North Crs *LSTA* FY8 49 E5
North Dr *CLV/TH* FY5 21 E4
KIRK/FR/WA PR4 42 D2
Northenden Rd *CHLY/EC* PR7 94 B4
Northfield Av *BPOOL* FY1 28 B2 2
Northfleet Av *FTWD* FY7 11 E4
Northgate *BISP* FY2 24 C3
LEY/BBR PR5 81 G2
Northgate Dr *CHLYE* PR6 87 H5
North Gv *LEY/BBR* PR5 77 H1
North Highfield *FUL/RIB* PR2 47 F2
North Houses La *LSTA* FY8 50 B2
Northlands *FUL/RIB* PR2 45 H2 2
LEY/BBR PR5 80 B5
Northleach Av *PRES* PR1 70 A4 4
North Meadowside
KIRK/FR/WA PR4 74 B4
North Park Dr *BPOOLE* FY3 3 K5
North Prom *LSTA* FY8 48 C4
North Ribble St *LEY/BBR* PR5 58 D5 6
North Rd *PRES* PR1 7 J1
Northside *CHLY/EC* PR7 85 H4 2
North Sq *BPOOLE* FY3 3 H2
CLV/TH FY5 16 C4
North St *CHLYE* PR6 87 F5
FTWD FY7 11 H1
PRES PR1 7 G1
Northumberland Av *BISP* FY2 28 B1
CLV/TH FY5 17 E5
Northumberland St
CHLY/EC PR7 91 G3 5
North Vw *KIRK/FR/WA* PR4 42 D3
LEY/BBR PR5 81 E4
North Warton St *LSTA* FY8 63 G3
Northway *FTWD* FY7 10 D5
FUL/RIB PR2 45 G2
GAR/LONG PR3 36 B2
Northwood Cl *LSTA* FY8 62 C2 8
Northwood Wy *PLF/KEOS* FY6 26 B5
Norwich Pl *BISP* FY2 24 D2 3
PRES PR1 7 K4 2
Norwood Av *BPOOLE* FY3 29 E2
Norwood Rd *LSTA* FY8 48 C3
Nottingham Rd *PRES* PR1 58 B2 5
Nursery Cl *CHLY/EC* PR7 94 A1 1
LEY/BBR PR5 81 E4
Nursery La *KIRK/FR/WA* PR4 75 F1
Nuttall Rd *BPOOL* FY1 5 G5
Nutter Rd *CLV/TH* FY5 20 D2
PRES PR1 6 E3

O

Oak Av *BPOOLS* FY4 32 D5
CHLY/EC PR7 86 A4
CLV/TH FY5 22 A4
KIRK/FR/WA PR4 43 E4
PRES PR1 6
Oak Cft *CHLYE* PR6 8
Oak Dr *CHLYE* PR6 8
KIRK/FR/WA PR4 6
Oakengate *FUL/RIB* PR2 4
Oakenhead St *PRES* PR1 59 F
Oakfield *FUL/RIB* PR2 4
FUL/RIB PR2 5
Oakfield Dr *LEY/BBR* PR5 8
Oakgrove *BPOOLS* FY4 38
Oak Gv *KIRK/FR/WA* PR4 7
Oakham Ct *PRES* PR1
Oakland Av *CLV/TH* FY5 24
Oakland Gln *PRES* PR1 7
Oaklands Dr *PRES* PR1 6
Oaklands Gv *FUL/RIB* PR2 56
Oakland St *LEY/BBR* PR5 71
Oak La *KIRK/FR/WA* PR4 5
Oakleaf Wy *BPOOLS* FY4 34
Oakmere *CHLYE* PR6 83
Oakmoor Av *BISP* FY2 2
Oakridge Cl *FUL/RIB* PR2 46
Oakshott Pl *LEY/BBR* PR5 7
The Oaks *CHLY/EC* PR7 9
LEY/BBR PR5 7
PLF/KEOS FY6 2
Oak St *FTWD* FY7 1
PRES PR1
Oaktree Av *FUL/RIB* PR2 4
LEY/BBR PR5 7
Oaktree Cl *FUL/RIB* PR2 44
Oak Vw *LEY/BBR* PR5 8
Oakwood Av *LEY/BBR* PR5 70
LSTA FY8 6
Oakwood Cl *BPOOLS* FY4 3
CLV/TH FY5 22
Oakwood Dr *FUL/RIB* PR2 3
Oakwood Rd *CHLY/EC* PR7 9
CHLY/EC PR7 9
Oakwood Vw *CHLY/EC* PR7 95
Oakworth Av *FUL/RIB* PR2 4
Oban Crs *PRES* PR1 4
Oban Pl *BISP* FY2 2
Ocean Wy *CLV/TH* FY5 2
Old Bridge La *PLF/KEOS* FY6 2
Old Bridge Wy *CHLYE* PR6 9
Oldbury Pl *CLV/TH* FY5 2
Old Cock Yd *PRES* PR1 7
Old Cft *FUL/RIB* PR2 36
Old Dawber's La *CHLY/EC* PR7 8
Oldfield *KIRK/FR/WA* PR4 7
PRES PR1 69
Oldfield Av *BISP* FY2 2
Oldfield Carr La *PLF/KEOS* FY6 3
Oldfield Cl *PLF/KEOS* FY6 3
Oldfield Crs *PLF/KEOS* FY6 2
Oldfield Rd *LEY/BBR* PR5 7
Old Hall Cl *LEY/BBR* PR5 7
Old Hall Dr *LEY/BBR* PR5 7
Old Hall La *CHLY/EC* PR7 8
Old Hey Cft *PRES* PR1 69
Old House La *BPOOLS* FY4 4
Old Lancaster La *FUL/RIB* PR2 5
Old Lostock La *LEY/BBR* PR5 7
Old Mains La *PLF/KEOS* FY6 2
Old Meadow La *BPOOLE* FY3 5
Old Mill Ct *KIRK/FR/WA* PR4 7
Old Millstones *PRES* PR1 6
Old Oak Gdns *PRES* PR1 7
Old Rw *KIRK/FR/WA* PR4 43
Old School La *CHLY/EC* PR7 86
CHLY/EC PR7 86
LEY/BBR PR5 7
Old Tram Rd *PRES* PR1 7
Old Vicarage *PRES* PR1 7
Olive Cl *CHLYE* PR6 8
Olive Gv *BPOOLE* FY3 3
KIRK/FR/WA PR4 5
Oliver's Pl *FUL/RIB* PR2 3
Ollerton Rd *LSTA* FY8 62
Onslow Rd *BPOOLE* FY3 2
Orchard Av *BPOOLS* FY4 3
KIRK/FR/WA PR4 7
PLF/KEOS FY6 3
Orchard Cl *CHLY/EC* PR7 8
CLV/TH FY5 17 H
FUL/RIB PR2 4
KIRK/FR/WA PR4 5
Orchard Cft *LEY/BBR* PR5 77 F
Orchard Dr *CHLYE* PR6 87
FTWD FY7 11
Orchard La *KIRK/FR/WA* PR4 7
Orchard Rd *LSTA* FY8 49
The Orchards *PLF/KEOS* FY6 25 H
Orchard St *LEY/BBR* PR5 81
PRES PR1 7
The Orchard *KIRK/FR/WA* PR4 53
Ord Av *BPOOLS* FY4 33
Orders La *KIRK/FR/WA* PR4 43
Ord Rd *FUL/RIB* PR2 57 F1

ion Av BPOOLE FY3 29 E2
ey Rd BPOOL FY1 5 F4
erod St CLV/TH FY5 21 H1
e St BPOOL FY1 5 F1
ond Av BPOOL FY1 28 B2
ont Av CLV/TH FY5 21 E2
skirk Rd PRES PR1 7 J2
l Cl LEY/BBR PR5 80 C3 6
st Rd PRES PR1 59 H2
orne Av CLV/TH FY5 21 E2
orne Dr CHLYE PR6 83 F2
orne Gv CLV/TH FY5 16 D4
orne Rd CLV/TH FY5 16 D4
Y/BBR PR5 71 E3
TA FY8 61 F1
orne St PRES PR1 6 E4
ourne Rd BPOOLS FY4 32 B5
r St BPOOLS FY4 33 F3 7
ald Rd FUL/RIB PR2 57 F2
TA FY8 63 H2 9
y Rd LSTA FY8 49 H4
rburn Cl BPOOLE FY3 29 H1 1
rs Cl FUL/RIB PR2 59 G1 5
ay St PRES PR1 57 H1 10
er Prom FTWD FY7 10 D1
am Wy LEY/BBR PR5 78 B1
rdale Gv BPOOLE FY3 29 G1
rton Rd FUL/RIB PR2 56 B3
ns St CHLYE PR6 91 H3 6
n St PRES PR1 58 C3 4
ram St PRES PR1 58 D3 5
ndale Rd CLV/TH FY5 22 B2
nholme Av CLV/TH FY5 16 D5
nhurst Rd BPOOLE FY3 29 G2 5
ord Dr KIRK/FR/WA PR4 43 G4
ord Rd BPOOL FY1 3 G4
V/TH FY5 20 C1
WD FY7 11 E3
L/RIB PR2 45 G4
Y/BBR PR5 78 C1
TA FY8 49 E4
ord St CHLY/EC PR7 91 F3 11
RES PR1 7 K4
ord Wy FTWD FY7 11 E3 2
eys St PRES PR1 57 G1 4
ill Pl CLV/TH FY5 21 E5
y Cl KIRK/FR/WA PR4 42 D3
y Rd PRES PR1 59 E2 16
y Rd North PRES PR1 59 E2 17

P

dock Dr BPOOLE FY3 34 A3
Paddock CLV/TH FY5 21 H4 2
L/RIB PR2 46 B2
F/KEOS FY6 26 A2 4
way PRES PR1 69 G4
es Ct LEY/BBR PR5 77 G2
ley Cl LSTA FY8 63 E2
tine Cl BPOOLE FY3 30 A4 1
tine Rd BPOOL FY1 2 E7
V/TH FY5 16 D5
y Rd PRES PR1 6 D3
rey Cl PLF/KEOS FY6 25 H1 1
Ml CHLY/EC PR7 91 F4
n Dr PLF/KEOS FY6 25 H1
ner Av BPOOL FY1 5 F3
adise La LEY/BBR PR5 80 A3
pold Cl BPOOLE FY3 29 F1 2
Av CHLY/EC PR7 86 A5
WD FY7 11 F3
RK/FR/WA PR4 68 B5
TA FY8 62 C3
RES PR1 58 C1
k Cl PRES PR1 69 G2
k Dr FUL/RIB PR2 56 A2
ker La KIRK/FR/WA PR4 76 B3
ker St BPOOL FY1 3 F4
HLY/EC PR7 91 F1
L/RIB PR2 57 G1
kfield Av FUL/RIB PR2 57 E1
kfield Cl LEY/BBR PR5 80 B4
kgate Dr LEY/BBR PR5 80 D5
k Hall Rd CHLY/EC PR7 93 E2
kinson Wy BPOOLS FY4 4 E6
kland Cl CLV/TH FY5 20 C3
klands Av PRES PR1 68 D2
klands Cl PRES PR1 68 D2 3
klands Dr FUL/RIB PR2 36 D5
klands Gv FUL/RIB PR2 36 D5
k La KIRK/FR/WA PR4 43 E2
LF/KEOS FY6 13 E2
RES PR1 69 H3
k Mill Pl PRES PR1 58 B2
k Pl LEY/BBR PR5 71 F2
RES PR1 7 J4
k Rd BPOOL FY1 3 F7
HLY/EC PR7 91 F1

CHLY/EC PR7 94 B4
CLV/TH FY5 21 H4
FUL/RIB PR2 46 B4
KIRK/FR/WA PR4 42 D4
LEY/BBR PR5 81 F5
LSTA FY8 49 E5
PLF/KEOS FY6 26 C3
PRES PR1 69 G2
Parkside FUL/RIB PR2 56 A1
PRES PR1 46 C5 1
Parkside Av CHLY/EC PR7 91 F2
Parkside Dr CHLYE PR6 87 E1
Parkside Dr South CHLYE PR6 87 E1
Parkside Rd LSTA FY8 49 G4
Parkstone Av CLV/TH FY5 22 B4
PLF/KEOS FY6 25 H2
Park St CHLY/EC PR7 88 B4 1
CHLY/EC PR7 91 F2
LSTA FY8 63 F3
Parksway PLF/KEOS FY6 12 B1
Park Vw PRES PR1 69 G2
Park View Av FUL/RIB PR2 57 E1 3
Park View Rd LSTA FY8 63 F2
Parkway BPOOLE FY3 29 G4
Park Wy PRES PR1 69 G2 1
Parlick Rd FUL/RIB PR2 59 H1 3
Parr Cottage Cl CHLY/EC PR7 88 B3 1
Parr La CHLY/EC PR7 88 A3
Parrock Cl PRES PR1 69 H3 2
Parrox Fold PLF/KEOS FY6 13 E1
Parson's Brow CHLY/EC PR7 91 F3 12
Partridge Av CLV/TH FY5 17 F5
Pasture Field Cl LEY/BBR PR5 80 B4
Pasture Field PLF/KEOS FY6 25 H1 2
Pastures New LEY/BBR PR5 77 H1 7
Patten St PRES PR1 7 G1
Patterdale Av BPOOLE FY3 33 F3
CLV/TH FY5 21 H1
FTWD FY7 16 D1
Paul's La PLF/KEOS FY6 23 G2
Pavey Cl BPOOLS FY4 33 F5
Paythorne Cl BPOOLE FY3 29 H1 2
Peachtree Cl FUL/RIB PR2 47 E2
Peacock Hall Rd LEY/BBR PR5 80 C5
Pearfield LEY/BBR PR5 81 F2
Pearl Av BISP FY2 29 E1 3
Pear Tree Av CHLY/EC PR7 94 C2
Pear Tree Cl LEY/BBR PR5 71 F4 5
Pear Tree Crs LEY/BBR PR5 71 F4
Pear Tree Cft KIRK/FR/WA PR4 74 B1
Pear Tree La CHLY/EC PR7 86 B4
Pear Tree Rd CHLYE PR6 83 E1
Pear Tree St LEY/BBR PR5 71 F4 6
Pechell St FUL/RIB PR2 57 F2 15
Pedder La PLF/KEOS FY6 23 F3
Pedders Gv FUL/RIB PR2 56 D3
Pedder's La BPOOLS FY4 38 D1
FUL/RIB PR2 56 D2
Pedder St PRES PR1 6 E1
Pedders Wy FUL/RIB PR2 56 D3 1
Peel Av BPOOLE FY3 28 D3
Peel Hall St PRES PR1 58 C2 7
Peel Hl BPOOLS FY4 40 C1
Peel Hill Br BPOOLS FY4 41 E2
Peel Rd BPOOLS FY4 40 D3
FTWD FY7 11 F3
Peel St CHLY/EC PR7 91 F3
PRES PR1 6 E1
Peg's La LSTA FY8 51 G3
Peg Wy KIRK/FR/WA PR4 53 H5
Pelham Av BPOOLE FY3 29 E2 6
Pembroke Av BISP FY2 24 B4
Pembroke Pl CHLY/EC PR7 91 E4
LEY/BBR PR5 81 F4 8
PRES PR1 7 K3 5
Pembroke Rd LSTA FY8 62 B3
Pembury Av PRES PR1 69 H3
Pendle Cl BPOOLE FY3 29 F1
Pendle Ct KIRK/FR/WA PR4 43 E2 3
Pendle Pl LSTA FY8 63 G2
Pendle Rd LEY/BBR PR5 82 A3
Penguin St PRES PR1 58 C1 3
Penhill Cl BISP FY2 28 D2 4
Pennine Av CHLY/EC PR7 90 A1
Pennine Cl BPOOL FY1 3 F7
Pennine Rd CHLYE PR6 91 H1 3
The Pennines FUL/RIB PR2 46 B1
Pennine Vw KIRK/FR/WA PR4 43 G3
Pennine Wy PLF/KEOS FY6 19 H2 1
Pennyfarthing La CLV/TH FY5 21 G2 5
Pennystone Rd BISP FY2 24 B3 4
Penny St PRES PR1 7 J1
Penrhos Av FTWD FY7 11 E5
Penrith Av CLV/TH FY5 16 D5
Penrose Av BPOOLS FY4 33 F4
Penswick Av CLV/TH FY5 21 E3
Penwortham Ct PRES PR1 69 G2
Penwortham Hall Gdns
PRES PR1 69 H3 3
Penwortham Wy PRES PR1 69 E4

Percy St BPOOL FY1 3 F1
CHLY/EC PR7 91 G3 6
FTWD FY7 11 F2
PRES PR1 7 K2
Peregrine Pl LEY/BBR PR5 80 C2 3
Pershore Gdns BPOOLE FY3 29 H2
Pershore Rd LSTA FY8 61 H1 1
Perth Cl CLV/TH FY5 21 F5 5
Peterfield Rd PRES PR1 69 H4 4
Peter St BPOOL FY1 3 F4
CHLY/EC PR7 91 F2
Petunia Cl LEY/BBR PR5 82 B2
Pharos Pl FTWD FY7 11 H1
Pharos St FTWD FY7 11 H1
Pheasant Wood Dr CLV/TH FY5 17 F4
Philip Av KIRK/FR/WA PR4 43 F4
Phillip St BPOOLS FY4 33 F3 8
Pickering Cl LSTA FY8 49 H4 1
The Pickerings LEY/BBR PR5 77 H1 8
Pickmere Av BPOOLS FY4 5 J7
Pickmere Cl CLV/TH FY5 17 G5 2
Pierston Av BISP FY2 28 C1
Pier St BPOOL FY1 4 C1
Pike Ct FTWD FY7 10 C4
Pilling Av LSTA FY8 49 H4
Pilling Cl CHLY/EC PR7 91 G4
Pilling Crs BPOOLE FY3 29 G1
Pilling La CHLY/EC PR7 91 F5
PLF/KEOS FY6 13 E1
Pincock Brow CHLY/EC PR7 89 H2
Pincock St CHLY/EC PR7 89 H2
Pine Av BPOOL FY1 5 J4
Pine Cl FUL/RIB PR2 47 G4 2
Pine Crs PLF/KEOS FY6 26 C5
Pine Gv CHLYE PR6 87 G4
Pines Cl LEY/BBR PR5 79 F5
Pineway FUL/RIB PR2 45 F4
Pine Wy KIRK/FR/WA PR4 43 F1
Pinewood Av BISP FY2 25 E3
CLV/TH FY5 21 H5
GAR/LONG PR3 36 B2
PLF/KEOS FY6 13 E1
Pinewood Crs LEY/BBR PR5 80 D4
LSTA FY8 62 B2
Pinfold KIRK/FR/WA PR4 74 B1
Pinfold St PRES PR1 59 E3
Pingle Cft CHLYE PR6 82 D2
Pippin St CHLYE PR6 79 H5
Pittman Ct FUL/RIB PR2 46 C1
Pittman Wy FUL/RIB PR2 37 G5
Pittsdale Av BPOOLE FY3 33 G3 2
Pitt St PRES PR1 7 F3
Plainmoor Dr CLV/TH FY5 21 F5
Plantation Av PLF/KEOS FY6 12 C1
Plant St FUL/RIB PR2 57 F2 16
Platt St BPOOL FY1 2 E3
Pleasant Gv CLV/TH FY5 21 H2
Pleasant St BPOOL FY1 2 C1
LSTA FY8 63 F3 8
Pleasant Vw CHLY/EC PR7 94 C3
Pleasington Cl BPOOLS FY4 33 G5
Pleck Pl PLF/KEOS FY6 25 H1 3
Plevna Rd PRES PR1 58 D3
Plover Cl CLV/TH FY5 17 F4
Plover St PRES PR1 58 C1
Plumpton Av BPOOLS FY4 39 F3
Plumpton Rd FUL/RIB PR2 57 F1 12
Plumtree Cl FUL/RIB PR2 46 D2 5
Plungington Rd FUL/RIB PR2 45 H5
PRES PR1 57 H1
Plymouth Av FTWD FY7 16 C1
Plymouth Gv CHLYE PR6 91 H2 9
Plymouth Rd BPOOLE FY3 29 E1
Poachers Wy CLV/TH FY5 17 G5
Pochard Pl CLV/TH FY5 21 F3 7
Polefield FUL/RIB PR2 45 H1
Pole St PRES PR1 7 K2
Pollard St PRES PR1 7 F1 3
Pollux Ga LSTA FY8 62 A2
Polperro Dr KIRK/FR/WA PR4 54 A5
Pool Ct FTWD FY7 10 D5 1
Poole Rd FUL/RIB PR2 46 B4
Pool Foot La PLF/KEOS FY6 27 H3
Poolhill Cl CLV/TH FY5 21 E5 2
Pool House La FUL/RIB PR2 44 C3
Pool La KIRK/FR/WA PR4 66 A2
Pope La FUL/RIB PR2 47 H5
KIRK/FR/WA PR4 69 E5
PRES PR1 69 F4
Pope Wk PRES PR1 69 G3
Poplar Av BPOOLE FY3 3 H4
CHLY/EC PR7 85 H3
KIRK/FR/WA PR4 43 E4
KIRK/FR/WA PR4 53 F5
KIRK/FR/WA PR4 74 C1
LEY/BBR PR5 71 G5
PLF/KEOS FY6 26 C5
Poplar Cl LEY/BBR PR5 71 G5
Poplar Dr KIRK/FR/WA PR4 65 H1
PRES PR1 69 F1

Poplar Gv FUL/RIB PR2 47 H4 2
LEY/BBR PR5 71 G5
Poplar St CHLY/EC PR7 91 G4
Poppy Av CHLYE PR6 87 G5
Poppyfield KIRK/FR/WA PR4 44 C2
Porter Pl PRES PR1 7 J5
Porter St PRES PR1 58 C2
Porter St East
KIRK/FR/WA PR4 42 D2 5
Portland Rd BPOOL FY1 3 G7
Portland St CHLY/EC PR7 91 G2 9
PRES PR1 6 D4
Portman St PRES PR1 58 C2
Portree Cl FUL/RIB PR2 46 D3 6
Portree Rd BISP FY2 25 E1
Portsmouth Cl CLV/TH FY5 17 F5 3
Portsmouth Dr CHLYE PR6 91 H2
Portway BISP FY2 25 E1 1
Port Wy FUL/RIB PR2 6 C4
Post La KIRK/FR/WA PR4 53 H5
Poulton Av LSTA FY8 49 G3
Poulton Crs LEY/BBR PR5 72 C3
Poulton Old Rd BPOOLE FY3 29 F1
Poulton Rd BPOOLE FY3 29 F2
FTWD FY7 11 E3
PLF/KEOS FY6 26 A3
Poulton St FTWD FY7 11 G2
FUL/RIB PR2 57 F2
KIRK/FR/WA PR4 43 E3
Powell Av BPOOLS FY4 32 D5
Powis Rd FUL/RIB PR2 56 D3
Poynter St PRES PR1 58 D2 13
Preesall Cl LSTA FY8 49 H4 2
Preesall Moss La PLF/KEOS FY6 13 H4
Preesall Rd FUL/RIB PR2 56 B2
Premier Wy PLF/KEOS FY6 26 D4
Prenton Gdns CLV/TH FY5 21 F5
Prescot Pl BPOOLE FY3 33 G3 3
CLV/TH FY5 22 A2 2
Press Rd LSTA FY8 48 D3 1
Prestbury Av BPOOLS FY4 38 C3
Preston New Rd BPOOLS FY4 41 E2
KIRK/FR/WA PR4 54 D4
Preston Nook CHLY/EC PR7 88 B5 1
Preston Old Rd BPOOLE FY3 5 K3
KIRK/FR/WA PR4 54 C5
Preston Rd CHLY/EC PR7 87 F5
CHLYE PR6 83 E1
LEY/BBR PR5 79 E4
LEY/BBR PR5 81 G2 9
LSTA FY8 63 H3
Preston St FTWD FY7 11 H2
KIRK/FR/WA PR4 43 F3
Price St BPOOLS FY4 4 C6
Priestfield CLV/TH FY5 21 F5
Primrose Av BPOOLS FY4 38 D2
Primrose Bank BISP FY2 25 F1 3
Primrose Gv PRES PR1 46 D5 4
Primrose Hl PRES PR1 58 C4 7
Primrose Hill Rd CHLY/EC PR7 85 G3
Primrose La PRES PR1 46 D5 5
Primrose Rd PRES PR1 46 D5 6
Primrose St CHLYE PR6 91 G2
Primrose Wy PLF/KEOS FY6 25 H1
Princes Ct PRES PR1 57 E5 1
Princes Dr FUL/RIB PR2 45 G2
Prince's Rd LEY/BBR PR5 71 F1 2
LSTA FY8 62 B2 3
PRES PR1 57 E5
Princess Av KIRK/FR/WA PR4 42 D2
PLF/KEOS FY6 26 B4
Princess Rd CLV/TH FY5 20 C2
Princess St BPOOL FY1 4 C1
CHLY/EC PR7 91 G4
LEY/BBR PR5 77 G2 4
LEY/BBR PR5 78 C1 13
LEY/BBR PR5 81 G3
PRES PR1 58 C4
Princess Wy CHLY/EC PR7 86 A5
Princes Wy CLV/TH FY5 20 C3
FTWD FY7 10 C4
Princeway BPOOLS FY4 38 C1
Pringle Wd GAR/LONG PR3 36 B3
Priory Cl LEY/BBR PR5 81 H2
Priory Crs PRES PR1 6 A5
Priory Ga BPOOLS FY4 38 C3
Priory La PRES PR1 6 A6
Priory St FUL/RIB PR2 6 D1
Progress St CHLYE PR6 91 H2
Progress Wy BPOOLS FY4 39 G3
Promenade BISP FY2 24 B3
BPOOL FY1 2 C3
BPOOLS FY4 38 A3
CLV/TH FY5 16 C4
Promenade North CLV/TH FY5 20 C1
Promenade Rd FTWD FY7 11 G1
Promenade South CLV/TH FY5 20 C2
Prospect Av LEY/BBR PR5 77 G1
Prospect Pl FUL/RIB PR2 57 E2 1
PRES PR1 69 H2 3

Prudy Hl *PLF/KEOS* FY6 26 B3 3
Pudding Pie Nook La
  GAR/LONG PR3 37 E1
Puddle House La *PLF/KEOS* FY6 30 D2
Pump St *PRES* PR1 7 K1

Q

Quaile Holme Rd *PLF/KEOS* FY6 12 B1
Quaker Brook La *LEY/BBR* PR5 73 F3
Quarrybank *CLV/TH* FY5 21 F4 4
Quarry Rd *CHLYE* PR6 91 H4
Quayle Av *BPOOLS* FY4 32 D5
Quebec Av *BISP* FY2 24 D4
Queen Mary Av *LSTA* FY8 61 G1
Queensbury Rd *CLV/TH* FY5 20 C3
Queen's Cl *PLF/KEOS* FY6 26 C4
Queenscourt Av *PRES* PR1 69 H4
Queen's Crs *KIRK/FR/WA* PR4 43 F4
Queensdale Cl *LEY/BBR* PR5 71 F1
Queens Dr *BPOOLE* FY3 30 B5
  FUL/RIB PR2 45 G2
Queensgate *CHLY/EC* PR7 91 E3 3
Queen's Gv *CHLY/EC* PR7 91 F2
Queens Pl *KIRK/FR/WA* PR4 42 D1
Queen's Prom *BISP* FY2 24 C1
  CLV/TH FY5 20 C4
Queen's Rd *CHLY/EC* PR7 91 E2
  FUL/RIB PR2 45 G5 7
  LEY/BBR PR5 71 F1 3
  LSTA FY8 61 F1
Queen's Sq *PLF/KEOS* FY6 26 B4 4
Queen's Ter *FTWD* FY7 11 H1
Queen St *BPOOL* FY1 2 D3
  FTWD FY7 11 G2
  LEY/BBR PR5 77 G2 5
  LSTA FY8 63 E3 7
  PRES PR1 58 C4
Queen St East *CHLY/EC* PR7 91 G4
Queens Wk *CLV/TH* FY5 16 D5
Queens Wy *PLF/KEOS* FY6 26 B3
Queensway *BPOOLS* FY4 38 C1
  CHLY/EC PR7 86 B5
  FUL/RIB PR2 56 C1
  KIRK/FR/WA PR4 53 G4
  LEY/BBR PR5 71 F5
  LEY/BBR PR5 80 D5
  LSTA FY8 49 H1
  PRES PR1 57 E5
Queensway Cl *PRES* PR1 57 E5
Queen Vera Rd *BPOOL* FY1 2 D4 1
Queen Victoria Rd *BPOOL* FY1 4 E2
Quernmore Av *BPOOLE* FY3 33 G2
Quin St *LEY/BBR* PR5 81 F3

R

Radburn Brow *CHLYE* PR6 83 E1
Radburn Cl *CHLYE* PR6 83 E1
Radcliffe Rd *FTWD* FY7 11 G3
Radley Av *BPOOLE* FY3 29 E2 7
Radnor Av *CLV/TH* FY5 21 F3
Radnor St *PRES* PR1 7 F1
Radway Cl *CLV/TH* FY5 21 F5 6
Radworth Crs *BPOOLS* FY4 33 H4 2
Raglan St *FUL/RIB* PR2 57 G1
Raikes Hl *BPOOL* FY1 3 F4
Raikes Pde *BPOOL* FY1 3 F5
Raikes Rd *CLV/TH* FY5 22 C3
  PRES PR1 58 D2
Railway Rd *CHLYE* PR6 91 G1
Railway St *CHLY/EC* PR7 91 G3
  LEY/BBR PR5 81 G2
Railway Ter *KIRK/FR/WA* PR4 42 D2
Rake La *KIRK/FR/WA* PR4 65 F1
Raleigh Av *BPOOLS* FY4 38 B3
Raleigh Cl *LSTA* FY8 48 D2 4
Raleigh Rd *FUL/RIB* PR2 45 H2
Ramper Ga *CLV/TH* FY5 20 D2 3
Ramsey Av *BPOOLE* FY3 28 D3
  PRES PR1 47 E5
Ramsey Cl *LSTA* FY8 48 D2
Ramsgate Cl *KIRK/FR/WA* PR4 53 G4
Ramsgate Rd *LSTA* FY8 49 F3
Ramshill Av *PLF/KEOS* FY6 25 H2 5
Ranaldsway *LEY/BBR* PR5 80 B4
Rangeway Av *BPOOLS* FY4 38 C1
Ranglet Rd *LEY/BBR* PR5 79 E2
Rangletts Av *CHLY/EC* PR7 91 F4
Rathlyn Av *BPOOLE* FY3 3 J1
Rathmell Cl *BPOOLE* FY3 29 H1 3
Ravenglass Cl *BPOOLS* FY4 39 E1
  KIRK/FR/WA PR4 43 E1
Ravenhill Dr *CHLY/EC* PR7 91 F1
Raven's Cl *BPOOLE* FY3 29 H3
Raven St *PRES* PR1 58 D1
Ravenswood *FUL/RIB* PR2 59 F1
Ravenswood Av *BPOOLE* FY3 29 H3
Ravenwood Av *BPOOLS* FY4 38 D3
Rawcliffe Dr *FUL/RIB* PR2 56 B3
Rawcliffe Rd *CHLY/EC* PR7 91 F3 13
Rawcliffe St *BPOOLS* FY4 4 C7
Rawlinson La *CHLY/EC* PR7 95 H4
Rawlinson St *KIRK/FR/WA* PR4 42 D2 6
Rawstorne Cl *KIRK/FR/WA* PR4 54 A5 2
Rawstorne Rd *PRES* PR1 69 E1
Raybourne Av *PLF/KEOS* FY6 26 A4
Raymond Av *BISP* FY2 28 D2
Read's Av *BPOOL* FY1 2 E7
Reaney Av *BPOOLS* FY4 39 E1 3
Rectory Cl *CHLY/EC* PR7 91 F1
Rectory Rd *BPOOLS* FY4 5 J5
Red Bank Rd *BISP* FY2 24 B3
Redcar Av *CLV/TH* FY5 17 E4
  FUL/RIB PR2 44 C4
Redcar Rd *BPOOL* FY1 28 B2
Red Cross St *PRES* PR1 6 E3
Rede Av *FTWD* FY7 10 C4
Redeswood Av *CLV/TH* FY5 20 D4
Redhill Gv *CHLYE* PR6 87 H4
Red House La *CHLY/EC* PR7 88 A4
Red La *CHLY/EC* PR7 88 D4
Red Marsh Dr *CLV/TH* FY5 18 A5
Redmayne St *PRES* PR1 59 E3 5
Redsands Dr *FUL/RIB* PR2 47 E3
Redstart Pl *CLV/TH* FY5 21 F3 8
Redvers Ter *BPOOL* FY1 28 B2 3
Redwing Av *CLV/TH* FY5 17 F5
Redwood Av *LEY/BBR* PR5 80 D4
Redwood Cl *BPOOLS* FY4 38 C4
Reedfield *LEY/BBR* PR5 79 F5
Reedfield Pl *LEY/BBR* PR5 78 C3
Reedy Acre Pl *LSTA* FY8 62 D2
Reeveswood *CHLY/EC* PR7 88 A4
Regal Av *BPOOLS* FY4 39 E2
Regency Av *LEY/BBR* PR5 78 A1 2
Regency Cl *KIRK/FR/WA* PR4 42 C3
Regent Av *LSTA* FY8 50 B5
Regent Ct *FUL/RIB* PR2 45 H3
Regent Dr *FUL/RIB* PR2 45 G4
Regent Gv *FUL/RIB* PR2 45 H3
Regent Pk *FUL/RIB* PR2 45 H2
Regent Rd *BPOOL* FY1 2 E5
  CHLY/EC PR7 91 E3
  LEY/BBR PR5 71 E2
  LEY/BBR PR5 81 E3 1
Regent Rd East *BPOOL* FY1 2 E5
Regents Ter *PLF/KEOS* FY6 26 C4 2
Regent St *CHLY/EC* PR7 94 B4
  PRES PR1 7 H5
Regents Wy *CHLY/EC* PR7 86 A5
Regentsway *LEY/BBR* PR5 78 B1
Reiver Rd *LEY/BBR* PR5 80 B1
Renshaw Dr *LEY/BBR* PR5 71 F4
Renwick Av *BPOOLS* FY4 32 D5
Repton Av *BPOOL* FY1 28 C1
Reta Dr *CLV/TH* FY5 21 G1
Rhoden Rd *LEY/BBR* PR5 80 B3
Rhodesway *LEY/BBR* PR5 72 D4
Rhyl St *FTWD* FY7 11 H1
Ribble Av *KIRK/FR/WA* PR4 54 A5
Ribble Bank *PRES* PR1 57 E5
Ribble Bank St *PRES* PR1 6 E3
Ribble Cl *KIRK/FR/WA* PR4 54 A5
  PRES PR1 69 H2 4
Ribble Crs *KIRK/FR/WA* PR4 43 F3
  LEY/BBR PR5 58 D5 7
Ribble Rd *BPOOL* FY1 2 E7
  FTWD FY7 11 F2
  LEY/BBR PR5 80 C4
Ribblesdale Cl *BPOOLS* FY4 33 G5 2
  KIRK/FR/WA PR4 42 D2
Ribblesdale Pl *CHLY/EC* PR7 91 E2 2
  PRES PR1 7 H5
Ribble St *LSTA* FY8 48 D5
  PRES PR1 7 F3
Ribbleton Av *FUL/RIB* PR2 47 F5 6
Ribbleton Hall Dr *FUL/RIB* PR2 47 G5 3
Ribbleton La *PRES* PR1 58 D2
Ribbleton Pl *PRES* PR1 58 C3 5
Ribbleton St *PRES* PR1 58 C3
Ribble View Cl *KIRK/FR/WA* PR4 53 H5
Ribby Av *KIRK/FR/WA* PR4 42 A4
  KIRK/FR/WA PR4 42 D3
Ribby Pl *BPOOLS* FY4 33 H4
  FUL/RIB PR2 56 C2
Ribby Rd *KIRK/FR/WA* PR4 42 A4
Ribchester Av *BPOOLE* FY3 33 H4
Ribchester Rd *LSTA* FY8 63 H2 10
Rice Gv *BPOOL* FY1 28 D2 5
Richardson Cl
  KIRK/FR/WA PR4 54 C5 3
Richardson St *BPOOL* FY1 2 D7
Richard's St *KIRK/FR/WA* PR4 42 D2 7
Richards Wy *CLV/TH* FY5 21 F3
  LSTA FY8 49 E1 1
Richmond Av *CLV/TH* FY5 21 E2
Richmond Ct *CHLY/EC* PR7 91 F4 8
  LEY/BBR PR5 80 A3 3
Richmond Rd *BPOOL* FY1 2 D1
  CHLY/EC PR7 88 B3
  CHLYE PR6 91 H4
  LSTA FY8 49 E5 6
Richmond St *PRES* PR1 58 C4 8
Ridgeford Gdns *FUL/RIB* PR2 45 G3
Ridgemont *FUL/RIB* PR2 45 F2
Ridge Rd *CHLYE* PR6 91 H3
Ridge Wy *PRES* PR1 69 H2
Ridgeway Dr *CLV/TH* FY5 22 B4
The Ridgeway *FTWD* FY7 10 D3
Ridgwood Av *BPOOLE* FY3 3 J4
The Ridings *CHLYE* PR6 87 F1
Riding St *PRES* PR1 58 A2
Ridley Rd *FUL/RIB* PR2 57 F1
Ridley St *BPOOLE* FY3 3 H4
Rigby Cl *KIRK/FR/WA* PR4 54 C5
Rigby Rd *BPOOL* FY1 4 D2
Rigby St *PRES* PR1 58 D2
Riley Av *LSTA* FY8 61 F2
Rimington Pl *LSTA* FY8 49 H5 2
Ring Dyke Wy *LSTA* FY8 63 E2
Rington Av *PLF/KEOS* FY6 25 H1
Ringway *CHLY/EC* PR7 90 D3
  CLV/TH FY5 17 E5
Ring Wy *PRES* PR1 7 K1
Ringwood Cl *LSTA* FY8 62 C3
Ringwood Rd *PRES* PR1 58 D1
Ripley Dr *LSTA* FY8 49 H5
Ripon Cl *CLV/TH* FY5 17 E4 1
Ripon Rd *BPOOL* FY1 3 G7
  LSTA FY8 62 B1
Ripon St *PRES* PR1 57 H1
Ripon Ter *PRES* PR1 59 G2 6
Rishton St *BPOOL* FY1 2 D7
Ritherham Av *CLV/TH* FY5 20 D1 1
River Hts *LEY/BBR* PR5 77 H1 9
River Pde *PRES* PR1 6 D6
River Rd *CLV/TH* FY5 22 C2
Riversedge Rd *LEY/BBR* PR5 80 B4
Riversgate *FTWD* FY7 11 F2
Riverside *LEY/BBR* PR5 78 B2
  PRES PR1 7 F7
Riverside Av *LEY/BBR* PR5 76 D5
Riverside Cl *LEY/BBR* PR5 76 D5 1
Riverside Dr *PLF/KEOS* FY6 23 F2
Riverside Rd *PRES* PR1 69 H1
Riversleigh Av *BPOOL* FY1 28 C1
  LSTA FY8 62 C3
River St *PRES* PR1 6 E3
Riversway *BPOOLE* FY3 29 F4
  FUL/RIB PR2 56 C3
  PLF/KEOS FY6 26 C2
Riverway Cl *LEY/BBR* PR5 78 A1 3
Rivington Av *BISP* FY2 24 C2
Rivington Cl *PLF/KEOS* FY6 26 B4
Rivington Rd *CHLYE* PR6 91 H1
Roach Rd *LEY/BBR* PR5 73 G2
Roberts St *CHLY/EC* PR7 91 F3 14
Robin Cl *CHLY/EC* PR7 94 A2 1
Robin Hey *LEY/BBR* PR5 80 A3
Robins Cl *PLF/KEOS* FY6 25 G3
Robins La *BISP* FY2 25 F1
  PLF/KEOS FY6 25 G3
Robinson St *FUL/RIB* PR2 45 G5
Robin St *PRES* PR1 59 E2
Robson Wy *BPOOLE* FY3 25 G5
Rochester Av *CLV/TH* FY5 17 F5
Rochford Av *CLV/TH* FY5 21 E3
Rockburgh Crs *KIRK/FR/WA* PR4 74 B4
Rockingham Rd *BISP* FY2 24 D4
Rock St *CLV/TH* FY5 17 H5
Rock Villa Rd *CHLYE* PR6 83 F4 1
Rockville Av *CLV/TH* FY5 21 E4
Rodney Av *LSTA* FY8 49 E2
Rodney St *PRES* PR1 7 G1
Rodwell Wk *BPOOLE* FY3 29 F2
Roebuck St *FUL/RIB* PR2 57 F1
Roehampton Cl *CLV/TH* FY5 21 G2 6
Roe Hey Dr *CHLY/EC* PR7 94 C3
Rogerley Cl *LSTA* FY8 63 E2
Roman Rd *PRES* PR1 58 C4
Roman Wy *CLV/TH* FY5 21 F3
  KIRK/FR/WA PR4 43 G4
Romford Rd *PRES* PR1 58 D1
Romney Av *BPOOLS* FY4 5 G6
  FTWD FY7 11 E3
Ronaldsway *PRES* PR1 47 E5
Rookery Cl *CHLY/EC* PR7 90 D4
  PRES PR1 69 H4
Rookery Dr *PRES* PR1 70 A4
Rook St *PRES* PR1 58 C1
Rookwood *CHLY/EC* PR7 88 A4
Rookwood Av *CHLY/EC* PR7 87 F5
  CLV/TH FY5 20 D4
Rosary Av *BPOOLS* FY4 5 K5
Roseacre *BPOOLS* FY4 3
Roseacre Pl *FUL/RIB* PR2 56
  LSTA FY8 49
Rose Av *BPOOL* FY1
  FUL/RIB PR2 4
Rosebank Av *BPOOLS* FY4 38
Roseberry Av *KIRK/FR/WA* PR4 4
Rosebery Av *BPOOLS* FY4 3
  LSTA FY8 6
Rose Cl *LEY/BBR* PR5 82
Rosedale Av *BPOOLE* FY3 3
Rosedene Cl *KIRK/FR/WA* PR4 44
Rose Fold *PRES* PR1 6
Rose La *PRES* PR1 4
Rose Lea *FUL/RIB* PR2 4
Roselyn Av *BPOOLS* FY4 38
Rosemary Av *BPOOLS* FY4 3
  CLV/TH FY5 21
Rosemary Ct *PRES* PR1 69
Rosemeade Av *LEY/BBR* PR5 7
Rosemede Av *BPOOLE* FY3 3
Rosemount Av *PLF/KEOS* FY6 1
Rose St *LEY/BBR* PR5 81
  PRES PR1 7
Rose Ter *FUL/RIB* PR2 5
Roseway *BPOOLS* FY4 3
  FUL/RIB PR2 5
  LSTA FY8 6
  PLF/KEOS FY6 26
Rosewood *KIRK/FR/WA* PR4 4
Rosewood Av *LEY/BBR* PR5 7
Rosewood Cl *CLV/TH* FY5 22
  LSTA FY8 62
Rosewood Dr *LEY/BBR* PR5 7
Rosklyn Rd *CHLYE* PR6 9
Rossall Cl *FTWD* FY7 1
  LEY/BBR PR5 72
Rossall Dr *FUL/RIB* PR2 4
Rossall Gdns *CLV/TH* FY5 1
Rossall Ga *FTWD* FY7 1
Rossall Grange La *FTWD* FY7 1
Rossall La *FTWD* FY7 1
Rossall Rd *BPOOLE* FY3
  CHLYE PR6 91
  CLV/TH FY5 1
  FUL/RIB PR2 45
  LSTA FY8 6
Rossall St *FUL/RIB* PR2 5
Rossendale Av North
  CLV/TH FY5 2
Rossendale Av South
  CLV/TH FY5 2
Rossendale Rd *LSTA* FY8 4
Rossett Av *BPOOLS* FY4 34
Rossington Av *BISP* FY2 2
Rosslyn Av *PLF/KEOS* FY6
Rosslyn Crs *PLF/KEOS* FY6 1
Rosslyn Crs East *PLF/KEOS* FY6 1
Rostrevor Cl *LEY/BBR* PR5 80
Rothay Av *FTWD* FY7 1
Rothbury Pl *LSTA* FY8 63
Rotherwick Av *CHLY/EC* PR7 9
Rothwell Ct *LEY/BBR* PR5 81
Rothwell Crs *FUL/RIB* PR2 47
Rothwell Dr *FTWD* FY7 1
Rough Heys La *BPOOLS* FY4 3
Rough Lea Rd *CLV/TH* FY5 2
Round Acre *LEY/BBR* PR5 7
Roundhay *BPOOLS* FY4 33
Round Meadow *LEY/BBR* PR5 8
Roundway *FTWD* FY7 1
Roundway Down *FUL/RIB* PR2 4
Round Wd *PRES* PR1
Rowan Av *FUL/RIB* PR2 47
Rowan Cl *PRES* PR1 6
Rowan Cft *CHLYE* PR6 8
Rowangate *FUL/RIB* PR2 46
Rowan Gv *CHLYE* PR6 8
The Rowans *PLF/KEOS* FY6 2
Rowberrow Cl *FUL/RIB* PR2 47
Rowland Cl *CLV/TH* FY5 21
Rowland La *CLV/TH* FY5 2
Rowntree Av *FTWD* FY7 1
Rowsley Rd *LSTA* FY8 4
Rowton Heath *FUL/RIB* PR2 45
Roxburgh Rd *BPOOLS* FY4 3
Royal Av *BPOOLE* FY3 33
  FUL/RIB PR2 4
  KIRK/FR/WA PR4 4
  LEY/BBR PR5 8
Royal Bank Rd *BPOOLE* FY3
Royal Pl *LSTA* FY8 5
Royal Troon Ct
  KIRK/FR/WA PR4 43
Royalty Av *KIRK/FR/WA* PR4 7
Royalty Gdns *KIRK/FR/WA* PR4 75
Royalty La *KIRK/FR/WA* PR4 7
Royds St *LSTA* FY8 61
Roylen Av *PLF/KEOS* FY6 2
Royle Rd *CHLY/EC* PR7 91

es Ct *CLV/TH* FY5 ... **21** H2
e St *BPOOL* FY1 ... **4** C5
ton Rd *PLF/KEOS* FY6 ... **26** D2
on Dr *CHLYE* PR6 ... **87** F2
vard Pl *BPOOLE* FY3 ... **29** F3 3
TA FY8 ... **49** E3 2
ord Rd *LSTA* FY8 ... **62** A1
s St *PRES* PR1 ... **58** D1
oy St *BPOOLS* FY4 ... **5** G6 2
corn Av *BISP* FY2 ... **25** F5
dle Rd *FUL/RIB* PR2 ... **45** G5
nymede Av *CLV/TH* FY5 ... **20** D2 4
shaw La *CHLY/EC* PR7 ... **84** C5
y Hey *LEY/BBR* PR5 ... **77** F1
in Av *BPOOL* FY1 ... **4** D4
V/TH FY5 ... **21** G1
Y/BBR PR5 ... **81** F2
kin Rd *KIRK/FR/WA* PR4 ... **54** B5
kin St *PRES* PR1 ... **58** C5
and Av *BPOOLS* FY4 ... **34** B4
and Dr *LEY/BBR* PR5 ... **72** D2
ell Av *CLV/TH* FY5 ... **20** D4
Y/BBR PR5 ... **81** H4
ES PR1 ... **59** H3
sell Sq *CHLYE* PR6 ... **91** G1
sell Sq West *CHLYE* PR6 ... **91** G1
erford Pl *BPOOLS* FY4 ... **38** B4 2
and Av *CLV/TH* FY5 ... **21** E1
WD FY7 ... **11** E3
RK/FR/WA PR4 ... **54** C4
Y/BBR PR5 ... **71** E3 4
F/KEOS FY6 ... **26** A4
and Ct *LSTA* FY8 ... **62** B1 5
and Rd *LSTA* FY8 ... **62** B1
and St *PRES* PR1 ... **58** D3
urn Av *BPOOLS* FY4 ... **5** J5
al Av *BPOOL* FY1 ... **5** F1
V/TH FY5 ... **21** H3
WD FY7 ... **11** E2
RK/FR/WA PR4 ... **54** A5
Y/BBR PR5 ... **71** E5
F/KEOS FY6 ... **26** B4
ES PR1 ... **69** F3
al Cl *FUL/RIB* PR2 ... **46** D4 5
al Pl *CHLY/EC* PR7 ... **91** F4
al Rd *LSTA* FY8 ... **49** E3
F/KEOS FY6 ... **23** G2
ES PR1 ... **59** E1
dingwood *PRES* PR1 ... **57** E5
en Av *CLV/TH* FY5 ... **20** D1
Y/BBR PR5 ... **81** H3
croft Av *PLF/KEOS* FY6 ... **23** G3
field Av *PRES* PR1 ... **69** G4
neys Rd *LSTA* FY8 ... **48** D3
ands Crs *FUL/RIB* PR2 ... **56** B3
St *PRES* PR1 ... **58** B2
nd Av *PLF/KEOS* FY6 ... **26** A4
nds Rd *CHLY/EC* PR7 ... **91** E3
on Pl *BPOOLS* FY4 ... **33** G3
on Av *BPOOLS* FY4 ... **33** F4

S

den Pl *LSTA* FY8 ... **50** A4
kville St *BPOOLS* FY4 ... **38** C1
LYE PR6 ... **91** H3
Cl *FTWD* FY7 ... **10** D3
ar Dr *KIRK/FR/WA* PR4 ... **54** A5
ar St *CHLY/EC* PR7 ... **88** B4
e Ct *PRES* PR1 ... **69** F4
e La *PRES* PR1 ... **46** C5
idans Pk *LEY/BBR* PR5 ... **71** F4
lban's Pl *CHLY/EC* PR7 ... **91** G5
lban's Rd *BPOOL* FY1 ... **3** G7
TA FY8 ... **49** F4
mbrose Ter *LEY/BBR* PR5 .. **81** G2 10
ndrew's Av *CLV/TH* FY5 ... **20** D2
L/RIB PR2 ... **56** D1
ndrew's Cl *LEY/BBR* PR5 ... **81** F5 2
ndrew's Rd *PRES* PR1 ... **58** B1 3
ndrew's Rd North *LSTA* FY8 ... **48** D4
ndrew's Rd South *LSTA* FY8 ... **49** E5
ndrews Wy *LEY/BBR* PR5 ... **81** F4
nnes Rd *BPOOLS* FY4 ... **5** F6
t Annes Rd *CHLYE* PR6 ... **91** H3 7
nne's Rd *LEY/BBR* PR5 ... **81** H2
nne's Rd East *LSTA* FY8 ... **49** E4 3
nne's Rd West *LSTA* FY8 ... **48** D5 2
nne's St *PRES* PR1 ... **58** B1 4
nthony's Cl *FUL/RIB* PR2 ... **45** F4 2
nthony's Crs *FUL/RIB* PR2 ... **45** F4
nthony's Dr *FUL/RIB* PR2 ... **45** F4
nthony's Pl *BPOOL* FY1 ... **3** F1
RK/FR/WA PR4 ... **43** E4
nthony's Rd *PRES* PR1 ... **58** B1 5
ustin's Pl *PRES* PR1 ... **7** K4
ustin's Rd *PRES* PR1 ... **7** K4
arnabas' Pl *PRES* PR1 ... **58** B2 6

St Bede's Av *BPOOLS* FY4 ... **4** C6
St Bernard Av *BPOOLE* FY3 ... **29** F3 4
St Bernard's Rd *PLF/KEOS* FY6 ... **12** C1
St Catherines Cl *LEY/BBR* PR5 .. **81** H2 3
St Catherine's Dr *FUL/RIB* PR2 ... **45** F4
St Catherines Wy *LEY/BBR* PR5 ... **77** H2
St Chads Cl *PLF/KEOS* FY6 ... **26** B5
St Chad's Rd *BPOOL* FY1 ... **4** C4
PRES PR1 ... **58** C2 8
St Christines Av *LEY/BBR* PR5 ... **77** H5
St Christopher's Rd *PRES* PR1 .. **58** B1 6
St Clares Av *FUL/RIB* PR2 ... **46** B2
St Clement's Av *BPOOLE* FY3 ... **3** K4
LEY/BBR PR5 ... **81** H1
St Cuthbert's Cl *FUL/RIB* PR2 ... **45** G5
LSTA FY8 ... **63** E3 8
St Cuthbert's Rd *LEY/BBR* PR5 ... **70** B5
PRES PR1 ... **58** B1 7
St David's Av *CLV/TH* FY5 ... **20** D2
St David's Gv *LSTA* FY8 ... **48** D3
St David's Rd *LEY/BBR* PR5 ... **81** H2
PRES PR1 ... **58** B1 8
St David's Rd North *LSTA* FY8 ... **48** D2
St David's Rd South *LSTA* FY8 ... **49** E5
St Edmund's Rd *BPOOLS* FY4 ... **5** K5
St Francis Cl *FUL/RIB* PR2 ... **46** B1
St George Ct *BPOOL* FY1 ... **3** G2
St George's Av *CLV/TH* FY5 ... **20** D3
LSTA FY8 ... **49** E4
St George's La *CLV/TH* FY5 ... **20** D2 5
LSTA FY8 ... **48** D5
St George's Rd *BPOOLS* FY4 ... **38** C2 3
LSTA FY8 ... **48** D5
PRES PR1 ... **58** C1 4
St George's Sq *LSTA* FY8 ... **48** D4 2
St George's St *CHLY/EC* PR7 ... **91** F3
St Gerrard's Rd *LEY/BBR* PR5 ... **70** B5
St Gregory Rd *PRES* PR1 ... **58** C1
St Gregory's Pl *CHLY/EC* PR7 ... **91** F5
St Helen's Rd *CHLYE* PR6 ... **83** F3
St Heliers Rd *BPOOL* FY1 ... **4** E4
St Hilda's Cl *CHLY/EC* PR7 ... **95** F1
St Hilda's Rd *LSTA* FY8 ... **48** D4
St Ignatius' Sq *PRES* PR1 ... **7** J1
St Ives Av *BPOOL* FY1 ... **5** H2
KIRK/FR/WA PR4 ... **54** A5
St Ives Crs *FUL/RIB* PR2 ... **44** D4 5
St James Cl *LEY/BBR* PR5 ... **77** G1
St James Rd *BPOOLS* FY4 ... **38** C2
Saint James's Pl *CHLYE* PR6 ... **91** H3 8
St James's Rd *PRES* PR1 ... **58** A1 12
St John Av *FTWD* FY7 ... **10** D4
St John's Av *CLV/TH* FY5 ... **22** B3
GAR/LONG PR3 ... **15** E1
KIRK/FR/WA PR4 ... **42** D4
PLF/KEOS FY6 ... **26** C2 1
St Johns Cl *CHLYE* PR6 ... **83** E5 2
St John's Gn *LEY/BBR* PR5 ... **80** D3
St John's Pl *PRES* PR1 ... **7** J3
St John's Rd *LEY/BBR* PR5 ... **71** E1
St John's St *LSTA* FY8 ... **63** G3 4
St Josephs Cl *BPOOLE* FY3 ... **3** K4
St Joseph's Ter *PRES* PR1 ... **58** D2 14
St Jude's Av *LEY/BBR* PR5 ... **71** E5
LEY/BBR PR5 ... **77** H5 1
St Leonard's Rd *BPOOLE* FY3 ... **33** F3
St Leonard's Rd East *LSTA* FY8 ... **49** E3
St Leonard's Rd West *LSTA* FY8 ... **48** D3
St Louis Av *BPOOLE* FY3 ... **29** F3 5
St Luke's Pl *PRES* PR1 ... **58** D2 15
St Luke's Rd *BPOOLS* FY4 ... **38** C2
St Margarets Cl *FUL/RIB* PR2 ... **44** D4
St Margaret's Rd *LEY/BBR* PR5 **81** H2 4
St Mark's Pl *BPOOLE* FY3 ... **29** E2 8
St Mark's Pl East *PRES* PR1 ... **6** C1
St Mark's Pl West *PRES* PR1 ... **6** C1 2
St Mark's Rd *PRES* PR1 ... **6** C1
St Marlow Av *LEY/BBR* PR5 ... **81** H1 2
St Martins Cl *PLF/KEOS* FY6 ... **25** H2 6
St Martin's Ct *CLV/TH* FY5 ... **21** F2
St Martin's Rd *BPOOLS* FY4 ... **38** C2
PRES PR1 ... **58** B1 9
St Mary Cl *BPOOLE* FY3 ... **29** H1 4
St Mary's Av *LEY/BBR* PR5 ... **71** E5
St Mary's Cl *LEY/BBR* PR5 ... **71** E5
PRES PR1 ... **58** D3 6
St Mary's Ct *PRES* PR1 ... **58** C3 6
St Mary's Ga *CHLY/EC* PR7 ... **85** H4
Saint Mary's Rd *LEY/BBR* PR5 ... **71** F5
St Mary's St *PRES* PR1 ... **58** C3
St Mary's St North *PRES* PR1 ... **58** C3 7
St Michael's Cl *CHLY/EC* PR7 ... **91** E1
St Michaels Rd *BISP* FY2 ... **25** E4
KIRK/FR/WA PR4 ... **43** G3
LEY/BBR PR5 ... **81** H1 3
PRES PR1 ... **58** B1 10
St Monica's Wy *BPOOLS* FY4 ... **34** B4 2
St Nicholas Rd *BPOOLS* FY4 ... **39** G3
St Oswalds Cl *PRES* PR1 ... **58** D1
St Patrick's Rd North *LSTA* FY8 ... **49** E3

St Patrick's Rd South *LSTA* FY8 ... **49** F4
St Paul's Av *LSTA* FY8 ... **61** H2
PRES PR1 ... **58** B2 7
St Pauls Cl *LEY/BBR* PR5 ... **77** E2
St Paul's Rd *BPOOL* FY1 ... **28** B2 4
PRES PR1 ... **58** B1
St Paul's Sq *PRES* PR1 ... **7** K1
St Peter's Pl *FTWD* FY7 ... **11** H2 2
St Peter's Sq *PRES* PR1 ... **7** F1
St Peter's St *CHLYE* PR6 ... **91** H1
PRES PR1 ... **7** G1
St Philip's Rd *PRES* PR1 ... **58** B1 11
St Saviour's Cl *LEY/BBR* PR5 ... **78** C2
St Stephen's Av *BISP* FY2 ... **24** B5
St Stephens Rd *KIRK/FR/WA* PR4 .. **42** D4
PRES PR1 ... **58** B1
St Teresa's Av *CLV/TH* FY5 ... **20** D3
St Theresa's Dr *FUL/RIB* PR2 ... **45** F4
St Thomas' Pl *PRES* PR1 ... **58** A2 8
St Thomas Rd *KIRK/FR/WA* PR4 ... **43** E4
LSTA FY8 ... **49** F5
PRES PR1 ... **58** A1
St Thomas's Rd *CHLY/EC* PR7 ... **91** E2
St Thomas' St *PRES* PR1 ... **58** A2 9
St Vincent Av *BPOOL* FY1 ... **5** H2
St Vincents Rd *FUL/RIB* PR2 ... **45** H3
St Walburga's Rd *BPOOLE* FY3 ... **29** F2
St Walburge Av *PRES* PR1 ... **6** E1
St Walburges Gdns *FUL/RIB* PR2 ... **6** D1
St Wilfrid St *PRES* PR1 ... **7** G3
Salcombe Av *BISP* FY2 ... **25** E5
Salcombe Rd *LSTA* FY8 ... **48** C2
Salisbury Av *PLF/KEOS* FY6 ... **12** C1
Salisbury Rd *BPOOL* FY1 ... **3** G7
PRES PR1 ... **6** D4
Salisbury St *CHLY/EC* PR7 ... **91** G3 7
PRES PR1 ... **59** E2 18
Salmesbury Av *BISP* FY2 ... **25** E5
Salmon St *PRES* PR1 ... **58** D4
Salop Av *BISP* FY2 ... **24** C3
Saltash Rd *CLV/TH* FY5 ... **17** H4
Saltcotes Pl *LSTA* FY8 ... **63** H2
Saltcotes Rd *LSTA* FY8 ... **63** H1 5
Salter St *PRES* PR1 ... **58** A2
Salthouse Av *BPOOL* FY1 ... **4** E1 2
Salt Marsh La *PLF/KEOS* FY6 ... **23** F3
Salwick Av *BISP* FY2 ... **24** D2
Salwick Pl *FUL/RIB* PR2 ... **56** B2
LSTA FY8 ... **49** G3
Samuel St *PRES* PR1 ... **59** E3
Sanderling Cl *CLV/TH* FY5 ... **21** F4 5
Sandersons Wy *BPOOLS* FY4 ... **33** F5
Sandfield St *LEY/BBR* PR5 ... **81** G3
Sandgate *BPOOLS* FY4 ... **38** D3
CHLY/EC PR7 ... **91** G5
LSTA FY8 ... **48** C4
Sandham St *CHLYE* PR6 ... **91** G2 10
Sandhills Av *BPOOLS* FY4 ... **38** B3
Sandhurst Av *BISP* FY2 ... **24** B2
LSTA FY8 ... **49** E4
Sandhurst Cl *KIRK/FR/WA* PR4 ... **42** D3
Sandicroft Av *PLF/KEOS* FY6 ... **23** G3
Sandicroft Pl *PLF/KEOS* FY6 ... **13** F2
Sandicroft Rd *BPOOL* FY1 ... **28** C1
Sandiways Cl *CLV/TH* FY5 ... **22** A4 4
Sandon Pl *BPOOLS* FY4 ... **38** C4
Sandown Cl *KIRK/FR/WA* PR4 ... **42** C3 2
Sandown Rd *CLV/TH* FY5 ... **21** H3 3
Sandridge Av *CHLY/EC* PR7 ... **91** E3
Sandridge Pl *BPOOLS* FY4 ... **38** B4 3
LSTA FY8 ... **38** B4 3
Sandringham Av *CLV/TH* FY5 ... **21** H3
LEY/BBR PR5 ... **81** H3
Sandringham Park Dr
KIRK/FR/WA PR4 ... **75** G1
Sandringham Rd *CHLY/EC* PR7 ... **88** B3
CHLY/EC PR7 ... **91** E2
LEY/BBR PR5 ... **71** E3
LSTA FY8 ... **61** G1
Sandsdale Av *FUL/RIB* PR2 ... **46** D3
Sands Wy *BPOOL* FY1 ... **4** D2
Sandwick Cl *FUL/RIB* PR2 ... **46** A1 5
Sandybrook Cl *FUL/RIB* PR2 ... **47** F3
Sandy Cl *CLV/TH* FY5 ... **20** C1
Sandycroft *FUL/RIB* PR2 ... **59** G1
Sandyfields *KIRK/FR/WA* PR4 ... **44** B2 3
Sandyforth Av *CLV/TH* FY5 ... **21** H1
Sandyforth La *KIRK/FR/WA* PR4 ... **44** D1
Sandygate La *GAR/LONG* PR3 ... **36** A3
Sandy La *BPOOLS* FY4 ... **39** G4
CHLYE PR6 ... **79** G5
FTWD FY7 ... **16** D2
KIRK/FR/WA PR4 ... **44** A1
LEY/BBR PR5 ... **81** F4
PLF/KEOS FY6 ... **13** F2
PLF/KEOS FY6 ... **23** G3
Sandy Pl *LEY/BBR* PR5 ... **81** F4 9
Santon Cl *KIRK/FR/WA* PR4 ... **43** E1
Saul St *PRES* PR1 ... **7** H2
Saunders' La *KIRK/FR/WA* PR4 ... **68** B5

Saunders Ms *CHLY/EC* PR7 ... **95** F2
Savick Av *FUL/RIB* PR2 ... **56** A2
Savick Cl *LEY/BBR* PR5 ... **78** C1
Savick Rd *FUL/RIB* PR2 ... **45** G4
Savick Wy *FUL/RIB* PR2 ... **44** C5
Saville Av *PLF/KEOS* FY6 ... **25** H1
Saville Rd *BPOOL* FY1 ... **4** E4
Saville St *CHLY/EC* PR7 ... **91** F5
Savoy St *PRES* PR1 ... **7** F3
Sawley Av *BPOOLS* FY4 ... **38** D3
LSTA FY8 ... **50** A5
Sawley Crs *FUL/RIB* PR2 ... **47** G5
Saxby Gv *BPOOLS* FY4 ... **33** F4
Saxon Cl *CLV/TH* FY5 ... **21** H4
Saxon Hey *FUL/RIB* PR2 ... **45** F5
Scafell Rd *LSTA* FY8 ... **49** G1
Scale Hall La *KIRK/FR/WA* PR4 ... **55** G1
Scarborough Rd *LSTA* FY8 ... **49** G2
Scarlet St *CHLYE* PR6 ... **91** H3 9
Scarsdale Av *BPOOLS* FY4 ... **38** C3
Scawfell Rd *CHLY/EC* PR7 ... **91** E5 6
Sceptre Wy *LEY/BBR* PR5 ... **79** E3
Schleswig St *PRES* PR1 ... **7** K1
Schleswig Wy *LEY/BBR* PR5 ... **80** B3
Schofield Av *BPOOLE* FY3 ... **29** H3 5
School Brow *CHLYE* PR6 ... **83** E5
School Fld *LEY/BBR* PR5 ... **79** E4
School La *CHLY/EC* PR7 ... **86** A4
KIRK/FR/WA PR4 ... **43** F3
KIRK/FR/WA PR4 ... **54** C4
KIRK/FR/WA PR4 ... **55** F1
KIRK/FR/WA PR4 ... **74** B1
LEY/BBR PR5 ... **71** G4
LEY/BBR PR5 ... **77** E2
LEY/BBR PR5 ... **81** E2
LSTA FY8 ... **63** E3
PLF/KEOS FY6 ... **13** F3 1
School Rd *BPOOLS* FY4 ... **39** G4
CLV/TH FY5 ... **22** A4
School St *KIRK/FR/WA* PR4 ... **74** A4
LEY/BBR PR5 ... **71** G3
LEY/BBR PR5 ... **81** G2
PRES PR1 ... **6** E3
Scorton Av *BPOOLE* FY3 ... **29** F3
Scotforth Rd *PRES* PR1 ... **58** D3
Scotswood Av *BPOOLS* FY4 ... **38** D2 4
Scott Cl *BPOOLS* FY4 ... **33** F5
Scott Ms *BPOOLS* FY4 ... **33** F5 4
Scott's Wd *FUL/RIB* PR2 ... **45** F2
Scudamore Crs *BPOOLS* FY4 ... **5** G6
Seabank Rd *FTWD* FY7 ... **11** G1
Seabourne Av *BPOOLS* FY4 ... **38** B1 2
Seabrook Dr *CLV/TH* FY5 ... **21** E4
Seacrest Av *BPOOL* FY1 ... **28** C2 2
Seafield Rd *BPOOL* FY1 ... **28** B2
LSTA FY8 ... **62** D3
Seaside Wy *BPOOL* FY1 ... **4** D3
Seathwaite Av *BPOOLS* FY4 ... **34** A4
Seaton Av *CLV/TH* FY5 ... **17** E5
Seaton Crs *LSTA* FY8 ... **48** C3
Seattle Av *BISP* FY2 ... **25** E4
Sea Vw *KIRK/FR/WA* PR4 ... **74** A4
Sea Wall *FTWD* FY7 ... **10** C2
Second Av *BPOOLS* FY4 ... **38** C1
Sedbergh Av *BPOOLS* FY4 ... **33** F3
Sedberg St *FUL/RIB* PR2 ... **45** G5 8
Sedgeley Ms *KIRK/FR/WA* PR4 .. **54** A5 3
Sedgfield Cl *BPOOLS* FY4 ... **39** F2
Sedgley Av *KIRK/FR/WA* PR4 ... **54** A5
Sedgwick St *PRES* PR1 ... **58** B2
Sedwell Cl *LSTA* FY8 ... **62** D2
Seedlee Rd *LEY/BBR* PR5 ... **78** D3
Seed St *BPOOL* FY1 ... **2** E3
PRES PR1 ... **7** G2
Sefton Av *PLF/KEOS* FY6 ... **30** B1
Sefton Rd *LEY/BBR* PR5 ... **71** E3
LSTA FY8 ... **49** F4 3
Segar St *KIRK/FR/WA* PR4 ... **42** D2
Selborne St *PRES* PR1 ... **7** K6
Selbourne Rd *BPOOL* FY1 ... **3** G2
Selby Av *BPOOLS* FY4 ... **38** D3
CLV/TH FY5 ... **17** F4
Selby Rd *KIRK/FR/WA* PR4 ... **42** D2
Selby St *PRES* PR1 ... **57** G2 7
Selkirk Dr *LEY/BBR* PR5 ... **71** E4
Sellers St *PRES* PR1 ... **58** D2
Senior Av *BPOOLS* FY4 ... **33** F4
Seniors Dr *CLV/TH* FY5 ... **21** F1
Sephton St *LEY/BBR* PR5 ... **77** F1 5
Sergeant St *LEY/BBR* PR5 ... **78** C1 14
The Serpentine *LSTA* FY8 ... **63** E3 9
Settle Pl *LSTA* FY8 ... **50** A4
Seven Acres *LEY/BBR* PR5 ... **79** F4
Sevenoaks *CHLY/EC* PR7 ... **95** F1
Sevenoaks Dr *CLV/TH* FY5 ... **21** F4
Seven Stars Rd *LEY/BBR* PR5 ... **80** B2
Seventh Av *BPOOLS* FY4 ... **38** C1
Severn Av *FTWD* FY7 ... **16** D1
Severn Dr *LEY/BBR* PR5 ... **71** E4
Severn Hl *FUL/RIB* PR2 ... **36** B5 3

Severn Rd BPOOLS FY4 38 B1
Seymour Rd BPOOL FY1 4 E4
FUL/RIB PR2 45 F5
LSTA FY8 62 B1
Seymour St CHLYE PR6 91 G3
FTWD FY7 11 F2 2
Shackleton Rd KIRK/FR/WA PR4 54 B1
Shady La LEY/BBR PR5 78 B5
Shaftesbury Av BISP FY2 24 C5
BPOOLE FY3 29 H4 3
CLV/TH FY5 16 C4
KIRK/FR/WA PR4 75 G1
PRES PR1 57 E5
Shaftesbury Cl LSTA FY8 62 B1
Shaftesbury Pl CHLY/EC PR7 91 E2
Shakespeare Rd FTWD FY7 11 E2
PRES PR1 59 E2 19
Shakespeare Ter CHLYE PR6 87 G5
Shalbourn Rd LSTA FY8 61 G2
Shalgrove Fld FUL/RIB PR2 45 F1
Shannon St BPOOL FY1 4 C1
Shap Ct FTWD FY7 10 D5
Shard La PLF/KEOS FY6 23 F4
Shard Rd PLF/KEOS FY6 27 F1
Sharman Rd LSTA FY8 49 F2
Sharoe Green La FUL/RIB PR2 45 H1
Sharoe Green Pk FUL/RIB PR2 46 B3
Sharoe Mount Av FUL/RIB PR2 46 A1
Sharow Gv BPOOL FY1 5 G3
Sharrats Pth CHLY/EC PR7 94 C1
Shawbrook Cl CHLY/EC PR7 85 H2
Shaw Brook Rd LEY/BBR PR5 84 D1
Shaw Brow CHLYE PR6 83 E5
Shaw Hl CHLYE PR6 87 E1
Shaw Hill Dr CHLYE PR6 87 E1
Shaw Hill St CHLY/EC PR7 91 F3
Shaw Rd BPOOL FY1 4 C6
Shaw's La GAR/LONG PR3 14 C3
Shaw St PRES PR1 58 B2 8
The Shay CLV/TH FY5 21 F5 7
Sheep Hill Brow CHLYE PR6 82 D2
Sheep Hill La CHLYE PR6 82 D1
Sheephill La KIRK/FR/WA PR4 75 G2
Sheffield Dr FUL/RIB PR2 56 A1
Shelley Cl CHLY/EC PR7 94 C5
Shelley Dr CHLY/EC PR7 88 C5
Shelley Gv CLV/TH FY5 20 D4
Shelley Rd FUL/RIB PR2 57 F1
Shenstone Rd BPOOLE FY3 3 K1
Shepherd Rd LSTA FY8 49 G4
Shepherd Rd North LSTA FY8 49 G3
Shepherd St LSTA FY8 63 F3 9
PRES PR1 7 K3
Shepherds Wy CHLY/EC PR7 91 G2
Sheppard St BPOOL FY1 2 D5
Sheraton Pk FUL/RIB PR2 44 D2
Sherbourne Cl PLF/KEOS FY6 26 A2
Sherbourne Crs PRES PR1 46 C5 2
Sherbourne Rd BPOOL FY1 28 B2
PLF/KEOS FY6 23 G2 1
Sherbourne St CHLYE PR6 91 G3 8
Sherburne Av
KIRK/FR/WA PR4 42 D3 4
Sherburn Rd PRES PR1 69 H3
Sherdley Rd LEY/BBR PR5 77 G2
Sheringham Av CLV/TH FY5 24 D1
Sheringham Wy PLF/KEOS FY6 26 C4
Sherwood Av BPOOLE FY3 29 E2
Sherwood Pl CHLYE PR6 91 G2 11
CLV/TH FY5 21 F3 9
Sherwood Rd LSTA FY8 50 A5
Sherwood Wy FUL/RIB PR2 46 B2
Shetland Rd BPOOL FY1 5 F4
Shipley Cl BPOOLE FY3 29 H1
Shipley Rd LSTA FY8 49 H4
Shire Bank Crs FUL/RIB PR2 45 H2
Shirley Crs BISP FY2 24 D1
Shirley Hts PLF/KEOS FY6 26 B3
Shop La LEY/BBR PR5 72 A2
Shore Gn CLV/TH FY5 21 F1
Shore Rd CLV/TH FY5 20 C4
Shortridge Rd BPOOLS FY4 33 F5
Shrewsbury Cl
KIRK/FR/WA PR4 43 G3 1
Shrewsbury Dr CLV/TH FY5 21 G2 7
Shuttleworth Rd PRES PR1 58 A1 13
Shuttling Fields La LEY/BBR PR5 72 A4
Sibbering Brow Preston Rd
CHLY/EC PR7 89 H3
Siding Rd FTWD FY7 11 G3
Sidmouth Rd LSTA FY8 48 C2
Sidney Av BISP FY2 25 E5
Silsden Cl BPOOLE FY3 29 H1 5
Silverdale BISP FY2 25 E1 2
Silverdale Av FTWD FY7 10 C5
Silverdale Cl LEY/BBR PR5 72 D2 2
LEY/BBR PR5 85 G1 2
Silverdale Dr FUL/RIB PR2 47 E3
Silverdale Rd CHLYE PR6 91 H3 10
LSTA FY8 50 A4
Silverwood Av BPOOLS FY4 5 F7
Silverwood Cl LSTA FY8 62 C2 10
Silvester Rd CHLY/EC PR7 91 F4
Silvia Wy FTWD FY7 11 E2
Simmons Av LEY/BBR PR5 70 C3
Simpson St BPOOLS FY4 32 B5
PRES PR1 7 G2 4
Singleton FUL/RIB PR2 46 A1
Singleton Av LSTA FY8 49 H4
Singleton Cl FUL/RIB PR2 46 A1
Singleton Rw PRES PR1 7 G1
Singleton St BPOOL FY1 4 C1 2
Sion Cl FUL/RIB PR2 47 G4
Six Acre La KIRK/FR/WA PR4 74 D3
Sixfields CLV/TH FY5 21 F5
Sixth Av BPOOLS FY4 38 C1
Sizehouse St PRES PR1 7 H1 4
Sizer St PRES PR1 58 A2 10
Skeffington Rd PRES PR1 58 C1
Skelwith Rd BPOOLE FY3 33 H3
Skiddaw Rd BPOOLS FY4 33 F5
Skippool Av PLF/KEOS FY6 26 C2
Skippool Br PLF/KEOS FY6 26 D1
Skippool Rd CLV/TH FY5 22 C5
Skipton Av PLF/KEOS FY6 26 A2
Skipton Cl BPOOLS FY4 33 F4
LEY/BBR PR5 71 F4
Skipton Crs FUL/RIB PR2 47 F3
Skipton Rd LSTA FY8 49 H5
Slade St PRES PR1 6 E3
Slaidburn Pl FUL/RIB PR2 59 H1 4
Slaidburn Rd FUL/RIB PR2 59 G1
Slater La LEY/BBR PR5 80 A4
Slater Rd CLV/TH FY5 20 C2 2
Slinger Rd CLV/TH FY5 20 C1
Smalley Cft PRES PR1 70 A3
Smallwood Hey Rd
GAR/LONG PR3 14 D1
Smithills Cl CHLYE PR6 91 H1
Smith Rd CLV/TH FY5 20 D2
Smith St CHLY/EC PR7 91 G4
CHLYE PR6 83 F4
KIRK/FR/WA PR4 42 D3 5
LEY/BBR PR5 78 C1
Smithy Brow WGNNW/ST WN6 92 B5
Smithy Cl PLF/KEOS FY6 19 F2
Smithy Cft LSTA FY8 50 A5
Smithy La BPOOLE FY3 30 B4
CHLYE PR6 79 H3
LSTA FY8 50 A5
PLF/KEOS FY6 13 F3 2
Smithy Ms BPOOL FY1 2 E1
Smithy St LEY/BBR PR5 78 B1 7
Snipe Cl BPOOLE FY3 29 H4
CLV/TH FY5 17 F4
Snipewood CHLY/EC PR7 88 A4
Snowdon Cl BPOOL FY1 5 H1
Snowdon Rd LSTA FY8 49 G1
Snowdrop Cl LEY/BBR PR5 82 B2 3
Snow Hl PRES PR1 7 H1
Snowshill Crs CLV/TH FY5 21 F5
Sod Hall La KIRK/FR/WA PR4 75 H3
Sollam's Cl LEY/BBR PR5 71 G4
Solway Cl BISP FY2 24 C1
PRES PR1 69 H3 4
Somerset Av BPOOL FY1 5 H1
CHLY/EC PR7 91 F1
Somerset Pk FUL/RIB PR2 45 E1
Somerset Rd LEY/BBR PR5 81 G2 11
PRES PR1 58 B2 9
Sorrel Cl CLV/TH FY5 17 F4
Sorrel Ct PRES PR1 69 F4
South Av CHLY/EC PR7 91 G4
CLV/TH FY5 16 C5
KIRK/FR/WA PR4 75 G1
Southbank Av BPOOLS FY4 39 G1
Southbourne Av PLF/KEOS FY6 26 A5
Southbourne Rd BPOOLE FY3 33 F3
Southbrook Rd LEY/BBR PR5 80 D3 2
South Cliff St PRES PR1 7 F5
South Clifton St LSTA FY8 63 F3 10
Southdown Dr CLV/TH FY5 22 B4
Southdowns Rd CHLY/EC PR7 91 G5
South Dr FUL/RIB PR2 36 D5
South End PRES PR1 6 E7
Southern Av PRES PR1 58 C5 2
Southern Pde PRES PR1 58 C5
Southey Cl FUL/RIB PR2 46 A1
Southfield Dr BPOOLE FY3 30 A2
KIRK/FR/WA PR4 75 G2
Southfleet Av FTWD FY7 11 E5
Southfleet Pl FTWD FY7 11 E5 1
Southfold Pl LSTA FY8 63 E2
Southgate FTWD FY7 16 D1
FUL/RIB PR2 45 G3
PRES PR1 58 A2
Southgates CHLY/EC PR7 94 A2
South Gv FUL/RIB PR2 36 D5
South Hey LSTA FY8 50 A5
South Holme LSTA FY8 63 F2
South King St BPOOL FY1 2 E5
Southlands KIRK/FR/WA PR4 43 E4
Southlands Av LEY/BBR PR5 70 C5
Southlands Dr LEY/BBR PR5 80 B5
South Meadow La PRES PR1 6 E6
South Meadow St PRES PR1 7 K1 3
South Moss Rd LSTA FY8 50 A4
South Pde CLV/TH FY5 21 E3
South Pk LSTA FY8 62 D2
South Park Dr BPOOLE FY3 33 F3
Southport Rd CHLY/EC PR7 90 D2
Southport Ter CHLYE PR6 91 H3 11
South Prom LSTA FY8 61 E1
South Ribble St LEY/BBR PR5 58 D5 8
South Rd CHLY/EC PR7 94 B4
Southside CHLY/EC PR7 85 H4 3
South Sq BPOOLE FY3 3 H3
CLV/TH FY5 16 C4
South Strd FTWD FY7 16 D2
South St LSTA FY8 63 H2
South Ter CHLYE PR6 86 A3
South Vw KIRK/FR/WA PR4 43 E4
South View Ter LEY/BBR PR5 81 F4 10
South Warton St LSTA FY8 63 G3 5
Southway FTWD FY7 10 D5
South Westby St LSTA FY8 63 F3
Southwood Av FTWD FY7 11 E3
Southwood Cl LSTA FY8 62 C2 11
Southworth Av BPOOLS FY4 39 E1 4
Sowerby Av BPOOLS FY4 32 D5
Sower Carr La PLF/KEOS FY6 19 H5
Spa Rd PRES PR1 6 D2
Spa St PRES PR1 6 C1
Speedwell Cl CLV/TH FY5 17 F4 5
Spencer Ct BPOOL FY1 3 F1
Spendmore La CHLY/EC PR7 94 A5
Spen Pl BPOOLS FY4 33 F5
Spey Cl LEY/BBR PR5 80 D4
Speyside BPOOLS FY4 38 D1
Spinners Sq LEY/BBR PR5 78 B2 2
Spinney Brow FUL/RIB PR2 47 E4
Spinney Cl CHLYE PR6 87 E1
KIRK/FR/WA PR4 75 G1
The Spinney CHLYE PR6 87 F4 1
CLV/TH FY5 21 F5 8
PLF/KEOS FY6 26 C3
PRES PR1 68 C3
Spires Gv KIRK/FR/WA PR4 44 B3
Spring Bank PRES PR1 6 E4
Springbank Av CLV/TH FY5 22 A2 3
Springbrook Av CLV/TH FY5 21 E4
Spring Crs CHLYE PR6 87 H1
Springcroft LEY/BBR PR5 81 H1 4
Springfield Av KIRK/FR/WA PR4 42 C3
Springfield Dr CLV/TH FY5 17 H5
Springfield Rd BPOOL FY1 2 C3
CHLY/EC PR7 91 F2 9
LEY/BBR PR5 80 C5
LSTA FY8 49 E5 7
Springfield Rd North
CHLY/EC PR7 94 B5 2
Springfield St PRES PR1 57 H2
Spring Gdns KIRK/FR/WA PR4 54 B3
LEY/BBR PR5 81 E4
LSTA FY8 49 F2 2
PRES PR1 70 A4
Spring Hl KIRK/FR/WA PR4 54 D4
Spring Meadow LEY/BBR PR5 82 B2
Spring Ms CHLYE PR6 87 H1
Springsands Cl FUL/RIB PR2 47 F3 4
Springs Rd CHLYE PR6 87 G5
Spring St LEY/BBR PR5 81 G3 4
Springwood Cl PRES PR1 70 B3
Springwood Dr CHLYE PR6 91 H5
The Square BPOOLE FY3 33 G3
CLV/TH FY5 16 D4
LEY/BBR PR5 81 G2 12
Squires Cl LEY/BBR PR5 72 D4
Squires Gate La LSTA FY8 38 A4
Squires Gate Link Rd
BPOOLS FY4 40 A1
Squire's Gate Rd FUL/RIB PR2 45 F5 6
Squires Rd PRES PR1 6 B6
Squires Wd FUL/RIB PR2 47 E2
Squirrel Fold FUL/RIB PR2 59 G1
Squirrel's Cha LEY/BBR PR5 77 F2
Stable Cl KIRK/FR/WA PR4 43 E2
Stable Yd GAR/LONG PR3 15 G1
Stack Cft CHLYE PR6 82 D2
Stadium Av BPOOLS FY4 38 D3
Stafford Av PLF/KEOS FY6 30 B1
Stafford Rd PRES PR1 58 B2 10
Stainforth Av BISP FY2 25 E2
Staining Av FUL/RIB PR2 56 C3
Staining Old Rd BPOOLE FY3 30 B3
Staining Ri BPOOLE FY3 30 B5
Staining Rd BPOOLE FY3 29 H3
Stakepool Dr GAR/LONG PR3 15 G1
Stamford Av BPOOLS FY4 38 D1
Stamford Dr CHLYE PR6 87 F2
Stanah Gdns CLV/TH FY5
Stanah Rd CLV/TH FY5
Standish St CHLY/EC PR7
Stanhope Rd BPOOL FY1 28
Stanhope St PRES PR1 57
Stanifield Cl LEY/BBR PR5 81
Stanifield La LEY/BBR PR5
Stanley Av CLV/TH FY5
KIRK/FR/WA PR4
LEY/BBR PR5
PLF/KEOS FY6
PRES PR1
Stanley Ct KIRK/FR/WA PR4
Stanley Cft KIRK/FR/WA PR4
Stanleyfield Cl PRES PR1 58
Stanleyfield Rd PRES PR1 58
Stanley Fold LEY/BBR PR5
Stanley Ga FTWD FY7 10
Stanley Gv PRES PR1
Stanley Park Cl BPOOLE FY3
Stanley Pl CHLY/EC PR7 91
PRES PR1
Stanley Rd BPOOL FY1
FTWD FY7
KIRK/FR/WA PR4
LEY/BBR PR5
LSTA FY8
Stanley St KIRK/FR/WA PR4
LEY/BBR PR5 81
PRES PR1
Stanley Ter PRES PR1
Stanmore Av BPOOLS FY4
Stanning Cl LEY/BBR PR5
Stanning St LEY/BBR PR5
Stansfield St BPOOL FY1
Stansford Ct PRES PR1 69
Stansted Rd CHLY/EC PR7
Starbeck Av BPOOLS FY4
Starfield Cl LSTA FY8
Starkie St LEY/BBR PR5 81
PRES PR1
Starr Ga BPOOLS FY4
Starrgate Dr FUL/RIB PR2
Startley Nook KIRK/FR/WA PR4
States Rd LSTA FY8
Station Rd CHLY/EC PR7
CLV/TH FY5
FTWD FY7
KIRK/FR/WA PR4 42
KIRK/FR/WA PR4
LEY/BBR PR5
LEY/BBR PR5
LSTA FY8
PLF/KEOS FY6
PLF/KEOS FY6
Station Sq LSTA FY8
Station Ter BPOOLS FY4
Staveley Pl FUL/RIB PR2 56
Staynall La PLF/KEOS FY6
Steeley La CHLYE PR6
Steeple Vw FUL/RIB PR2
Steeton Rd BPOOLE FY3
Stefano Rd PRES PR1 58
Stephendale Av LEY/BBR PR5
Stephenson St CHLYE PR6 91 H
Stephen St LSTA FY8
Stevenson Av LEY/BBR PR5 81
Stewart St PRES PR1
Stirling Cl CHLYE PR6 91 H
LEY/BBR PR5 81
Stirling Rd BPOOLE FY3
Stockdale Crs LEY/BBR PR5
Stockdove Wy CLV/TH FY5
Stockdove Wd CLV/TH FY5
Stocks La CHLY/EC PR7
PLF/KEOS FY6
Stocks Rd FUL/RIB PR2
Stocks St PRES PR1
Stockydale Rd BPOOLS FY4
Stoke Av BPOOL FY1
Stokes Hall Av LEY/BBR PR5
Stonebridge Cl LEY/BBR PR5 77 H
Stonechat Cl BPOOLE FY3
Stone Cft PRES PR1
Stonecroft Rd LEY/BBR PR5 80
Stonefield KIRK/FR/WA PR4
PRES PR1 69
Stonehouse Gn CHLYE PR6 83
Stone Park Rd GAR/LONG PR3
Stoneway Rd CLV/TH FY5
Stoney Butts FUL/RIB PR2
Stoneygate CLV/TH FY5
PRES PR1
Stoney Holt LEY/BBR PR5
Stoneyhurst Av CLV/TH FY5
Stoney La KIRK/FR/WA PR4
LEY/BBR PR5
PLF/KEOS FY6
Stonycroft Av BPOOLS FY4
Stony Croft Pl BPOOLS FY4 38

y Hill Av *BPOOLS* FY4 **38** B2
yhurst *CHLY/EC* PR7 **95** F1
ford Av *BISP* FY2 **25** E5
k Cl *CLV/TH* FY5 **21** F3
r Ldg *FUL/RIB* PR2 **45** F2
nd Rd *PRES* PR1 **6** D4
nd St West *FUL/RIB* PR2 **6** B1
Strand *BPOOL* FY1 **2** C4
WD FY7 **16** C1
tfield Pl *LEY/BBR* PR5 **81** G3 7
tford Dr *FUL/RIB* PR2 **45** G4
tford Pl *BPOOL* FY1 **5** J3
tford Rd *CHLYE* PR6 **91** G2
TA FY8 **49** H5
thdale *BPOOLS* FY4 **39** F1
thmore Gv *CHLY/EC* PR7 **91** E3 4
thmore Rd *FUL/RIB* PR2 **45** H4 4
thyre Cl *BISP* FY2 **25** F2 2
tton Av *BPOOLS* FY4 **5** K7
kland's La *PLF/KEOS* FY6 **19** H3
RES PR1 **69** G2
ke La *KIRK/FR/WA* PR4 **54** B3
nsay Pl *BISP* FY2 **25** F1
tt St *PRES* PR1 **58** C2 9
rt Cl *FUL/RIB* PR2 **47** F5
rt Rd *CLV/TH* FY5 **22** A2
JL/RIB PR2 **47** F5
dfold *CHLY/EC* PR7 **87** E5
dholme Av *PRES* PR1 **69** H4
dholme Cl *PRES* PR1 **69** H4 5
dholme Crs *PRES* PR1 **69** H3
mp La *CHLYE* PR6 **91** G2
minster Cl *PRES* PR1 **69** H4 6
n St *FTWD* FY7 **11** G2
folk Rd *BPOOLE* FY3 **33** G3 4
RES PR1 **58** B2 13
y Dr *FUL/RIB* PR2 **47** G3
y Gv *FUL/RIB* PR2 **47** H3
mmerfield *LEY/BBR* PR5 **81** E1
mmerfield Cl *PRES* PR1 **70** B4
mmerfields *LSTA* FY8 **48** C3
mmer Trees Av *FUL/RIB* PR2 **44** A5
mmerville *BPOOLS* FY4 **38** C2 4
mmerville Av *BPOOLE* FY3 **30** B5
mmerwood Cl *BISP* FY2 **24** D5
mmit Dr *KIRK/FR/WA* PR4 **54** C5
nner St *LEY/BBR* PR5 **81** F3 7
pter Cft *PRES* PR1 **69** H4
bury Av *PRES* PR1 **69** G3
derland Av *CLV/TH* FY5 **17** E5
LF/KEOS FY6 **23** H2
field Cl *BPOOLS* FY4 **39** G1
nningdale *GAR/LONG* PR3 **36** A2 1
nningdale Av *BPOOLS* FY4 **33** G3
TWD FY7 **16** D2
nningdale Cl
RK/FR/WA PR4 **43** E4 3
nningdale Ct *LSTA* FY8 **49** G5 2
nningdale Dr *CLV/TH* FY5 **22** B4
nny Bank *KIRK/FR/WA* PR4 **42** D3
nny Bank Av *BISP* FY2 **24** C3
RK/FR/WA PR4 **55** G1 1
nny Brow *CHLY/EC* PR7 **94** D3
nnyhurst Av *BPOOLS* FY4 **38** D2 5
nnyside Av *KIRK/FR/WA* PR4 **53** G5 3
nnyside Cl *KIRK/FR/WA* PR4 **54** B4
geon's Ct *PRES* PR1 **7** G3
rey St *PRES* PR1 **58** D3
sex Rd *BPOOLE* FY3 **3** J2
sex St *PRES* PR1 **58** B2 14
cliffe St *CHLY/EC* PR7 **91** G3 9
herland Rd *BPOOL* FY1 **28** C3
ton Pl *BPOOL* FY1 **3** F7
ainson St *BPOOL* FY1 **2** E3
STA FY8 **62** D3
allow Av *PRES* PR1 **69** H2 6
allow Cl *CLV/TH* FY5 **17** G5
allow Ct *CHLYE* PR6 **83** F3 1
anage Av *BPOOLS* FY4 **38** B2 2
an Dr *CLV/TH* FY5 **21** F3
ansea St *FUL/RIB* PR2 **57** F2
ansey La *CHLYE* PR6 **83** E3
an St *PRES* PR1 **58** C3
arbrick Cl *BPOOL* FY1 **3** G1
arbrick St *KIRK/FR/WA* PR4 **43** E4
ll Brook La *PRES* PR1 **58** D5
ndon Av *BPOOLS* FY4 **5** H7
ords Cross Cl *CHLY/EC* PR7 **90** D5 7
amore Av *BPOOLS* FY4 **39** F3 5
HLY/EC PR7 **86** A4
amore Cl *FUL/RIB* PR2 **46** D2
amore Ct *CHLY/EC* PR7 **91** E5 7
amore Dr *PRES* PR1 **69** H3
amore Rd *CHLYE* PR6 **87** G5
JL/RIB PR2 **59** F1
ney St *LSTA* FY8 **49** F5 1
e Hl *PRES* PR1 **7** K4
e St *PRES* PR1 **7** J4
vancroft *FUL/RIB* PR2 **44** D3
van Gv *LEY/BBR* PR5 **71** H4
Symonds Rd *FUL/RIB* PR2 **45** H5

T

Tag Cft *FUL/RIB* PR2 **44** C3
Tag Farm Ct *FUL/RIB* PR2 **44** C3 2
Tag La *FUL/RIB* PR2 **44** C2
KIRK/FR/WA PR4 **44** C2
Talbot Dr *CHLY/EC* PR7 **86** A5
Talbot Rd *BPOOL* FY1 **2** C4
BPOOLE FY3 **3** G1
LEY/BBR PR5 **80** D2
LSTA FY8 **63** G1
PRES PR1 **6** D3
Talbot St *CHLYE* PR6 **91** H1 5
FUL/RIB PR2 **45** G5
Talbot Ter *LSTA* FY8 **63** F3 11
Tamar Cl *LEY/BBR* PR5 **81** G5
Tamar St *PRES* PR1 **59** F3
Tanglewood *FUL/RIB* PR2 **46** C3 1
Tansley Av *CHLY/EC* PR7 **94** A4
Tanterton Hall Rd *FUL/RIB* PR2 **44** C2
Tanyard Cl *CHLY/EC* PR7 **94** A4
Tarnbrick Av *KIRK/FR/WA* PR4 **54** C4
Tarnbrook Dr *BPOOLE* FY3 **29** G3
Tarn Cl *PRES* PR1 **68** C2
Tarn Ct *FTWD* FY7 **10** D5
Tarn Hows Cl *CHLY/EC* PR7 **91** E5 8
Tarn Rd *CLV/TH* FY5 **22** B5
Tarnway Av *CLV/TH* FY5 **22** B4
Tatham Ct *FTWD* FY7 **10** C5
Taunton St *BPOOLS* FY4 **5** G6 3
PRES PR1 **59** E2 20
Taybank Av *BPOOLS* FY4 **38** D1
Taylors Cl *PLF/KEOS* FY6 **26** A2 5
Taylor St *CHLY/EC* PR7 **91** E5 9
PRES PR1 **6** D5
Taymouth Rd *BPOOLS* FY4 **39** G2 6
Tay St *PRES* PR1 **6** D6
Taywood Cl *PLF/KEOS* FY6 **26** D3
Taywood Rd *CLV/TH* FY5 **21** G1
Teal Cl *CLV/TH* FY5 **17** G5
LEY/BBR PR5 **80** C5
Tebay Av *CLV/TH* FY5 **16** D5
KIRK/FR/WA PR4 **43** G3
Teenadore Av *BPOOLS* FY4 **39** E1 5
Tees Ct *FTWD* FY7 **10** D4
Teesdale Av *BISP* FY2 **28** D2
Tees St *PRES* PR1 **58** D1
Teil Gn *FUL/RIB* PR2 **47** F2
Temperance St *CHLYE* PR6 **91** H2 10
Temple Ct *PRES* PR1 **7** H4 2
Temple St *BPOOL* FY1 **2** C5
Temple Wy *CHLYE* PR6 **87** G4
Tenby Rd *PRES* PR1 **7** K5
Tennyson Av *CHLY/EC* PR7 **91** F4
CLV/TH FY5 **21** G1
KIRK/FR/WA PR4 **53** F5
LSTA FY8 **63** H2
Tennyson Pl *LEY/BBR* PR5 **71** E4
Tennyson Rd *BPOOLE* FY3 **29** F3 6
FTWD FY7 **11** G2 4
PRES PR1 **59** E2 21
Tensing Av *BISP* FY2 **24** D2
Tenterfield St *PRES* PR1 **7** H2
Terance Rd *BPOOLS* FY4 **5** K6
Terrace St *PRES* PR1 **58** D2 16
Teven St *LEY/BBR* PR5 **71** F5
Teviot Av *FTWD* FY7 **10** D3
Tewkesbury Av *BPOOLS* FY4 **38** D3
Tewkesbury Dr *LSTA* FY8 **63** H1
Thames Rd *BPOOLS* FY4 **38** B1
Thames St *KIRK/FR/WA* PR4 **55** F1
Theatre St *PRES* PR1 **7** G4
Third Av *BPOOLS* FY4 **38** C1
Thirlemere Av *FTWD* FY7 **16** C1
Thirlmere Av *PLF/KEOS* FY6 **25** H3
Thirlmere Cl *KIRK/FR/WA* PR4 **74** C1
Thirlmere Rd *BPOOLS* FY4 **32** C5
CHLY/EC PR7 **90** D4
PRES PR1 **59** G2
Thirsk Av *LSTA* FY8 **49** H4
Thirsk Gv *BPOOL* FY1 **5** H3
Thistle Cl *CHLYE* PR6 **91** H2
CLV/TH FY5 **17** F4
Thistlecroft *FUL/RIB* PR2 **44** D3
Thistleton Rd *FUL/RIB* PR2 **56** B2
Thomas St *PRES* PR1 **58** D4 7
Thompson St *KIRK/FR/WA* PR4 **42** D2 9
PRES PR1 **59** E1
Thornbank *BPOOLE* FY3 **29** H3
Thornber Gv *BPOOL* FY1 **5** G2
Thorneycroft Cl *PLF/KEOS* FY6 **25** H2 7
Thornfield Av *FUL/RIB* PR2 **47** G5
Thorngate *PRES* PR1 **69** E2
Thorngate Cl *PRES* PR1 **69** E2
Thorn Gv *BPOOL* FY1 **5** J3
Thornhill Av *PLF/KEOS* FY6 **13** E1
Thornhill Cl *BPOOLS* FY4 **39** F3 6
Thornhill Rd *CHLYE* PR6 **87** G5
LEY/BBR PR5 **80** B4
Thornleigh Cl *CLV/TH* FY5 **21** G2 8
Thornley Pl *FUL/RIB* PR2 **47** H5
Thornley Rd *FUL/RIB* PR2 **47** H5
Thornpark Dr *FUL/RIB* PR2 **56** A3
Thorn St *PRES* PR1 **58** D1
Thornton Av *FUL/RIB* PR2 **45** E4
LSTA FY8 **49** H3
Thornton Dr *LEY/BBR* PR5 **72** D3
LEY/BBR PR5 **76** D5
Thornton Ga *CLV/TH* FY5 **16** C5
Thorntrees Av *FUL/RIB* PR2 **56** A2
Thornway Av *CLV/TH* FY5 **22** B4
Thornwood Cl *LSTA* FY8 **62** C2
Thorpe Cl *PRES* PR1 **58** A2 11
Threefields *FUL/RIB* PR2 **44** D3
Three Nooks *LEY/BBR* PR5 **79** F4
Threlfall *CHLY/EC* PR7 **86** C5
Threlfall Rd *BPOOL* FY1 **5** G5
Threlfall St *FUL/RIB* PR2 **57** F2 17
Thropps La *KIRK/FR/WA* PR4 **74** D3
Throstle Wy *CLV/TH* FY5 **21** F3
Thurnham Rd *FUL/RIB* PR2 **56** B3
Thursby Av *BPOOLS* FY4 **38** D2
Thursfield Av *BPOOLS* FY4 **5** K7
Thurston Rd *LEY/BBR* PR5 **81** F3 8
Tiber St *PRES* PR1 **58** C4
Tinkerfield *FUL/RIB* PR2 **45** H1
Tintern Av *CHLY/EC* PR7 **91** G5
Titan Wy *LEY/BBR* PR5 **80** A3
Tithebarn Ga *PLF/KEOS* FY6 **26** B3
Tithe Barn La *LEY/BBR* PR5 **85** E2
Tithebarn Pl *PLF/KEOS* FY6 **26** B3
Tithebarn St *PLF/KEOS* FY6 **26** A3
PRES PR1 **7** J3 2
Tiverton Cl *FUL/RIB* PR2 **37** E5
Todd La North *LEY/BBR* PR5 **70** D5
Todd La South *LEY/BBR* PR5 **77** H1
Todmorden Rd *LSTA* FY8 **48** D5
Tollgate *PRES* PR1 **69** H2 7
Tolsey Dr *KIRK/FR/WA* PR4 **68** A4
Tom Benson Wy *FUL/RIB* PR2 **44** C1
Tomlinson Rd *FUL/RIB* PR2 **57** F1 13
LEY/BBR PR5 **81** E1
Tongues La *GAR/LONG* PR3 **8** C5
Tootell St *CHLY/EC* PR7 **91** E4
Topping St *BPOOL* FY1 **2** D4
Toronto Av *BISP* FY2 **25** E4
FTWD FY7 **10** D4
Torquay Av *BPOOLE* FY3 **33** G3
Torsway Av *BPOOLE* FY3 **29** F4
Totnes Cl *PLF/KEOS* FY6 **26** A2
Tower Cl *CLV/TH* FY5 **17** G5
Tower Gn *FUL/RIB* PR2 **46** A1
Tower La *FUL/RIB* PR2 **37** F5
Tower St *BPOOL* FY1 **2** D5
Tower Vw *PRES* PR1 **6** A4
Town Brow *CHLYE* PR6 **82** C2
Townfield Cl *KIRK/FR/WA* PR4 **74** A2 2
Towngate *CHLY/EC* PR7 **88** A2
LEY/BBR PR5 **81** E5
Town La *CHLY/EC* PR7 **92** B4
CHLYE PR6 **83** F5
Townley Av *BPOOLS* FY4 **33** E5
Townley La *PRES* PR1 **68** A2
Townley St *CHLYE* PR6 **91** G3
Townsway *LEY/BBR* PR5 **77** H1
Trafalgar Cl *FUL/RIB* PR2 **45** G5 9
Trafalgar Rd *BPOOL* FY1 **4** C3
Trafalgar St *CHLY/EC* PR7 **91** F1 6
LSTA FY8 **49** F4
Trafford St *PRES* PR1 **57** H1 11
Tramway La *LEY/BBR* PR5 **79** E3
Tranmere Rd *BPOOLS* FY4 **5** H6
Tranmoor *KIRK/FR/WA* PR4 **74** A3 1
Travers Pl *FUL/RIB* PR2 **57** F2
Trawden Crs *FUL/RIB* PR2 **47** F4 7
Trefoil Cl *CLV/TH* FY5 **17** G4
Trent Rd *BPOOLS* FY4 **38** B1
Trent St *LSTA* FY8 **63** H3
The Triangle *FUL/RIB* PR2 **45** H4
Trinity Gdns *CLV/TH* FY5 **21** G1
Trinity Pl *PRES* PR1 **7** H2 1
Trinity Rd *CHLY/EC* PR7 **91** E3 5
Tristan Av *KIRK/FR/WA* PR4 **74** B4
Troon Av *CLV/TH* FY5 **22** B4
Troon Ct *PRES* PR1 **56** D5 3
Troughton Crs *BPOOLS* FY4 **5** K6
Troutbeck Av *FTWD* FY7 **10** D4 4
Troutbeck Crs *BPOOLS* FY4 **34** B5
Troutbeck Pl *FUL/RIB* PR2 **47** F3
Troutbeck Rd *CHLY/EC* PR7 **91** E5
LSTA FY8 **48** D2 5
Trout St *PRES* PR1 **58** D4 8
Trower St *PRES* PR1 **58** C5
Trunnah Gdns *CLV/TH* FY5 **21** H1 5
Trunnah Rd *CLV/TH* FY5 **21** H1
Truro Pl *PRES* PR1 **59** E2 22
Truro St *BPOOLS* FY4 **5** G6 4
Tudor Av *PRES* PR1 **59** G3
Tudor Cl *CLV/TH* FY5 **21** F3
PLF/KEOS FY6 **25** G3
Tudor Cft *LEY/BBR* PR5 **77** H2
Tudor Dr *KIRK/FR/WA* PR4 **54** B1
Tudor Pl *BPOOLS* FY4 **38** B2
Tudor Rd *LSTA* FY8 **48** D3
Tuer St *LEY/BBR* PR5 **81** E2
Tulketh Av *FUL/RIB* PR2 **57** E2
Tulketh Brow *FUL/RIB* PR2 **57** F2
Tulketh Crs *FUL/RIB* PR2 **57** F2 18
Tulketh Rd *FUL/RIB* PR2 **57** E2
Tunbridge Pl *PRES* PR1 **59** E2 23
Tunley Holme *LEY/BBR* PR5 **79** E4
The Turbary *FUL/RIB* PR2 **45** F5 7
Turks Head Yd *PRES* PR1 **7** J3
Turnberry Av *CLV/TH* FY5 **22** B4
Turnberry Cl *KIRK/FR/WA* PR4 **43** E4 4
Turnbury Cl *CHLYE* PR6 **86** A3
Turner Av *LEY/BBR* PR5 **77** F3
Turner St *PRES* PR1 **58** B2 15
Turnfield *FUL/RIB* PR2 **44** C2
The Turnpike *FUL/RIB* PR2 **45** G2
Turnstone *BPOOLE* FY3 **29** H4
Turpin Green La *LEY/BBR* PR5 **81** G3 8
Turton Dr *CHLYE* PR6 **91** H1 6
Tuson Cft *KIRK/FR/WA* PR4 **74** A1
Tuson Dr *PRES* PR1 **6** E1
Tuxbury Cl *CLV/TH* FY5 **22** B4 2
Tuxford Rd *LSTA* FY8 **50** A5
Twickenham Pl *LSTA* FY8 **50** B5 4
Two Acre La *PRES* PR1 **69** F5 2
Tyldesley Rd *BPOOL* FY1 **4** C2
Tyne Av *BPOOLE* FY3 **3** H6
Tyne Cl *CLV/TH* FY5 **17** E4
Tynedale Rd *BPOOLE* FY3 **29** G1
Tyne St *LEY/BBR* PR5 **71** G5 4
PRES PR1 **6** D6
Tyrone Av *BISP* FY2 **24** D5

U

Ullswater Av *CLV/TH* FY5 **21** H2
FTWD FY7 **16** D1
Ullswater Cl *PLF/KEOS* FY6 **23** G2 2
Ullswater Rd *BPOOLS* FY4 **32** C5
CHLY/EC PR7 **91** E4
FUL/RIB PR2 **46** D4
Ulverston Crs *LSTA* FY8 **50** A4
Underbank Rd *CLV/TH* FY5 **22** C3
Under Wd *FUL/RIB* PR2 **45** F5
Union Pas *KIRK/FR/WA* PR4 **43** E3 5
Union St *CHLY/EC* PR7 **91** F2
CHLYE PR6 **83** F4
PRES PR1 **7** G2
Unsworth Av *PLF/KEOS* FY6 **13** E2 2
Uplands Cha *FUL/RIB* PR2 **45** E2
Upper Lune St *FTWD* FY7 **11** H1
Upper Westby St *LSTA* FY8 **63** E3
Upwood Cl *BISP* FY2 **25** E2 3

V

Valentia Rd *BISP* FY2 **24** D4
Valentines Meadow
KIRK/FR/WA PR4 **44** B4
Vale Royal *KIRK/FR/WA* PR4 **43** G3
The Vale *FUL/RIB* PR2 **46** A3
Valeway Av *CLV/TH* FY5 **20** D4
Valley Rd *PRES* PR1 **6** C7
Valley Vw *CHLYE* PR6 **91** H3
FUL/RIB PR2 **46** B4
Valley View Rd *PRES* PR1 **70** B3
Vance Rd *BPOOL* FY1 **2** D6
Varley St *PRES* PR1 **58** B1 12
Ventnor Pl *FUL/RIB* PR2 **44** D4
Ventnor Rd *BPOOLS* FY4 **38** B2
CHLY/EC PR7 **91** E4 5
Venture Rd *FTWD* FY7 **17** G3 1
Vermont Gv *CLV/TH* FY5 **21** E4
Vernon Av *BPOOLE* FY3 **5** K1
Vernon Rd *LSTA* FY8 **49** E2
Vernon St *PRES* PR1 **58** A2 12
Vevey St *LEY/BBR* PR5 **81** F4
Vicarage Av *CLV/TH* FY5 **20** D2
Vicarage Cl *CHLY/EC* PR7 **86** A4
FUL/RIB PR2 **46** A4 2
LSTA FY8 **49** F4 4
Vicarage La *BPOOLS* FY4 **5** K6
FUL/RIB PR2 **46** A4
Vicarage Rd *PLF/KEOS* FY6 **26** B4
Vicarage St *CHLYE* PR6 **91** G1
Vicarsfields Rd *LEY/BBR* PR5 **81** F5
Victoria Ct *GAR/LONG* PR3 **36** B3 1

Victoria Pde FUL/RIB PR2 57 E2
Victoria Park Av FUL/RIB PR2 56 A2
LEY/BBR PR5 80 B5
Victoria Park Dr FUL/RIB PR2 56 A2
Victoria Rd FUL/RIB PR2 46 A5
KIRK/FR/WA PR4 42 D3
LEY/BBR PR5 58 D5
LSTA FY8 61 F1
PLF/KEOS FY6 26 C3
Victoria Rd East CLV/TH FY5 21 G3
Victoria Rd West CLV/TH FY5 20 C2
Victoria St BPOOL FY1 2 C5
CHLY/EC PR7 91 G3
FTWD FY7 11 H1
LEY/BBR PR5 77 G1
LSTA FY8 63 G3 6
PRES PR1 57 H2
Victoria Ter CHLYE PR6 91 G1 2
Victory Rd BPOOL FY1 3 F2
Village Cft CHLY/EC PR7 85 H4
Village Dr FUL/RIB PR2 59 G1
Village Green La FUL/RIB PR2 44 C2
Village Wy BISP FY2 24 D2
The Villas KIRK/FR/WA PR4 44 B3
Villiers Ct PRES PR1 57 H1
Villiers St PRES PR1 57 G1 6
The Vinery KIRK/FR/WA PR4 75 G1
Vine St CHLY/EC PR7 91 F1
PRES PR1 6 D2
Vulcan Rd KIRK/FR/WA PR4 54 B2

W

Waddington Rd FUL/RIB PR2 59 H1 5
LSTA FY8 50 A5
Wades Cft KIRK/FR/WA PR4 54 C5
Wadham Rd PRES PR1 58 C5 3
Wakefield Rd BISP FY2 25 E3
Waldon St PRES PR1 59 E2
Walesby Pl LSTA FY8 62 B1 6
Walgarth Dr CHLY/EC PR7 90 D3
Walkdale KIRK/FR/WA PR4 68 A4
Walker La FUL/RIB PR2 44 D1
Walker Pl PRES PR1 58 C4
Walkers Hl BPOOLS FY4 39 G1
Walker St BPOOL FY1 2 C3
PRES PR1 7 H1
Walker Wy CLV/TH FY5 17 H5 3
The Walled Gdn CHLYE PR6 87 E1 1
Wallend Rd FUL/RIB PR2 56 A4
Waller Av BISP FY2 24 C2
Walletts Rd CHLY/EC PR7 91 E4
Wall St BPOOL FY1 2 E1
Walmer Gn KIRK/FR/WA PR4 74 A4
Walmer Rd LSTA FY8 49 F3
Walmsley St FTWD FY7 11 G2
Walney Pl BPOOLE FY3 29 G3
Walnut Cl PRES PR1 69 E3
Walpole Av BPOOLS FY4 38 B3
Walter Av LSTA FY8 49 G1
Waltham Av BPOOLS FY4 38 D3
Walton Av PRES PR1 69 E3
Walton Gn LEY/BBR PR5 71 E2 3
Walton's Pde PRES PR1 7 F4
Walton Summit Rd LEY/BBR PR5 78 D3
Walton Vw PRES PR1 59 E3
Walverden Av BPOOLS FY4 5 G7
Wansbeck Av FTWD FY7 10 D4
Wanstead Crs BPOOLS FY4 5 J6
Wanstead St PRES PR1 59 F3 1
Warbreck Dr BISP FY2 24 C5
Warbreck Hill Rd BISP FY2 28 D1
Warbury St PRES PR1 59 F2 12
Ward Av CLV/TH FY5 20 D1
Wardle Dr CLV/TH FY5 21 F1
Wardley's La PLF/KEOS FY6 19 E5
Ward's End PRES PR1 7 J3
Ward St BPOOL FY1 4 D5
CHLYE PR6 91 H3
KIRK/FR/WA PR4 43 E3
LEY/BBR PR5 77 G2
Wareham Rd BPOOLE FY3 29 F1
Waring Dr CLV/TH FY5 21 G1
The Warings CHLY/EC PR7 92 C1
Warley Rd BISP FY2 28 D2
BPOOL FY1 28 B2
Warner Rd PRES PR1 59 E2
Warren Av North FTWD FY7 11 F2
Warren Av South FTWD FY7 11 F2
Warren Dr CLV/TH FY5 20 D4
Warrenhurst Rd FTWD FY7 11 F3
Warren St FTWD FY7 11 H2
Warton Pl CHLY/EC PR7 90 D2
Warton St LSTA FY8 63 G3
PRES PR1 6 E6 1
Warwick Av CLV/TH FY5 17 E5
Warwick Cl FUL/RIB PR2 45 H4 5
Warwick Pl BPOOLE FY3 29 H2
Warwick Rd BPOOLE FY3 3 G2
CHLY/EC PR7 88 B3
LEY/BBR PR5 71 E2
LEY/BBR PR5 80 D5 2
LSTA FY8 49 F5
Warwick St PRES PR1 7 G1
Wasdale Cl LEY/BBR PR5 85 G1 3
Wasdale Rd BPOOLS FY4 33 G5
Washington Av BISP FY2 25 E5
Washington Ct BISP FY2 25 E5 4
Washington La CHLY/EC PR7 86 B5
Waterdale BISP FY2 25 E2 4
Waterfoot Av BPOOLE FY3 3 J3
Waterford Cl FUL/RIB PR2 46 D3 7
Waterhead Crs CLV/TH FY5 24 C1
Watering Pool La LEY/BBR PR5 70 C5
Water La FUL/RIB PR2 6 B1
Waterloo Rd BPOOLS FY4 4 E6
FUL/RIB PR2 57 E1
Waterloo St CHLY/EC PR7 91 F1 7
CHLY/EC PR7 91 G1 3
Waterloo Ter FUL/RIB PR2 57 F2 19
Water's Edge FUL/RIB PR2 44 C5
Water St CHLY/EC PR7 91 F2
LEY/BBR PR5 71 F4 7
Watery La FUL/RIB PR2 6 B1
PRES PR1 59 E3
Watkin La LEY/BBR PR5 77 G2
Watkin Rd CHLYE PR6 83 E4
Watling Street Rd FUL/RIB PR2 45 H5
Watson Rd BPOOLS FY4 38 B1
Waverley Av BPOOL FY1 28 C2
FTWD FY7 10 D3
Waverley Dr KIRK/FR/WA PR4 75 G2
Waverley Gdns FUL/RIB PR2 59 F1 2
Waverley Rd PRES PR1 59 E2
Waxy La KIRK/FR/WA PR4 54 C4
Way Ga CLV/TH FY5 16 D4 1
Wayman Rd BPOOLE FY3 3 H3
Wayside PLF/KEOS FY6 12 B1
Webster Av BPOOLS FY4 39 E1
Webster St FUL/RIB PR2 57 F2 20
Weeton Av BPOOLS FY4 39 E3
CLV/TH FY5 20 D1
LSTA FY8 49 G3
Weeton Pl FUL/RIB PR2 56 B2 8
Weeton Rd KIRK/FR/WA PR4 42 C1
Weirden Cl PRES PR1 69 F5
Welbeck Av BPOOLS FY4 5 K6
FTWD FY7 11 F2
Weld Av CHLY/EC PR7 91 F5
Weldbank La CHLY/EC PR7 91 F5
Weldbank St CHLY/EC PR7 91 F5 2
Welland Cl BISP FY2 25 E3 2
Wellfield Av LEY/BBR PR5 81 E3
Wellfield Rd LEY/BBR PR5 77 F2
PRES PR1 6 D2
Wellington Av LEY/BBR PR5 81 G4 3
Wellington Pl LEY/BBR PR5 71 E4
Wellington Rd BPOOL FY1 4 C4
FUL/RIB PR2 57 E2
Wellington St CHLY/EC PR7 91 F1 8
KIRK/FR/WA PR4 42 D3
LSTA FY8 63 H2 11
PRES PR1 6 C1
Wellogate Gdns BPOOLS FY4 38 D2
Well Orch LEY/BBR PR5 79 E4
Wellow Pl LSTA FY8 62 B1
Wells Cl CLV/TH FY5 21 G2
Wells Fold Cl CHLYE PR6 83 F3
Wells St PRES PR1 59 E2 24
Welsby Rd LEY/BBR PR5 80 D4 4
Welwyn Pl CLV/TH FY5 20 D3 2
Wembley Av BPOOLE FY3 29 E2
PLF/KEOS FY6 26 C4
PRES PR1 69 E1
Wembley Rd CLV/TH FY5 17 H5
Wendover Rd PLF/KEOS FY6 25 G1
Wensley Av FTWD FY7 11 E5
Wensleydale Av BPOOLE FY3 29 G3
Wensleydale Cl CLV/TH FY5 22 B4 3
Wensley Pl FUL/RIB PR2 47 E4
Wentworth Av FTWD FY7 16 D2
Wentworth Cl PRES PR1 56 D5
Wentworth Dr CLV/TH FY5 22 A4
GAR/LONG PR3 36 B2
Wentworth Ms LSTA FY8 49 G5 3
Werneth Cl KIRK/FR/WA PR4 70 A5 1
Wesham Hall Rd
KIRK/FR/WA PR4 43 E2
Wesley St LEY/BBR PR5 78 C1
West Av FUL/RIB PR2 44 D2 2
West Bank CHLY/EC PR7 91 F2 11
Westbank Av BPOOLS FY4 39 G1 5
West Bank Av LSTA FY8 62 C3
West Beach LSTA FY8 62 D4
Westbourne Av BPOOL FY1 4 E5
Westbourne Rd CHLY/EC PR7 91 E4 6
CLV/TH FY5 16 C4
PLF/KEOS FY6 12 B1
Westbrook Crs FUL/RIB PR2 44 D4
Westbury Cl CLV/TH FY5 20 C5
Westby Av BPOOLS FY4 39 E3
Westby Pl FUL/RIB PR2 56 C2
Westby Rd LSTA FY8 49 E3
Westby St LSTA FY8 63 E3
Westby Wy PLF/KEOS FY6 26 B5
West Cliff PRES PR1 6 E5
West Cliffe LSTA FY8 63 G3 7
Westcliffe Dr BPOOLE FY3 29 E2
West Cliff Ter PRES PR1 7 F5
West Ct CLV/TH FY5 16 C4
West Crs GAR/LONG PR3 36 B2
LSTA FY8 49 E5
West Dr CLV/TH FY5 20 D1
KIRK/FR/WA PR4 42 C1
LEY/BBR PR5 82 A1
West End PRES PR1 56 D5
Westend Av CHLY/EC PR7 94 A4
West End La KIRK/FR/WA PR4 52 D5
Westerlong FUL/RIB PR2 56 A2
Western Dr LEY/BBR PR5 80 C3
Westfield LEY/BBR PR5 77 F1
Westfield Av BPOOLE FY3 29 H3
FTWD FY7 11 E4
Westfield Dr FUL/RIB PR2 47 E4
KIRK/FR/WA PR4 65 G1
LEY/BBR PR5 72 C5
LEY/BBR PR5 80 C3
Westfield Rd BPOOL FY1 5 G4
West Ga FTWD FY7 10 D2
Westgate FUL/RIB PR2 45 G3
LEY/BBR PR5 81 E4
Westgate Rd LSTA FY8 38 C4
Westhead Wk FTWD FY7 11 E4 5
Westlands LEY/BBR PR5 80 B5
Westlands Ct CLV/TH FY5 21 H4
Westleigh Rd FUL/RIB PR2 56 C2 3
West Meadow FUL/RIB PR2 44 B5 1
Westminster Pl KIRK/FR/WA PR4 68 A5
Westminster Rd BPOOL FY1 28 C2
CHLY/EC PR7 91 F3 15
Westmorland Av BPOOL FY1 5 G1
CLV/TH FY5 16 D5
Westmorland Cl PRES PR1 69 E2 4
West Moss La LSTA FY8 50 B2
Weston Pl BPOOL FY1 5 F5
Weston St FUL/RIB PR2 6 D1
West Paddock LEY/BBR PR5 80 D4
West Park Av FUL/RIB PR2 56 B1 5
West Park Dr BPOOLE FY3 3 K6
BPOOLE FY3 33 F2 7
West Park La FUL/RIB PR2 56 D1
West Rd FUL/RIB PR2 46 A5
Westside BPOOLS FY4 33 F5 5
West Sq KIRK/FR/WA PR4 74 B1 3
West Strd PRES PR1 6 B1
West St BPOOL FY1 2 C4
CHLY/EC PR7 91 F3
West Ter CHLYE PR6 86 A3
West Vw BPOOL FY1 4 E1
KIRK/FR/WA PR4 42 D1
KIRK/FR/WA PR4 74 B1
LEY/BBR PR5 78 B2
PRES PR1 58 D1
West View Av BPOOL FY1 4 D4 3
West View Ter FUL/RIB PR2 6 B1
West Wy CHLY/EC PR7 86 D5
FTWD FY7 16 C2
Westway FUL/RIB PR2 46 B4
KIRK/FR/WA PR4 53 H5
Westwell Gv BPOOL FY1 2 E6
Westwell Rd CHLYE PR6 91 G1 4
Westwood Av BPOOLE FY3 3 J6
FTWD FY7 11 E3 3
PLF/KEOS FY6 26 C4
Westwood Ms LSTA FY8 63 E3
Westwood Rd LEY/BBR PR5 79 F5
LSTA FY8 63 E3
Wetherall St FUL/RIB PR2 57 G2 8
Wetherby Av BPOOLS FY4 38 B3
Weymouth Rd BPOOLE FY3 33 F2
Whalley Crs BPOOLE FY3 30 C5 1
Whalley La BPOOLS FY4 33 G5
Whalley Pl LSTA FY8 49 H5 3
Whalley Rd CHLY/EC PR7 92 D1
Whalley St CHLY/EC PR7 91 F3 16
LEY/BBR PR5 71 G4 2
Wham Hey KIRK/FR/WA PR4 75 H2
Wham La KIRK/FR/WA PR4 74 D5
Wharfedale BPOOLS FY4 39 E1
Wharfedale Av CLV/TH FY5 21 G1
FUL/RIB PR2 47 F3 5
Wharfedale Cl LEY/BBR PR5 85 F1
Wharf St LSTA FY8 63 G3 8
Wharton Av CLV/TH FY5 22 B3
Wheatfield Cl CLV/TH FY5 21 F5 9
Wheatlands Crs BPOOLE FY3 34 A3
Wheel La GAR/LONG PR3 9 G5
Wheelton La LEY/BBR PR5 81 F2
Whernside BPOOLS FY4 3
Whernside Crs FUL/RIB PR2 4
Whernside Wy LEY/BBR PR5 8
Whimberry Cl CHLYE PR6 91 H
Whimbrel Dr CLV/TH FY5 1
Whinfield Av CHLYE PR6 91
FTWD FY7 1
Whinfield La FUL/RIB PR2 5
Whinfield Pl FUL/RIB PR2 5
Whinney Heys Rd BPOOLE FY3 2
Whinny La CHLY/EC PR7 8
PLF/KEOS FY6 1
Whinpark Av BPOOLE FY3 2
Whinsands Cl FUL/RIB PR2 4
Whitby Av FUL/RIB PR2 4
Whitby Pl FUL/RIB PR2 44
Whitby Rd LSTA FY8 4
Whitebeam Cl CLV/TH FY5 17
PRES PR1 6
White Carr La CLV/TH FY5 2
Whitecotes Dr LSTA FY8 63 H
Whitecrest Av CLV/TH FY5 1
Whitefield Rd PRES PR1 6
Whitefield Rd East PRES PR1 6
Whitefield Rd West PRES PR1 68
Whitefriar Cl FUL/RIB PR2 44
Whitegate Dr BPOOLE FY3
White Gate Fold CHLY/EC PR7 9
Whitehead Cl BPOOLE FY3 30
Whitehill Rd BPOOLS FY4 4
Whiteholme Dr PLF/KEOS FY6 2
Whiteholme Pl FUL/RIB PR2 56
Whiteholme Rd BISP FY2 2
CLV/TH FY5 2
Whitelees Wy PLF/KEOS FY6 2
White Meadow FUL/RIB PR2 44
Whitemoss Av BPOOLE FY3 2
Whitendale Dr LEY/BBR PR5 7
Whiteside St BPOOL FY1
Whiteside Wy CLV/TH FY5 2
Whitethorn Cl CHLYE PR6 8
Whitethorne Ms CLV/TH FY5 2
Whitethorn Ms LSTA FY8 4
Whitethorn Sq FUL/RIB PR2 56
Whitewood Cl LSTA FY8 6
Whitley Av BPOOLE FY3
CLV/TH FY5 1
Whitmore Dr FUL/RIB PR2 5
Whitmore Gv FUL/RIB PR2 59
Whitmore Pl FUL/RIB PR2 5
Whittaker Av BPOOLE FY3
Whittam Av BPOOLS FY4
Whittam Rd CHLY/EC PR7 9
Whittle Pk CHLYE PR6 8
Whitwell Av BPOOLS FY4 38
Whitworth Ct KIRK/FR/WA PR4 43
Whitworth Dr CHLY/EC PR7 9
Whitworth St KIRK/FR/WA PR4 4
Wholesome La KIRK/FR/WA PR4 7
Wicklow Av LSTA FY8 6
Widgeon Cl CLV/TH FY5 1
Wigan Rd CHLY/EC PR7 8
CHLYE PR6 8
Wignall St PRES PR1 58 D
Wigton Av LEY/BBR PR5 8
Wilbraham St PRES PR1 5
Wilderswood Cl CHLYE PR6 8
Wilding's La LSTA FY8 4
Wild La BPOOLS FY4 4
Wildman St BPOOLE FY3 3
PRES PR1 5
Wildoaks Dr CLV/TH FY5 2
Wilford St BPOOLE FY3 2
Wilkinson Av BPOOLE FY3
Wilkinson St LEY/BBR PR5 7
Wilkinson Wy PLF/KEOS FY6 1
William Henry St PRES PR1 58
Williams La FUL/RIB PR2 4
William St BPOOLE FY3 29 E
LEY/BBR PR5 77
William Young Cl PRES PR1 58
Willoughby Av CLV/TH FY5 2
Willowbank Av BPOOLS FY4 3
Willow Cl CLV/TH FY5 2
KIRK/FR/WA PR4 6
LEY/BBR PR5 7
LEY/BBR PR5 7
PRES PR1 68
Willow Coppice FUL/RIB PR2 44
Willow Crs FUL/RIB PR2 5
LEY/BBR PR5 8
Willowcroft Dr PLF/KEOS FY6 2
Willow-dale CLV/TH FY5 2
Willowdene CLV/TH FY5 2
Willow Dr CHLY/EC PR7 94
KIRK/FR/WA PR4 4
KIRK/FR/WA PR4 6
PLF/KEOS FY6 3
Willow Fld CHLYE PR6 8
Willow Field Cha LEY/BBR PR5 73

w Gn FUL/RIB PR2 .... 56 D3
w Gv BPOOLE FY3 .... 29 G1 2
=/KEOS FY6 .... 23 F2
wmead Pk LSTA FY8 .... 52 B1
w Rd CHLYE PR6 .... 87 H5
ws Av CLV/TH FY5 .... 21 E3
A FY8 .... 62 C3
ws La KIRK/FR/WA PR4 .... 42 D3
w St FTWD FY7 .... 11 G2 5
w Tree Av GAR/LONG PR3 .... 36 C2
w Tree Crs LEY/BBR PR5 .... 80 C3
w Wy KIRK/FR/WA PR4 .... 75 G2
haw Rd BISP FY2 .... 28 B1
ar Rd LEY/BBR PR5 .... 81 H2
ot Rd FUL/RIB PR2 .... 47 F5
on Sq CLV/TH FY5 .... 20 C5
on Gv PRES PR1 .... 68 D2
on Pde BPOOL FY1 .... 28 B3
on Pl LEY/BBR PR5 .... 81 G3 9
ere Dr CLV/TH FY5 .... 20 C4
bledon Av CLV/TH FY5 .... 24 D1
bourne Pl BPOOLS FY4 .... 38 A2
hcombe Rd CLV/TH FY5 .... 21 E5
hester Av BPOOLS FY4 .... 5 G6
LY/EC PR7 .... 95 H2
hester Dr PLF/KEOS FY6 .... 25 G1
ckley Rd PRES PR1 .... 6 D6
ckley Sq PRES PR1 .... 7 H4
dermere Av FTWD FY7 .... 16 D1
Y/BBR PR5 .... 81 F1
dermere Rd BPOOLS FY4 .... 32 B5
LYE PR6 .... 91 H3 14
L/RIB PR2 .... 46 D4
ES PR1 .... 59 H2
dermere Sq LSTA FY8 .... 49 F1 2
dmill Av KIRK/FR/WA PR4 .... 43 F4
dmill Cl BPOOLE FY3 .... 30 C5
dmill Pl BPOOLS FY4 .... 39 F2 4
dmill Vw KIRK/FR/WA PR4 .. 43 E2 4
dsor Av BPOOLS FY4 .... 32 B5
V/TH FY5 .... 21 H2
L/RIB PR2 .... 45 E5
RK/FR/WA PR4 .... 68 D5
ES PR1 .... 69 F3
dsor Cl CHLY/EC PR7 .... 91 E3 6
dsor Ct PLF/KEOS FY6 .... 26 C4 3
dsor Dr FUL/RIB PR2 .... 45 G2
dsor Rd BPOOLE FY3 .... 29 H3
LY/EC PR7 .... 88 B3
LY/EC PR7 .... 91 E3
Y/BBR PR5 .... 71 E3
TA FY8 .... 61 G1 1
TA FY8 .... 62 B2
dsor Ter FTWD FY7 .... 11 H1 7
ery La LEY/BBR PR5 .... 70 D1
gate Av CLV/TH FY5 .... 20 D5
gate Pl CLV/TH FY5 .... 20 D4 3
gates PRES PR1 .... 69 F3
grove Rd FTWD FY7 .... 11 F4
fred St BPOOL FY1 .... 2 C6
marleigh Rd FUL/RIB PR2 .... 57 E2
nipeg Pl BISP FY2 .... 25 E4
sford Crs CLV/TH FY5 .... 20 C4
slow Av PLF/KEOS FY6 .... 25 H2
slow Cl PRES PR1 .... 69 H4 7
sor Av LEY/BBR PR5 .... 81 G4
stanley Gv BPOOL FY1 .... 2 E4 4
ster Cl LEY/BBR PR5 .... 72 D2 3
ster Pl BPOOLS FY4 .... 34 B4

Winston Av CLV/TH FY5 .... 21 F2
LSTA FY8 .... 49 H5
Winton Av BPOOLS FY4 .... 33 G4
FUL/RIB PR2 .... 46 A2 2
Winton Rd BPOOLS FY4 .... 33 G3
Withington La CHLY/EC PR7 .... 92 D3
Withnell Gv CHLYE PR6 .... 91 H1
Withnell Rd BPOOLS FY4 .... 32 B5
Withy Grove Cl LEY/BBR PR5 .... 71 G5
Withy Grove Crs LEY/BBR PR5 .... 71 G5
Withy Grove Rd LEY/BBR PR5 .... 71 G5
Withy Pde FUL/RIB PR2 .... 45 H4 6
Withy Trees Av LEY/BBR PR5 .... 71 G5
Withy Trees Cl LEY/BBR PR5 .... 71 G5
Witton Av FTWD FY7 .... 11 E5
Witton Gv FTWD FY7 .... 11 E5
Witton St PRES PR1 .... 58 C3 9
Woburn Gn LEY/BBR PR5 .... 81 G3
Woburn Rd BPOOL FY1 .... 28 C3 13
Wolseley Cl LEY/BBR PR5 .... 81 F4 11
Wolseley Pl PRES PR1 .... 7 J4 1
Wolseley Rd PRES PR1 .... 6 E7
Wolsey Cl CLV/TH FY5 .... 21 E1
Wolsley Rd BPOOL FY1 .... 4 D6
FTWD FY7 .... 11 F2 3
Wolverton Av BISP FY2 .... 24 B5
Woodacre Rd FUL/RIB PR2 .... 59 H1 7
Wood Bank PRES PR1 .... 69 F3
Woodcock Cl CLV/TH FY5 .... 17 G4
Woodcock Fold CHLY/EC PR7 .... 88 B3
Woodcroft Cl PRES PR1 .... 69 F4
Wood End PRES PR1 .... 69 F4
Wood End Rd CHLYE PR6 .... 82 D1
Woodfall CHLY/EC PR7 .... 87 E5
Woodfield LEY/BBR PR5 .... 79 F3
Woodfield Av BPOOL FY1 .... 4 C4
Woodfield Rd BPOOL FY1 .... 4 C4
CHLY/EC PR7 .... 91 F1 9
CLV/TH FY5 .... 22 B3
Woodford Copse CHLY/EC PR7 .... 90 C3
Wood Gn KIRK/FR/WA PR4 .... 43 F1
LEY/BBR PR5 .... 80 D2
Wood Green Dr CLV/TH FY5 .... 21 F4
Woodhall Crs LEY/BBR PR5 .... 72 D2
Woodhall Gdns PLF/KEOS FY6 .. 23 G2 3
Woodhart La CHLY/EC PR7 .... 88 B5
Woodhouse Rd CLV/TH FY5 .... 22 C4
Woodland Av CLV/TH FY5 .... 21 H2
Woodland Cl PLF/KEOS FY6 .... 23 H2
Woodland Crs PLF/KEOS FY6 .... 8 A5
Woodland Dr PLF/KEOS FY6 .... 30 C1
Woodland Gv BPOOLE FY3 .... 3 J7
PRES PR1 .... 69 E1
Woodlands Av FUL/RIB PR2 .... 59 F1
KIRK/FR/WA PR4 .... 42 D3 6
LEY/BBR PR5 .... 71 H4 1
PRES PR1 .... 69 G3
Woodlands Dr FUL/RIB PR2 .... 36 D5 2
KIRK/FR/WA PR4 .... 43 F1
KIRK/FR/WA PR4 .... 65 E1
LEY/BBR PR5 .... 81 E4
Woodlands Meadow
CHLY/EC PR7 .... 95 F2
Woodlands Rd LSTA FY8 .... 62 B2
The Woodlands FUL/RIB PR2 .. 56 B2 10
Woodlands Wy KIRK/FR/WA PR4 .. 74 A1
Wood La CHLY/EC PR7 .... 92 D1

Woodlea Rd LEY/BBR PR5 .... 81 E4
Woodley Av CLV/TH FY5 .... 22 B3
Woodmancote CHLY/EC PR7 .... 87 E5 2
Wood Park Rd BPOOL FY1 .... 5 H5
Woodplumpton La
GAR/LONG PR3 .... 36 B3
Woodplumpton Rd FUL/RIB PR2 .. 45 E4
Woodridge Av CLV/TH FY5 .... 20 C4
Woodruff Cl CLV/TH FY5 .... 17 F4
Woods Gn PRES PR1 .... 7 F7
Woodside CHLY/EC PR7 .... 85 H4
CHLY/EC PR7 .... 95 H1
LEY/BBR PR5 .... 77 H5 2
Woodside Av CHLYE PR6 .... 83 E3
FUL/RIB PR2 .... 45 H4
FUL/RIB PR2 .... 47 F5
KIRK/FR/WA PR4 .... 75 G2
Woodside Dr BPOOLE FY3 .... 29 G5
Woodstock Av CLV/TH FY5 .... 22 A4
Woodstock Cl LEY/BBR PR5 .... 77 H1 11
Woodstock Gdns BPOOLS FY4 .... 38 B1
Wood St BPOOL FY1 .... 2 D4
FTWD FY7 .... 17 E1
LSTA FY8 .... 49 E5
PLF/KEOS FY6 .... 26 D5
Woodvale Rd CHLYE PR6 .... 83 E1 4
Woodville Rd CHLY/EC PR7 .... 91 F2 12
PRES PR1 .... 69 G4
Woodville Rd West PRES PR1 .... 69 F4 5
Woodville St LEY/BBR PR5 .... 81 G1
Woodville Ter LSTA FY8 .... 62 D3
Woodway FUL/RIB PR2 .... 45 F4
Wookey Cl FUL/RIB PR2 .... 47 E2 7
Woolman Rd BPOOL FY1 .... 3 F7
Worcester Av LEY/BBR PR5 .... 81 G4
Worcester Pl CHLY/EC PR7 .... 95 H2
Worcester Rd BPOOLE FY3 .... 33 F2
Worden Cl LEY/BBR PR5 .... 81 E5
Worden La LEY/BBR PR5 .... 81 F5
Worden Rd FUL/RIB PR2 .... 45 G5 10
Wordsworth Av BPOOLE FY3 .... 33 H3
CLV/TH FY5 .... 21 F2
KIRK/FR/WA PR4 .... 53 G5 4
LSTA FY8 .... 63 H2 13
Wordsworth Pl LEY/BBR PR5 .... 71 E4 3
Wordsworth Ter CHLYE PR6 .... 87 G5
Worsley Av BPOOLS FY4 .... 38 C1
Worsley Cl PLF/KEOS FY6 .... 12 B1
Worsley Rd LSTA FY8 .... 62 A1
Worthing Rd FUL/RIB PR2 .... 44 D4
Worthington Rd BPOOLS FY4 .... 39 G4 1
Worthy St CHLYE PR6 .... 91 H3
Wray Crs KIRK/FR/WA PR4 .... 42 A4
Wray Gv CLV/TH FY5 .... 20 D4 4
Wraywood Ct FTWD FY7 .... 10 C5 2
Wren Av PRES PR1 .... 69 H1 5
Wren Cl CLV/TH FY5 .... 22 B4
PLF/KEOS FY6 .... 25 G3
Wren Gv BPOOLE FY3 .... 5 K3
Wrennalls La CHLY/EC PR7 .... 88 A5
Wren St PRES PR1 .... 58 C1 5
Wrights Fold LEY/BBR PR5 .... 81 H4
Wright St CHLYE PR6 .... 91 H2
KIRK/FR/WA PR4 .... 42 D2 10
Wroxton Cl CLV/TH FY5 .... 21 F5 10
Wychnor FUL/RIB PR2 .... 45 E1
Wycombe Av BPOOLS FY4 .... 38 B2 3

Wykeham Rd LSTA FY8 .... 63 F2
Wymundsley CHLY/EC PR7 .... 90 C1
Wyndene Gv KIRK/FR/WA PR4 .... 54 B5
Wyndham Gdns BPOOLS FY4 .... 38 D2
Wynfield LEY/BBR PR5 .... 71 G4
Wynnwood Av BPOOL FY1 .... 28 C1
Wyre Av KIRK/FR/WA PR4 .... 43 F3
Wyredale Rd LSTA FY8 .... 48 C3
Wyrefields PLF/KEOS FY6 .... 27 E4
Wyre Gv BPOOL FY1 .... 5 F3
Wyre Rd CLV/TH FY5 .... 26 D1
Wyresdale Av BISP FY2 .... 24 D3
PLF/KEOS FY6 .... 26 A4
Wyresdale Crs FUL/RIB PR2 .... 47 E4
Wyresdale Dr LEY/BBR PR5 .... 85 G1
Wyresdale Rd PLF/KEOS FY6 .... 12 B1
Wyreside Dr PLF/KEOS FY6 .... 23 F3
Wyre St FTWD FY7 .... 11 F3
FUL/RIB PR2 .... 57 F2 21
KIRK/FR/WA PR4 .... 42 D2 11
Wyvern Wy PLF/KEOS FY6 .... 25 H2

Y

Yarrow Ga CHLY/EC PR7 .... 91 H4
Yarrow Pl LEY/BBR PR5 .... 80 C4 2
Yarrow Rd CHLYE PR6 .... 91 H4
LEY/BBR PR5 .... 80 C4 3
Yates Rd CHLY/EC PR7 .... 91 E5
Yates St BPOOL FY1 .... 2 D2
Yeadon Gv CHLY/EC PR7 .... 90 D3
Yeadon Wy BPOOLS FY4 .... 4 E6
Yew Ct FTWD FY7 .... 10 C5
Yew Gn KIRK/FR/WA PR4 .... 43 F1
Yewlands Av CHLY/EC PR7 .... 93 E2 1
FUL/RIB PR2 .... 45 H2
LEY/BBR PR5 .... 71 G5 5
LEY/BBR PR5 .... 81 E3
Yewlands Crs FUL/RIB PR2 .... 45 H2
Yewlands Dr FUL/RIB PR2 .... 45 H2
LEY/BBR PR5 .... 81 E3
Yew Tree Av CHLY/EC PR7 .... 85 H3
Yewtree Av FUL/RIB PR2 .... 47 H3
Yewtree Cl CHLY/EC PR7 .... 95 E2 1
Yewtree Gv LEY/BBR PR5 .... 77 F2
Yew Tree Rd BPOOLE FY3 .... 29 G1
York Av CLV/TH FY5 .... 20 D2
FTWD FY7 .... 11 E3
FUL/RIB PR2 .... 45 H4
York Cl LEY/BBR PR5 .... 80 D5
York Dr KIRK/FR/WA PR4 .... 54 B1 2
York Rd BISP FY2 .... 24 B3 5
LSTA FY8 .... 61 F1
Yorkshire St BPOOL FY1 .... 4 C1
York St BPOOL FY1 .... 4 C1
CHLY/EC PR7 .... 91 G3 10
Young Av LEY/BBR PR5 .... 81 H3

Z

Zetland St PRES PR1 .... 58 D4 9

Index - featured places

ey Road Clinic
POOLS FY4 .... 38 C2
Cinema
POOL FY1 .... 2 D4
urst Business Park
HLY/EC PR7 .... 90 C1
urst Park Industrial Estate
HLY/EC PR7 .... 90 B2
ny High School
HLYE PR6 .... 91 H5
allows RC High School
RES PR1 .... 68 D3
aints C of E Primary School
HLY/EC PR7 .... 91 E5
Bowling
POOL FY1 .... 4 E2
orsholme Primary School
LV/TH FY5 .... 21 E4
ell CP School
STA FY8 .... 62 A1
educt Street
ndustrial Estate
UL/RIB PR2 .... 57 G2

Archbishop Temple School
FUL/RIB PR2 .... 46 A3
Arnold Medical Centre
BPOOLS FY4 .... 38 D1
Arnold School
BPOOLS FY4 .... 38 C1
Ashton Health Centre
FUL/RIB PR2 .... 56 D2
Ashton on Ribble High School
FUL/RIB PR2 .... 56 C1
Astley Park School
CHLY/EC PR7 .... 91 E2
Atlas Foundry Estate
PRES PR1 .... 6 D2
Baines Endowed C of E School
BPOOLS FY4 .... 33 F4
Baines Endowed CP School
CLV/TH FY5 .... 22 A4
Baines School
PLF/KEOS FY6 .... 30 B1
Balshaws C of E High School
LEY/BBR PR5 .... 81 G5

Bamber Bridge Clinic
LEY/BBR PR5 .... 71 G4
Bamber Bridge Football Club
LEY/BBR PR5 .... 78 A1
Bamber Bridge Methodist
Primary School
LEY/BBR PR5 .... 78 C1
Bamber Bridge (Withy Park)
Leisure Centre
LEY/BBR PR5 .... 71 G5
Bank View Industrial Estate
PLF/KEOS FY6 .... 23 G3
Bates Swimming Pool
PLF/KEOS FY6 .... 23 G2
Beech Drive Surgery
FUL/RIB PR2 .... 45 G1
The Beeches Medical Centre
KIRK/FR/WA PR4 .... 74 B1
Beech Tree School
LEY/BBR PR5 .... 79 E5
Beehive Industrial Estate
BPOOLS FY4 .... 33 H5

Birchwood Medical Centre
FUL/RIB PR2 .... 57 E1
Bispham Endowed
Junior School
BISP FY2 .... 24 D3
Bispham High School
BISP FY2 .... 25 E5
Blackpool and Flyde College
FTWD FY7 .... 17 E2
Blackpool Borough Council
BISP FY2 .... 25 F2
Blackpool Borough Council
BPOOL FY1 .... 2 D4
Blackpool Borough Council
BPOOL FY1 .... 4 E2
Blackpool Borough Council
BPOOLS FY4 .... 34 B5
Blackpool Business Park
BPOOLS FY4 .... 39 E3
Blackpool County Court
BPOOL FY1 .... 2 C7
Blackpool Cricket Club
BPOOLE FY3 .... 3 K6

Blackpool Football Club *BPOOL* FY1 2 D5
Blackpool Football Club *BPOOL* FY1 4 E3
Blackpool & Fylde College *BISP* FY2 25 E1
Blackpool & Fylde College *BPOOL* FY1 3 F6
Blackpool & Fylde College *LSTA* FY8 62 A1
Blackpool & Fylde College *PLF/KEOS* FY6 26 C5
Blackpool Reform Jewish Synagogue *BPOOL* FY1 3 F5
Blackpool Rugby Club *CLV/TH* FY5 20 D5
The Blackpool Sixth Form College *BPOOLE* FY3 25 G5
Blackpool Sports Centre *BPOOLE* FY3 3 K7
Blackpool Victoria Hospital NHS Trust *BPOOLE* FY3 29 G4
Blackpool Victoria Hospital NHS Trust *PLF/KEOS* FY6 26 D4
Blackpool Welfare Clinic *BPOOLE* FY3 29 F3
Blackpool Wyre & Fylde Community Health Services NHS Trust *KIRK/FR/WA* PR4 42 D2
Blackpool Wyre & Fylde Health Authority *BPOOLE* FY3 29 G5
Blackpool Zoo Park *BPOOLE* FY3 33 H1
Blessed Sacrament RC Primary School *FUL/RIB* PR2 47 G5
Bloomfield Medical Centre *BPOOL* FY1 5 F3
Breck CP School *PLF/KEOS* FY6 26 D2
Broadfield County Junior School *LEY/BBR* PR5 81 E3
Brookfield CP School *FUL/RIB* PR2 47 F3
Broughton C of E Primary School *GAR/LONG* PR3 36 C4
Broughton High School *GAR/LONG* PR3 36 B3
Broughton Park Private Hospital *GAR/LONG* PR3 36 D4
Brownedge St Marys RC School *LEY/BBR* PR5 71 G5
Buckshaw CP School *CHLY/EC* PR7 86 D5
Burn Hall Industrial Estate *FTWD* FY7 17 G3
Burn Naze CP School *CLV/TH* FY5 21 H1
Cardinal Allen RC School *FTWD* FY7 16 D1
Cardinal Newman College *PRES* PR1 58 C4
Carleton C of E Primary School *PLF/KEOS* FY6 25 H2
Carleton Green CP School *PLF/KEOS* FY6 25 H1
Carr Head CP School *PLF/KEOS* FY6 26 C5
Carr Hill High School *KIRK/FR/WA* PR4 43 F4
Centurion Industrial Estate *LEY/BBR* PR5 77 G5
Centurion Industrial Estate *LEY/BBR* PR5 81 G1
Chandlers Business Park *LEY/BBR* PR5 80 D2
Chapel Lane Business Park *CHLY/EC* PR7 94 C5
Charles Saer County School *FTWD* FY7 10 D3
Charnley Fold Industrial Estate *LEY/BBR* PR5 71 G4
Charnock Richard C of E Primary School *CHLY/EC* PR7 94 A1
Chaucer CP School *FTWD* FY7 11 G2
Chequers Gallery *BPOOL* FY1 2 E5
Chiropody Surgery *CLV/TH* FY5 24 C1
Chorley Associated Football Club *CHLY/EC* PR7 91 F4
Chorley Cricket Club *CHLY/EC* PR7 91 E2
Chorley & District Hospital *CHLY/EC* PR7 87 F5
Chorley Mayfield School *CHLY/EC* PR7 91 F5
Chorley North Business Park *CHLYE* PR6 87 G4
Chorley & South Ribble Health Authority *CHLY/EC* PR7 94 A4
Chorley Sports Centre *CHLY/EC* PR7 91 G1
Chorley West Business Park *CHLY/EC* PR7 90 C2
Christ the King High School *PRES* PR1 58 C5
Christ the King Primary School *BPOOLE* FY3 29 G3
Civic Centre *LEY/BBR* PR5 81 E4
Claremont Junior & Infant School *BPOOL* FY1 28 C2
Clayton Brook County School *LEY/BBR* PR5 79 E4
Clayton Brook Surgery *LEY/BBR* PR5 79 E4
Clayton Green Business Park *LEY/BBR* PR5 79 E5
Clayton Green Sports Centre *LEY/BBR* PR5 79 E5
Clayton-le-woods C of E Primary School *CHLYE* PR6 82 D2
Cleveleys Health Centre *CLV/TH* FY5 20 D2
Clifton CP School *LSTA* FY8 50 A5
Clifton Retail Park *BPOOLS* FY4 34 B5
Cocker Trading Estate *BPOOL* FY1 2 E1
Collegiate High School *BPOOLE* FY3 29 G1
Common Bank Employment Area *CHLY/EC* PR7 90 B3
Common Bank Industrial Estate *CHLY/EC* PR7 90 C3
Cop Lane C E Primary School *PRES* PR1 69 F3
Coppice School *LEY/BBR* PR5 71 G5
Coppull CP School *CHLY/EC* PR7 94 B4
Coppull Medical Practice *CHLY/EC* PR7 94 B5
Coppull Parish Church School *CHLY/EC* PR7 94 C4
Copse View Business Park *FTWD* FY7 11 F4
Corn Exchange *PRES* PR1 7 G3
Corpus Christi RC High School *FUL/RIB* PR2 45 H3
Cottam CP School *KIRK/FR/WA* PR4 44 A3
Council Office *BPOOL* FY1 2 E4
Coupe Green CP School *LEY/BBR* PR5 72 D2
Cowling Brow Industrial Estate *CHLYE* PR6 91 H4
Crossley House Industrial Estate *PRES* PR1 69 H2
Crown Stage & Theatre *LEY/BBR* PR5 80 B1
Deepdale County Junior & Infant School *PRES* PR1 58 C1
Deepdale Surgery *PRES* PR1 58 C2
Dental Health Centre *PRES* PR1 46 C5
Devonshire Junior School *BPOOLE* FY3 3 G2
Dewhurst Industrial Estate *PRES* PR1 57 G2
Docklands Medical Centre *FUL/RIB* PR2 57 F2
Duke Street County Infant School *CHLY/EC* PR7 91 F4
Dunkirk Hall Industrial Estate *LEY/BBR* PR5 80 B4
Duxbury Park Golf Club *CHLY/EC* PR7 95 G1
Earnshaw Bridge County Infant School *LEY/BBR* PR5 80 D2
East Chorley Business Centre *CHLYE* PR6 91 G2
Eccleston CP School *CHLY/EC* PR7 88 A4
Eccleston Health Centre *CHLY/EC* PR7 88 A3
Eldon Street CP School *PRES* PR1 57 H1
Elmslie Girls School *BPOOLE* FY3 5 J1
English Martyrs Junior School *PRES* PR1 57 H2
Euxton C of E Primary School *CHLY/EC* PR7 85 H4
Euxton CP School *CHLY/EC* PR7 85 G3
Euxton Hall Hospital *CHLY/EC* PR7 89 H1
Fairhaven Golf Club Ltd *LSTA* FY8 62 C2
Farington Business Park *LEY/BBR* PR5 81 F2
Farington CP School *LEY/BBR* PR5 81 G1
Farington St Pauls C of E School *LEY/BBR* PR5 77 E2
Fernlea Hotel & Leisure Complex *LSTA* FY8 48 D5
Fishergate Hill Surgery *PRES* PR1 6 D5
Fishergate Shopping Centre *PRES* PR1 7 G4
Flakefleet County Junior & Infant School *FTWD* FY7 11 E4
Fleetwood Cricket Club *FTWD* FY7 17 E1
Fleetwood Football Club *FTWD* FY7 11 F3
Fleetwood Health Centre *FTWD* FY7 11 H2
Fleetwood Hesketh High School *FTWD* FY7 11 E3
Fleetwood Hospital *FTWD* FY7 11 H1
Fleetwood Museum *FTWD* FY7 12 A1
Forte Posthouse Hotel *PRES* PR1 7 J1
The Forward Industrial Estate *LEY/BBR* PR5 80 D2
Fox Industrial Estate *BISP* FY2 29 E1
Freckleton C of E School *KIRK/FR/WA* PR4 54 C4
Freckleton Cricket Club *KIRK/FR/WA* PR4 54 B5
Frenchwood CP School *PRES* PR1 58 C5
Fulwood & Cadley CP School *FUL/RIB* PR2 45 G4
Fulwood Hall Hospital *FUL/RIB* PR2 46 C2
Fulwood High School *FUL/RIB* PR2 45 G2
Fulwood Leisure Centre *FUL/RIB* PR2 45 G3
Fylde Borough Council *KIRK/FR/WA* PR4 42 D3
Fylde Borough Council *LSTA* FY8 48 D5
Fylde Cricket Club *PLF/KEOS* FY6 26 C3
Fylde Road Industrial Estate *PRES* PR1 57 G2
Fylde Rugby Club *LSTA* FY8 62 B1
Gillibrand Primary School *CHLY/EC* PR7 91 E4
Glades Clinic *FUL/RIB* PR2 59 G1
Grand Theatre *BPOOL* FY1 2 D5
Grange CP School *FUL/RIB* PR2 47 G4
Grange Park County Infant School *BPOOLE* FY3 2
Grange Park County Junior School *BPOOLE* FY3 2
Grange Park Health Centre *BPOOLE* FY3 2
Great Arley Special School *CLV/TH* FY5 2
Great Arley Swimming Pool *CLV/TH* FY5 2
Green Drive Golf Club *LSTA* FY8 6
Greenlands CP School *FUL/RIB* PR2 4
Gregson Lane Primary School *LEY/BBR* PR5 7
Grove Park Industrial Estate *CHLY/EC* PR7 8
Guardian Sports Club *LSTA* FY8 6
Guild Community Healthcare NHS Trust *FUL/RIB* PR2 4
Guild Community Healthcare NHS Trust *FUL/RIB* PR2 4
Guild Community Healthcare NHS Trust *PRES* PR1 5
Guild Trading Estate *PRES* PR1 5
Gynn Gallery *BPOOL* FY1 2
Haida Galleries *LSTA* FY8 4
Hall Park CP School *LSTA* FY8 6
Hambleton County School *PLF/KEOS* FY6 2
Hambleton Health Centre *PLF/KEOS* FY6 2
Harris CP School *FUL/RIB* PR2 4
Harris Museum & Art Gallery *PRES* PR1
Harrison Trading Estate *PRES* PR1 5
Hawes Side Clinic *BPOOLS* FY4 3
Hawes Side Primary School *BPOOLS* FY4 3
Heskin Football Club *CHLY/EC* PR7 9
Heskin Pembertons Primary School *CHLY/EC* PR7 9
Heyhouses Endowed C of E Infant School *LSTA* FY8 4
Heyhouses Endowed C of E Junior School *LSTA* FY8 4
Higher Walton C of E Primary School *LEY/BBR* PR5 7
Higher Walton C of E School *LEY/BBR* PR5 7
Highfield CP School *CHLYE* PR6 9
Highfield Industrial Estate *CHLYE* PR6 8
Highfield Priory School *FUL/RIB* PR2 4
Highfurlong Special School *BPOOLE* FY3 2
HM Prison *KIRK/FR/WA* PR4 4
Hodgson High School *PLF/KEOS* FY6 2
Holme Slack C P School *PRES* PR1 4
Holy Cross RC High School *CHLY/EC* PR7 9
Holy Family Primary School *KIRK/FR/WA* PR4 5
Holy Family RC Primary School *BPOOL* FY1 2
Holy Family RC Primary School *FUL/RIB* PR2 4
Hoo Hill Industrial Estate *BPOOLE* FY3 2
Houndsmill Shopping Centre *BPOOL* FY1
Howick Gallery *PRES* PR1 6

ck Primary School
RK/FR/WA PR4 68 C3
on Grammar School
RK/FR/WA PR4 68 A4
or Bowls
POOL FY1 2 E3
CP School
L/RIB PR2 44 C4
Pool House School
L/RIB PR2 44 D2
ic Community
entre & Mosque
POOL FY1 4 E2
nar Industrial Estate
RES PR1 58 D4
ts Trading Estate
RES PR1 69 H2
aig Primary
Junior School
SP FY2 25 F1
Edward School
TA FY8 61 G2
fold Medical Centre
RES PR1 69 F3
sfold Primary School
RES PR1 69 G4
am Baths
RK/FR/WA PR4 43 E3
am Grammar
nior School
RK/FR/WA PR4 42 D4
am Grammar School
RK/FR/WA PR4 42 D3
am Museum
RK/FR/WA PR4 43 E3
am & Wesham CP School
RK/FR/WA PR4 42 D3
ashire Area
ealth Authority
POOL FY1 3 G1
ashire Area
ealth Authority
POOLS FY4 38 C3
ashire College for Adult
ducation
HLY/EC PR7 90 C2
ashire County Council
POOL FY1 2 E5
ashire County Council
POOLE FY3 3 J7
ashire County Council
V/TH FY5 21 G2
ashire County Council
WD FY7 11 H1
ashire County Council
EY/BBR PR5 71 G4
ashire County Council
EY/BBR PR5 78 A2
ashire County Council
EY/BBR PR5 80 D4
ashire County Council
TA FY8 48 D3
ashire County Council
TA FY8 49 F3
ashire County Council
RES PR1 7 G6
ashire County Council
RES PR1 47 E5
ashire County Council
RES PR1 58 A1
ashire County Council
RES PR1 58 C4
ashire County
useum Service
RES PR1 58 C3
ashire Schools ICT Centre
HLY/EC PR7 90 D2
aster Lane CP School
EY/BBR PR5 82 A3
Ends Trading Estate
JL/RIB PR2 57 F1
dale Preparatory School
SP FY2 28 C1
holme County
econdary School
WD FY7 10 D4
holme CP School
WD FY7 16 D1
Courts
RES PR1 7 J1
on Medical Centre
POOLE FY3 29 F3
on Primary School
POOLE FY3 29 F2
P School
JL/RIB PR2 56 A2
and Golf Club
EY/BBR PR5 82 A4

Leyland Leisure Centre
LEY/BBR PR5 81 E4
Leyland Methodist
Junior & Infant School
LEY/BBR PR5 81 G3
Lidun Park Industrial Estate
LSTA FY8 64 A1
Light Industrial Estate
KIRK/FR/WA PR4 74 A4
Lisieux Hall Hospital
CHLYE PR6 82 D4
Little Hoole CP School
KIRK/FR/WA PR4 74 B4
Little Theatre
CHLY/EC PR7 91 F2
Longsands CP School
FUL/RIB PR2 47 E2
Longton School
KIRK/FR/WA PR4 74 B1
Lostock Hall CP School
LEY/BBR PR5 70 C5
Lostock Hall High School
LEY/BBR PR5 70 D5
Lostock Hall Primary School
LEY/BBR PR5 77 G1
Louis Tussauds Waxworks
BPOOL FY1 2 C7
Lytham C of E Primary School
LSTA FY8 63 F2
Lytham Cricket Club
LSTA FY8 62 D3
Lytham Hospital
LSTA FY8 63 H3
Lytham Leisure Centre
LSTA FY8 62 B1
Lytham Posey Bowl
LSTA FY8 63 F3
Lytham St Annes High School
LSTA FY8 62 A1
Lytham Windmill
LSTA FY8 63 G3
Manor Beach CP School
CLV/TH FY5 20 D1
Marine Business Centre
LSTA FY8 64 A2
Market Halls
PRES PR1 7 H2
Marsh Mill Museum
CLV/TH FY5 21 H2
Martin Gallery
BPOOLE FY3 5 K3
Marton CP School
BPOOLS FY4 39 F1
Marton Medical Centre
BPOOLE FY3 5 K3
Mayfield County School
LSTA FY8 49 E3
Medicare Unit Surgery
LEY/BBR PR5 77 F1
Mereside Junior
& Infant School
BPOOLS FY4 33 H4
Methodist School
KIRK/FR/WA PR4 74 A1
Metropolitan Business Park
BPOOLE FY3 33 H3
Middleforth C of E School
PRES PR1 69 G3
Middleforth Industrial Estate
PRES PR1 69 H2
Millfield High School
CLV/TH FY5 22 A4
Montgomery High School
BISP FY2 24 D2
Moorbrook School
FUL/RIB PR2 45 H5
Moorhey School
LEY/BBR PR5 70 B5
Moor Nook CP School
FUL/RIB PR2 47 H5
Moor Park High School
PRES PR1 58 B1
Moor Park Industrial Estate
BISP FY2 25 F3
Moor Park Junior
& Infant School
BISP FY2 25 E4
Moor Park Swimming Pool
BISP FY2 24 D3
Mosque
PRES PR1 58 B2
Moss Side CP School
LEY/BBR PR5 80 A3
National Football Museum
FUL/RIB PR2 46 A4
The Natural Health Centre
PRES PR1 7 K1

Natural Therapy Clinic
BPOOLE FY3 29 F3
New Longton C of E School
KIRK/FR/WA PR4 75 G2
New Mill Industrial Estate
LEY/BBR PR5 78 C2
Newton Bluecoat School
KIRK/FR/WA PR4 55 G1
Norbreck Primary School
CLV/TH FY5 20 D4
Northfold CP School
CLV/TH FY5 17 E5
Odeon Cinema
BPOOL FY1 4 E1
Old Brewery Trading Estate
PRES PR1 6 D2
Our Lady of Assumption
RC School
BPOOLS FY4 39 F3
Our Lady & St Edwards
RC Primary School
GAR/LONG PR3 36 C5
Our Ladys High School
FUL/RIB PR2 45 F4
Over Wyre Medical Centre
PLF/KEOS FY6 12 D1
Oxford Medical Centre
BPOOL FY1 5 K4
Oxhey Trading Estate
PRES PR1 57 G1
Parker Street Industrial Estate
FUL/RIB PR2 57 G2
Park Hall Leisure Centre
CHLY/EC PR7 93 F1
Park School
BPOOLE FY3 3 J7
Penwortham Broad
Oak County School
PRES PR1 69 F4
Penwortham County
Primary School
PRES PR1 68 D1
Penwortham Cricket Club
PRES PR1 69 H2
Penwortham Girls High School
PRES PR1 69 F1
Penwortham Holme Recreation
Centre
PRES PR1 6 C6
Penwortham Leisure Centre
PRES PR1 68 D1
Penwortham Sports Club
PRES PR1 69 H2
Phoenix Sporting
& Leisure Centre
CLV/TH FY5 21 E5
Picture Gallery
BPOOLS FY4 5 J6
Picture Gallery
CLV/TH FY5 21 G2
Picture Gallery
& Framing Service
LEY/BBR PR5 81 E4
Playhouse Theatre
PRES PR1 7 G2
Police Headquarters
PRES PR1 7 H1
Post Graduate Medical Centre
FUL/RIB PR2 46 A4
Poulton C of E School
PLF/KEOS FY6 26 B4
Preesall Fleetwood
Charity School
PLF/KEOS FY6 13 F3
Preesall Mill Industrial Estate
PLF/KEOS FY6 13 F4
Preston Borough Council
FUL/RIB PR2 59 F1
Preston Borough Council
PRES PR1 58 B2
Preston Bowl
PRES PR1 57 G1
Preston College
FUL/RIB PR2 46 A3
Preston College
PRES PR1 7 H4
Preston College Park School
PRES PR1 58 A1
Preston Cricket Club
PRES PR1 7 F7
Preston Grasshoppers
Rugby Football Club
KIRK/FR/WA PR4 36 A5
Preston Muslim Girls
Secondary School
PRES PR1 58 C2
Preston North End Football Club
PRES PR1 58 C1

Preston Sports Club
PRES PR1 7 F6
Priory High School
PRES PR1 68 D1
Progress Business Park
KIRK/FR/WA PR4 43 E4
Queen Mary School
LSTA FY8 61 G2
Queens Drive Primary School
FUL/RIB PR2 45 G3
Queens Retail Park
PRES PR1 58 C3
Raza Mosque
PRES PR1 58 B2
Redmarsh School
CLV/TH FY5 21 H1
Red Rose Cosmetic Surgery
PRES PR1 7 H5
Red Rose Radio Station
PRES PR1 7 K1
Regent House Surgery
CHLY/EC PR7 91 E3
Register Office
BPOOL FY1 2 E5
Revoe CP School
BPOOL FY1 5 F2
Ribbleton Avenue County Infant
School
PRES PR1 58 D1
Ribbleton Avenue
Methodist Junior School
PRES PR1 59 E1
Ribbleton Hall High School
FUL/RIB PR2 47 G5
Ribbleton Hospital
FUL/RIB PR2 59 G1
Ribbleton Lane Trading Estate
PRES PR1 58 C3
Ribble Village Health Centre
FUL/RIB PR2 59 F1
Ribble Village Surgery
FUL/RIB PR2 59 G1
Ripleys Belive It Or Not Museum
BPOOLS FY4 38 B1
Riverside Medical Centre
LEY/BBR PR5 71 E1
Roebuck Street CP School
FUL/RIB PR2 57 G1
Roseacre CP School
BPOOLS FY4 38 C3
Rossall Hospital
FTWD FY7 16 C1
Rossall School
FTWD FY7 16 C3
Royal Cross Primary School
FUL/RIB PR2 56 B2
Royal Preston Hospital
FUL/RIB PR2 46 A2
Royles Brook Primary School
CLV/TH FY5 21 G2
Runshaw College
CHLY/EC PR7 85 G1
Runshaw College
CHLY/EC PR7 91 F3
The Ryan Medical Centre
LEY/BBR PR5 71 F5
Sacred Heart RC Primary School
CHLYE PR6 91 H3
Sacred Heart RC School
FUL/RIB PR2 57 F2
Sacred Heart School
CLV/TH FY5 21 H1
St Aidans C of E High School
PLF/KEOS FY6 13 F3
St Aidans School
LEY/BBR PR5 71 G5
St Andrews C of E Infant School
LEY/BBR PR5 81 E4
St Andrews Primary School
FUL/RIB PR2 57 E2
St Annes College
Grammar School
LSTA FY8 61 E1
St Annes Cricket Club
LSTA FY8 49 E2
St Annes Old Links Golf Club
LSTA FY8 48 D2
St Annes School
LEY/BBR PR5 80 C4
St Annes Swimming Pool
LSTA FY8 61 E1
St Anthonys School
FUL/RIB PR2 45 F4
St Augustines RC
Primary School
PRES PR1 7 K4
St Bedes RC High School
LSTA FY8 63 G2

St Bernadettes RC Primary School *BISP* FY2 .... 24 D2
St Clares RC School *FUL/RIB* PR2 .... 46 A2
St Cuthberts Primary School *BPOOLS* FY4 .... 5 F7
St Edmunds RC Junior School *FTWD* FY7 .... 17 E1
St Georges Chiropody Surgery *CLV/TH* FY5 .... 20 D2
St Georges High School *BPOOLS* FY4 .... 33 G4
St Georges Primary School *CHLY/EC* PR7 .... 91 H5
St Georges Road Surgery *PRES* PR1 .... 58 B1
St Georges Shopping Centre *PRES* PR1 .... 7 H3
St Gerrards School *LEY/BBR* PR5 .... 77 G1
St Gregorys RC Primary School *PRES* PR1 .... 46 C5
St James C of E School *CHLYE* PR6 .... 91 H3
St James C of E School *LEY/BBR* PR5 .... 80 A4
St Johns Centre *PRES* PR1 .... 7 J2
St Johns C of E Primary School *BPOOL* FY1 .... 2 E5
St Johns RC Primary School *PLF/KEOS* FY6 .... 26 C2
St John Vianney RC Primary School *BPOOL* FY1 .... 5 K4
St Josephs RC Primary *KIRK/FR/WA* PR4 .... 42 D1
St Josephs RC Primary School *PRES* PR1 .... 58 D2
St Josephs RC School *CHLYE* PR6 .... 87 G5
St Kentigerns RC Primary School *BPOOLE* FY3 .... 3 H4
St Leonards C of E Primary School *LEY/BBR* PR5 .... 70 D2
St Maria Goretti School *FUL/RIB* PR2 .... 47 G3
St Mary Magdelenes School *PRES* PR1 .... 69 H2
St Marys C of E Primary School *CHLY/EC* PR7 .... 88 B4
St Marys Health Centre *PRES* PR1 .... 69 E1
St Marys Primary School *LEY/BBR* PR5 .... 81 E3
St Marys RC High School *BPOOLE* FY3 .... 29 F3
St Marys RC Primary School *CHLY/EC* PR7 .... 90 D3
St Marys RC Primary School *FTWD* FY7 .... 11 G1
St Marys RC School *LEY/BBR* PR5 .... 80 D5
St Marys & St Benedicts RC Primary School *LEY/BBR* PR5 .... 71 F5
St Marys School *CHLY/EC* PR7 .... 85 H4
St Matthews C of E Primary School *PRES* PR1 .... 59 E3
St Michaels C of E High School *CHLY/EC* PR7 .... 87 F5
St Michaels Primary School *KIRK/FR/WA* PR4 .... 43 F3
St Nicholas C of E School *BPOOLS* FY4 .... 39 G4
St Oswalds RC Primary School *CHLY/EC* PR7 .... 93 H5
St Patricks School *LEY/BBR* PR5 .... 71 F2
St Pauls School *KIRK/FR/WA* PR4 .... 65 G1
St Pauls Surgery *PRES* PR1 .... 7 K1
St Peters C of E Junior School *CHLYE* PR6 .... 87 H5
St Peters Primary School *FUL/RIB* PR2 .... 46 A1
St Peters RC School *LSTA* FY8 .... 63 G1
St Pius X Preparatory School *FUL/RIB* PR2 .... 45 H3
St Saviours C of E Primary School *LEY/BBR* PR5 .... 78 C2
St Stephens School *PRES* PR1 .... 6 E6
St Teresa's Primary School *PRES* PR1 .... 68 D1
St Teresas RC Primary School *PRES* PR1 .... 59 F3
St Teresas School *CLV/TH* FY5 .... 20 D3
St Thomas C of E Primary School *LSTA* FY8 .... 49 F5
St Williams RC School *GAR/LONG* PR3 .... 15 G2
St Wulstans RC School *FTWD* FY7 .... 11 E3
Sandy Lane Clinic *LEY/BBR* PR5 .... 81 F4
Savick County Junior School *FUL/RIB* PR2 .... 56 B1
Sawmill Industrial Estate *BPOOL* FY1 .... 3 G3
Sealife Centre *BPOOL* FY1 .... 2 C7
Sealife Centre *BPOOL* FY1 .... 4 C2
Selby Industrial Estate *KIRK/FR/WA* PR4 .... 42 D2
Seven Stars CP Infants School *LEY/BBR* PR5 .... 80 C4
Shakespeare CP School *FTWD* FY7 .... 11 E2
Sharoe Green Hospital *FUL/RIB* PR2 .... 46 A4
Sherburn School *PRES* PR1 .... 46 B5
Sherwood County Primary School *FUL/RIB* PR2 .... 46 B1
Southlands High School *CHLY/EC* PR7 .... 90 D5
South Ribble Borough Council *KIRK/FR/WA* PR4 .... 74 A2
South Ribble Borough Council *LEY/BBR* PR5 .... 80 D3
South Ribble Industrial Estate *LEY/BBR* PR5 .... 70 D1
South Ribble Museum & Exhibition Centre *LEY/BBR* PR5 .... 81 F4
Spen Farm Business Park *BPOOLS* FY4 .... 34 A5
Springfield Industrial Estate *PRES* PR1 .... 57 H2
Squires Gate Industrial Estate *BPOOLS* FY4 .... 39 E3
Staining C of E School *BPOOLE* FY3 .... 30 B5
Stanah CP Infant School *CLV/TH* FY5 .... 22 B3
Stanah CP Junior School *CLV/TH* FY5 .... 22 B3
Stanley Infant School *BPOOLE* FY3 .... 33 H3
Stanley Junior School *BPOOLE* FY3 .... 33 H3
Starkie Industrial Estate *FUL/RIB* PR2 .... 57 G1
Station Surgery *LEY/BBR* PR5 .... 81 G2
Strike Lane County School *KIRK/FR/WA* PR4 .... 54 C3
Sunnybank Industrial Estate *PLF/KEOS* FY6 .... 23 H3
Superbowl Leisure Parcs *BPOOL* FY1 .... 2 C5
Swimming Pool *LEY/BBR* PR5 .... 81 E4
Sycamore Trading Estate *BPOOLS* FY4 .... 39 F4
Talbot Road Industrial Centre *LEY/BBR* PR5 .... 80 C2
Tardygate Trading Estate *LEY/BBR* PR5 .... 77 F1
The Temple *PRES* PR1 .... 59 E2
Thames Road Primary School *BPOOLS* FY4 .... 38 B1
The Theatre Coffee Shop *PRES* PR1 .... 7 G4
Thornton Cleveleys Cricket Club *CLV/TH* FY5 .... 26 D1
Thornton Cleveleys Rugby Union Football Club *CLV/TH* FY5 .... 21 G2
Three Worlds Business Centre *LSTA* FY8 .... 63 H2
Towngate Healthcare Clinic *LEY/BBR* PR5 .... 81 F4
Town Hall Annexe *PRES* PR1 .... 7 H2
Town Hall & Municipal Buildings *BPOOL* FY1 .... 2 C4
Toy & Teddy Bear Museum *LSTA* FY8 .... 48 D4
Traceys Industrial Estate *LEY/BBR* PR5 .... 82 A3
University of Central Lancashire *PRES* PR1 .... 7 G2
Victoria Business Park *FTWD* FY7 .... 11 G3
Victoria Market Hall *BPOOLS* FY4 ....
Walton-le-dale County Primary School *LEY/BBR* PR5 ....
Walton-le-dale County Secondary School *LEY/BBR* PR5 ....
Walton-le-dale School Clinic *LEY/BBR* PR5 ....
Warbreck High School *BISP* FY2 ....
Warner Brothers Cinema *LEY/BBR* PR5 ....
Waterfront Marine Business Park *LSTA* FY8 ....
The Waterloo Crown Green Bowling *BPOOL* FY1 ....
Waterloo Medical Centre *BPOOL* FY1 ....
Waterloo Primary School *BPOOL* FY1 ....
Watling Street County Primary School *FUL/RIB* PR2 ....
Wellfield Business Park *PRES* PR1 ....
Wellfield County Secondary School *LEY/BBR* PR5 ....
Wesham C of E Primary School *KIRK/FR/WA* PR4 ....
Westcliffe Infant School *BISP* FY2 ....
West View Leisure Centre *PRES* PR1 ....
Westwood County Primary School *LEY/BBR* PR5 ....
Whitefield Road Primary School *PRES* PR1 ....
Whitegate Galleries *BPOOL* FY1 ....
Whittle-le-woods C of E Primary School *CHLYE* PR6 ....
Whittle Surgery *CHLYE* PR6 ....
Woodlands School *BPOOLE* FY3 ....
Woodlands School *FUL/RIB* PR2 ....
Woodlea School Junior School *LEY/BBR* PR5 ....
Worden High School *LEY/BBR* PR5 ....
World Wide Travel & Theatre Agency *BISP* FY2 ....
Wyre Borough Council *CLV/TH* FY5 ....
Wyre Borough Council *FTWD* FY7 ....
Wyre Borough Council *PLF/KEOS* FY6 ....
Wyredale School *PLF/KEOS* FY6 ....

ge 11

hitstead Ct
okall Cl
nondsen Pl
shaw Cl
enfield Cl
gson Dr
field Ms
nderson Rd
plett Ct

ge 17

ckthorn Cl
ony Cl
npion Cl
erberry Cl
edwell Cl
itebeam Cl

ge 21

ating Pl
dstone Wy
lenook Cl
iwake Cl
orhen Pl
rman Cl
chard Pl
dstart Pl
erwood Pl

dgewater Av
nberra Cl
ardonnay Crs
oy Cl
th Cl
dway Cl
e Shay
e Spinney
eatfield Cl
oxton Cl

enden Pl
chester Cl
ham Cl
donstoun Pl
nnyfarthing La
ehampton Cl
ewsbury Dr
ornleigh Cl

ge 28

k Ashburton Rd
k Eaves St
k Pleasant St
ithwaite St
de St
perial St
n Gv
orhouse St

ngdon St
k High St
k Warbreck Rd
cker Sq
kson Rd
ncis St
sdowne Pl
d St
lker St

elphi St
k Church St
ey St
ter St
dar Sq
ton St
ronation St
rporation St
ansgate
t Topping St
vard St
pold Gv
rket St
een Vera Rd
e Strand
nple St
ping St
ver St
st St

horp Cl
resford St
remont Ct
ofters Ms
rdeners Ms
fton St
ntham Rd
mpstead Ms
ndsworth Ct
Anthony's Pl
ithy Ms
nhope Rd
burn Rd

red St
nesbury Pl
ansgate
orge St
g's Sq
g St
coln Rd
rker St
kes Hl
kes Pde
gent Rd
gent Rd East
uth King St
nstanley Gv

D3
1 Catterall Cl
2 Cooper's Wy
3 Cypress Gv
4 Empire Gv
5 Kyston Cl
6 Laburnum St
7 Rossall Rd
8 Stirling Rd
9 Swarbrick Cl
10 Warwick Rd
11 Wildman St

Page 29

E2
1 Benson Rd
2 Cannock Av
3 Chelford Av
4 Eastwood Av
5 Humber Av
6 Pelham Av
7 Radley Av
8 St Mark's Pl

E3
1 Alder Gv
2 Caledonian Av
3 Cameron Av
4 Croydon Rd
5 Cumbrian Av
6 Garrick Gv
7 Gisburn Gv
8 Huntley Av
9 Whittaker Av
10 William St

E5
1 Felgate Brow
2 St Josephs Cl

Page 32

B3
1 Amberbanks Gv
2 Back Clarendon Rd
3 Back Moon Av
4 Back Woodfield Rd
5 Cadsby St
6 Hopton Rd
7 Hyde Rd
8 John St
9 Trafalgar Rd
10 West View Av
11 Woodfield Av

B4
1 Austin Gv
2 Back Waterloo Rd
3 Britannia Pl
4 Castlegate
5 Commercial St
6 Elland Pl
7 Frazer Gv
8 Garden Ter
9 Gordon St
10 Lawrence St
11 Miller St
12 Price St
13 Royle St
14 Ruskin Av
15 St Bede's Av
16 Wolsley Rd

C4
1 Exeter St
2 Stansfield St

Page 33

E5
1 Morley Rd
2 Troughton Crs

F3
1 Cadby Av
2 Dunmail Av
3 Halifax St
4 Higham Gv
5 John Hill St
6 Maltby Pl
7 Oscar St
8 Phillip St

Page 45

G5
1 Boundary Rd
2 Douglas Ct
3 Fowler St
4 Haddon Pl
5 Mill Ga
6 Mill Hvn
7 Queen's Rd
8 Sedberg St
9 Trafalgar Cl
10 Worden Rd

Page 46

C3
1 Tanglewood

Page 49

E5
1 Avon St
2 Back Springfield Rd North
3 Back West Crs
4 Dee St
5 Garden St
6 Richmond Rd
7 Springfield Rd

F3
1 Headroomgate Back Rd
2 Mayfield Rd

Page 57

F1
1 Arnott Rd
2 Belmont Rd
3 Bulmer St
4 Colenso Rd
5 Ecroyd Rd
6 Gathurst Rd
7 Hampton St
8 Kimberley Rd
9 Ladysmith Rd
10 Mafeking Rd
11 Ord Rd
12 Plumpton Rd
13 Tomlinson Rd
1 Blanche St
2 Brampton St
3 Bray St
4 Brunswick Pl
5 Cannon Hl
6 Elton St
7 Fazackerley St
8 Flett St
9 Francis St
10 Hanbury St
11 Holland Rd
12 Kane St
13 Markham St
14 Nares St
15 Pechell St
16 Plant St
17 Threlfall St
18 Tulketh Crs
19 Waterloo Ter
20 Webster St
21 Wyre St

G2
1 Bath St
2 Brierley St
3 Brookhouse St
4 Dewhurst St
5 Malthouse Ct
6 Newsham St
7 Selby St
8 Wetherall St

G3
1 Abbey St
2 Bromley St
3 Cheviot St
4 The Cloisters
5 Ingot St
6 Maddy St
7 Mill St
8 Nelson Ter
9 Priory St
10 St Mark's Pl East
11 St Mark's Pl West
12 St Walburges Gdns
13 Spa St
14 Steeple Vw
15 Stewart St
16 Vine St
17 West View Ter

G4
1 Carnarvon Rd
2 Cooper Rd
3 Hunt St
4 Northcote Rd
5 Paley Rd

H4
1 Birk St
2 Burleigh Rd
3 Kay St
4 Kingswood St
5 Ladyman St
6 Markland St
7 Nutter Rd
8 Red Cross St
9 Savoy St
10 School St
11 Spring Bank
12 Stanley Ter

Page 58

A1
1 Albert Rd
2 Barlow St
3 Brackenbury St
4 Butler Pl
5 Derwentwater Pl
6 English Martyrs' Pl
7 Hammond St
8 Havelock St
9 Haysworth St
10 Kenmure Pl
11 Lockhart Rd
12 St James's Rd
13 Shuttleworth Rd

A2
1 Broomfield Mill St
2 Bushell St
3 Castle St
4 Emmett St
5 Fish St
6 Hanover St
7 Kilshaw St
8 St Thomas' Pl
9 St Thomas' St
10 Sizer St
11 Thorpe Cl
12 Vernon St

A3
1 Adelphi Pl
2 Back Seed St
3 Birley St
4 Bispham St
5 Bowran St
6 Chandler St
7 Clayton's Ga
8 Earl St
9 Fylde St
10 Gardner St
11 Hope St
12 Kendal St
13 Lowthian St
14 Lund St
15 Market St West
16 Marsh La
17 Melbourne St
18 Melling St
19 Orchard St
20 Patten St
21 Rodney St
22 St Peter's St
23 Saul St
24 Seed St
25 Simpson St
26 Sizehouse St
27 Tenterfield St
28 Trinity Pl
29 Union St

A5
1 Camden Pl
2 Regent St
1 Charnock Fold
2 Charnock St
3 St Andrew's Rd
4 St Anne's St
5 St Anthony's Rd
6 St Christopher's Rd
7 St Cuthbert's Rd
8 St David's Rd
9 St Martin's Rd
10 St Michael's Rd
11 St Philip's Rd
12 Varley St

B2
1 Alma St
2 Cromwell St
3 Dorset Rd
4 Norfolk Rd
5 Nottingham Rd
6 St Barnabas' Pl
7 St Paul's Av
8 Shaw St
9 Somerset Rd
10 Stafford Rd
11 Stanleyfield Cl
12 Stanleyfield Rd
13 Suffolk Rd
14 Sussex St
15 Turner St

B3
1 Agnes St
2 Bishopgate
3 Crooked La
4 Cunliffe St
5 Danewerke St
6 East St
7 Egan St
8 Hardwicke St
9 High St
10 Lord's Wk
11 Margaret St
12 Old Vicarage
13 Ormskirk Rd
14 Penny St
15 Pump St
16 St Ignatius' Pl
17 St Paul's Sq
18 Schleswig St
19 South Meadow St

B4
1 Arundel Pl
2 Back Grimshaw St
3 Birley St
4 Blelock St
5 Blue Bell Pl
6 Bostock St
7 Charlotte Pl
8 Charlotte St
9 Church Rw
10 Greaves St
11 Guildford Rd
12 Guild Rw
13 Hammond's Rw
14 Harris St
15 Jacson St
16 Knowsley St
17 Library St
18 Main Sprit Weind
19 Norwich Pl
20 Oakham Ct
21 Pembroke Pl
22 St John's Pl
23 Stoneygate
24 Tithebarn St
25 Turks Head Yd
26 Wolseley Pl

B5
1 Avenham Pl
2 Cadogan Pl
3 Frenchwood St
4 Great Avenham St
5 Tenby Rd

C2
1 Bleasdale St East
2 Bullfinch St
3 Deepdale Mill St
4 Golbourne St
5 Herbert St
6 Isherwood St
7 Peel Hall St
8 St Chad's Rd
9 Strutt St

C5
1 Malvern Rd
2 Southern Av
3 Wadham Rd

D2
1 Ansdell St
2 Caroline St
3 Collinson St
4 Crescent St
5 Curwen St
6 Denville Rd
7 Eccles St
8 Fitzgerald St
9 Gillett St
10 Holman St
11 Landseer St
12 Lonsdale Rd
13 Poynter St
14 St Joseph's Ter
15 St Luke's Pl
16 Terrace St
17 Wignall St

D3
1 Cromford Wk
2 John William St
3 Maitland Cl
4 Maitland St
5 Owtram St
6 St Marys Cl
7 Stefano Rd
8 William Henry St

D5
1 Bridge Bank
2 Bridge Ter
3 Hillside Rd
4 Hoghton Vw
5 Mellings Fold
6 North Ribble St
7 Ribble Crs
8 South Ribble St

Page 59

E2
1 Alston St
2 Asheldon St
3 Bagnold Rd
4 Beenland St
5 Bodmin St
6 Braddon St
7 Cecilia St
8 Crowle St
9 Dymock Rd
10 Dymock Rd North
11 Grimsargh St
12 Hermon St
13 Levens St
14 Maitland St
15 Malcolm St
16 Oxley Rd
17 Oxley Rd North
18 Salisbury St
19 Shakespeare Rd
20 Taunton St
21 Tennyson Rd
22 Truro Pl
23 Tunbridge Pl
24 Wells St

G1
1 The Glen
2 The Green
3 Grizedale Cl
4 Grizedale Pl
5 Otters Cl

Page 62

C2
1 Birchwood Cl
2 Cedarwood Cl
3 Cherrywood Av
4 Fernwood Cl
5 Firswood Cl
6 Greenwood Cl
7 Kingswood Cl
8 Northwood Cl
9 Rosewood Cl
10 Silverwood Cl
11 Southwood Cl

Page 81

F3
1 Balfour St
2 Charnock St
3 Chatsworth Rd
4 Meadow St
5 Newsome St
6 Northcote St
7 Sumner St
8 Thurston Rd

F4
1 Balcarres Pl
2 Broad Sq
3 Broad St
4 Deighton Av
5 Edward St
6 Liege Rd
7 Morris Cl
8 Pembroke Pl
9 Sandy Pl
10 South View Ter
11 Wolseley Cl

G3
1 Bretherton Ter
2 Burghley Ct
3 Murray St
4 Spring St
5 Stanley St
6 Starkie St
7 Stratfield Pl
8 Turpin Green La
9 Wilton Pl

Page 91

E3
1 Chelmsford Gv
2 Clifton Gv
3 Queensgate
4 Strathmore Gv
5 Trinity Rd
6 Windsor Cl

F1
1 Bengal St
2 Commercial Rd
3 Congress St
4 Cross St
5 Nichol St
6 Trafalgar St
7 Waterloo St
8 Wellington St
9 Woodfield Rd

F4
1 Catherine St
2 Cottam St
3 Coventry St
4 Gilbert St
5 Knowles St
6 Lupton St
7 Norris St
8 Richmond Ct

G2
1 Bowland Av
2 Brunswick St
3 Byron St
4 Cameron Cft
5 Friday St
6 Houghton St
7 Mackay Cft
8 Mackenzie Cl
9 Portland St
10 Sandham St
11 Sherwood Pl

G4
1 Gin Bow
1 Brownley St
2 Cavendish St
3 Clarendon St
4 Cuerden St
5 Lawson St
6 Owens St
7 St Annes Rd
8 St James's Pl
9 Scarlet St
10 Silverdale Rd
11 Southport Ter
12 Stephenson St
13 Stirling Cl
14 Windermere Rd

Notes

Notes

Notes